Fanny Burney: Her Life
1752–1840

Fanny Burney: Her Life

1752–1840

Kate Chisholm

Chatto & Windus
London

Published by Chatto & Windus 1998

2 4 6 8 10 9 7 5 3 1

First published in the USA in 1998 by Farrar, Straus & Giroux

Copyright © Kate Chisholm 1998

Kate Chisholm has asserted her right under the
Copyright, Designs and Patents Act 1988 to
be identified as the author of this work

First published in Great Britain in 1998 by
Chatto & Windus
Random House, 20 Vauxhall Bridge Road,
London SW1V 2SA

Random House Australia (Pty) Limited
20 Alfred Street, Milsons Point, Sydney,
New South Wales 2061, Australia

Random House New Zealand Limited
18 Poland Road, Glenfield,
Auckland 10, New Zealand

Random House South Africa (Pty) Limited
Endulini, 5A Jubilee Road, Parktown 2193, South Africa

Random House UK Limited Reg. No. 954009

A CIP catalogue record for this book is available from the British Library

ISBN 0 7011 16378 X

Papers used by Random House UK Limited are natural,
recyclable products made from wood grown in sustainable forests.
The manufacturing processes conform to the environmental
regulations of the country of origin.

Typeset by Deltatype Limited, Birkenhead, Merseyside

Printed and bound in Great Britain by
Mackays of Chatham PLC

To Rosemary Elvira,
Hannah Nelum
and Thomas Arthur

Next to the Balloon, Miss Burney
is the object of public curiosity.

Mrs Barbauld, January 1784

As to Les Muses – they are the most
skittish ladies Living – one, with Bowls
& Daggers, pursues – another with a
Mask escapes – However, I wind round
& round their Recesses, where of old I
found them – or where, rather, they
found *me* & perhaps we may yet
meet in some Green Retreat.

Fanny Burney, May 1793

CONTENTS

LIST OF ILLUSTRATIONS

Maps and Family Tree

A Plan of the Cities of London and Westminster, and Borough of
Southwark, with the new buildings, 1772 *(Guildhall Library,
Corporation of London)*

Wallis's Guide for Strangers, through London, and its Environs, 1821
(Guildhall Library, Corporation of London)

Paris, 1802 *(From* Paris de 1800 à 1900 D'après les Estampes et les
Memoires du Temps. Volume I: 1800–1830, Le Consulat; Le
Premier Empire; La Restauration *by Charles Simond, Paris, 1900)*

Burney Family Tree

Section 1

Fanny Burney, by Edward Francisco Burney *(Courtesy of The
Brooklyn Museum)*

James Macburney, by Michael Dahl *(By courtesy of The National
Portrait Gallery, London)*
Dr Charles Burney, by Edward Francisco Burney, after Sir Joshua
Reynolds's portrait of 1781 *(The Osborn Collection, with kind
permission of Yale University Library)*
Esther Sleepe Burney, by Edward Francisco Burney, after Gervase
Spencer's miniature of 1748 *(R. A. Lynex Collection, with kind
permission of Penelope and Anthea Lynex)*
Elizabeth Allen Burney, by an unknown artist *(with kind permission of
Professor Lars Troide)*

James Burney *(Berg Collection of English and American Literature, The
New York Public Library, Astor, Lenox and Tilden Foundations)*
Susan Burney, by Edward Francisco Burney *(By courtesy of The
National Portrait Gallery, London)*

Charles Burney, DD, by Thomas Lawrence *(John Comyn/By courtesy of The National Portrait Gallery, London)*

Charlotte Burney, by an unknown artist *(By courtesy of The National Portrait Gallery, London)*

Susan Burney, Richard Burney, Fanny Burney and Mr Samuel Crisp, 1780, by Paul Sandby *(© Christie's Images)*

A Sunday Concert, 1782 by Charles Loraine Smith *(© The British Museum)*

Commerce, or the Triumph of the Thames, 1777–83, by James Barry *(Royal Society for the encouragement of Arts, Manufactures and Commerce)*

Fanny Burney's first draft for the title-page of *Evelina (John Comyn/ By courtesy of The National Portrait Gallery, London)*

A scene from *Evelina,* 1780, by Edward Francisco Burney *(John Comyn/By courtesy of The National Portrait Gallery, London)*

Remarkable Characters at Mrs Cornelys' Masquerade, engraved for the *Oxford Magazine (By courtesy of The National Portrait Gallery, London)*

Samuel Crisp of Chesington Hall, 1782, by Edward Francisco Burney *(By courtesy of The National Portrait Gallery, London)*

Dr Samuel Johnson, *c* 1781, by Theophila Palmer *(Courage Ltd)*

Mrs Thrale and her Daughter Hester (Queeney), 1781, by Sir Joshua Reynolds *(Gift of Lord Beaverbrook, The Beaverbrook Art Gallery, Fredericton, New Brunswick, Canada)*

Sketch of the interior of Covent Garden Theatre showing the Royal Box, 16 October 1776, by Fanny Burney *(From Charles Beecher Hogan's* The London Stage, Part V: 1776–1800, *Southern Illinois University Press)*

The Witlings: cast-list and page one of text in Fanny Burney's handwriting *(Berg Collection of English and American Literature, The New York Public Library, Astor, Lenox and Tilden Foundations)*

David Garrick as Richard III, 1771, by Nathaniel Dance *(Courtesy of Stratford-upon-Avon Town Council)*

Edward Francisco Burney, *c* 1784, by Henry Edridge *(© The British Museum)*

An Elegant Establishment for Young Ladies by Edward Francisco Burney *(© The Board of Trustees of the Victoria & Albert Museum)*

Section 2

Monsieur d'Arblay, *c* 1793, by an unknown artist *(By courtesy of The National Portrait Gallery, London)*

George III, by Edward Francis Burney, after Thomas Gainsborough's portrait of 1783 *(Courtesy of the Huntington Library, Art Collections, and Botanical Gardens, San Marino, California)*

Queen Charlotte, by Edward Francis Burney, after Thomas Gainsborough's portrait of 1783 *(Courtesy of the Huntington Library, Art Collections, and Botanical Gardens, San Marino, California)*

Fanny Burney, *c*, 1787, silhouette by Thomas Wheeler *(The Royal Collection © Her Majesty The Queen)*

South East View of Windsor Castle, with the Royal Family on the Terrace and View of the Queen's Lodge, 1783, by James Fittler, after George Robertson *(The Royal Collection © Her Majesty The Queen)*

Madame de Staël, after the portrait by François Gérard *(From Austin Dobson's 1904 edition of* The Diaries and Letters of Madame d'Arblay, *volume vi, Macmillan)*

The Comte Louis de Narbonne, by an unknown artist *(By courtesy of The National Portrait Gallery, London)*

Juniper Hall, *c* 1793, possibly by William Lock junior *(© John Bebbington, FRPS)*

Playbill for the only performance of *Edwy and Elgiva*, 21 March 1795, at the Theatre Royal, Drury Lane *(From Joyce Hemlow's 1972–84 edition of* The Journals and Letters of Fanny Burney, *volume iii, Clarendon Press)*

Sarah Siddons Rehearsing in the Green Room with her father and John Kemble, 1789, by Thomas Rowlandson *(© The British Museum)*

Camilla Cottage, *c* 1797, by Monsieur d'Arblay

Camilla Cottage: Monsieur d'Arblay's sketch-plans of the interior *(Both from Joyce Hemlow's 1972–84 edition of* The Journals and Letters of Fanny Burney, *volume iv, Clarendon Press)*

Alexander d'Arblay at three years old, a page of silhouettes by Amelia Lock *(Berg Collection of English and American Literature, The New York Public Library, Astor, Lenox and Tilden Foundations)*

Alexander d'Arblay, *c* 1815, silhouette *(By courtesy of The National Portrait Gallery, London)*

LONDON IN 1772

1	Bolt Court	8	Marylebone Gardens
2	Covent Garden Theatre	9	Mitre Tavern
3	Fleet Prison	10	Opera House, Haymarket
4	Great Queen Street	11	Orange Coffee House, Haymarket
5	Grigg's Coffee House, York Street	12	Poland Street
6	King's Arms Tavern, Cornhill	13	Queen's House
7	Leicester Fields	14	Queen Square

To Streatham

LONDON, 1821

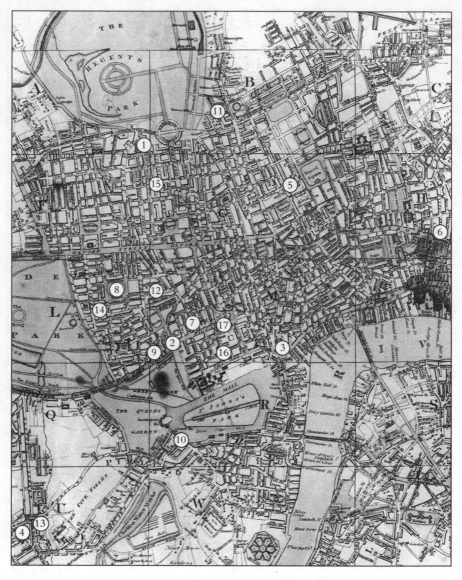

PARIS 1802

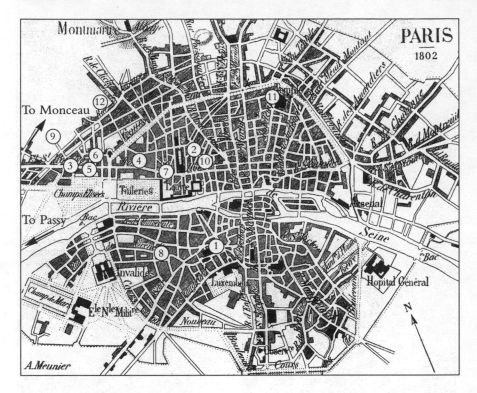

1   faubourg St Germain
2   Opéra-Comique
3   Place Beauvau
4   Place Vendôme
5   rue d'Aguesseau
6   rue d'Anjou
7   rue du faubourg St Honoré
8   rue de Grenelles
9   rue de Miroménil
10   rue Nôtre Dame des Victoires
11   Théâtre (or Cirque) Olympique
12   Tivoli Gardens

BURNEY FAMILY TREE

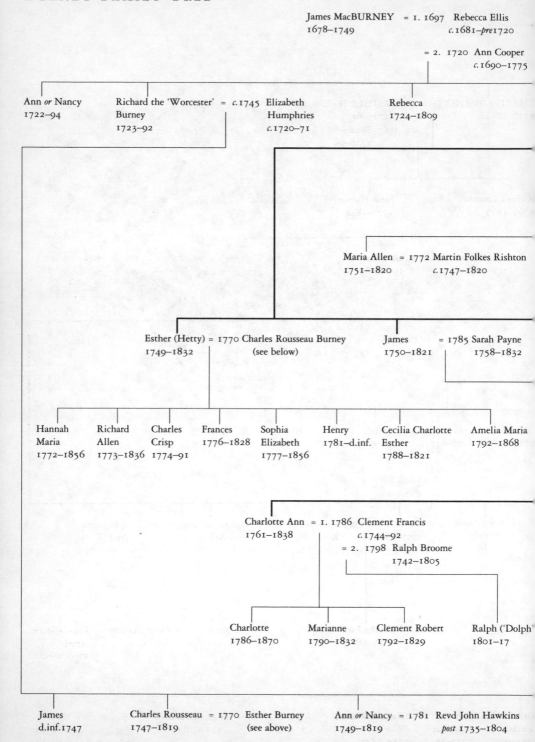

James MacBURNEY = 1. 1697 Rebecca Ellis
1678–1749   c.1681–pre1720

= 2. 1720 Ann Cooper
       c.1690–1775

Ann or Nancy   Richard the 'Worcester' = c.1745 Elizabeth   Rebecca
1722–94   Burney   Humphries   1724–1809
              1723–92   c.1720–71

Maria Allen = 1772 Martin Folkes Rishton
1751–1820   c.1747–1820

Esther (Hetty) = 1770 Charles Rousseau Burney   James   = 1785 Sarah Payne
1749–1832   (see below)   1750–1821   1758–1832

Hannah   Richard   Charles   Frances   Sophia   Henry   Cecilia Charlotte   Amelia Maria
Maria   Allen   Crisp   1776–1828   Elizabeth   1781–d.inf.   Esther   1792–1868
1772–1856   1773–1836   1774–91   1777–1856   1788–1821

Charlotte Ann = 1. 1786 Clement Francis
1761–1838   c.1744–92
          = 2. 1798 Ralph Broome
                1742–1805

Charlotte   Marianne   Clement Robert   Ralph ('Dolph'
1786–1870   1790–1832   1792–1829   1801–17

James   Charles Rousseau = 1770 Esther Burney   Ann or Nancy = 1781 Revd John Hawkins
d.inf.1747   1747–1819   (see above)   1749–1819   post 1735–1804

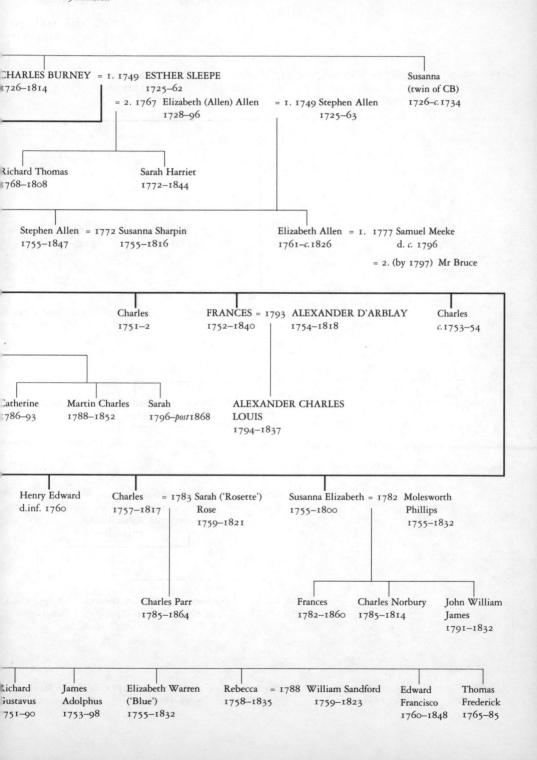

15 children

CHARLES BURNEY = 1. 1749 ESTHER SLEEPE
1726–1814   1725–62
                = 2. 1767 Elizabeth (Allen) Allen = 1. 1749 Stephen Allen
                         1728–96   1725–63

Susanna
(twin of CB)
1726–c.1734

Richard Thomas   Sarah Harriet
1768–1808   1772–1844

Stephen Allen = 1772 Susanna Sharpin   Elizabeth Allen = 1. 1777 Samuel Meeke
1755–1847   1755–1816   1761–c.1826   d. c. 1796
                                                            = 2. (by 1797) Mr Bruce

Charles   FRANCES = 1793 ALEXANDER D'ARBLAY   Charles
1751–2   1752–1840   1754–1818   c.1753–54

Catherine   Martin Charles   Sarah   ALEXANDER CHARLES
1786–93   1788–1852   1796–post1868   LOUIS
                                                1794–1837

Henry Edward   Charles   = 1783 Sarah ('Rosette')   Susanna Elizabeth = 1782 Molesworth
d.inf. 1760   1757–1817   Rose   1755–1800   Phillips
                                   1759–1821   1755–1832

                Charles Parr   Frances   Charles Norbury   John William
                1785–1864   1782–1860 1785–1814   James
                                                                              1791–1832

Richard   James   Elizabeth Warren   Rebecca = 1788 William Sandford   Edward   Thomas
Gustavus   Adolphus   ('Blue')   1758–1835   1759–1823   Francisco   Frederick
1751–90   1753–98   1755–1832   1760–1848   1765–85

ONE

A Most Feeling Girl
1752–68

What a slight piece of machinery is the terrestrial part of thee, our Fannikin! – a mere nothing; a blast, a vapour disorders the spring of thy watch; and the mechanism is so fine that it requires no common hand to set it a-going again.

Samuel Crisp, c. 1781

The portrait of Fanny Burney – novelist, diarist, playwright, courtier to George III and Queen Charlotte and witness to the Battle of Waterloo – that hangs alongside Dr Johnson, Laurence Sterne and David Garrick in the National Portrait Gallery in London shows a young woman in half-profile, shyly looking away from the artist (and her audience). She has soft blue eyes, full and shapely lips, rosy cheeks and lightly powdered fair hair, gently curling on to her shoulders. Her simple grey dress is tightly waisted and has long tapered sleeves; a cream muslin fichu is tucked into the bodice. She wears no jewellery, but a large strawberry-pink bow is pinned to her petite bosom. Black gloves and a black lace shawl would complete the impression that here is a woman of gentle spirit and modest pretensions – except that she is also wearing a magnificent hat. This dusky-gold 'Lunardi', ruffled, trimmed and flounced, was the height of fashion in the autumn of 1784, named after the daring exploits of the balloonist, Vicenzo Lunardi. It dominates the portrait and quite transforms Fanny from an unexceptional society belle into someone who compels our attention. For what thoughts lie hidden beneath this fantastical head-dress? Was its wearer really as demure as her pensive expression suggests?[1]

Fanny was painted by her cousin Edward Francisco Burney when she was in her early thirties. Already an established writer, her first two novels, *Evelina* and *Cecilia*, had entertained and amazed her contemporaries with their witty, and sometimes biting, caricatures of fashionable society and their richly inventive plots. This was Edward's second attempt to capture her likeness. His first (which can be seen in the Long Gallery at Parham Park in Sussex and shows Fanny in an elegant 'Vandyke' ballgown) she did not like because, she said, it was too flattering: 'I have taken pains incredible to make him *magnify* the Features & darken the complection ... for it really makes me uneasy to see a Face in which the smallest resemblance of my own can be traced looking almost *perfectly* handsome.'[2] Edward was thought to be a little in love with his cousin, and perhaps painted her as he wished her to appear to others. She would have preferred, one feels, to remain anonymous, and there are no other portraits regarded now as being definitely of her.[3] Fortunately, Edward has given us a memorable impression of Fanny as, in her own description of one of her fictional creations, 'a woman of character'.[4]

Frances Burney (1752–1840) was the second daughter of the musician Dr Charles Burney and his first wife Esther. With her brothers James and Charles and her sisters, Hetty, Susan and Charlotte, the Burneys were a close-knit family of talented musicians and scholars, of whom Dr Johnson once said, 'I love all of that breed, whom I can be said to know, and one or two whom I hardly know I love upon credit, and love them because they love each other.'[5] But as a young girl, growing up in the Norfolk port of King's Lynn, no one could have foreseen that Fanny would be the Burney who would be more famous in her own time than Jane Austen or Maria Edgeworth, and still so well known and admired some two hundred years later.

Frances, who was always affectionately known as 'Fanny',[6] was described by her family as a quiet, retiring girl, who blushed easily and spoke very little. In comparison with her musical elder sister Hetty and quick-witted brother James, she was dull company and a poor student. Dr Burney would recall many years later that Fanny 'was wholly unnoticed in the nursery for any talents, or quickness of study: indeed at eight years old she did not know her letters; and her brother, the tar [James], who in his boyhood had a natural genius for hoaxing, used to pretend to teach her to read; and gave her a book topsy-turvy, which he said she never found out!' Whereas Hetty excelled at the harpsichord, Fanny was 'silent, backward and timid, even to sheepishness', according to her father, and 'from her shyness, had such profound gravity and composure of features that, those of my friends who came often to my house ... never called Fanny by any other name, from the time she had reached her eleventh year, than The Old Lady.'[7] Her mother, however, knew otherwise. When friends and neighbours talked of her short-sighted, dumpy eight-year-old as 'a little dunce', she would reply crisply that 'she had no fear about Fanny'.[8]

Life in King's Lynn was frustrating for Dr Burney. Ill-health had forced him to leave the polluted air of London and seek a healthier environment in which to live. But when he moved out of the capital in 1751, he left behind a successful career as a professional musician, employed not just by the orchestras at Drury Lane and in Vauxhall Gardens but also by the most prolific composer in London, Handel. This was a remarkable achievement for the nineteenth child of a penniless artist. Charles was sent away from home as a three-year-old and was brought up with his elder brother Richard by an illiterate nurse, Dame Ball, in the tiny village of Condover, some four miles from Shrewsbury. Fanny later painted a sad picture of her father's childhood: 'The dissipated facility & negligence of his Witty & accomplished, but careless Father; the niggardly unfeelingness of his nearly unnatural Mother . . . opening to the public view a species of Family degradation to which the name of Burney now gives no similitude.'[9]

The Burney family had started out as aristocratic and well connected; indeed, they were descended from the Macburneys, who were said to have come south from Scotland in 1603 as members of the Court of James I. But impetuous marriages and a love of the theatre had dissipated their wealth – and their standing in society. Charles's grandfather, James Macburney, was secretary to the Earl of Ashburnham and had a house in Whitehall. He educated his son, also called James, at Westminster School, in the hope that he would enter the legal profession, but James junior was lured away from such a respectable career by his dream of becoming famous as an actor. Before he was nineteen, he eloped with a fifteen-year-old actress, Rebecca Ellis, cutting himself off from his family and his inheritance. He spent the rest of his life struggling to make enough money as an itinerant actor, musician and portrait-painter to support Rebecca and their large family. She died some time in 1719 or 1720, after enduring fifteen pregnancies in twenty years (only nine of her babies survived into adulthood).[10]

When James married again in 1720 he took more notice of his financial requirements, and his second wife, Ann Cooper, the daughter of a respected burgher of Shrewsbury, brought with her a considerable dowry (she is reputed to have turned down the proposal of the elderly

3

dramatist, William Wycherley). The future Dr Burney was their last surviving child, born with his twin sister Susanna on 7 April 1726 in Shrewsbury. He was christened 'Charles Mackburney' (where and when he dropped the 'Mack' is not known) after his godfather, Charles Fleetwood, the theatre manager. Fleetwood was later to promote the career of David Garrick at the Drury Lane Theatre and defend the life of his stage manager Charles Macklin, when he stood trial for the manslaughter of a fellow thespian after poking his eye out in a backstage brawl. But Fleetwood was no role model: according to his contemporaries, he was an 'irregular and expensive man', who 'took a strange delight in the company of the meanest of the human species' and gambled away his fortune on cards and boxing. He died in middle age in the late 1740s, destitute and in great pain with 'a generalized gout'.[11]

Despite Fanny's aspersions, however, Charles appears to have had a happy childhood. He barely knew his half-brothers and -sisters, but he always remained close to his three 'Cooper' siblings, Richard, Ann and Rebecca. His twin Susanna died when she was eight, yet he always cherished her memory with 'a particular fondness' and mourned her loss. He was fond, too, of his Nurse Ball, and suffered an 'agony of grief' when his father took him away and sent him to board at the cathedral school in Chester.[12] Richard, too, agreed that they had been 'so happy' in Condover, that 'the remembrance remain'd with them during life'.[13]

Once at Chester, Charles soon displayed a talent for music, singing in the cathedral choir and learning to play the organ. But he also showed, while still a teenager, his determination to become more than a performing musician. In the memoir of his childhood that he wrote as an old man, he recalled: 'I had a great passion for angling, & whenever I could get time to pursue that sport, I ran no risk of losing my time if the Fish did not bite, for I had always a book in my Pocket, which enabled me to wait with Patience their Pleasure.' Charles dreamed of a better life than the precarious existence led by his father. 'The aerial Castles I now built, & The plans I formed . . . '[14]

He was given his 'first trial' when Matthew Dubourg, an old friend of his father and by then Master of the King's Band in Ireland, stopped off in Chester in the summer of 1743 on his way to Dublin. Charles, then aged seventeen, was invited to play a duet with 'the great player'. Afterwards he was 'very proud of being able to acquit myself tolerably', yet what most affected him was not the experience of playing with a 'Master' but his observation that Dubourg 'was a man of wit, who had been admitted into good company *without, as well as with*, his fiddle'.[15] As a talented teenager, Charles already understood that to play well was not sufficient: success for him depended on being able to overcome the disadvantages of his family connections and lack of private means.

Chester was in those years a fruitful place for an ambitious and gifted musician. Two years earlier Handel had spent several days in the town, delayed by autumnal gales while waiting for a boat that would take him to Dublin for the first performance of the *Messiah*. Charles, curious to see 'so extraordinary a man', followed the composer (then sixty-six) into the Exchange Coffee House and watched him 'smoke a pipe, over a dish of coffee'. A couple of days later he listened in as a scratch choir tried out the new choruses for the oratorio, and later told how they 'failed so egregiously, that Handel let loose his great bear' on them, 'swearing in four or five languages'.[16]

Thomas Arne, highly regarded for composing 'Rule, Britannia!',[17] also stopped off in Chester while on his way from Ireland to London to take up his appointment as composer to the Drury Lane Theatre. He was apparently shown some of Charles's musical compositions and thought so highly of them that he suggested that the young organist should study music in the capital. Indeed, Arne was so convinced of Charles's talent that when he realised such a proposition was impossible, given the Burneys' lack of money, he decided to take him on as an unpaid apprentice.

Charles left Chester for London in September 1744, and was given a room in Dr Arne's house in Great Queen Street, off Lincoln's Inn Fields. Five years' earlier, Dr Johnson had described the capital in his poem *London* as a place where 'falling houses thunder on your head', bewailing the speedy and slapdash way in which new houses were springing up in response to the growth in population: by the time of the 1801 Census, the city had almost doubled in size over the past century to just under one million inhabitants. For Henry Fielding, the novelist and magistrate, the capital was like 'a vast wood or forest in which the thief may harbour with as great security as wild beasts do in the deserts of Arabia and Africa'.[18] Many of these new Londoners lived in cramped and decrepit lodgings (another reason for Johnson's 'falling houses') and idled away their free time by wandering through this 'vast wood' of narrow, noisy streets looking for alehouses, chandler's shops (which sold gin and bread) and places of 'entertainment', such as the arenas where bull-baiting and cock-fighting took place. When Dr Johnson came to London in the spring of 1737 to make a career out of writing, he had very little money and moved from room to room, sometimes finding himself without a bed for the night. On such evenings he would saunter up to the West End, from the print-shops of Fleet Street to the more stately boulevards of St James's, passing on the way Child's Coffee-House, the Mitre Tavern, Clifton's Chop-House and the Turk's Head.[19]

But this was not just the age of the coffee-house and club: by the mid-eighteenth century London was full of foreign visitors attracted by the city's flourishing musical life. The pleasure gardens of Vauxhall, Marylebone and Ranelagh were open nightly during the season for musical (and other) entertainments; subscription concerts were organised at assembly rooms like Hickford's Rooms in Brewer Street (now part of Soho), and in several taverns in the City. Singers, violinists and harpsichordists from Germany, France and especially Italy were attracted to the capital by the money they could make. Arne's youthful apprentice soon found paid employment in the theatre orchestra at Drury Lane, and at Vauxhall.

Opened in 1660, Vauxhall Gardens covered twelve acres, its tree-lined walks dotted with supper-boxes where the modish *ton* could first promenade and later dine to music from some of the finest performers in Europe. The concerts were better than the food: the ham at Vauxhall was said to be sliced so thinly it was possible to read the evening's programme through it. Charles was a regular member of the orchestra, which could on occasion include a hundred players. He also provided new music for organ and harpsichord, afterwards mingling with the fashionable society that frequented the gardens.

In 1746 he was introduced by his friend, the harpsichord-maker Jacob Kirkman, to the rich and well-born Fulke Greville (who claimed descent from Sir Philip Sidney). Charles made the most of this fortuitous encounter, if the story recounted in Fanny's biography of her father is to be believed. Greville, a keen amateur musician, challenged Kirkman to find him a harpsichordist who could amuse him as much by his conversation as by his musicianship. Kirkman invited Charles to play for Greville, who immediately asked the talented, personable *and* well-read Burney to join his country-house party at Wilbury House in Wiltshire.[20]

Charles had first to extricate himself from his indenture to Arne, which was legally binding for seven years. According to Charles's later memoir, Arne was so 'selfish & unprincipled, that finding me qualified to transcribe music, teach, & play in public, all which I could do before I was connected with him, he never wished I should advance further in the Art. And besides not teaching or allowing me time to study & practice, he locked up all the Books in his possession, by the perusal of which I could improve myself.' Charles was particularly annoyed that he was denied the chance to learn the 'Lessons of Scarlatti & Handel, & Madrigals of Palestrina', except on Sunday nights, when he was encouraged to take the tenor part in the impromptu concerts organised by the Arnes and their friends.[21] But Arne at least had the good grace to allow Charles to spend several weeks with Greville at Wilbury, where he found himself mixing with the highest echelons of English society.

Greville once said that he would have nothing to do with *fogrums* – the old-fashioned, the inelegant, the ignorant – surrounding himself instead with the *ton*, who whiled away their days hunting, racing and gambling and spent their evenings listening to music or dancing. Charles kept his head in such company, if his memoir is to be believed, focusing his energies instead on the opportunity to play on Greville's fine collection of harpsichords and make use of the extensive library. Greville took him to Bath, where he performed in the Assembly Rooms before a distinguished audience, after which Greville offered to free Charles from his invidious position with Arne and to employ him as a music-teacher and companion. Arne, however, was unwilling to lose his invaluable assistant and only agreed to let Charles go after months of wrangling. In late 1748, Greville paid £300 to release Charles from his servitude in the household of the unhappy Arnes. (Charles had watched with disapproval as the irascible Dr Arne cheated on his wife.)

Greville had by this time married Frances Macartney, the poet, and planned to take her on a Grand Tour of the Continent; Charles was expected to go with them. It would have been a very useful experience, enabling him to broaden his repertoire beyond Scarlatti, Corelli, Geminiani and Handel, and to learn the music of composers such as Rousseau (known at that time more for his operettas than as a writer and philosopher) and J.S. Bach, few of whose works were yet available in Britain. But he, too, had fallen in love. Charles's brother Richard was also in London, working as a dancing master. He organised social evenings for his pupils in Hatton Garden, at one of which Charles met a 'Lady of great strength of mind, possessing a taste for literature, with an engaging manner, & much beauty'.[22] Esther Sleepe was the daughter of a musician, the leader of the Lord Mayor's band, and grand-daughter of a fan-maker with a shop in Cheapside. She was twenty-three, clever, well read and a gifted harpsichordist. Charles was in a dilemma: whether to risk offending Greville by refusing to travel with him or follow the dictates of his heart.

Charles let his emotions win – but he played a clever diplomatic game so that he would not lose his new-found role in high society. He later told his children how he had shown his patron a miniature of Esther, which he always carried with him,[23] knowing full well that her fine features and sweet smile would appeal to Greville, who prided himself on being a connoisseur of women. Greville fell for Charles's ploy, teasingly suggesting that since Esther was such a beauty, Charles should marry her. Charles replied – rather more readily, one suspects, than Greville expected – 'May I?' And, with remarkable alacrity, Charles and Esther were married the next day, 25 June 1749, at St George's Chapel, Hyde Park, well known as a venue for clandestine weddings. Greville was their witness.

The reason for the haste would soon have become obvious to Greville: Charles and Esther already had a young daughter, born a month earlier and christened Esther after her mother (but always known as Hetty). This detail, however, was so effectively suppressed by Fanny that it was not actually known until Joyce Hemlow's revelations in her *History of Fanny Burney*, which was published in 1958.[24] Fanny did a marvellous cover-up job when she came to edit the memoirs of her father, carefully obfuscating the details of her parents' courtship and marriage. In the typically high-flown language of her later years, she describes how Charles and Esther fell in love:

> who shall be surprised, that two such beings, where, on one side, there was so much beauty to attract, and on the other so much discernment to perceive the value of her votary, upon meeting each other at the susceptible age of ardent youth, should have emitted, spontaneously, and at first sight, from heart to heart, sparks so bright and pure that they might be called electric, save that their flame was exempt from any shock?

And she ascribes their rush to get married to their mutual lack of money: 'for if they had not, in their matrimonial preparations, the

8

luxuries of wealth, neither had they its fatiguing ceremonies; if they had not the security of future advantage, they avoided the torment of present procrastination; and if they had but little to bestow upon one another, they were saved, at least, the impatiency of waiting for the seals, signatures, and etiquettes of lawyers'.[25]

So when the Grevilles departed on their continental tour Charles stayed behind, and was then reliant on what he could earn from giving harpsichord lessons and from his job as Handel's *répétiteur*, rehearsing the singers for the composer's new oratorios, *Solomon*, *Susanna* and *Hercules*. Fortunately, at about this time he was offered the post of organist at the fashionable City church of St Dionis Backchurch, in Fenchurch Street (rebuilt by Wren after the Great Fire of London), which gave him a regular salary of £30 per annum. He was also put in charge of the concerts at the King's Arms Tavern in Cornhill, inviting Italian visitors such as Gaetano Guadagni, the castrato, and Sipruttini, the violoncellist, to perform with him.[26]

Charles also began composing for the theatre. While living with the Arnes, he had met and ingratiated himself with Dr Arne's sister-in-law, the actress Mrs Cibber. Her house in Scotland Yard had become a popular meeting-place for actors and musicians, and one evening Charles happened to be there when in walked David Garrick, who was then in his mid-twenties and already drawing audiences to his performances as Hamlet, Lear and Abel Drugger.[27] In 1747, Garrick took over the management of the Drury Lane Theatre and, seeking to outdo his rival at Covent Garden, John Rich, began extending the repertoire to include musical entertainments, for which he asked Charles to provide the songs and interludes. Their most successful collaboration was *Queen Mab*, a comic musical with characters such as Puck the Fairy and Harlequin, which opened on 26 December 1750. According to Garrick's biographer, Thomas Davies (writing a year after the actor's death in 1779), 'The people crowded for above forty nights to see this exhibition.'[28] Charles also worked with Garrick on adapting Arne's *The Masque of Alfred*, which became another popular hit after its first performance on 23 February 1751.

Charles by then had established himself in the capital as a performer and composer; he was also happily married, with two children, Hetty and James. But in March 1751 he fell ill with what appeared to be an incurable fever – probably brought on by overwork. Weakened by a hacking cough, he was unable to recover enough strength to continue his hectic schedule, and, in desperation, he took Esther and the

9

children away from the smoky, dank atmosphere of the City to the healthier climes of Canonbury, then a small village north of the capital (and now part of Islington), encouraged by his friend, the poet Christopher Smart. But Charles needed to earn money to support his growing family: on 3 June, Esther gave birth to another son, Charles (who died at sixteen months). Adept at making friends and useful contacts, Charles was soon offered a suitable job – as organist of St Margaret's Church in King's Lynn, a busy Norfolk port. Indeed, the local MP, Sir John Turner, was so keen to persuade Charles to accept that he arranged for the salary to be increased from £20 to £100.[29] And by the winter of 1751 the Burneys were settled there in lodgings in Chapel Street.

Charles was appalled that he had to leave behind a flourishing career to retire, at only twenty-five, to a provincial market town. In a letter sent to Esther in September, before she and the children had joined him in Lynn Regis (as the town was then known), he wrote, 'it Shames me to think How little I knew myself, when I fancy'd I should be Happy in this Place. O God! I find it impossible I should ever be so . . . Nothing but the Hope of acquiring an independent Fortune in a Short Space of Time will keep me Here.'[30] Even today, the local newspaper grumbles about the way the Burneys denigrated the town; and no plaque adorns the site of the house where Fanny spent her first years.[31] Charles's comments about the congregation's 'Total Ignorance of the most known and Common Musicall Merits' still rankle, as does his condemnation of the organ in St Margaret's. He was so offended by the poor sound of this 'execrably bad' instrument that he persuaded the parish to import from Germany a fine Snetzler organ, which is still in use.

But the Burneys' years in Lynn were not without happiness. On 13 June 1752, Esther gave birth to their fourth child – a girl – who was baptised Frances (after her godmother, Frances Greville, the wife of Charles's former patron).[32] Of Fanny's early years in Lynn Regis, we know little: Charles was far too busy to keep a diary, while Esther was burdened with almost continual pregnancy and breastfeeding. Another son, the second Charles, followed Fanny in 1753 (he died within a year) and Susanna, named after her father's twin but fondly called Susan, arrived in 1755. A third Charles, who lived to become a famous classical scholar and chaplain to George III, was born in 1757. Three years later, Esther gave birth to another son, Henry Edward, who died within a few months.

The home of the Burneys must have been noisy, chaotic and perpetually short of money. Charles and Esther, however, appear to have been well suited to each other, with similar interests and a shared ability to charm whomsoever they met. Both enjoyed reading poetry, learning new languages and discussing philosophical ideas. Charles recalled that Esther

> had a most agreeable turn for conversation; entered into the humours of her company; seasoned her conversation with agreeable wit & pleasing manners; which with the beauty of her person occasioned her more invitations than she chose to accept: as she was very domestic, had a young family on her hands, generally, one of them at her breast, and when we could spend an evening at home, we had a course of reading: history, voyages, poetry, and science, as far as Chambers's Dictionary, the French Encyclopédie, & the Philosophical transactions, which set her greatly above the generality of Lynn ladies.[33]

Charles fancied himself as a poet, writing loving verses dedicated to his wife. In an example, quoted by Fanny, he describes Esther as 'my matchless mate'; 'My help! companion! wife! and friend!'; 'Sweet partner of my hopes and fears'.[34] They appear to have sustained each other through the deaths of their three baby sons. In the same poem, Charles writes:

> 'Tis thou alone can'st dry my tears.
> 'Tis thou alone can'st bring relief,
> Partner of every joy and grief!
> E'en when encompass'd with distress,
> Thy smile can every ill redress.

And, with touching fatherly concern, he requested in 1754 that 'five stools be provided for the organist's family, to be placed in the organ loft' so that his wife and children could sit with him during the services.[35]

By this time, the Burneys had moved into a much grander house on the High Street close to the quay. Like the Chapel Street building, this house no longer exists, although a photograph of its elegant wooden staircase can be seen in the biography of Charles written by Dr Percy Scholes in 1948, who visited it before its demolition and commented that 'It has a fine staircase and good ceilings and, in its best days, has clearly been a really superior sort of dwelling.' According to the rate-books, Charles paid £10 13s. 4d. annually for the house, a considerable proportion of his salary.[36] Perhaps he was trying to reflect his increasing social status in the town by moving on to a street where other local bigwigs lived. For Charles soon recovered from his debilitating ill-health to become a pivotal figure in the life of Lynn Regis, organising subscription concerts in the Town Hall and recitals by visiting organists at St Margaret's.

He was close friends with the two families who dominated the town – the Turners, who had made their fortune in brewing, and the Walpoles, who owned Houghton Hall nearby, with its collection of pictures famous throughout Europe. He once rather proudly asserted, 'I may be said to have been at home, not only at Houghton Hall, but at Rainham, at Sir Andrew Fountaine's, at Halcombe, Blickling, Wolterton, and Sir Harry l'Estrange's. At all which places there was painting, sculpture, architecture and antiquities to examine.' While at Houghton, Charles met John Hayes, the natural son of Sir Robert Walpole, who was later to bequeath his London house in James Street, Westminster, to Charles's eldest son James – an example of the strong bonds of friendship that Charles made throughout his life, a characteristic shared by many of his children.[37]

Lynn Regis was a journey of some twelve hours by post-chaise from the capital, but it was by no means a dead-end. Its long quayside on the estuary of the River Ouse was crammed in the mid-eighteenth century with boats from Russia, the Baltic States and the German ports. The Russians arrived with tobacco, snuff and soap; and left with grain and wool produced by the Norfolk farmers. Beer and ale were exchanged for coal from Newcastle, while dried fruits, tea and spices arrived from further afield. The large mansions of Felbrigg, Houghton, Raynham and Blickling were within a day's ride, and Charles was a regular guest, paid to teach music but often staying on for dinner afterwards.[38] His horse, Peggy, was so used to the journeys he made each week that Charles read volumes of Italian and French poetry on the way. No time was wasted by the industrious and largely self-taught musician, who compiled his own dictionaries of French and Italian (tiny notebooks just six by three inches in size) to carry in his pocket wherever he went.[39]

Esther, in between nursing and teaching her children, and protecting them from the smallpox epidemic that ravaged Lynn in 1754,[40] became close friends with two of the leading ladies of the town: Mrs Elizabeth Allen, three years her junior and the vivacious wife of a successful wine-merchant, and her sister-in-law, Miss Dorothy ('Dolly') Young, whose amiability and common sense made her a lifelong friend of all the Burneys, especially Fanny, who wrote that 'Miss Young's were the kind arms that first welcomed to this nether sphere the writer of these memoirs'.[41] The three friends met for reading afternoons and what they regarded as 'real' conversation, so different from the tittle-tattle exchanged in the assembly rooms at Lynn.

Fanny grew up in a house that revolved around music, and where books were read aloud, ideas discussed – and evenings were spent dressing-up and play-acting. In later life the Burneys all called each other by pet names, and when together they used a special shorthand of tag words and expressions invented by them when they were children ('take the veil', 'the wig is wet', 'an alive'), which were incomprehensible to anyone outside the family. The brothers, especially James, played practical jokes on their sisters, and came home with lurid tales of adventures at sea told them by the sailors they met on the quayside. Along with the rush and tumble of excitable youngsters competing for the attention of their approachable but often preoccupied father, there were always dogs in the house, and, of course, the sound of someone practising the violin or harpsichord.

Fanny's elder sister Hetty showed early promise as a musician and by the age of ten was performing in front of a paying audience. But it was with her younger sister, Susan, that Fanny had the closest relationship. Before Susan was born on 7 January 1755 two babies had died, and her arrival filled the gap left by the absent toddlers. The sisters were almost as close as twins; indeed, a family friend, the Italian castrato Gaspare Pacchierotti, was to observe of them in the 1780s (when they were both in their late twenties) that it was as if there was between them 'but one Soul – but one Mind between you – You are two in One!'[42]

As Dr Burney noted in his memoirs, Fanny was a late developer, not learning to read until after Susan. But she revealed early on that she had an extraordinarily acute memory, reciting word-for-word to her mother passages from Dryden, Pope and Shakespeare that had been read to her just once. She also impressed the troubled poet, Christopher Smart, who was so entertained by her that he once presented her with a pink rose. Her ability to memorise – perhaps born of her extreme shyness and poor eyesight, which meant that she concentrated on listening – came to fruition when she grew up, for it is the accuracy of her dialogue that gives zest to both the diaries and the novels.

Fanny, then, was quiet, thoughtful, teased for being 'slow', but in fact she was learning in her own way the skills she was later to use to such pertinent effect. A sensitive child, she was also, no doubt, overawed by her elder sister. Of all Charles's children, Fanny appears to have been the least musical and the only one really to dislike performing, whether on the stage or concert platform. While Fanny watched Hetty being shown off by their father to his friends and patrons, she perhaps felt keenly that she could match neither her sister's musical gift nor her outgoing personality. 'I, also, was so peculiarly backward,' she later wrote to Hetty, 'that even our Susan stood before me; she could read when I knew not my letters. But though so sluggish to learn, I was always observant.'[43]

By Fanny's eighth birthday in June 1760, Charles was making plans to go back to London. The restorative air of Norfolk had done its work, and his friends in the capital were urging him to return. During his nine years in Lynn, Charles had visited London every winter 'in order to rub off rust and revive friendships',[44] and some time in 1758 or 1759 he had been asked to provide the musical settings for a burlesque, *Ode to St Cecilia's Day*, written by the satirist Bonnell Thornton, to be performed in Ranelagh Gardens. Charles's music is now lost, but it caused quite a stir because of Thornton's request that the instruments should include a salt-box, cleaver, and 'bladder and string'. Charles was unable to attend the performance (he was still living in Lynn), but he described the *Ode* in a fragment of his memoir that has survived. It must have been rather like the *Toy Symphony* composed by Mozart's father, Leopold, some ten years earlier, with the orchestra carrying the tune, interrupted by solos from an assortment of unorthodox instruments played by famous London personalities: 'Beard sung the salt-box song, which was admirably accompanied on that instrument by Brent, the Fencing-master, and father of Miss Brent, the celebrated singer; Skeggs on the broomstick, as bassoon; and a remarkable performer on the Jew's-harp.'[45]

In the spring of 1760, Charles took Hetty with him to London for her first public performance before a prestigious audience in the Little Theatre on the Haymarket. On 23 April, the *Public Advertiser* announced that 'Miss Burney' (i.e. Hetty, who is inaccurately described as being 'nine years old') was expected to give 'a Lesson on the Harpsichord' as well as 'to perform in a quartet with other child prodigies'. This was a fashionable event: tickets were sold at half a guinea for a box or a seat in the pit and five shillings for the gallery (there were no cheap one-shilling seats), and 'Ladies' were 'desired to send their servants to keep places'.[46] The Duke of York attended and remarked favourably on Hetty's performance of some Scarlatti sonatas, using the virtuoso technique devised by her father. Hetty's success also brought her father to the attention of a Mrs Sheeles, who ran a boarding-school in Queen Square, Bloomsbury later attended by Boswell's daughters and known as 'The Ladies' Eton'. She offered Charles the post of music-master there, providing him with a small but reliable source of income, which gave him the impetus and the means to move his family back to London.

By September 1760 the Burneys were living in Poland Street, an unpretentious row of houses between Oxford Road (as Oxford Street was then known) and Broad Street (now Broadwick Street in Soho). Fanny later described their new home: 'The new establishment was in Poland-street; which was not then, as it is now, a sort of street that, like the rest of its neighbourhood, appears to be left in the lurch . . . Oxford-road . . . into which Poland-street terminated, had little on its further side but fields, gardeners' grounds, or uncultivated suburbs.' Their neighbours included the Duke of Chandos and Lady Augusta Bridges: Charles was determined this time to make a success of his London sojourn, living not in the City but in the more genteel West End, where he would be closer to the wealthy homes into which he hoped to be invited to give lessons. William Chambers, the architect, lived at No. 58 until 1766, while the watercolourist Paul Sandby was also a neighbour.[47]

From these years, we are given a picture of Fanny as a serious girl with a wisdom way beyond her age. Next door to the Burneys lived a wig-maker with young children, and one afternoon while playing together in the back-yard they found a trunk filled with old and dusty perukes, with which they had a lot of fun dressing–up and inventing imaginary characters. But inevitably one of the wigs, worth about ten guineas, fell off into a tub of rainwater and was ruined. Suddenly, all went quiet. Who was going to own up? Fanny, her family always fondly remembered, was the only child not afraid to tell the irate *perruquier*: 'What signifies talking so much about an accident. The wig is wet, to be sure; and the wig was a good wig, to be sure; but it's of no use to speak of it any more; because what's done can't be undone.'[48] The wig-maker was so nonplussed that he let all the children go unpunished, and 'The wig is wet!' became Burney code for 'It can't be helped'. Wigs – and their masking effect – play a significant role in the fictions that Fanny was later to write, almost like a personal signature.

Charles was soon as busy in London as he had ever been, and before long had 'more scholars than he could undertake'. Fanny later recalled how during the height of the London season, which ran from the beginning of January to the King's birthday on 4 June, her father often left the house at eight o'clock and 'his tour from house to house was scarcely ever finished sooner than eleven o'clock at night'. There were times when he gave as many as fifty-seven lessons in a week, eating his dinner of 'sandwiches prepared in a flat tin box; and wine and water ready mixed, in a wickered pint bottle' while travelling between pupils in his coach.[49]

On 4 November 1761, Esther gave birth without difficulty to another girl, Charlotte Ann, but afterwards became dangerously ill, weakened by nine pregnancies in thirteen years. In desperation, Charles took his wife to Bristol Hotwells, in the hope that the mineral waters would revive her. But she developed an inflammation of the bowels and died on 27 September 1762, after eight days of agony. Charles was inconsolable. As he recalled bitterly many years later, it was 'the greatest domestic calamity that could befal a fond & tender husband, in the death of the best Wife, friend & companion, with which a mortal could be blessed!'[50] He also had to find some way of caring for his six young children. James had been sent off to sea two years earlier as captain's servant on a man-of-war, the *Princess Amelia*,[51] but Hetty, Fanny, Susan, Charles and their ten-month-old baby sister all still needed their mother.

Of the children, it seems that it was ten-year-old Fanny who was most affected by Esther's death. The loss or absence of a parent, usually the mother, is a theme that runs through what she was later to write, suggesting that her own experience of being motherless was something with which she could never come to terms, and which she needed to work through by writing it out. Perhaps, as the shyest of the Burney brood, she had been closest to her quiet-spoken mother, clinging to her side when visitors called. Mrs Sheeles of Queen Square, who took care of the girls during those first few weeks of mourning, remarked of Fanny that 'she never saw such affliction in one before – that Fanny would take no comfort – & was almost killed with crying'.[52] Certainly, at ten, Fanny was of an age to be most affected by Esther's death, old enough to know and appreciate her mother's character but not yet independent enough to cope without her. Indeed, when five years later her father remarried, Fanny's stepmother remarked, 'Here's a Girl will *never* be happy! *Never* while she Lives! – for she possesses perhaps as feeling a Heart as ever Girl had!'[53]

When the girls returned to Poland Street, the house must have seemed empty without the warm, steadying influence of Esther. Charles shut himself up in his room, and the children were left very much to themselves. His letters from that time, which Fanny found after his death, are stained by his tears and speak of 'the total deprivation of domestic comfort and converse – that converse from which I tore myself with such difficulty in a morning, and to which I flew back with such celerity at night!' He mourned that he had 'lost the spur, the stimulus to all exertions ... From an ambitious, active, enterprizing Being, I am become a torpid drone, a listless, desponding wretch!'[54] His only release was to write reams of poetry, whose emotional nature suggests that Fanny's 'feeling Heart' was inherited from her father.

Other Burneys rallied round to help the lost and aimless Charles and his bemused children. His older sisters Rebecca ('Becky') and Ann ('Nancy') lived in York Street (close to Covent Garden market) with their mother, the former Ann Cooper. Fanny recalls fondly how she and the others would go there for tea – a fifteen-minute walk from Poland Street. She was even more attached to Esther's mother, 'my darling grandmother', whom she later described as 'a pattern of a perfect fine lady, a real fine lady, of other days'.[55] Charles, however, was concerned about his childrens' education. The sons were no problem: James went to sea, while Charles, who was already bookish, was destined for boarding-school.[56] But how were the girls to be taught without Esther? He had no time himself, but could not tolerate the idea of having a governess, a stranger to the family, in the house; nor did he want to send them away to school. Yet he recognised that a fine education was an essential attribute for daughters without prospects: his girls had no fortune to attract husbands, nor were they outstandingly beautiful. To know French and Italian and be able to play the harpsichord, dance a quadrille and stitch a sampler would ensure that they could at least find employment as governesses.

The family muddled along for more than a year before Charles finally decided to take two of his daughters to France, where he hoped they might learn to speak French fluently. 'Learning French, for females in servitude was absolutely necessary', he wrote many years later. And he understood that the best way for his girls to do this was by 'being boarded in a house where nothing else was spoken . . . and they being young and the Organs of speech ductile, they would acquire a better pronunciation & idiom in a few weeks, than at home in as many years, where it is book French which children learn & English translated'.[57] Charles may have been preoccupied with furthering his own career, but he also took great trouble over the welfare of his children, encouraging them to nurture and fulfil their talents.

The trip to Paris enabled Charles to acquaint himself with the latest trends in music on the Continent – and make up for that missed opportunity with the Grevilles. He originally intended to take the two older girls, Hetty and Fanny, but in the end Fanny was left behind, and on 6 June 1764 Charles set off for Dover with Hetty (then aged fifteen) and young Susan, who was nine. They were to live with a Madame Saintmard in Paris, who had been recommended to Charles by one of his aristocratic patrons, Lady Clifford, sister of the Duchess of Norfolk. It is likely that Lady Clifford also provided financial assistance since the cost of boarding the two girls, some £200 each year, was a substantial sum of money for Charles, who was totally reliant on his own resources.

At eleven, Fanny would have gained more from the experience than Susan, but her father perhaps feared that she would be too influenced by French Catholicism, being more sensitive than her sisters.[58] Certainly, Charles decided against settling his girls in a convent – even though this would have been a much cheaper way of educating them – because he feared for their religious upbringing. 'I thought it best,' he once wrote, 'whatever might be the expence, to avoid putting them in the way to be prejudiced in favour of any religion but our own [i.e. Anglican Protestantism], as it might distract their mind, &, if opposed, render them miserable for the rest of their lives.'[59] Indeed, if any of the girls had been tempted to convert to Catholicism, it might well have endangered more than their peace of mind: several years later, during the Gordon Riots of 1780, Catholics feared for their lives as their homes were ransacked and set on fire.

Maybe, too, Charles could not bear to part with the daughter who most resembled his shy, retiring but spirited wife? Whatever the reason, Fanny was left behind with only Charles junior, who was six, and two-year-old Charlotte for company. How could she fill the long days while her father was out and about in town? Fanny never went to school but, like her father, she had an enquiring mind. With the same dogged determination and keen intelligence as Charles, she taught herself French and Italian by reading Dante, Petrarch and Voltaire in the original language. The lists she kept of the books she had read also suggest her enthusiasm for Cicero, Pliny and Thucydides. These latter, however, she read in translation, as she knew neither Latin nor Greek. Her father (in keeping with many of his friends and contemporaries) considered that while their female companions needed to be cultured enough to conduct informed and lively conversation, too much learning in a woman was disagreeable, and when Dr Johnson later offered to give Fanny lessons in the classical languages, Charles refused to give his permission.[60]

Novels, too, were forbidden, as being dangerous fodder for malleable young minds, and Fanny later claimed that the only fiction in her father's library was Henry Fielding's *Amelia*. Scraps and fragments of notebooks kept by Fanny in her teenage years (and now in the Berg Collection of Burney family papers in the New York Public Library) indicate that Fanny was influenced instead by books on self-improvement and devotional meditations, such as *Moore's Fables for the Female Sex*, *Fordyce's Sermons to Young Women* and the *Letters Moral and Entertaining* of Mrs Elizabeth Rowe. On four sheets entitled 'Lessons of Conduct & Sentiment', which were for her 'Daily Perusal', Fanny copied out advice under the headings 'Religion', 'Duty', 'Sincerity', 'Charity', 'Self-denial' and 'Delicacy'. Blank spaces were left alongside 'Humility' and 'Housewifery', but under 'Activity' she wrote, 'Those who slight this, lose half their lives. Those who court it, enjoy Two. Have employments adapted to all Times, situations & companies. Be never entirely idle. Youth will ill bear neglect, whose very existence is but a few moments, & age has need of every resource Early industry can give, to render it agreeable.'

On another fragment, dated 31 December 1767, she made lists of advice on Love, Duty, Romance and Care, warning that 'The woman who owns a clandestine affection subjects herself to the most cutting mortification her sex can receive, namely, *the familiar assurance* of a Lover'.[61] Fanny took such advice seriously and her novels are peppered with improving mottoes. In her diary, however, she confided that she was 'charmed' by Laurence Sterne's *A Sentimental Journey through France and Italy*, which she confessed she was about to read for the third time. Her enjoyment of a book in which Sterne wittily tells his readers of his amorous adventures, rather than giving them a precise account of his travels, suggests that Fanny, although serious, moral and religious, also had a lively sense of humour.

Another, and far more important influence on her writing, was a friend of her father, to whom she was introduced in those lonely months just after Susan and Hetty left for France. Samuel Crisp (1709–83) was a wealthy and cultured gentleman who had travelled much on the Continent. He was once described by Sterne as being a member of the army of 'peregrine martyrs' who rushed around Europe in the 1730s and 1740s in search of learning and amusement, and is remembered as being the first man in Britain to have a pianoforte, bought and transported home from Rome. Crisp first met Charles Burney while staying at Fulke Greville's country home in 1747. They became friends through their common interests – both men championed the new Italian music (Crisp had a fine tenor voice), and both pursued the dream of writing for the theatre (Crisp's tragedy *Virginia* ran for eleven nights at Drury Lane in February 1754).

It was Crisp who most encouraged Charles to leave Lynn Regis and return to London: 'is not settling at Lynn, planting your youth, genius, hopes, fortune, &c, against a north wall? Can you ever expect ripe, high-flavoured fruit from such an aspect? . . . In all professions, do you not see every thing that has the least pretence to genius, fly up to the capital – the centre of riches, luxury, taste, pride, extravagance . . . Take, then, your spare person, your pretty mate, and your brats, to that propitious mart.'[62] Crisp knew how dull life could be away from the metropolis: by the time he wrote this letter to Charles in 1759 he himself had retreated from the world to a remote house in Chesington, Surrey (modern Chessington), which was often cut off in bad weather, the track submerged in mud. Charles once became so lost in the surrounding marshland that he was forced to return to London without seeing his friend: 'I wrote my friend Crisp an account of my Quixoteism in seeking him with as much zeal & ill success as La Manca's Knight ever wandered after his Dulcinea.'[63]

Samuel Crisp was said to have been embittered by his failure to persuade Garrick to revive *Virginia*, but his retreat from society is more likely to have been because he simply ran out of money. The portrait of him by Edward Francisco Burney shows a genial, ruddy-faced man with kindly eyes and unpretentious clothes, a gentleman-farmer rather than an aesthete. His letters reveal a wise and witty man who never ceased to encourage the young Burneys to make the most of their talents:

My dear Fanny, I tell you what – You are a Jew – an Ebrew Jew – of the line of Shylock, & I shall henceforth call you, Jessica,' [he once wrote to her,] 'because you, an overgrown Rich Jew, can give me an Entertainment of a hundred Dishes, do you expect the like from such a poor, forked unbelieving Christian as I am – You riot in Provisions of all sorts, I have nothing to do, but choose, or reject; & your Cookery is at your fingers ends, & to do you Justice has the true relish, & is highly season'd; all this I give you credit for; I devour the feast you give me, finish the desert, lick up the Jellies & Ic'd Creams to the last drop, & am thankful – but all this must do it seems – the Mosaic Law says – '*the Eye for an Eye & a Tooth for a Tooth*' – And if I have neither, *then I must have your pound of Flesh says Jessica* – The truth is, Chesington produces nothing beyond Bacon & Greens, with a new laid Egg, or so.[64]

Fanny never forgot her first meeting with her 'earliest and dearest friend', which took place in late 1764 when Mr Crisp (as she wrote to him) was tempted back to London to visit his old friend in Poland Street. She was fascinated by the breadth of Mr Crisp's conversation, which veered from scholarly allusion to flippant comments about human nature, while he in turn was bewitched by her combination of thoughtfulness and impish humour. He became Fanny's mentor and inspiration; a substitute parent – and husband, too. Fanny wrote in her diary for 1768, 'My Papa always mentions him by the name of my *Flame* – indeed he is not mistaken, – himself is the *only* man on Earth I prefer to him.' It was to be thirty years before Fanny met anyone who could match this courtly, distinguished man with 'bright, hazel, penetrating, yet arch eyes; an open front; a noble Roman nose; and a smile of a thousand varied expressions', whom she would address in her letters as 'My dear Daddy'. In return Mr Crisp has given us perhaps the most perceptive and vivid description of Fanny: 'What a slight piece of machinery is the terrestrial part of thee, our Fannikin! – a mere nothing; a blast, a vapour disorders the spring of thy watch; and the mechanism is so fine that it requires no common hand to set it a-going again.'[65]

Other, less welcome visitors arrived in Poland Street. Shortly after Esther's death, the Burneys' old friend in Lynn Regis, Mrs Allen, was also widowed and, quietly, secretly, she and Charles began a courtship that was to end in marriage in October 1767.[66] Esther, in her last illness, had expressed the hope that her husband would marry again, and that his choice would be Dolly Young, whom she knew was fondly loved by all her children. But Charles succumbed to a not uncommon weakness, preferring to wed not the plain and unprepossessing Dolly but 'the celebrated beauty of Lynn', Elizabeth Allen.[67] His new wife was, like Esther, intelligent, educated and a great conversationalist, but Fanny was never to accept her. Reading between the lines of Fanny's description of her stepmother in her *Memoirs of Doctor Burney*, one suspects that little love was lost between them: 'She had wit at will; spirits the most vivacious and entertaining; and, from a passionate fondness for reading, she had collected stores of knowledge which she was always able, and "*nothing loath*" to display.'[68]

Charles, however, was devoted to his 'beloved Mrs Allen'. In old age he recalled how: 'He used to sit up whole nights pleading my cause in letters addressed to her in a feigned hand or under cover to D. Young' and that they behaved like '2 young lovers under age trying to out-wit our parents and guardians'. Mrs Allen had three children of her own – Maria (a year older than Fanny), Stephen (born in 1755, the same year as Susan) and Elizabeth (known as Bessy and then aged four, like Charlotte) – and her mother was anxious that a freelance musician would never have sufficient income to support them all. Charles was more concerned that all the children should get along: 'It was my wish & hope that our children would not be in each other's way, & that the children of my former marriage would be loved and regarded by my new partner as her own, being myself perfectly disposed & resolved to treat Mrs Allen's children with the same care and tenderness as my own.'[69] In the summer of 1767, Charles travelled to Bristol Hotwells, taking Fanny with him (to her delight, as it was her first jaunt with her father by herself), so that he could visit Mrs Allen's brother and persuade him to give his approval to the match. Charles had last visited the spa with Esther, so the return must have been difficult, filled with memories of her.

Needless to say, nothing of Charles's ardent devotion to his new wife appears in Fanny's *Memoirs*. She does admit, very stiffly, that 'The four daughters of Mr Burney, – Esther, Frances, Susan, and Charlotte, – were all earnest to contribute their small mites to the happiness of one of the most beloved of parents, by receiving, with the most respectful alacrity, the lady on whom he had cast his future hopes of regaining domestic comfort.' But she later launches into a veiled demolition-job on her stepmother, subtly hinting at the second Mrs Burney's lack of gentility: 'The friends of Mr Burney were not slack in paying their devoirs to his new partner, whose vivacious society, set off by far more than remains of uncommon beauty, failed not to attract various visitors to the house; and whose love, or rather passion, for conversation and argument, were of that gay and brilliant sort, that offers too much entertainment to be ever left in the lurch for want of partakers.'[70]

At first Mrs Allen kept her home in Lynn Regis, and when in London stayed in separate rented accommodation in Poland Street, so as not to cause too much disruption. Nevertheless, the freedoms of Fanny's quiet and rather lonely life were at an end. There were compensations: Hetty and Susan were brought back home from France and Maria Allen proved a lively and irreverent addition to the family, tempting her new sisters to gossip over midnight feasts of cheese on toast. Many years later she recalled: 'I feel the same unreserved friendship towards my "Old friends and companions" as I did when our highest Luxury was sitting in Elegant undress over a few dying embers in my bedchamber relating the disasters of the day and afterwards sleeping three in a bed in a charming warm night in July.'[71] But Fanny was never reconciled to her stepmother.

In retrospect, though, what Fanny felt as a betrayal by her father might well have impelled her to find some release for her pent-up emotions. Not long after her mother's death, she had begun to scribble secretly 'little works of invention', as she was later to call them. Sadly, these early 'schoolgirl fictions' are now lost, destroyed by Fanny on her fifteenth birthday after she had been discovered in mid-flow by her stepmother. Fanny resolutely determined to give up her 'clandestine delight' and burn all that she had written so far. At that time she 'considered it her duty to combat this writing passion as illaudable, because fruitless'. Looking back on that afternoon, when she had 'committed to the flames' her stories, elegies, odes, verses and plays, she solemnly recorded in the *Memoirs* how she took the opportunity of being alone in the house except for Susan (Dr Burney and his wife were staying with Mr Crisp in Chesington), and 'made over a bonfire, in a paved play-court, her whole stock of prose goods and chattels; with the sincere intention to extinguish for ever in their ashes her scribbling propensity'.[72]

Writing, however, was to be a passion that Fanny could not – and would not – suppress.

TWO

To Nobody
1768–78

> To Nobody, then, will I write my Journal! since To Nobody can I be
> Wholly unreserved – to Nobody can I reveal every thought, every wish
> of my Heart, with the most unlimited confidence.
>
> Fanny Burney, March 1768

Having burnt to cinders all her stories and poems in a huge bonfire,
Fanny discovered that it was not so easy to give up her addiction. Nine
months later, she sat down at her bureau with sheets of crisp paper and
sharpened quill and resolved that from this day, 27 March 1768, she
would begin writing a journal. From the outset, this was not just for
her own amusement: 'To have some account of my thoughts, manners,
acquaintance & actions, when the Hour arrives in which time is more
nimble than memory,' she wrote, 'is the Reason which induces me to
keep a Journal.' This was to be, she continued, 'a Journal in which I
must confess my every thought, must open my whole Heart!'[1]

Once begun, she was to continue her journal for seventy years.[2] A
good deal of what she wrote she later destroyed when, as a forgetful
old lady, she steadily worked through all her papers either obliterating
certain passages or, in some cases, incinerating them in a series of little
bonfires. Fanny, always over-cautious, feared that she had been too
revealing both of herself and of her family. She had resolved at the
start that 'I must imagion myself to be talking – talking to the most
intimate of friends – to one in whom I should take delight in confiding,
& remorse in concealment.'[3] And this she did – to such effect that she
was probably right to be concerned that she had been too free with her
pen.

Fanny was not the only Burney to be a perceptive observer of
people *and* a gifted writer. Susan, who began her own journal in 1764
when she left home and travelled to Paris with Hetty, wrote an
illuminating comparison of her sisters Hetty and Fanny: 'The

characteristics of Hetty seem to be wit, generosity, and openness of heart; Fanny's, – sense, sensibility, and bashfulness, and even a degree of prudery.' Indeed, she thought that Fanny was cleverer than Hetty, but that 'My eldest sister [i.e. Hetty] shines in conversation, because, though very modest, she is totally free from any mauvaise honte . . . I am afraid that my eldest sister is too communicative, and that my sister Fanny is too reserved.'[4] While Hetty was an unabashed extrovert – confident enough to walk into a crowded ballroom playing a hurdy-gurdy and carry it off without blushing (she is the only sister for whom we have no record of a diary; that preserve of the shy, secretive and reserved) – Fanny fled from the room in embarrassment if anyone made a personal comment about her. She was, too, always anxious to preserve her 'reputation', cutting former friends dead if she thought their behaviour had gone beyond the limits of social acceptability.

In the privacy of her diary, however, Fanny allowed herself the freedom to be someone quite different. She may not have had the courage or musical talent to perform in public but, ironically, through her pen she was to play to a far larger audience than either her father (shortly to become Dr Burney, with the award of a doctorate in music from Oxford University) or her sister Hetty.

At first, she wondered to whom she should address her innermost thoughts: 'To *whom*, then, *must* I dedicate my wonderful, surprising & interesting adventures?' she wrote, in a cheeky reference to Daniel Defoe's *The Life and Strange and Surprizing Adventures of Robinson Crusoe*.[5] 'To *whom* do I reveal my private opinion of my nearest Relations? My secret thoughts of my dearest friends? My own hopes for & affections & dislikes?' Her diary was to be hcr confessional, her emotional release, and so she decided that 'To Nobody, then, will I write my Journal! since To Nobody can I be Wholly unreserved – to Nobody can I reveal every thought, every wish of my Heart, with the most unlimited confidence, the most unremitting sincerity to the end of my Life! . . . No secret *can* I conceal from No-body, & to No-body can be *ever* unreserved.' She had 'nothing to fear' from Nobody, because 'secrets sacred to friendship, Nobody will not reveal'.[6]

Fanny's intention was to write as if to a close friend who would remain forever nameless. She had no interest in making a daily record of dinners eaten, walks taken and visits made to the dressmaker or milliner. Indeed, over seventy years of diary-writing, she made surprisingly little reference to the minutiae of her life, which at times can be very frustrating: what, for instance, did she wear to her wedding? Fanny was bored by fashion and idle gossip (observing in a letter to Mr Crisp that 'perpetual Dress requires perpetual replenishment');[7] she preferred to use her journal as a commonplace book in which she could express her thoughts, ideas, observations – and to pen a whole gallery of character studies, rather like an artist and her sketch-pad. 'I cannot express the pleasure I have in writing down my thoughts, at the very moment – my opinion of people when I first see them, & *how* I alter, or *how* I confirm myself in it,' she wrote on 27 March. The journal was to be a record of *her* life, an assertion of *her* self. 'There is something to me very Unsatisfactory in passing year after year without even a memorandum of what you did, &c. And then, all the happy Hours I spend with particular Friends and Favourites, would fade from my recollection.'[8]

It was also a valuable way to occupy her days and nights when she was alone. The Burney family at this time lived a double life – half in Lynn Regis, where the second Mrs Burney still had a large, accommodating house on the quayside, and half in Poland Street. Charlotte was sent to school in Lynn and Susan was taken there in February 1769 by her stepmother after suffering a 'dangerous illness' described by Fanny as an 'inflammation of the breast'. Hetty was often engaged to play for Dr Burney's friends, leaving Fanny at home in Poland Street on her own (Charles was away at Charterhouse):

> How delightful, how enviable a tranquility and content do I at present enjoy! I have scarse a wish, and am happy & easy as my Heart can desire. My Papa has more Business of late than ever, & he is almost always out . . . Hetty now aged twenty has perpetually visits to pay – so that I am very much alone, but to that I have no objection . . . I write now from a pretty neat little Closet of mine that is in the Bed Chamber, where I keep all my affairs – Tell me, my dear, what Heroine ever yet existed without her own Closet.[9]

Being by herself – with 'a room of her own' – was preferable, Fanny suggests, to being plagued by the officious presence of the new Mrs Burney. Much of what Fanny said about her stepmother in her diary she later tried to delete, which is hardly surprising, for the text that underlies her heavy black scoring-out (much of which has now been recovered for the new edition of her diaries) is full of recriminations. The Burney and Allen girls appear to have been united in their antipathy to their interfering, inquisitive mother, whom they secretly called 'The Lady'. They were also agreed that, compared with the 'amusements' of London, Lynn Regis was horribly small, petty-minded and provincial. Fanny confided in her journal for March 1768 that 'they had amused themselves with railing against Lynn, every thing, every body in it'. She, however, felt obliged to say 'some few words in favour of my poor old abused Town – the Land of my Nativity' before being interrupted by Hetty:

'Hush – hush – Mama's in the next Room – if she hears us – we shall be whipt – & Fanny will have a sugar plumb.' 'Ay, cried A [Fanny's code for Maria Allen]. 'Tis her defending Lynn which makes Mama – & my Grandmama so fond of her.' 'Fond of me,' cried I. – 'What makes you imagion Mrs Allen fond of me?'[10]

Only a few months after that 'secret' conference of the 'cabal' of sisters (as their stepmother once accused them of being), the second Mrs Burney wrote Fanny a most heartfelt letter. She was just about to give birth to Richard Thomas (born on 20 November 1768) and, understandably worried (she was over forty), she asked Fanny to look after her new stepbrother: 'Allow me my dear Fanny to take this moment (if there proves occasion) to recommend a helpless Infant to your Pity and Protection, you will ev'ry day become more and more Capable of the Task – & you will, I do trust you will, for your same dear Father's sake, cherish & support His Innocent Child – tho' but half allied to you – My Weak Heart speaks in Tears to you my Love.'[11]

Mrs Burney evidently found it necessary almost to beg for acceptance by her silent sixteen-year-old stepdaughter. Yet she was fond of Fanny and recognised that she had 'a feeling heart' and a great deal of common sense. With good reason Fanny was known as the prudent 'Old Lady' of the family; she was the daughter most often called upon by Dr Burney to sit up with him on those nights when he could not sleep (for he hated to be alone), and was first choice as secretary and copyist when he came to write his history of music in the 1770s. Much later, her stepsister Maria remembered how she was 'the prop and support of the Family in all Emergencies'.[12] Fanny, as Susan observed had both sense and sensibility.

She tells us disappointingly little about her physical appearance in the diaries: without Edward's portraits, we would have little idea of how she looked. We know that she was shorter than her sisters (barely five feet two inches in height)[13] and very short-sighted – yet she did not take advantage of the new spectacles, her 'Miracle Machine', until

1794 and always had difficulty recognising people when she entered a crowded room.[14] She was not entirely pleased with her appearance, believing herself to be not half so pretty as either Hetty or Susan, nor so good-natured, while her comments on food suggest that she took little enjoyment in it (she was forever on diets restricted to turnips, bread and asses' milk). The weather, the seasons, the arrival of the first snowdrop or swallow never impinge on Fanny's narrative. And yet, in her 'Juvenile Journal', she gives us a vivid impression of what it was like to be a teenage girl in the mid-eighteenth century.

'I am going to tell you something concerning myself,' she wrote while staying in Lynn Regis in the summer of 1768, 'which, if I have not chanced to mention it before will I believe a little surprise you – it is, that I scarse wish for any thing so truly, really & greatly, as to be *in love*.' Some weeks later, she continued on the same theme: 'Alas, alas, my poor Journal! – how dull, unentertaining, uninteresting thou art! – oh what would I give for some Adventure worthy reciting – for something which would surprise – astonish you! – Would to Cupid I was in love! – Shall I never feel that so much desired passion.'[15]

There was, however, an ambivalence in Fanny. Maybe she sensed that there was some bigger 'Adventure' awaiting her; maybe, like her father, she was driven by an ambition to create something that would make her famous; maybe she knew instinctively that her talent was to write, and that this gift was more important than anything else. Whatever the reason, she dreamed of love but was already wary of marriage and its consequences for a woman. One afternoon, while writing in the 'Cabin' at the end of the garden of Mrs Burney's house in Lynn Regis, from which she could see the ships moored along the riverside – and overhear the 'oaths & ribaldry' of the sailors and porters as they unloaded; she would retreat back to the house when they became too shocking – she watched a wedding-party first processing along the lane beside the garden into St Margaret's Church opposite, and then emerging some fifteen minutes later. 'O heavens!' she commented ruefully, 'how short a time does it take to put an eternal end to a Woman's liberty! I don't think they were a $\frac{1}{4}$ of an Hour in the Church altogether . . . Well of all things in the World, I don't suppose any thing can be so dreadful . . . as a public Wedding – my stars! – I should never be able to support it.'[16]

She was only sixteen, yet she was not bewitched by the aura of happiness encapsulated in such rituals. She may not have had much experience of the world – and she had missed the warmth and guidance of her mother – but Fanny had read widely and had learned to think for herself. She had been shocked by *The Iliad*, for instance, at the passage where Venus tempts Helen with riches and power, and Helen resists at first only to weaken when she is threatened with the loss of her beauty: 'Thus has Homer proved his opinion of our poor sex,' wrote Fanny, 'that the Love of Beauty is our most prevailing passion. It really grieves me to think that there certainly must be reason for the insignificant opinion the greatest men have of Women – At least I *fear* there must. – But I don't in fact *believe* it – thank God!'[17]

She understood that marriage could mean a life of miserable dependence for the wife. She had also begun to resent the constrictions imposed on women, confined by strict rules of etiquette to waste their time paying calls on other women whose company was valuable merely because they might be of use socially:

> O how I hate this vile custom which obliges us to make slaves of ourselves! to sell the most precious property we boast, our Time; & to sacrifice it to every prattling impertinent who chuses to demand it! – yet those who shall pretend to defy this irksome confinement of our happiness, must stand accused of incivility . . . For why should we not be permitted to be masters of our Time . . . 'tis Custom – Custom – which is so woven around us – which so universally commands us – which we all blame – and all obey, without knowing why or wherefore.[18]

She was encouraged in these rebellious views by her stepsister Maria, who shared Fanny's sense of humour but had none of her reserve. Fanny remarked of her:

> The strongest *trait* of her own Character is sincerity, – one of the most noble of virtues, &, perhaps, without any exception, *the most* uncommon – but if it is possible, she is *too* sincere; she pays too little regard to the World, & indulges herself with too much freedom of raillery & pride of disdain, towards those whose vices or follies offend her. Were this a *general* rule of conduct, what real benefit might it bring to society! but being *particular*, it only hurts & provokes Individuals.[19]

Nevertheless, Fanny enjoyed Maria's company, declaring that she was 'the life of our House & family'. For a while, too, Maria stood in for 'Nobody', and Fanny wrote copious letters and poems to her, in one of which, entitled 'Female Caution', she bemoaned the curse of 'faithless', 'deceiving' men. She advised her stepsister to 'learn to guard the heart, Nor let it's softness be its bane!'

The stepsisters discussed ways of negating the effects of living in a society dominated by men; Maria's solution is worthy of the most militant feminist. She wrote to Fanny, 'I like your Plan immensely of Extirpating that vile race of beings called man but I (who you know am clever (VERRÉE) clever) have thought of an improvement in the sistim: suppose we were to Cut of [sic] their *prominent members* and by that means render them Harmless innofencive Little Creatures.'[20] Soon afterwards, Maria followed the predictable route of rebellious but naïve young women, first falling victim to the charms of the wealthy dilettante Martin Rishton, of whom her mother did not approve, and then eloping with him to Ypres (in Flanders) in May 1772.[21] Her initial happiness soon turned to boredom and misery as Martin fled his debts to a remote farmhouse in Norfolk. Maria became a lonely, domesticated farmer's wife, while, unbeknown to her, Martin carried on a long affair with her best friend.

Though by her own admission 'awkward & abashed', Fanny made a more successful entry into London society. On 10 January 1770, she and Hetty were invited to a masquerade given by the Lalauzes, who ran a fashionable dancing academy in Leicester Fields. Fanny later noted every detail of the evening, which she and Hetty looked forward to for three months and then spent a whole day dressing up in preparation.[22] Having decided not to disguise herself as a nun or Quaker – because 'there is a gravity & extreme reserve required to support them, which would have made me necessarily so dull & stupid that I could not have met with much entertainment – she opted to go in 'a meer *fancy Dress*', of which she was so proud that she has left an elaborate description: 'A close pink persian *Vest*, with long close sleeves, to my Wrists, it was covered with Gauze, in loose pleats behind, & drawn half tight & half loose at the sleeve, puckered before, with very small pink Flowers fastened on to look like buttons; it came up high in the Neck, & had a Gauze frill round the Waist.' Over this, she wore a coat of white silk, 'trimmed also with small artificial flowers before, & a Gauze train looped up behind, & pink ribband round the Bottom'. Her demure appearance was completed by 'pink silk shoes & Roses, a very small black collar about my Neck, a little Garland or Wreath of Flowers on the left side of my Head, & looped Pearl Earrings'.

Hetty, dressed as a shepherdess in blue and white, walked into the ballroom playing her hurdy-gurdy and was immediately the centre of attention. 'The Company flocked about her with much pleasure,' wrote Fanny, who was soon courted herself by a harlequin, merlin, a witch, two or three Turks, a pink domino,[23] and a Dutchman. After supper everyone unmasked, revealing, to Fanny's amusement, just how much appearances could deceive:

> Nothing could be more droll . . . to see the pleasure which appeared in some Countenances, & the disappointment pictured in others . . . in short every Face appeared different from what we expected. The old Witch in particular we found was a young Officer; the Punch who had made himself as Broad as long, was a very young and handsome man; but what surprised me, was the shepherd, whose own face was so stupid that we could scarsely tell whether he had taken off his mask or not.

Meanwhile, the Dutchman, whom Fanny had thought was at least fifty, revealed himself as young and very handsome: 'I believe my surprise was very manifest, for Mynheer could not forbear Laughing. On his part he paid me many Compliments, repeatedly & with much civility congratulating himself on his Choice.' A few days later he sent a note to Poland Street with three tickets for the Chelsea assembly, intended for Fanny, Hetty and a chaperone. Hetty teased Fanny that she had made her 'first serious Conquest'. Dr Burney was less amused, and, fearing that this presumptuous suitor 'must either be a very bold man, or a young man who knew nothing of the world', told Fanny to return the tickets at once.

Neither Dr Burney nor his wife accompanied Fanny and Hetty to their first ball (Mrs Burney was again in Lynn Regis visiting her mother). But Dr Burney was a much-loved father, who took care to ensure that *all* his children were well read and never failed to write to them when he was away:

> I'm not such a Churl
> To deny my dear Girl
> So small & so trifling a favour;
> For I always shall try
> With her wish to comply
> Though of Nonsense it happen to savour

31

he wrote to Fanny from Berkshire when she was ten.[24] However, he appeared to have little interest in the fate of his daughters as they entered the marriage market, preferring perhaps that they should remain with him as companions and assistants in his work. Mrs Burney, meanwhile, was too preoccupied with her second family – Richard Thomas and Sarah Harriet, born in August 1772 – to care for the welfare of her stepdaughters. (Her own daughters fared little better: Bessy copied Maria by running away to Ypres to marry an 'adventurer'.)

As the eldest, Hetty was the first to suffer from this lack of guidance through the sophisticated nuances of courtship. She had been assiduously wooed (or so she thought) by a Mr Alexander Seton, who was handsome, wealthy and, as the son of a titled Edinburgh brewer, an advantageous catch. But he was fickle and Fanny soon saw through him, writing in April 1770:

> Mr Seton is artful: I have seen that he courts my good opinion, & I know why, – he flatters me in a peculiar style, always affecting a serious air, & assuring me he speaks his real sentiments: – I some times think he does not know *how* to do that; – though there is an insinuating air of sincerity in his manner when ever he is serious, which often staggers me, in spight of the prejudice I have conceived against him for his unworthy trifling with so sweet, so amiable a Girl as Hetty.[25]

Hetty was not so perceptive and became thin and wan from the sleepless nights she spent waiting for her suitor to declare himself. Mr Seton disappeared suddenly from the 'Juvenile Journal' and was never mentioned again, while Hetty was diverted by a series of private concert engagements with her cousin, Charles Rousseau Burney (the son of Dr Burney's brother Richard). A virtuoso violinist and harpsichordist (he played the organ at Ranelagh Gardens, the rival pleasure garden to Vauxhall), Charles Rousseau was regarded as an ideal partner for Hetty, with whom he is pictured in a painting thought to be by Thomas Hudson or William Hoare and still owned by the family. Hetty is seated at the harpsichord while Charles Rousseau strums his violin and his father Richard looks on.[26] Maybe the possibility of an engagement between Hetty and Mr Seton prompted Dr Burney to encourage a match between the cousins, fearing that otherwise the unorthodox circumstances of Hetty's birth might have to be disclosed. (The taint of illegitimacy could well have endangered her prospects and besmirched his professional reputation.)

Maybe Hetty found relief in Charles Rousseau's straightforwardness and familiarity.[27]

Six months after the masquerade at which Hetty had shown her 'partial preference' for Mr Seton, she wrote to her sisters Fanny and Susan who were in Lynn Regis for the summer with the news that she was engaged to Charles Rousseau and that the wedding was to take place very soon, on 20 September, in St Paul's Church, Covent Garden. Dr Burney was away in Italy, gathering material for his history of music and did not know of the marriage until 27 October, when he was told by a fellow traveller with whom he had spent the day walking up Vesuvius that, 'The English papers say that Dr B's daughter is married to one of his own name – I hope felicementa and with his concent.' Dr Burney added, 'If it had been otherwise, the Captain's manner of breaking it to me would not have been the most gentle in the world.'[28]

According to Fanny, her new brother-in-law appeared at his wedding as 'a shy, modest, embarrassed, half-formed youth'. Fanny also mentions that Charles Rousseau had 'nothing to offer her [Hetty] but the fruits of his profession', implying that Hetty could have secured for herself a better match.[29] Charles Rousseau was kindly but too retiring and gentle a man to make a success of a career as a music-teacher and performer. Marriage for Hetty brought with it years of poor health (she suffered a number of miscarriages and had eight children between 1772 and 1792) and much sadness. One son, Henry, died at only a few weeks, while boarded out with a wet nurse in Chesington (Hetty was in London caring for her other children), while another, Charles Crisp, ran away to India as a teenager, where he died of dysentery soon afterwards.[30] Her daughters often stayed for several months with their Burney aunts and uncles, presumably because Charles Rousseau and Hetty could not afford to have them at home. It should be said, though, that Charles Rousseau was acknowledged to be a brilliant musician and when he died in 1819 the obituary in the *New Monthly Magazine* declared him to be 'one of the finest performers in the British Empire'.[31] That he found it difficult to earn a living despite his talent suggests that his uncle, Dr Burney, was truly remarkable in his success.

While Dr Burney was away in France and Italy, his resourceful wife sold her property in Lynn Regis so that she could afford to buy a house in Queen Square, Bloomsbury, that was large enough for both the Burney and Allen families. The house she chose, at the northern end of the square, had a literary connection – Dean Swift's friend, John Barber (Lord Mayor of London in 1733), had once lived there – which much gratified Dr Burney. Its rooms were elegantly proportioned, spacious and airy, and from the back looked across fields to the hilltop villages of Hampstead and Highgate. Dr Burney arrived back from Italy on Christmas Eve 1770 after an absence of almost seven months and went straight to Queen Square. But he soon abandoned his family again, rushing off to stay with Mr Crisp in Chesington so that he could work on his book, *The Present State of Music in France and Italy, or the Journal of a Tour through those Countries, undertaken to collect Materials for a General History of Music*, which was published the following May. (It was praised at the time for its prose style, rather than its musical scholarship; which pleased Dr Burney, who wanted his book to be 'so divested of Pedantry & Jargon that every Miss, who plays *o' top' the Spinet* should make it her manual'.[32] On 8 May, Fanny noted plaintively that 'Last Sunday 5 May was the first Day for some Time past, that my Father has favoured us with his company, in the parlour stile, having been so exceedingly occupied by writing in those few Hours he spends at Home, that he really seemed lost to his Family, & the comfort of his society & Conversation are almost as new as grateful to us.'[33]

Her journal in the months after Hetty's marriage and the move from Poland Street has many gaps. 'Alas! my poor forsaken Journal! how long have I neglected thee!' She had lost her '*Goût* for Writing', and although there had been a time when she 'could enjoy Nothing, without relating it', there had since been too many changes: 'too many subjects . . . of sorrow, have I met with of late, without the least wish of applying to my old friend for participation or relief'.[34] She does not reveal what these 'sorrows' were, but Fanny was always to feel confused and dejected when the tightly knit bonds between the Burneys were disrupted, as if it reminded her of the grief she experienced when her mother died. She also admitted, half ironically, that she had to 'accomodate herself' to the dire business of having turned nineteen. The excitements of London were already becoming dull and tarnished for Fanny and, after an outing with Mama and Maria to Ranelagh Gardens (by the river in Chelsea, with a huge domed rotunda and picture gallery), she declared, 'The Room was extremely Crowded & very brilliant . . . I saw few people there that I knew, & none that I cared for.'[35]

Fanny turned elsewhere for friendship, beginning at about this time a frequent and lengthy correspondence with Mr Crisp. 'My design upon Mr Crisp has succeeded to my wish,' she wrote on 30 April 1772. 'He has sent me the kindest & most flattering Answer – which encourages me to write again. He says more in three lines, than I shall in a hundred while I live.'[36] With her 'dear Daddy' she could talk of real matters – not the trivia of the ballroom and card-table – and also bask in his admiration without fear of wandering into the dangerous territory of flirtation and coquetry. In return, he nurtured her talent for writing; for although Mr Crisp never achieved the literary success he wanted, he was of crucial importance in launching Fanny upon her life as a writer.

It was Mr Crisp who encouraged her passion for 'scribbling', declaring that he 'shall set up for a Critic, or schoolmaster, or Observer of Composition – Damn it all! – I hate it if once You set about framing studied letters, that are to be correct, nicely grammatical & run in smooth Periods'. Fanny had asked him to 'deal sincerely' with her and to tell her of her faults; he replied forthwith: 'let this *declaration serve* once for all . . . the sudden sallies of imagination, clap'd down on paper, just as they arise, are worth Folios . . . never think of being correct, when You write to me'.[37]

Mr Crisp's stimulating advice was a valuable counterpoint to her stepmother's suspicion of her secret vice and to the warnings of Dolly Young, who told Fanny that keeping a diary was 'the most dangerous employment young persons can have', because 'it makes them often record things which ought *not* to be recorded, but instantly forgot'. Fanny retaliated by insisting that she wrote only for her own amusement and perusal, and that Miss Young thought 'worse of my poor Journal than it deserves'. But Miss Young was too wise for Fanny: 'I know very well the nature of these things. I know that in journals, thoughts, actions, looks, conversations – *all* go down; do they not?' Fanny risked all by calling Miss Young's bluff. She let her choose one day's entry to read out loud, a day that fortunately for Fanny proved 'harmless', so that even Dolly was forced to agree that there could be no harm in Fanny continuing to write.[38]

Mr Crisp, however, did more than give his approval. Fanny would retire to Chesington when she wanted to escape her duties at home and get on with her writing undisturbed. At Chesington Hall she was given her own room, called by Mr Crisp 'the conjuring Closet', where if she wished she could spend the whole day with Miss Nobody. 'There is no place where I more really *enjoy myself* than at Chesington,' she wrote in 1777.

> All the Household are kind, hospitable & partial to me; there is no sort of restraint, – every body is disengaged & at liberty to pursue their own inclinations, – & my Daddy, who is the soul of the place, is, at once, so flatteringly affectionate to *me*, & so infinitely, so beyond comparison in *himself*, – that were I to be otherwise than happy in his company, I must either be wholly without feeling or utterly destitute of under-standing.[39]

He also provided Fanny with an audience, and a reason for her to describe in detail her life in London. By October 1774 the Burneys had moved out of Bloomsbury and into a house 'nearly in the Centre of the Town' in St Martin's Street, off Leicester Fields. It was, according to Fanny, 'an odious street', but the house had the cachet of once belonging to Sir Isaac Newton, who had built an observatory in the roof.[40] It was, too, very well situated, being close to the theatre in the Haymarket and the Opera House in Covent Garden; Sir Joshua Reynolds was a neighbour in Leicester Fields.

The Burneys' home in St Martin's Street became a meeting-place for many of the actors, singers and personalities in London, especially on Sunday evenings when Dr Burney organised concerts in the drawing-room, to which he invited foreign ambassadors, characters such as James Bruce the explorer, Edmund Burke – and the by then elderly and greatly revered Dr Johnson.[41]

Mr Crisp insisted that Fanny sent him detailed accounts of all these visitors, and this she did – to brilliant effect. Through her eyes, we see David Garrick surprising the Burneys by calling on them first thing in the morning before they were out of bed:

> One morning he called at 8 o'clock, & unfortunately, Susette & I were not come down stairs [Mrs Burney was again visiting her mother in Lynn]. We hurried in vain – for he discovered our laziness, & made us monstrously ashamed by his raillery – 'I shall tell Mrs Garrick,' said he – 'that I found the Doctor reading Petrarch – in *Flannels*, like a *young man* – but where,' says I, 'where the young ladies? – Where do you think were my Favourites? – Why *in Bed*!' When he went away, he caught Charlotte in his Arms, & ran with her down the steps, & to the Corner of the square – protesting he intended taking her off.[42]

The young Burneys had always seen a lot of the Garricks: without children themselves, the actor and his wife Eva-Maria Veigel (an Austrian singer and dancer who gave up the stage when she married) had virtually adopted the motherless children in the years after Esther's death. Garrick often rushed in on his way to and from the Drury Lane Theatre, still in his make-up and reeling off speeches from *Hamlet* and *Richard III* (or from his latest success, *The Clandestine Marriage*). He teased and joked with them, calling Charles junior 'Cherry Nose Charlie' because his nose was always 'rather of the brightest', while Charlotte was his 'little Dumpling Queen'. He gave them his dog, Phil, to look after. Dr Burney recalled that even Fanny was brought out of her shell by the excitement of seeing the actor's performances, describing how she 'used, after having seen a play in Mrs Garrick's box, to take the actors off, and compose speeches for their characters'.[43]

Garrick lent the Burneys his private box at Drury Lane, giving Fanny the best view of the stage. 'Garrick was sublimely horrible!' she wrote after seeing him as Richard III in May 1772. 'Good Heaven – how he made me shudder whenever he appeared! it is inconceivable, how terribly great he is in this Character. I will never see him so disfigured again – he seemed so truly the monster he performed, that I felt myself glow with indignation every time I saw him.'[44] She never forgot the powerful charisma of his stage presence, forever comparing other actors with 'The fire of Genius' that she had seen 'in his Eye'.[45]

When Garrick turned up on Sunday evenings, he was often persuaded to entertain Dr Burney's guests with impersonations and speeches from Shakespeare. Even he, though, could be upstaged by some of the other visitors such as Omai, the South Seas tribal chief, who arrived in Britain in December 1774 on board the *Adventure*, one of the ships to take part in Captain Cook's botanical and geographical exploration of the Pacific. Omai called at St Martin's Street because of his friendship with James ('Jem the tar'), who had travelled with Cook on that expedition as Second Lieutenant of the *Adventure*, and who had impressed both Cook and the Admiralty by learning to speak Otaheite fluently.

Omai arrived in full Court dress after attending a Drawing-Room at St James's Palace, where he was presented to George III and Queen Charlotte. Fanny, who had been confined to bed for three days with 'a violent cold', was enticed out of the sick-room wrapped in several blankets to meet their extraordinary guest:

I found Omai seated on the Great Chair, & my Brother next to him, & talking Otaheite as fast as possible . . . Jem introduced me, and told him I was another sister. He rose, & made a very fine Bow & then seated himself again. But when Jem went on, & told him that I was not well, he again directly rose, & muttering something of the *Fire*, in a very polite manner, without *speech*, insisted upon my taking his seat.

Fanny remarked on Omai's command of English and his ability to appear at ease in the tight breeches, close-buttoned tunic and powdered hair of a Georgian courtier:

He makes *remarkably* good Bows – not for *him*, but for *any body* . . . Indeed he seems to shame Education, for his manners are so extremely graceful, & he is so polite, attentive, & easy, that you would have thought he came from some foreign Court . . . He never looked at his Dress, though it was on for the first time. Indeed he appears to be a perfectly rational & intelligent man, with an understanding far superior to the common race of *us cultivated gentry*; he could not else have borne so well the way of life into which he is thrown.[46]

Another exotic foreigner turned up late one evening in November 1775. Prince Aleksei Grigorevich Orlov was rumoured to be the leader of the band of officers who assassinated the husband of the Russian Empress Catherine the Great.[47] Fanny was mesmerised by his imposing appearance and the thought of what he might have done:

The Prince . . . immensely Tall, & stout in proportion . . . is a handsome & magnificent Figure. His Dress was very superb. Besides a Blue Garter, he had a star of Diamonds, of prodigious brilliancy; he had likewise a *shoulder knot* of the same *precious Jewels*, & a Picture of the Empress hung from his Neck, which was set round with Diamonds of such magnitude & lustre that, when near the Candle, they were too dazzling for the Eye.

Fanny later mentioned that one of these jewels was the size of a nutmeg. She concluded crisply that Orlov was so gracious and polite that he appeared to be '*addicted to pleasantry*'. But his tallness intimidated her, 'I felt myself so *Dwarfish* by his *high* Highness . . . Lord how I hate those enormous Tall men! I only *hated* them, because they made *me*, & such as me, look so very insignificant.'[48]

In such pen-portraits, Fanny was practising her skills as a scene-setter and student of character. She does not describe Orlov's actual physical appearance; her skill was in highlighting the salient features – his great height and love of jewels – and then adding just a few words giving us her own opinion. We can imagine, for instance, Fanny's reaction as a short young woman to this immensely tall and arrogant Russian. As Mr Crisp once told her: 'To do you justice, Fanny, you paint well.'

All this diary-writing was a preparation, a talent moulding itself for something bigger than a private journal. In her huge birthday bonfire of 1767, Fanny had not only destroyed poems, odes, epic histories, plays and romances, she had also burned the manuscript of an almost completed novel, 'The History of Caroline Evelyn'. But she never forgot her heroine and, secretly, on scraps of paper of all shapes and sizes, in fear of being discovered wasting her time on idle and dangerous fictions, she rescued Caroline Evelyn's infant daughter from the flames and brought her back to life as Evelina.[49]

Evelina is, like her creator, a motherless girl who is launched into London society without proper guidance; she, too, is embarrassed by relatives with whom she feels she has nothing in common. The resemblance between author and heroine ends there – but there was enough of Fanny in her novel to give it bite. *Evelina* is no feeble romance – for where Fanny's first fiction triumphs is in its satirical sketch of the follies into which eighteenth-century codes of conduct could lead the unsuspecting or unwary. As she described her novel in a letter to her publisher, Thomas Lowndes: 'The plan of the first Volume is the Introduction of a well educated but inexperienced young woman into public company, and a round of the most fashionable Spring Diversions of London. I believe it has not before been executed, though it seems a fair field open for the Novelist, as it offers a fund inexhaustible for Conversation, observations, and probable Incidents.'[50]

Fanny kept her novel hidden from her family – but this did not mean that it was to survive only as a private indulgence. She was determined that 'Evelina' should not share the fate of 'Caroline Evelyn' and, by the end of 1776, she had begun writing letters with a view to having the book published. In her Preface, she wrote that her novel was merely 'the trifling production of a few idle hours', but this was disingenuous. She was proud of what she had written, and in that same Preface dares to call herself an author alongside Johnson, Marivaux, Fielding, Richardson and Smollett.[51]

Her first choice of printer was James Dodsley of Pall Mall, whose father had published Dr Johnson's *Rasselas* and *The Vanity of Human Wishes*. But he refused to look at the manuscript unless its author's name was revealed. Fanny, however, knew that she must conceal her identity, fearing that if it became known that she was the author of a fiction in which she had dared to be satirical, she might cause a rumpus and bring the Burney name into disrepute. So, undeterred by Dodsley's negative response, she tried elsewhere, sending off her manuscript a few days later to Thomas Lowndes in Fleet Street.[52]

The draft of her letter shows that she was no novice when it came to dealing with printers. After an initial preamble – 'As an author has a kind of natural claim to a connexion with a Bookseller, I hope that, in the character of the former, you will pardon me, although a stranger, for the liberty I take of requesting you to favour me with an Answer to the following queries' – she made three crisply worded requests. First: 'Whether You will take the trouble of candidly perusing a MS Novel?' Second: 'Whether it is now too late in the Year for printing the first volume . . . this season?' And finally: 'Whether if, after reading, you should think it worth printing, you would buy the Copy without ever seeing, or knowing, the Author?' She asked for the reply to be directed to a 'Mr King' – actually her brother Charles who was let into the secret of her audacious experiment so that he could collect the correspondence from Fanny's suggested poste restante, a local coffee-house.[53]

The letter she *actually* sent was less forthright. She explained the reason for the need to remain anonymous: 'such is my situation in Life, that I have objections unconquerable to being known in this transaction', and then (in a less precise and more obsequious fashion than in the draft version) she requested 'a candid and impartial Reading, to a Book that has no *recommendation* to previously prejudice you in its favour?' And she asked, 'if, upon perusal, the work should meet with your approbation, you will Buy the Copy of a Friend whom I shall commission to wait upon you, without ever seeing or knowing the Editor?'[54]

By 23 December, Lowndes had replied, agreeing to look at the manuscript 'for now is the time for a Novel'. Charles was dispatched to Fleet Street, heavily disguised (or so Fanny would have us believe, in the account she wrote much later in the *Memoirs of Doctor Burney*): 'The young agent was muffled up now by the laughing committee, in an old great coat, and huge hat, to give him a somewhat antique as well as vulgar disguise; and was sent forth in the dark of the evening with the two first volumes to Fleet-street, where he left them to their fate.'[55] It was the kind of adventure in which the Burneys loved to indulge; Charles modelling himself on Garrick, who often arrived at St Martin's Street flourishing a cloak and large red hat. Four days later, Thomas Lowndes wrote back with the encouraging news: 'I've read & like the Manuscript & if you'll send the rest I'll soon run it over.'[56]

This presented Fanny with a problem. She had hoped that Lowndes would be prepared to publish the novel as a serial, with two volumes appearing first as a teaser, followed by two more some months later. But he was unwilling to do this, fearing that it would affect the success of the book. He wrote to her on 17 January 1777: 'Sir, I have read your Novel, & can't see any reason why you should not finish & publish it compleat. I'm sure it will be to your interest as well as the Bookseller's. You may well add one volume to these, and I shall more eagerly print it . . . I would rather print in July than now to publish an unfinished book. This I submit to your consideration & with best wishes that you may come into my way of thinking.'

Fanny's reply again indicates that she was well versed in the business of publishing:

Sir, I am well contented with the openness of your proceedings, & obliged to you for your advice. My original plan was, to publish 2 volumes now, & two more next year. I yield, however, to your experience in these matters, & will defer the publication till the work is completed, – though I should have been better pleased to have *felt the pulse* of the public before I had proceeded. I will write to you again, when I am ready for the press. In the mean time, I must beg the favour of a line, directed as before, to acquaint me how long I may delay printing the novel, without losing the proper season for its appearance.[57]

By March, however, she had made little progress with volume three, and commented wryly in her diary:

Now, this man, knowing nothing of my situation, supposed, in all probability, that I could seat myself quietly at my Bureau, & write on with all expedition and ease till the work was finished: but so different was the case, that I had hardly Time to write half a page in a Day; & niether my Health, nor inclination, would allow me to continue my *Nocturnal* scribbling for so long a Time as to write first, & then copy, a whole volume. I was, therefore, obliged to give the attempt & affair entirely over for the present.[58]

Fanny was not only expected to help her father, who was rushing to finish the second volume of his history of music, but had also set herself a laborious task. To ensure that no one would guess at the authorship of her novel, she copied her entire manuscript *in a feigned hand*, as her usual handwriting would have been familiar to the printers of Fleet Street after her years of acting as Dr Burney's secretary.

At the end of the month, she was at last given her freedom to pay 'a long & happy Visit to my ever-dear & ever-kind Mr Crisp'.[59] But after only a few days she was forced to return to town by the arrival of her Uncle Richard and her cousins, James and Becky, from Worcester. They, in turn, whisked her off to their home at Barborne Lodge, where she was obliged to stay until someone offered to escort her back to London. In desperation, she confessed to her father that she was writing a book. His response was not what she expected – 'He could not help Laughing' – which, perhaps, is not surprising. After all, his daughter, whom he had trained to be the perfect secretary, was now challenging him and setting herself up as a writer in her own right! He did ask Fanny 'to acquaint him, from Time to Time, how my *work* went on, called himself the *Père confident*, & kindly promised to guard my secret as cautiously as I could wish'. But his interest appeared to go no further for, she says, 'he forbore to ask me its name, or make any enquiries'. Fanny, with considerable grace and intuition, suggested that he was 'not sorry to be saved giving me the pain of his criticism'.[60]

Nothing, however, was to deflect Fanny from her desire to publish. By mid-September, she had written to Lowndes informing him that 'the MS concerning which I troubled you last winter, is at length finished'. Her original scheme for *Evelina* had run to four volumes, but in the end she managed to tie up the threads of her plot in three. She now had to wait anxiously for Lowndes's final verdict. She spent an agonising two months before, on 11 November, she finally received the news that was to change her life: 'I've read this 3d vol & think it better than 1 & 2d. If you please I'll give you Twenty Guineas for the manuscript and without loss of time put it to Press.'[61]

The terms were not to Fanny's liking, and the letter in which she decisively rejected them is a model for any budding author. It showed that, at twenty-five, Fanny fully understood the value of her work. So much so, indeed, that she was prepared to bargain for a better deal:

Sir,
    I am much gratified by your good opinion of the MS, with which I have troubled you; but I must acknowledge, that though it was originally written merely for amusement, I should not have taken the pains to copy & correct it for the press had I imagined that 10 Guineas a volume would have been more than its worth. As yet the work has been seen by no human eye, but your own & mine; if, however, you think its value inadequate to this sum, I would by no means press an unreasonable Demand. I shall, therefore, for the present, only beg the favour of you to deliver the 3rd volume to my Friend, who will call for it tomorrow Evening. My intention is to submit it to the perusal of a Gentleman who is much more Experienced in Authorship business than myself, & to abide by his Decision. Should his opinion co-incide with yours, as to the value of the MS I will immediately & frankly return you the three volumes upon your own terms – but if this should not be the case will give you no further trouble than that of begging you to receive my apologies & thanks for what you have already taken.
    I am, Sir,
    your most obedient and most willing Servant.[62]

Her ruse worked. Lowndes evidently realised that he had a bestseller on his hands, and that thirty guineas was a bargain price. He agreed to publish, and must have acted very quickly upon this decision. By January 1778 Fanny recorded in her diary how the New Year had been 'ushered in by a grand & most important Event'.

THREE

Evelina
1778

I have an exceeding odd *sensation*, when I consider that . . . a Work which was so lately Lodged, in all privacy, in my Bureau may now be seen by every Butcher & Baker, Cobler & Tinker, throughout the 3 Kingdoms, for the small tribute of 3 pence.

Fanny Burney, March 1778

Fanny received the first proofs of her book on 7 January, 1778. Three weeks later, bound copies were available for sale at nine shillings for the three volumes. The novel could also be borrowed from Bell's Circulating Library at 132 Strand for 'the small tribute of 3 pence'. But Fanny herself was unaware of this. It was not until her stepmother pointed out over breakfast one morning that *Evelina, or, A Young Lady's Entrance into the World* was being advertised in the *London Chronicle* that she discovered that her book had been given life beyond her closet and could now be read by 'every Butcher & Baker, Cobler & Tinker, throughout the 3 kingdoms'.[1] The advertisement, which appeared on Thursday 29 January, was tucked away at the bottom of a column amid news of the trial of an armed robber in Bristol (judged by Sir John Fielding, brother of the novelist Henry Fielding) and an advertisement for salt of lemons as the essential cure for ink spots, iron mould and red-wine stains on linen and cambric. It read: '*This Day was published* In 3 vols, 12 mo, price 7s-6d sewed or 9s bound, EVELINA or, A Young Lady's Entrance into the World. Printed for T. Lowndes in Fleet-street.'

Susan rushed out to buy a copy, surreptitiously, for fear of their stepmother discovering Fanny's secret. No author's name appeared on the title page. Unlike her predecessor, Charlotte Lennox, who had published *The Female Quixote* (a parody of Cervantes, wittily satirising the chivalric conventions of romance in fiction) under her own name in 1752, with a dedication by Dr Johnson, Fanny had remained strictly

44

anonymous in her dealings with Mr Lowndes. The first proofs had been left for collection by a 'Mr Grafton' at 'Gregg's Coffee House' on York Street, Covent Garden and were not received by Fanny until some ten days later. So great was the haste with which her publisher wished to treat the public (and his own purse) to *Evelina* that he rushed the book out, even before her corrections had been made.

'Mr Grafton' had replaced the 'Mr King' of Fanny's original letters to her publisher because of a family drama that beset the Burneys in late 1777. Charles junior, who had matriculated at Caius College, Cambridge earlier that year, was caught stealing (and defacing) books from his college library at the end of October. Although the case was never brought before a criminal court, he was expelled from the university with a blackened reputation. Dr Burney was furious and barred his son from the house in St Martin's Street. Charles went to stay with friends in Reading, Berkshire, leaving Fanny without an agent to act for her in her dealings with Mr Lowndes. Someone else had to be let in on her secret, and she chose her cousin from Worcester, Edward Francisco, who was staying with his London relatives while studying art at the Royal Academy.[2] Edward willingly donned hat and cloak and became 'Mr Grafton'.

Fanny does not mention Charles's disgrace in her diary, which she neglected throughout the winter months. When she did at last pick up her pen again at the end of March 1778, it was to record that she had ventured out with her sister Charlotte and cousin Edward to attend a benefit concert given for the great Italian violinist, Felice de Giardini. This was, according to Fanny, 'the first Public place to which we went, after Our long, melancholy, voluntary confinement to the House'.[3] Dr Burney had evidently retreated from society, fearing that his family might become the subject of malicious gossip. He had every reason to be concerned, for in the same month that Charles was sent down from Cambridge his stepdaughter Bessy Allen had, like her sister Maria before her, run off to Ypres to marry a man described by an acquaintance of the family as 'a Bankrupt in fame as well as Fortune'. (This 'friend' was Mrs Elizabeth Draper, the 'Eliza' of Laurence Sterne's *A Sentimental Journey* and *The Journal to Eliza*.)[4] At first, no one knew whether Bessy had actually married her 'adventurer', Samuel Meeke, but even when it was ascertained (by Mr Crisp, who wrote anxious letters to Ypres on Dr Burney's behalf) that a wedding had taken place, her family believed that she had ruined her life and was 'doomed to Experience Poverty and Wretchedness'. From the little we hear of her later from Fanny's diaries, it would seem that this was indeed Bessy's fate. She was taken to Geneva by her husband and returned to England only after their marriage ended, and then just for a short visit before returning to the Continent. How and where she died (and under what name) is not known.

Bessy's story reads like the plot of a bad romantic novel – and was carefully hushed up by the Burneys.[5] But it was all too common in real life: both of Fanny's stepsisters married young and foolishly; and her stepbrother, Stephen Allen, eloped to Gretna Green with the seventeen-year-old daughter of a physician from East Dereham (near Lynn Regis, where Stephen was then living with his grandmother). Fanny had every opportunity to observe at first hand what happened to young girls who allowed their passions to get the better of them. It was a lesson that her fictional creation, Evelina, was also to learn: those females (not, it has to be said, the males) who offended against the moral code of the mid-eighteenth century did so at their peril.

After Maria Allen's escapade in 1772, Fanny wrote in her journal for Thursday, 21 May: 'Miss Allen – for the last time I shall so call her – came home on Monday last. Her *novel* is not yet over; nevertheless, she was married last Saturday! Good Heaven! what a romantic life has this beloved friend lived!' Mr Crisp, however, reprimanded her for letting such sentimental notions obscure the reality of Maria's 'imprudent' behaviour. In a letter written from Chesington on 11 August, he warned Fanny, 'what is done, is past recall – She still may be, as the common word is, very happy – he is, I believe, a man of Sense, & if he does not use her ill, or spend her Fortune, he may be of use to her, in checking her little imprudent sallies, & regulating her Conduct; which hitherto appears to me to have been wild, childish, trifling to a high degree'.[6] Like Evelina, Fanny was to learn from the 'sermons' of Mr Crisp that there was a price to be paid for short-term happiness.

These family affairs once again prevented Fanny from pursuing her own interests; just at the time that *Evelina* was arriving at the booksellers and being talked about in the circulating libraries she was virtually incarcerated in St Martin's Street unable to relish her book's success – even in secret. At the end of March, she announced to 'Nobody': 'This Year was ushered in by a grand & most important Event, – for, at the latter end of January, the Literary World was favoured with the first publication of the ingenious, learned, & most profound Fanny Burney – I doubt not but this memorable affair will, in future Times, mark the period whence chronologers will date the Zenith of the polite arts in this Island!'[7] Indeed, her pride was not misplaced: by July the first edition of 500 copies[8] had sold out, and there have been innumerable new editions of *Evelina* ever since. (German and Dutch translations appeared in 1779 and 1780, and a French version in 1797; in 1796 *Evelina* crossed the Atlantic with the publication of an American edition.)

Fanny's story of 'a young female, educated in the most secluded retirement', who makes 'her first appearance upon the great and busy stage of life; with a virtuous mind, a cultivated understanding, and a feeling heart', but whose 'ignorance of the forms, and inexperience in the manners, of the world, occasion all the little incidents which these volumes record' was the number-one success of its time.[9] Yet these words in the Preface to her novel were dashed off by Fanny at four o'clock in the morning: much of *Evelina* was written through the night – it was the only way she could get her 'secret history' finished without detection, and without interrupting the work she was doing for her father.

The novel follows Evelina's 'Entrance into Life' in a series of letters between her and her substitute father, Mr Villars.[10] When we first meet her, she is a shy seventeen-year-old, orphaned, and living with her guardian, the Revd Villars, in the tiny village of Berry Hill in Dorset. All this changes, however, when Evelina is taken up to London for 'the season' by the family of her schoolfriend, Miss Mirvan. Here, her striking looks (we are told that she is beautiful but never learn the colour of her eyes or even her hair) and her unusual naïvety and unselfconsciousness draw to her side all the best-looking and wealthiest bachelors in the ballroom. Who is she, they want to know? What is her name? Her fortune? Her lineage? Evelina herself is unsure of her identity. She ends her first letter to Mr Villars by asking him: 'I cannot to you sign Anville, and what other name may I claim?'[11] In the secluded safety of Berry Hill such a question had never arisen but, out on the stage of London society, Evelina is made all too aware of her invidious position: while her friend, Maria Mirvan, is both personable *and* the granddaughter of Lady Howard of Howard Grove, Evelina has neither birth nor fortune. Such a girl – with beauty but no connections or wealth – is liable to fall prey to characters such as the foppish libertine, Sir Clement Willoughby.

Even Lord Orville, to whom Evelina is inexorably drawn from their first meeting, is guilty of this obsession with class. At first, she observes, 'his conversation was sensible and spirited; his air and address were open and noble; his manners gentle, attentive, and infinitely engaging'. But she next overhears him talking about her rather too freely with the definitely not-to-be-trusted Sir Clement.[12] Mr Villars warns her, 'Alas, my child . . . The supposed obscurity of your birth and situation, makes you liable to a thousand disagreeable adventures.'[13] Evelina's genteel upbringing enables her to make an entrance into society, but she is bound to suffer humiliation once it is discovered that she is, in fact, a *Nobody* (she is actually called a 'Nobody' by Mr Lovel, a vain, stupid character whom she offends by laughing at him, because of his foolish obsession with appearance).[14]

There is, however, a worse fate than having *no* connections – and that is having the *wrong* connections. One evening, as Evelina returns with the Mirvans from an outing to the theatre, it begins to rain. A 'tall, elderly woman' with a foreign accent asks for help because she cannot find her friends or a carriage to take her home. She is invited by the Mirvans to take a seat in their coach and, in the course of their conversation, reveals herself to be none other than Madame Duval, the long-lost grandmother of Evelina. Fanny could have turned the encounter into a sentimental reconciliation scene – but she has other plans for this Widow Twankey-like character.

Madame Duval offends on all counts. A brash, blowsy woman with whom a young girl might die of embarrassment to be seen, she has a French boyfriend, who accompanies her everywhere. Evelina finds it odd and vulgar that someone of such advanced years (approaching forty) should still be trying to attract men and fussing like a young girl about her wardrobe: 'During this conversation, she endeavoured to adjust her head dress, but could not at all please herself. Indeed, had I not been present, I should have thought it impossible for a woman at her time of life to be so very difficult in regard to dress.'[15] Madame Duval's language and uncouth behaviour – slapping the coachmen and haranguing them, ' "Take that back for your answer, sirrah," cried she, "and learn to grin at your betters another time" ' – betray her. Worse still, she has relatives who, '*ma foi*', are in trade and live '*in the City*!'

Here, Fanny displays her knowing touch as a comic writer – and the advantages of being herself of no fixed class. While emphasising that Evelina feels more at home in the fashionable world of the ballroom, opera house and Vauxhall Gardens (the world to which Fanny had access as the daughter of the sought-after socialite Dr Burney), she now introduces her heroine to a quite different cast of characters – the Branghtons, the Smiths and the Browns. This allows her to delve into another side of London life, which Fanny knew through her paternal aunts in Covent Garden and her maternal grandfather, who lived in Cheapside. The Branghtons live above their silversmith's shop on Snow Hill and have a lodger, the silly and affected 'Holborn Beau', Mr Smith,[16] another rich source of comedy. Not for them the fashionable ridottos, or dancing-parties, and drawing-rooms of the West End. Instead of going to see Garrick at Drury Lane or Signor Millico at the Opera House in the Haymarket, Evelina is taken by her cousins to the music-hall at Sadler's Wells, and to White-Conduit House in Islington, a tea-garden where shopkeepers, tradesmen, housemaids and footmen enjoyed their afternoons off watching the bowling and cricket matches. She visits the menagerie at the Tower of London, and 'George's' in Hampstead – a museum of curious mechanical devices, collapsing chairs and fanciful fountains.[17]

With these new companions, Evelina is placed in some awkward situations. She goes to see a fireworks display in Marylebone Gardens, but in the confusion and excitement finds herself alone and lost in the 'dark walks'. There she falls into the clutches of a group of prostitutes, whom she mistakenly believes can rescue her from the untoward advances of the men who accost her as she rushes about in search of her cousins. (The Marylebone Gardens were closed in 1778 because they had acquired such an unsavoury reputation.) While in their company, she is seen by, of all people, Lord Orville, who does not (or pretends not to) recognise her.

It's a risqué scene – and a surprise to discover just how much the prudish Fanny knew about 'alternative' London. Is she merely using the scene as a device for creating comic drama, tension, uncertainty as to whether Evelina will finally win Lord Orville's heart? Or does she intend it to be a lesson on the dangers for young girls of wandering at will in the world, of being given the freedom to roam in the dangerous labyrinth of society where they can be tempted by evil men? I suspect the latter, for although *Evelina* is a comic novel, it can also be read as a biting satire in which Fanny airs some of her own views on the absurdities and injustices of eighteenth-century society. When, for instance, Evelina describes her first shopping trip to Bond Street, it is almost as if Fanny herself is writing to her stepsister Maria Allen: 'But what most diverted me was, that we were more frequently served by men than by women, and such men! so finical, so affected! they seemed to understand every part of a woman's dress better than we do ourselves; and they recommended caps and ribbands with an air of so much importance, that I wished to ask them how long they had left off wearing them.'[18]

In Evelina's next letter to Mr Villars, it is again as if Fanny is using her heroine to say those things that she would never have dared to air herself in public. Evelina is describing her first dance, where you might have expected her to have been overwhelmed by the occasion and by her naïve ignorance of the rituals of the ballroom. Not at all; with semi-detached amusement, she observes: 'The gentlemen . . . looked as if they thought we were quite at their disposal, and only waiting for the honour of their commands; and they sauntered about, in a careless indolent manner, as if with a view to keep us in suspense – and I thought it so provoking, that I determined, in my own mind, that, far from humouring such airs, I would rather not dance at all.'[19]

The premise upon which Fanny based her novel – that Evelina should fall in love with a lord and then suffer the pangs of being removed from his social circle – is essentially romantic, but Fanny does not focus on Evelina's feelings; nor does she attempt to evoke an emotional response. What she does do – brilliantly – is make the reader laugh by her witty, darting comments on the odd ways in which people behave in an effort to impress, bewitch or mislead. So vivid is her dialogue, so sharp her delineations of character that a dramatic cast emerges from the pages of her novel, parading in their silk waistcoats, powdered wigs and rose-pink gowns. And the experience of reading *Evelina* today is to be taken back to the Mall in St James's Park on a balmy afternoon in the late spring of 1778.

Fanny's attempts to recreate in her diary the conversations she had heard in the drawing-room at St Martin's Street had honed her skills as a dramatic writer. Turn to almost any page in *Evelina* and you will not find long passages of descriptive narrative; instead, you will listen in on the conversations of a roomful of characters. Fanny reveals Sir Clement, Captain Mirvan, Madame Duval, Mr Smith and company not through descriptions of what they *look* like, but through the way in which they *talk*. Madame Duval's lack of 'class' is shown by her ungrammatical speech and smattering of slang; Mr Villars's letters are filled with the classical allusions of a cultured man. Fanny builds up a richly coloured scene purely through dialogue. On one occasion, for example, Madame Duval is being teased unmercifully by Maria Mirvan's father, whose unconventional behaviour and uncouth language are excused because he is a sea captain (a noble profession in those days of constant naval engagements with France and Spain). She has slipped and muddied her dress after her carriage was involved in an accident on the way home from an evening at Ranelagh:

> 'Now, Madam,' says the Captain, 'you that have lived abroad, please to tell me this here; Which did you like best, the *warm room* at Ranelagh, or the *cold bath* you went into afterwards? though, I assure you, you look so well that I should advise you to take another dip.'
>
> '*Ma foi*, Sir,' cried she, 'nobody asked for your advice, so you may as well keep it to yourself: besides, it's no such great joke to be splashed, and to catch cold, and spoil all one's things, whatever you may think of it.'
>
> '*Splashed*, quoth-a! – why I thought you were soused all over – Come, come, don't mince the matter, never spoil a good story; you know you had n't a dry thread about you – 'Fore George, I shall never think onto without hallowing! such a poor, forlorn, draggle-tailed – *gentlewoman*! and poor Monsieur French, here, like a drowned rat, by your side!'
>
> 'Well, the worse pickle we was in, so much the worser in you not to help us, for you knowed where we was fast enough, because, while I laid in the mud, I'm pretty sure I heard you snigger.'

When Sir Clement appears in the middle of this quarrel and is asked to intervene between Madame Duval and the Captain, we know immediately that he is well-bred by the manner of his speech:

> 'I should have hoped,' (said Sir Clement, with the utmost gravity) 'that the friendship subsisting between that lady and gentlemen, would have guarded them against any actions professedly disagreeable to each other; but, probably, they might not have discussed the matter previously; in which case, the gentleman, I must own, seems to have been guilty of inattention, since, in my humble opinion, it was his business first to have enquired whether the lady preferred soft, or hard ground, before he dropt her.'[20]

The incident provides plenty of opportunities for the misogynistic, jingoistic Captain to lambast the hapless Madame Duval for the follies of womanhood, and for her supposedly French origins. (An English barmaid, she reputedly seduced Evelina's grandfather, John Evelyn, and ran off with him to France. When John Evelyn died soon

afterwards, she married a Monsieur Duval, who conveniently disappears.) Captain Mirvan uses the kind of language with which you
might not expect the timid Miss Burney to have been acquainted.[21]

Evelina is full of such scenes. Fanny may not have been very good at
constructing a clearly thought-through plot, but there is no lack of
dramatic interest in her novel. Incest, blackmail, patricide, fraud,
deception, gambling are all touched upon – and even the 'minor'
players find themselves with a message for the youthful Evelina. One
such is Macartncy, the Branghtons' Scottish lodger, whose mournful
story and melancholy personality were to engage both Dr Johnson and
Mrs Thrale. 'I always liked Macartney, – he is a very pretty Character,
& I *took to him,* as the folks say,' said Mrs Thrale, according to Fanny;
to which Dr Johnson replied, 'Yes, poor fellow, I liked the *man,* – but
I love not the *Nation.*'[22]

Macartney is discovered by Evelina with pistols in hand and about
to put an end to his life, having lost all hope of being able to marry the
girl he loves (he is led to believe that she is his sister) and being faced
with debts incurred in Paris that he can never hope to repay. Evelina
valiantly saves him by forcing him to drop the pistols (before daintily
swooning with the shock of such extremities of behaviour), and then
listens to the lonely 'Scotchman' as he confides in her his desperate
story.[23] All ends happily when it is revealed that his supposed sister
was in fact exchanged at birth with Evelina (yes, the plot does become
fearfully complicated).

But the character of Macartney is not simply a plot device, through
whom Evelina can be reunited with her father. His woeful tale may
shed more light on why the Burneys were so distraught at the end of
1777. According to Mrs Thrale's diary (later published as the
Thraliana), she was asked by Mrs Crewe, daughter of Fulke and
Frances Greville,

> if the Story in Fanny Burney's Book – Evelina – about Mr Macartney
> was not founded on Fact, for said She I had heard it was true, and that
> She had told you so; and that you had told many, how the Anecdote or
> Circumstance or what you will of Macartney's going to shoot himself
> actually did happen to her own Brother Charles Burney, who having
> been expelled by the University & forbidden his Fathers house was
> actually discovered by his Sister Fanny in the desperate State
> mentioned of Macartney.

Mrs Thrale claimed not to have heard any such thing, but when Dr

Burney next visited her at her home in Streatham, she hinted to him 'that I had heard somebody observe that the Story of Macartney was written with such *feeling*, it must *absolutely* be founded on Fact; at this Discourse he changed Colour so often, and so apparently that tho' I instantly got quit of the Conversation, I left it however well perswaded that all Mrs Crewe had said – or great part of it – was but too true. A Strange World after all!²⁴

A strange tale indeed, for, if it is true, then Fanny showed great fortitude and presence of mind in protecting her brother from his own despair. Charles's disgrace, however, took place in late autumn 1777, by which time Fanny had already completed the first two volumes of her novel; and the dramatic scene with Macartney occurs half-way through the second volume. Fanny could well have embellished her characterisation of Macartney *after* witnessing such scenes with Charles; whether or not based on fact, the scene is certainly written with great feeling and emotion. We know, too, from comments that appear later in the diaries, that Charles, as a young man, was often in debt, often depressed and was a cause of much anxiety to his family after a failed love affair. Indeed, the letter in which Evelina tells Mr Villars of her heroic attempt to save Macartney reads as if Fanny is releasing some of the pent-up concern she felt for her brother:

I saw, passing by the door, with a look perturbed and affrighted, the same young man I mentioned in my last letter. Not heeding, as I suppose, how he went, in turning the corner of the stairs, which are narrow and winding, his foot slipped, and he fell, but, almost instantly rising, I plainly perceived the end of a pistol, which started from his pocket, by hitting against the stairs.

I was inexpressibly shocked. All that I had heard of his misery occurring to my memory, made me conclude, that he was, at that very moment, meditating suicide! Struck with the dreadful idea, all my strength seemed to fail me; – I sat motionless; – I lost all power of action, – and grew almost stiff with horror . . . [Evelina here follows him up to his room.]

In a moment, strength and courage seemed lent me as by inspiration: I started, and rushing precipitately into the room, just caught his arm, and then, overcome by my own fears, I fell down at his side, breathless and senseless. My recovery, however, was, I believe, almost instantaneous; and then the sight of this unhappy man, regarding me with a look of unutterable astonishment, mixed with concern, presently restored to me my recollection . . .

53

Unwilling to leave the pistols, and, indeed, too weak to move, I leant one hand upon the table, and then stood perfectly still: while he, his eyes cast wildly towards me, seemed too infinitely amazed to be capable of either speech or action. [She then takes hold of Macartney by the arm, forcing him to drop the pistols, upon which she seizes them and rushes out of the room.][25]

Charles has tended to be thought of as a light-hearted, fun-loving fellow who stole books to pay off the debts he incurred by his lavish, gambling lifestyle, and who was the model for all the practical jokers in his sister's novels. But his scholarly, bookish interests would suggest that he had a more introverted disposition. It seems to me all too likely that Charles's chequered years as a depressive teenager were the basis for the character of Macartney. Throughout her early diaries, Fanny implies that Charles was the brother on whom the family focused their worries. James, the tar, is a far more likely inspiration for Fanny's pranksters and comic wits. In later life he became a dining companion of Hazlitt, Lamb and Leigh Hunt, playing whist and chess into the early hours, and affectionately known as 'Captain Battle'.

Dr Johnson and Mrs Thrale both admired the character of Macartney, because they felt that his story complemented the rough ribaldry of Captain Mirvan and the inane foppery of Mr Lovel and Sir Clement. Herein lies the key to *Evelina*'s success – the richness of its portrait of eighteenth-century society, and the vitality of its scenes of life in London, Bristol and Bath. On 1 March 1778 however, Fanny, was still awaiting the verdict of the critics 'with fear & fidgets'. Although she had heard from Charles junior in Reading that he had enquired at a circulating library for *Evelina* and been told that the novel was much in demand and was considered to be 'one of the best publications we have had for a long Time',[26] she was expecting to be 'horribly mauled' in the periodicals.

She need not have worried. When the first reviews did eventually appear, they were glowing in their praise of this 'sprightly, entertaining, and agreeable' novel. The anonymous critic of the *London Review* judged that 'There is much more merit, as well respecting stile, character & Incident, than is usually to be met with in modern Novels.'[27] Such praise was not common for first novels written by unknown or anonymous authors; and *Evelina* was only one among several fictions with similar themes to be published at that time. In May 1778, for example, a number of novels – *The History of Eliza*

Warwick, The History of Miss Maria Barlow in a Series of Letters and *The History of Melinda Harley* – received brief mentions in the *Monthly Review*. All, without exception, were dismissed as 'inoffensive' or 'perfectly insipid'. Not so *Evelina*, which fast became the book that everyone wanted to read.

But at the beginning of June, its author retreated to Chesington Hall to recover from 'a severe inflammation of the lungs'. The strain of rushing to finish that final volume, and then the anxious weeks awaiting *Evelina*'s entrance into the world, had been too much for Fanny. She appears to have suffered a complete nervous and physical collapse and was unable to eat, or to walk unaided. When at last she was fit enough to travel to Chesington, she was accompanied in the post-chaise by both Susan and their cousin Edward. Susan took with her a vial of smelling salts to revive Fanny, who was so weak on arrival at Mr Crisp's that she had to be carried into the house by Edward.

While at Chesington, Fanny heard from her publisher that '*all the polite World* send to him to *Buy* my Book' and that 'a Lady of Fashion told him to send it her, for she was reckoned quite unfashionable for not having read it'. Much heartened, Fanny wrote to Susan (who had returned immediately to St Martin's Street to take over from Fanny as their father's secretary and librarian), with barely concealed triumph, that Mr Lowndes's attitude to 'Mr Grafton' had subtly changed: 'Lowndes Letter is *so* civil! . . . he shall be *proud* of my commands, & signs himself my *obliged* servant'. Fanny made a rapid recovery: 'Good God! My dear Susy!' she wrote on 5 or 6 July, 'what a wonderful affair has this been! – & how extraordinary is this *torrent* of success, which sweeps down all before it!'[28]

The '*polite world*' had as yet no idea that the author of this surprise bestseller was a 'young lady', in a position not so very different from that of her heroine. Fanny's family, however, had now been let in on the secret. Dr Burney had seen the review of *Evelina* in the April edition of the *Monthly Review* and had discussed it with Susan, who had then confessed that she knew the book's author. Dr Burney sent straight to Fleet Street for a copy and, the following day, Fanny received a letter from Susan: 'My Father, she said, was highly pleased with the Dedication & the Preface, & said they were *vastly strong* & well written, better than he could have expected, though he did not think he should meet with *Trash*.' (Since the Dedication was written as an ode to the 'author of my being! – far more dear/To me than light, than nourishment, or rest', Dr Burney's appreciation of the novel that followed is perhaps not surprising.)[29]

Fanny's father read the book aloud in the company of his friends Lady Hales and Miss Coussmaker, and was so impressed that he told Susan, 'Upon my soul I think it the best Novel I know excepting Fieldings, – &, in some respects, *better* than his! I have been *excessively* pleased with it . . . I protest I think it will scarce bear an Improvement. I wish I may die, if I do not believe it to be the very best Novel in the Language, except Fielding's! for Smollets, with all their Wit, are quite too gross.'[30]

Fanny was much relieved. But perhaps even more important to her peace of mind was the verdict of her stepmother, who might well have been mortally offended that Fanny had continued to write romantic nonsense. On 20 July, however, Fanny noted jubilantly that Mrs Burney had been impressed *and* entertained by the story of Evelina, and had written to Fanny to congratulate her: 'She declares it has given her more pleasure than any Book she has read of a *long, long* while, & that it has *revived* in her both pleasure & sensation, by alternate Tears & Laughter.' Indeed, Mrs Burney, despite her stepchildren's reservations, was a discerning critic. She told Fanny, 'In the sportive way of holding up Ignorance, Conceit & Folly to ridicule, I thought I discovered Your attentive Ear, & observing Eye; but there is a knowledge of the ill manners & absurd conduct of Bon Ton in domestic Life, that almost puzzled me, – till a Leaf I had over looked at the beginning, brought me back, & gave it *all* to you.'[31]

Dr Burney, meanwhile, was so proud of his daughter's achievement that he wanted her to be acknowledged as *Evelina*'s creator – and he knew where best to divulge the secret. By the summer of 1778 he had become a regular dining-guest at the home of Mrs Thrale in Streatham, having first been invited there to give lessons on the harpsichord to her eldest daughter, 'Queeney'. The seven miles from St Martin's Street to the rural setting of Streatham Park were a long way to go for a one-hour lesson (for which he was paid one guinea). But Dr Burney hoped to meet there his scholarly hero and inspiration, Dr Johnson, who was at this time also dining weekly with the Thrales, arriving on Tuesday afternoons and staying until Thursday.

The 'clubable' Dr Burney was soon more than just a music teacher to the Thrales: 'such was the fertility of his Mind, & the extent of his Knowledge, such the Goodness of his Heart and Suavity of his Manners that we began in good earnest to sollicit his Company, and gain his Friendship,' wrote Mrs Thrale in her diary for August to September 1777. 'Few People possess such Talents for general Conversation, and fewer still for select Society, where no Restraint is laid upon one's Expressions & where Humour and good humour charm more than Wit and Philosophy.'[32] She was relieved to find in Dr Burney someone prepared to stay up with her other guest, drinking tea and talking into the early hours: Dr Johnson could only be persuaded to go to bed after the candles had burned down, so fearful was he of those wakeful pre-dawn hours.

Mrs Thrale prided herself on being an arbiter of literary fashion, and already had a copy of *Evelina* on display in her library. It was easy, then, for Dr Burney to raise the subject of the mystery surrounding its author and to tease his friend with the suggestion that he knew the secret. First he told her that it was definitely not written by Christopher Anstey, author of the spoof *New Bath Guide*, as was suspected by many. Then he said he was certain that it was not the work of a man. He agreed that, yes, the author must be the same age as its heroine. And, yes, he did know her identity: it was none other than his daughter, Fanny!

Mrs Thrale was delighted: not only could she be the first to broadcast the name of this mysteriously modest author, but she could also be the first to entertain her. It was a perfect way to outwit her rival hostesses, Mrs Cholmondeley (sister of the famous actress Peg Woffington) and Mrs Montagu. These 'Bluestockings' prided themselves on their ability to amuse themselves with conversation on *important* subjects, and refused to waste endless evenings on idle gossip or card games. They abhorred 'fashion', and flagrantly disregarded the rules of 'full dress', encouraging their male visitors to turn up at their salons in heavy worsted 'blue' stockings, instead of the more elegant (and more expensive) black silk (or so the story goes). Each sought to outdo the other in the calibre of guests attending their early-evening soirées.

Mrs Thrale immediately invited Dr Burney to bring Fanny with him on his next visit to Streatham. Fanny was at first understandably nervous about acknowledging herself publicly as the author of such a satirical novel. She asked her father, in a letter written from Chesington on 8 July: 'if you do tell Mrs Thrale, – won't she think it very strange where I can have *kept Company*, to draw such a family as the Branghtons . . . so that, I am afraid she will conclude I must have an *innate vulgarity of ideas* to assist me with such coarse colouring for the objects of my Imagination'. She added: 'I should certainly have been more finical, had I foreseen what has happened, or had the most *remote* notion of being known by *Mrs Thrale* for the scribe.'[33] But these fears soon disappeared when she realised the significance of being accepted as 'an authoress' by such an opinion-maker as Mrs Thrale, and she ended her letter to Dr Burney by begging him to let her know Mrs Thrale's reaction when he set off 'the *Great gun*'.

Fanny was soon reassured by her father that Mrs Thrale had so enjoyed *Evelina* that she had given the first volume to Dr Johnson for him to read on his journey home from Streatham to Bolt Court (off Fleet Street). Mrs Thrale told Dr Burney that Dr Johnson had been 'full of the praises of the *Book* I had lent him & protesting that there were passages in it which might do *honour* to Richardson'. He was, she said, 'ardent after the denouement' and had demanded to borrow the other volumes. In her diary, she confided her own, rather different opinion: 'I was shewed a little Novel t'other Day which I thought pretty enough & set Burney to read it, little dreaming it was written by his second Daughter Fanny, who certainly must be a Girl of good Parts, & some Knowledge of the World too, or She could not be the Author of Evelina – flimzy as it is, compar'd with the Books I've just mentioned by Charlotte Lennox, Smollett and Fielding'! Though she added, 'Johnson says Harry Fielding never did any thing equal to the 2nd Vol of Evelina.'[34]

Fanny, however, never forgot the moment when she realised that her book was receiving such approval, and especially from Dr Johnson, whose philosophical tale, *Rasselas: Prince of Abyssinia*, she quoted from several times in *Evelina*, in appreciation of its analysis of human behaviour. She was staying at Chesington Hall when she heard the news and was so thrilled that she dashed out into the garden like a young girl and danced a jig round the mulberry tree. The afternoon remained forever etched on her memory as marking an irrevocable change in her life, and she was still talking about it some fifty years later when Sir Walter Scott, who was much influenced by her novels, visited her as an old lady in Mayfair.

All this praise (despite Mrs Thrale's private disparagement) was not just hot air: Fanny's characters had entered the popular imagination, and the diaries and letters of the time are filled with references to 'Madame French', the 'Holborn Beau' (Mr Smith) and the 'old sea dog' (Captain Mirvan). Sir Joshua Reynolds's niece, Theophila Palmer, remarked to Fanny how Mrs Cholmondeley's favourite character was Madame Duval: 'she acts her from morning to night, & *ma-fois* every body she sees. But though we all want so much to know the Author, both Mrs Cholmondeley, & my Uncle himself, say they should be frightened to Death to be in her Company, because she must be such a very nice observer, that there would be no escaping her with safety.'[35] Having such women as Mrs Cholmondeley as her champions was a huge compliment to Fanny for, as Dr Burney was to remark, 'they were *d—d severe, & d—d knowing, & afraid* of praising *à tort & à travers* as their opinions are liable to be quoted, which makes them extremely shy of speaking favourably'.[36] Thirty years later, Jane Austen revealed her affection for the novel and its characters in a letter to her sister Cassandra: 'What a contretemps! – in the Language of France; What an unluckiness in that of Mme Duval!'[37]

But when Fanny first visited Streatham Park on Monday, 27 July 1778, she little knew what a transformation she would experience herself because of *Evelina*. Typically, she says little in her diary about the appearance of the Thrale's house and its furnishings, other than the fact that it was 'white, & very pleasantly situated, in a fine Paddock'.[38] Instead, she launches straightway into what was said: 'Mrs Thrale was strolling about & came to us as we got out of the Chaise. "Ah," cried she, "I hear Dr Burney's Voice! – & you have brought your Daughter? – well, now you *are* good!" '

Dr Johnson was there too. Fanny had met the ageing scholar (who was by now sixty-eight, and overweight, gouty and irritable) once before, when he called at St Martin's Street, brought by Mrs Thrale to view Dr Burney's considerable library of foreign literature. Hetty and Susan played a duet for the visitors, while Fanny noted her first impressions of 'the acknowledged Head of Literature in this kingdom':

He is, indeed, very ill favoured, – he is tall & stout, but stoops terribly, – he is almost bent double. His mouth is in perpetual motion, as if he was chewing; – he has a strange method of frequently twirling his Fingers, & twisting his Hands; – his Body is in continual agitation, *see-sawing* up & down; his Feet are never a moment quiet, – &, in short, his whole person is in perpetual motion: His Dress, too . . . was as much out of the common Road as his Figure: he had a large Wig, snuff colour coat, & Gold Buttons; but no Ruffles to his Wrist & Black Worsted Stockings . . . He is shockingly near sighted, & did not, till she held out her Hand to him, even know Mrs Thrale. He *poked his Nose* over the keys of the Harpsichord, till the Duet was finished, &

then, my Father introduced Hetty to him, as an old acquaintance, & he instantly kissed her. His attention, however, was not to be diverted five minutes from the Books, as we were in the Library; he pored over them, almost brushing the Backs of them, with his Eye lashes, as he read their Titles; at last, having fixed upon one, he began, without further ceremony, to Read, all the time standing at a distance from the Company. We were very much provoked, as we perfectly languished to hear him talk; but, it seems, he is the most silent creature, when not particularly drawn out, in the World.[39]

Apart from that last comment on Dr Johnson's reluctance to talk except when spoken to, what Fanny says is much the same as the portrait drawn by Boswell and other members of the Literary Club. But the description of the scholar and conversationalist whom she came to know at Streatham Park sheds a very different light on his character. Here we see him as a tease, a flirt, and the author of ribald rhymes. With the Thrales, Dr Johnson was sufficiently at home to indulge his passion for talking, and Fanny listened intently and memorised every word:

this man ... who has the most extensive knowledge, the clearest understanding, & the greatest abilities of any Living Author, – has a Face the most ugly, a Person the most awkward, & manners the most singular, that ever were, or ever can be seen. But all that is unfortunate in his *exterior*, is so greatly compensated for in his *interior*, that I can only, like Desdemona to Othello, '*see his Visage in his mind*'. His Conversation is so replete with instruction & entertainment, his Wit is so ready, & his Language at once so original & so comprehensive, that I hardly know any satisfaction I can receive, that is equal to listening to him.

Fanny does not appear to have been overawed by Dr Johnson. She was usually shy and withdrawn, but was never so with him – perhaps because he, too, was awkward in company, yet loved to talk. Fanny may not have received any formal education, yet Dr Johnson was never bored by her conversation (or at least not according to *her* diary), and this gave her a social poise and confidence that she had never had before. She impressed him with the acuity of her perceptions about people and her lack of illusions about life; yet she had an inner strength which enabled her to face up to what she saw.

'When we were summoned to Dinner,' she recalled of that first meal at Streatham Park, 'Mrs Thrale made my Father & me sit each side of her: I said I hoped I did not take Dr Johnson's place? – for he had not yet appeared. "No," answered Mrs Thrale, "he will sit by you, – which I am sure will give him great pleasure."' In the middle of dinner, Dr Johnson:

> asked Mrs Thrale what was in some little pies that were near him? 'Mutton,' answered she; 'so I don't ask you to Eat any, because I know you despise it.' 'No, Madam, no,' cried he, 'I despise *nothing* in its way that is good of its sort: – but I am too proud *now* to Eat of it; – sitting by Miss Burney makes me very proud to Day!' 'Miss Burney,' said Mrs Thrale, Laughing, 'you must take great care of your heart if Dr Johnson attacks it! – for I assure you he is not often successless.' 'What's that you say, Madam?' cried he, 'are you making mischief between the young lady & me already?'

Dr Johnson was not above flattery, entertaining the company with a story that made Fanny blush: 'And this ... reminds me of a Gentleman & Lady with whom I travelled once; I suppose I *must* call them so according to form, because they travelled in their own Coach & 4 Horses: But at the first Inn where we stopt, the Lady called for – a pint of Ale! – & when it came, quarrelled with the Waiter for not giving full measure! – Now *Madame Duval* could not have done a grosser thing!'

Madame Duval was not the only character to amuse Dr Johnson. Of the Branghtons' upwardly mobile lodger Mr Smith, he was later to say, 'O, Mr Smith, Mr Smith is the Man! ... Harry Fielding *never* drew so good a Character! – such a fine *varnish* of low politeness! – such a *struggle* to appear a Gentleman! – Madam, there is *no* Character better drawn any where – in *any* Book, or by *any* Author.' Mrs Thrale agreed that Mr Smith was well drawn: 'I *know* Mr Smith, too, very well; – I always have him before me at the Hampstead Ball, Dressed in a White Coat, & a Tambour waistcoat, worked in Green Silk.' And Dr Johnson teased her other guests, '"Why Seward," said he, "how smart you are Dressed! – why you only want a *Tambour waistcoat* to look like Mr Smith!"'

Even Mrs Thrale was forced to admit that 'it is a sweet Book – & the great beauty of it is, that it reflects back all our own ideas & observations: for every body must have seen *something* similar to almost all the incidents.' This, no doubt, explains its success: it was unusual then for a novelist to attempt to recreate *actual* incidents and emotions, without dressing them up as lessons in correct behaviour. Indeed, what seemed most to surprise and please Dr Johnson about *Evelina* was that its author displayed a full and spirited understanding of how the world worked. '"Richardson would have been really *afraid* of her; – there is merit in Evelina which he could not have borne. – No, it would not have done!" . . . (Then shaking his Head at me, he exclaimed) "O, you little *Character-monger*, you!"'[40]

Not everyone approved of *Evelina*. Edmund Burke claimed that he sat up all night to finish it, and Sir Joshua Reynolds boasted that he would give fifty pounds to know the author and 'make Love to the Author, if ever he met with her'. But the fearsome critic Mrs Montagu thoroughly disliked it, according to Mrs Thrale, who told Dr Johnson in a letter of 19 October that she had overheard Mrs Montagu saying that she 'cannot bear *Evelina* . . . her Silver-Smiths are Pewterers . . . & her Captains Boatswains'.[41] Dr Johnson dismissed this as jealousy: 'Montagu has got some vanity in her head . . . Vanity always oversets a Lady's Judgement.' He despised Mrs Montagu, never forgetting how she had criticised his own work when he was a writer struggling to make his way on Grub Street in the 1750s.[42] And she was not popular at Streatham Park: 'If I am like the Rattlesnake,' wrote Mrs Thrale in her diary in 1780, 'Mrs Montagu is like the Peccary; who when it hears the Serpent's Approach which fills every other Tenant of the Desart with Fear, runs and devours it.'[43]

But, as the 'Queen of the Bluestockings', Mrs Montagu's opinion could be crucial to a book's success, and she was not alone in her disapproval of Fanny's use of colloquial language and depiction of low-life characters. The writer of the brief notice in the *Monthly Review* also did not like Captain Mirvan: though commending the 'ease & Command of Language', the critic added that 'we must, however, except the Character of a son of Neptune, whose manners are rather those of a rough, uneducated Country 'squire, than those of a genuine sea Captain'.[44] Even Dr Burney felt that the scene in which Captain Mirvan lets loose an irate monkey on the unbearably effete Mr Lovel was too cruel and overdone. 'I don't hate that young man enough,' he wrote to Fanny, 'ridiculous as he is, to be pleased or diverted at his having his ear torn by a monkey; there is something even disgusting in it.' Dr Burney's objection was to an episode at the end of the novel where Captain Mirvan, infuriated by Mr Lovel's silly obeisance to 'fashion', turns a monkey on him to show him what a fool he is to ape other people. It is an extraordinarily violent scene for a genteel novel – the monkey bites off Lovel's ear. Yet it is extremely vivid and could not have offended everyone, since it was later used as one of the illustrations in the fourth edition of the novel, which appeared in 1779.[45]

Surprisingly, no one appears to have complained about another scene in which Lord Orville's friend Lord Merton, and Mr Lovel, organise a race between two old women, laying bets on who will win. It is comic, but only at the expense of the women, who have no choice but to follow the orders of the aristocratic and authoritarian men. Fanny's point is to show up the foolishness of Lord Merton and Mr Lovel, who are so desperate to gamble that they concoct this ridiculous charade in order to satisfy their addiction. It makes, however, for uncomfortable reading now, although no one remarked upon it in 1778; Fanny was, it seems, attuned to the comic pressure-points of her time.[46]

But the extraordinary acclaim that virtually all of the critics gave to this young, previously unknown and *female* writer provoked something of a backlash. Before 1778 was over, the cynics of Grub Street had begun to imply that the praise lavished on *Evelina* was misplaced, and was only expressed because its author had falsely led everyone to believe that she was, like her heroine, only seventeen, and not twenty-six. Rumours began to circulate that Dr Johnson had been so bored by the novel that he had only read part of it,[47] while Mrs Thrale wrote in a letter to Dr Johnson on 19 October, 'The Attorney General says you must have all commended it out of a Joke.'[48]

It was also insinuated that Fanny had not been wholly responsible for her book. Mr Earle, a bookseller on Albemarle Street, off Piccadilly, hinted that he had often visited Dr Johnson in his rooms at Bolt Court to collect the writer's corrections to essays for the *Public Advertiser*, and that on some of these visits he had observed lying on a table a 'MS novel previous to its delivery to the Publisher, which Novel the said Dr Johnson spoke highly in praise of mention & that it was entitled Evelina & intended to be publish'd by Mr T. Lowndes. It has been asserted that previous to its publication Evelina was submitted to the revision of Dr Johnson.'[49] This story was never denied by Fanny or substantiated by Dr Johnson. But it seems *most* unlikely: Fanny did not really become acquainted with him until some months after her book's publication, her letters to Mr Lowndes never mention the need for extra time or revision, and it would have been very presumptuous to ask Dr Johnson to revise her book – a novel – on the basis of his very slight acquaintance with her father.

Fanny, in any case, had always wanted to keep her book a secret – and was only happy to be known as its author once its success was guaranteed. Like most writers, she was *very* wary of exposing herself to criticism: 'I had written my little Book simply for my amusement,' she says. 'I printed it, by the means first of my Brother, Charles, next of my cousin, Edward Burney, merely for a frolic, to see how a production of my own would figure in that Author like form: but as I had never read anything to any human being but my sisters Susan and Charlotte, I had taken it for granted that They, only, could be partial enough to endure my compositions.'[50] However, the rumour refused to go away, and over twenty years later Jane Austen mentioned to her sister Cassandra that she had been told by a young student at Oxford that it was Dr Johnson who wrote *Evelina*.[51]

Fanny herself understood that success would bring its own perils. How, for instance, could she hope to produce another novel that would match *Evelina*'s popularity? On 5 July – even before her momentous visit to Streatham Park – she had confided her fears to Susan: 'I am now at the *summit* of a high Hill, – my prospects, on one side, are bright, glowing, & invitingly beautiful; – but when I turn round, I perceive, on the other side, sundry Caverns, Gulphs, pits & precipices ... I have already, I fear, reached the *pinnacle* of my Abilities, & therefore to *stand still* will be my best policy.'[52] Fanny Burney was ever a realist.

FOUR

My Dear Little Burney
1778–9

Dr Johnson [has] more *fun*, & comical humour, & Laughable
& . . . nonsense about him, than almost any body I ever saw.
                                        Fanny Burney, March 1779

Fanny was to say of her first visit to Streatham Park in July 1778 that
it was 'the most *Consequential* Day I have spent since my Birth'.
Indeed, it was to mark for her a more significant change than even the
publication of *Evelina*. Hitherto, Fanny, as the daughter of the
musical, scholarly and sociable Dr Burney, had been introduced to
singers, songwriters, actresses, politicians and explorers. But while
Hetty as the musician took centre-stage, and Susan proved herself a
clever and entertaining conversationalist, Fanny had always preferred
to be the 'silent, observant Miss Burney'.[1] With this invitation to be a
house-guest of the Thrales, however, she embarked on a quite
different journey through life, writing many years later that it was '*le
commencement d'une nouvelle existence*'.[2]

Everyone wanted to be introduced to the young woman who had so
successfully lampooned the extravagances and follies of society, and
who was now championed by none other than Mrs Thrale. When
Fanny walked into a room, it was to her that everyone looked, to her
that they wanted to talk. She was often daunted by all the attention,
yet at the same time she could not help admitting that it was most
satisfying. She often noted in her diary how she had been forced to run
out of the room, blushing furiously, after someone had commented on
her book. But the manner in which she painstakingly recorded all the
praise and adulation suggests that she also enjoyed it.

Mr Crisp was given every detail of that first visit to the Thrales. A
fortnight later, he replied to his 'adopted' daughter: 'Well, the Ice is
now broke, & your perturbation ought to be in a great Measure at an
end.' He then encouraged Fanny to embrace this new life: 'When You

65

went into the Sea at Tinmouth, did not You shiver & shrink at first, & almost lose your breath when the Water came up to your Chest? – I suppose You afterwards learn'd to plunge in boldly overhead & Ears at once, & then Your pain was over – You must do the like now; & as the Public have thought proper to put You on a Cork Jacket, your Fears of drowning would be unpardonable.'[3]

Fanny had need of such advice, for she was never to lose her extreme sensitivity to public scrutiny. A month later, she committed to her diary a farewell to nonentity:

Heigh ho! – I part with this my dear, long loved, long cherished *snugship* with more regret than any body will believe, except my dear sisters who *Live with* me, & know me too well & too closely to doubt me: but yet, I am niether insensible to the *Honours* which have wrested my secret from my Friends, nor Cold to the *pleasures* attending a success so unhoped for: yet my fears for the *future* – & my dread of getting into *Print*, & thence into *Public Notice*, – I niether now can, – or believe I ever shall, wholly Conquer![4]

Fanny's fears were not unfounded: the popular press was as eager then as it is today to deflate those in the public eye. By December she was bewailing to Susan that her name was being bandied around in print. In a satirical pamphlet, *Warley: A Satire. Addressed to the First Artist in Europe* (that is, Sir Joshua Reynolds, who had founded the Royal Academy ten years earlier), attacking the quantities of bad verse being published, the writer George Huddesford questioned whether such verse would 'gain approbation from dear little Burney?'

Fanny was horrified, and claimed that she could not eat, drink or sleep for a week. She hated to think that people were discussing her – *and* using the term of endearment coined for her by Dr Johnson. She became obsessed with her embarrassment – magnifying it out of all proportion. On 20 December, Mrs Thrale wrote to her, snappily urging her to forget the whole business:

Why will you, my lovely Friend, give Consequence to Trifles by thus putting your Peace in their Power? Is not the World full of severe Misfortunes, & real Calamities? & will you fret and look pale about such Nonsense as this? let me see you on Thursday next 24 December if but for an hour, and let me see you chearful I insist. Your looking dismal can only advertise the paltry Pamphlet which I firmly believe no one out of your own Family has seen and which is now only lying like a dead Kitten on the Surface of a dirty Horsepond.

Mrs Thrale knew that talking in such plain terms might offend, but she explained why she believed Fanny was making an inordinate fuss about nothing:

This World is a rough road, and those who mean to tread it many Years must not think of beginning their Journey in Buff Soles. What hurts me most is lest you should like me the less for this Letter; yet I will be true to my own Sentiments & send it; you will think me coarse & indelicate: – I can't help it! – you are twenty Years old and I am past thirtysix there's the true Difference. I have lost seven Children and been cheated out of two thousand a Year, & I cannot, indeed I cannot, sigh & sorrow over Pamphlets & Paragraphs.[5]

Fanny commented, after copying this letter into her journal, that it was a 'spirited, charming, & rational Remonstrance', but this belied the vehemence with which it had been written. Mrs Thrale was still not fully recovered from a catalogue of personal tragedies, the pain of which Fanny (despite losing her mother when she was only ten) could have had little comprehension. By 1778 Mrs Thrale had buried seven of her twelve children – including her only son. Harry Thrale junior had died shockingly in 1776, just a few hours after suffering a ruptured appendix; he was nine. Her last child, Henrietta, who was born in June 1778, was to die four years later – of swollen glands, measles and a cough. No wonder Mrs Thrale wrote such a reprimand. It must have been extraordinary to her that Fanny could make such a fuss over a trifling matter of hurt pride.

Mrs Thrale's relationship with her newly adopted friend was tinged, indeed, with more than a hint of ambivalence. She had at first desired an acquaintance with the author of *Evelina*, surprised by the novel's slightly racy language and intrigued that its satirical stabs at the pretensions of the socially ambitious had been written by a woman. However, on first meeting Fanny, although she admired her conversation, she was disappointed to find her anything but a true radical. For, unlike Fanny, Mrs Thrale had no qualms about what people thought of her, and she had suffered enough to regard such sensitivity as misplaced.

Hester Lynch Salusbury Thrale was the daughter of a celebrated Welsh family, in which she took great pride. She claimed descent from

Adam de Salzburg – reputed to have come over to England with the Conqueror in the eleventh century – and also from Katherine of Beraine, the grand-daughter of an illegitimate son of Henry VII. Hester described herself as being 'so little that the Description of it ought by no means to be large: The Height four feet eleven only, and the Waist though not a taper one quite in proportion . . . with Chestnut Hair & Eyebrows of the same Colour strongly mark'd over a pair of large – but light Grey Eyes'.[6] She was the only child of Sir John Salusbury and Hester Maria Cotton, and was, according to her memoir, 'their Joynt Play Thing'. Indulged with affection, she was also given an unusually fine education for a girl. Both her parents were well read and enjoyed literary pursuits, and they ensured that, 'although Education was a Word then unknown, as applied to Females; They had taught me to read, & speak, & think, & translate from the French, till I was half a Prodigy.'[7] At seventeen, she was privately tutored in Latin and French by a cleric, Dr Parker, later Chaplain to George III.

Mrs Thrale thus confidently knew herself to be both upper class *and* unusually well informed for a woman. When, however, she married Henry Thrale in 1763, it was more out of family duty than personal desire. As the wealthy owner of a brewery in Southwark, Henry had been courted by Hester's parents, rather than by herself, as a means by which they could rescue their own fortunes (though of aristocratic descent, they were an improvident couple). The marriage was unlikely ever to be a success: he was a businessman and Londoner, who before his marriage had enjoyed the rakish lifestyle of a wealthy bachelor – gambling, drinking and womanising (there is a cartoon of him as the 'Southwark Macaroni'); Hester, in contrast, had attempted from the age of fourteen to establish herself as a poet, writing frequently to the newspapers in verse and letters. Although they never quarrelled, and Henry was always a genial and welcoming host, Hester could not find in her husband a like mind and companion. She sought friendship elsewhere, surrounding herself with scholars, conversationalists and wits to whom she could air her views on the latest scurrilous pamphlet or debate in Parliament.

In the winter of 1765, Dr Johnson paid his first visit to the Thrales' new home in Streatham, and before long Hester was playing host to playwrights, artists, singers and politicians eager to meet 'the Great Cham of Literature',[8] including Oliver Goldsmith, Sir Joshua Reynolds, Edmund Burke and the Italian writer and translator of Johnson's *Rasselas*, Giuseppe Baretti. In some years Henry Thrale made as much as £14,000 profit from his brewery (a vast sum, equivalent to over £250,000 today), and there was plenty of disposable income to spend on extravagant improvement projects to his newly acquired house and estate. Dinners at Streatham Park were elaborate affairs – 'two courses of 21 dishes each, besides Removes; and after that a dessert of a piece with the Dinner – Pines and Fruits of all Sort, Ices, Creams, &c, &c, &c,' recorded Mr Crisp after dining there with Fanny and her father in September 1780.[9] When Dr Johnson stayed there during the summer months, he would eat six or seven peaches before breakfast, the fruit grown in Mr Thrale's specially built hothouses. Fanny often complained in the privacy of her diary that the meals were too large, and that her small appetite was unable to cope with them.

Her new friendship was important to her not just because it brought her within the orbit of an exalted literary circle, but also because she found in Mrs Thrale a lively, independent-minded, female counsellor and adviser. But, one suspects, the friendship always meant more to Fanny than to Mrs Thrale. Every moment, every precious conversation is minutely recorded by Fanny, yet no mention of her can be found in the *Thraliana* until some six months after that first visit; even then, Fanny (and her father) are described rather caustically by their hostess. 'The Doctor,' wrote Mrs Thrale on 10 February 1779, 'is a Man quite after my own Heart, if he has any Fault it is too much Obsequiousness, though *I* should not object to a Quality *my* Friends are so little troubled with. – his following close upon the heels of Johnson or Baretti makes me feel him softer though; like turning the Toothpick after you have rubbed your Gums with the *Brush* & immediately applying the *Spunge* to them.'

Of Fanny she wrote, 'his Daughter is a graceful looking Girl, but 'tis the Grace of an Actress not a Woman of Fashion – how should it? her Conversation would be more pleasing if She thought less of herself; but her early Reputation embarrasses her Talk, & clouds her Mind with scruples about Elegancies which either come uncalled for or will not come at all: I love her more for her Father's sake than for her own.'[10] In Fanny's defence, Mrs Thrale was known for being snobbish, perhaps enhanced by a sense that she had demeaned herself by marrying for money, rather than personal happiness or family connection. And her irritation with Fanny's egocentric concern for her own reputation may well have been inspired by jealousy (after all,

Fanny had achieved what Mrs Thrale most aspired to – literary acclaim).

There was, too, a huge gulf between Fanny's knowledge of the world and the experience of Mrs Thrale, who was far more preoccupied at this time with the humiliation of watching her husband fall victim to the charms of the coquettish Sophia Streatfeild. 'Mr Thrale is fallen in Love *really & seriously* with Sophy Streatfield [*sic*],' she noted on 10 January 1779, part humorously, part bitterly. 'But there is no wonder in that: She is very pretty, very gentle, soft & insinuating; hangs about him, dances round him, cries when She parts from him, squeezes his Hand slyly, & with her sweet Eyes full of Tears looks so fondly in his Face – & all for *Love of me* as She pretends; that I can hardly sometimes help laughing in her Face. A Man must not be a *Man* but an *It* to resist such Artillery.[11] Miss Streatfeild, at twenty-four, was thirteen years younger than Mrs Thrale. In the brutal terms of eighteenth-century society, Henry Thrale was quite at liberty to flaunt his passion before his wife, but when some years later the widowed Mrs Thrale indulged her own feelings by marrying the Italian tenor Gabrieli Piozzi, she was vilified even by those closest to her (including Fanny).

Mrs Thrale was also burdened by worries over her husband's increasing financial difficulties. The late 1770s were a time of economic uncertainty, brought on by the outbreak of war with both France and Spain, which necessitated the imposition of ruinous taxes, and by the 'fashionable Frenzy' for speculation in commodities like alum, malt and hemp, whose future value was unpredictable. Many investors lost huge fortunes in 1779–80. In this climate, Mr Thrale's brewing profits had slumped, yet he refused to curtail the extravagance of his hospitality.

Fanny was oblivious to these concerns, and from the first believed herself to be regarded by Mrs Thrale almost like a sister. She describes how when staying at Streatham Park her bedroom adjoined that of her hostess, who would fling open the door first thing in the morning before breakfast, or late at night, and begin a 'delightful confab' about the other guests. The Burney household had always been informal: meals were often interrupted by the arrival of unexpected visitors and by heated arguments over the rival merits of singers at the Opera. Susan and Fanny had overheard their father and stepmother chuckling over passages in *Evelina* as they read it to each other before getting up for breakfast. But Fanny was perhaps too sensitive to her stepmother's moods, and too emotionally obligated to her father, to feel relaxed at home. She found the atmosphere at Streatham Park quite different, and, it seems, more congenial and stimulating. She told Susan, 'There can be no better House for rubbing up the memory, – as I hardly ever Read, saw, or heard of *any* Book that by some means or other, has not been mentioned here.'[12]

During the winter of 1778-9, Fanny spent more time at Streatham Park than she did either with Mr Crisp at Chesington Hall or at St Martin's Street. She was succumbing to the attractions of life with Mrs Thrale, who introduced her to the other celebrated Bluestockings – Mrs Cholmondeley and Mrs Montagu – as well as to Dr Johnson. By 11 March 1779, she was writing to Mr Crisp, 'The kindness & honours I meet with from this charming Family are greater than I can mention . . . sweet Mrs Thrale hardly suffers me to leave her, & Dr Johnson is another Daddy Crisp to me.' One can imagine that Mr Crisp felt neglected and hurt at being pushed aside. Indeed, he complained to his sister that Fanny 'now in a manner lives at Streatham . . . She is become so much the fashion, is so carried about, so fêted from one fine house to another, that if she wished it, it is now really almost out of her power to see her old Friends, as she us'd to do.' Fanny had not written to him for several weeks.[13]

Her diary is taken over during these months by the author of *The Idler* essays and the *Lives of the Poets*, and through her eyes we see Dr Johnson in a rather different light. According to Fanny, he had 'more *fun* & comical humour, & Laughable & . . . nonsense about him, than almost any body I ever saw'.[14] His conversation fills her letters to Susan – talk that was as much witty and flippant as it was learned and philosophical. 'We [Fanny and Mrs Thrale] had been talking of *Colours*, & of the fantastic *names* given to them: & why the palest lilac should be called a *soupire étouffer* – & when Dr Johnson came in, she applied to him, – "Why, Madam," said he, with wonderful readiness, – "it is called a *stifled sigh*, because it is *checked in its progress*, & only half a Colour."'[15] Fanny writes with infectious excitement, and her precise recollections of the after-dinner wordgames enjoyed by Mrs Thrale and her guests vividly evoke the atmosphere in the large, airy drawing-room of Streatham Park, with its french windows on to the garden, where the company spent their evenings sparking off ripostes.

In the Evening, the Company divided pretty much into Parties, & almost every body walked upon the Gravel Walk before the Windows.

I was going to have joined some of them, when Dr Johnson stopt me, & asked how I did . . . 'I was afraid. Sir,' cried I, 'You did not intend to *know* me again, for you have not spoken to me before, since your return from Town.'

'My dear,' cried he, taking both my Hands, 'I was not *sure* of you, I am so near sighted, & I apprehended making some mistake.' Then, drawing me, very unexpectedly towards him, he actually kissed me! –

To be sure I was a little *surprised*, having no idea of such *facetiousness* from him . . .

So Fanny describes an evening in September 1778, which continued with a conversation that 'chiefly was upon the Hebrides, for he [Dr Johnson] always talks to me of Scotland for *sport*: & he *wished* I had been of that Tour! – quite *gravely*, I assure you!' (He was referring to the tour of the Western Isles that he made with Boswell in 1773.) She adds, 'I fancy the folks had all drunk too much Champagne!'[16]

On another occasion, Fanny won one shilling and sixpence in a game of backgammon with Mrs Thrale and her other guests, after which the Doctor wished her goodnight with the words, '*There is none like you*, my dear little Burney! *There is none like you*! – good night, my darling!'[17] Dr Johnson was – in this company at least – quite the ladies' man. He once gave Fanny 'an account of the *celebrated Ladies* of his Acquaintance', which, she told Susan, 'had you heard from *himself*, would have made you *die* with Laughing'. Fanny also told her sister how relieved she was that she had taken her 'best becomes' to Streatham, for Dr Johnson '*scrutinies* into every part of almost every body's appearance'. While oblivious to his own dirty necktie and ragged cuffs, he always, she said, 'speaks his mind concerning the Dress of Ladies, & all Ladies who are here *obey* his injunctions implicitly, & *alter* whatever he disapproves'. Their stepmother discovered this to her cost when she visited Streatham in August 1778 with Dr Burney, experiencing the humiliation of being told that her outfit was quite unsuitable for church and that it was just not the thing to wear 'a Black Hat & Cloak, in summer'.[18]

Despite her shyness, Fanny evidently felt at home at Streatham and in such august company. She was, it seems, not afraid to let rip the ribald sense of humour that peppers her writing, but which she revealed only rarely when in company. Wordplay, rhyming competitions, teasing allusions were as much a part of the after-dinner conversations led by Mrs Thrale as politics and philosophy. One evening, for example, Fanny, Mrs Thrale and Dr Johnson must have amused themselves by parodying an elegy that they had found in a 'Trumpery Book'. The silliness of the rhymes, and its somewhat lewd theme, are not what you might expect from the great scholar and the proud Bluestocking – or from Fanny:

> Here's a Woman of the Town,
>   Lies as Dead as any Nail!
> She was once of high renown –
>   And so here begins my Tale.
>
> She was once a cherry plump
>   Red her cheek as Cath'rine Pear,
> Toss'd her nose, & shook her Rump,
>   Till she made the Neighbours stare.
>
> There she soon became a Jilt,
>   Rambling often to & fro,
> All her life was nought but guilt,
>   Till Purse & Carcase both were low.
>
> But there came a country 'Squire
>   He was a seducing Pug!
> Took her from her friends & sire,
>   To his own House her did Lug.
>
> Black her eye with many a Blow,
>   Hot her breath with many a Dram,
> Now she lies exceeding low,
>   And as quiet as a Lamb.[19]

Fanny copied this word-for-word into her journal, not at all embarrassed by its tone and subject-matter.

Surprising, too, is a reference made by Mrs Thrale to an idea that she discussed with Fanny for a new weekly newspaper to be called *The Flasher*, whose intended readers were the gentlemen guests, 'who desert us most grievously for the sake of attending Parliament'. (Henry Thrale was MP for Southwark until 1781.) She explained, 'we have a Hack Phrase here at Streatham of calling ev'ry thing *Flash* which we want other folks to call *Wit*'. Fanny promised to write the introductory issue, while Mrs Thrale agreed to 'put in a Song', which began with a verse that sets the facetious, 'flashy' tone of the enterprise:

> How bold the Streatham Muse is grown
> To *flash* when all her *Sparks* are flown

> Will nothing then abash her?
> Our solitary Copse can blaze
> Without the Sun's concentred Rays
> To animate our Flasher.

By the 'Streatham Muse', Mrs Thrale meant Sophia Streatfeild, and she went on:

> The meek Minerva's radiant Eyes
> May lead a Man away sure.[20]

Among Fanny's jottings, a string of epithets has survived, scribbled on the back of a piece of printed paper from 1796, which Fanny perhaps remembered from the time she spent at Streatham:

> I'm as sick as a Horse
> I'm as tired as a dog –
> as constant as the turtle
> as tender as a Dove
> as gruff as a bear
> as spotless as a Leopard
> as brisk as a doe
> as strong as a Horse
> as swift as a Hare
> as slow as a Tortoise
> Creep like a snail
> buz like a Bee.[21]

Her fascination with their table talk was shared by Mrs Thrale, who noted in her journal: 'We were playing the fool today & saying every body was like some Colour; & I think some Silk – Sophy Streatfield [*sic*] was to be a pea Green Satten . . . Miss Burney a lilac Tabby, & myself a Gold Colour'd Watered Tabby: My Master a mouse Dun & Johnson who helped this Folly forward was to be a marone. Marone comes from maron I suppose the French Word for a Chestnut.' In another game, Fanny was described as a 'Ranunculus', while Sophy Streatfeild was a 'Jessamine' and Mrs Thrale herself 'a Sprig of Myrtle – which the more it is *crushed*, the more it discloses its *Sweetness*'. While Dr Johnson was once described as a 'haunch of Venison', Dr Burney was 'a dish of fine Green Tea', Miss Burney a 'Woodcock' and Mrs Montagu 'Soup – à la *Reine*'.[22]

There must also have been much talk of the troubled political situation – England was threatened by invasion from France (which had taken advantage of the turmoil in the rebel American colonies to threaten its old enemy) – but little of this emerges from Fanny's diaries and letters. She reassured Susan several times that she would not bore her with such matters. More important to Fanny was her desire to record for her audience (for undoubtedly she wrote these journal-letters as a record, which she and others in her family were to look back on in their old age) the character of the Dr Johnson who came to Streatham Park to be entertained and beguiled, away from the domestic concerns and scholarly labours that obsessed him when at home in Bolt Court.

Mrs Thrale, meanwhile, is portrayed as taking a special interest in her protégée's future. When Fanny first went to stay at Streatham Park, she was already twenty-six and well past marriageable age. Mrs Thrale had married at twenty-two (after a long and involved wrangle over the financial conditions of the marriage settlement between her father and her future husband). Fanny's older sister Hetty had been married for eight years and was already mother to five children. Yet Fanny herself had no suitors at this time (as far as we know), and her new celebrity meant that she was less (rather than more) likely to attract a husband, unless he was famous in his own right and therefore unconcerned that he might be upstaged by his talented wife. Indeed, she was verging dangerously on that territory reserved for maiden aunts.

Fanny had once assured Mr Crisp that she did not care if she became an old maid, but those were the words of an inexperienced girl, who had not fully contemplated the fate of women without a husband or personal wealth. *Evelina* had scarcely earned her a fortune (thirty guineas was only three-fifths of the average annual working wage at the time), and Fanny was totally dependent on her father, who in turn valued her assistance with his work. While he researched his volumes on the history of music in the 1770s by travelling through France, Italy and Germany, Fanny, Susan and Charlotte were busily employed at home in St Martin's Street organising his notes, copying out his manuscripts for the printers, and keeping his huge library of books and musical references in order. Why, then, should he encourage them to abandon him, and impose on himself the need to earn extra money to provide dowries for them and a paid clerical assistant for himself?

Mrs Thrale, however, saw clearly that if Fanny was to develop as a writer she needed to escape from St Martin's Street. And she took it upon herself to find an eligible husband, believing this to be the only way for Fanny to secure her future. 'The present chief sport with Mrs Thrale is disposing of me in the holy state of matrimony – & she *offers* me who–ever comes to the House,' Fanny jokingly wrote to Susan from Streatham Park in September 1778.[23] But Fanny was not so eager for marriage. She had often scorned it as being a stifling condition for a woman – unless it was the outcome of a true meeting of minds. And her resolution had been strengthened by her narrow escape three years earlier, when a Mr Thomas Barlow had proposed marriage and her family had ranged themselves against her, telling her that it was an offer she should not refuse. Fanny was adamant: Mr Barlow was not the man for her.

It was Hetty who organised a tea–party at which Fanny was introduced to this eminently suitable young man – an East End merchant with prospects, who was known to her maternal grand-mother and aunts. Mr Barlow responded dutifully, falling for Fanny at first sight and sending her a letter four days later that expressed his ardent love. Fanny was appalled: she had absolutely nothing in common with this presentable but dull man. On 8 May 1775 she confided in her diary:

> This month is Called a *tender* one – It has proved so *to* me – but not *in* me – I have not breathed one sigh, – felt one sensation, – or uttered one folly the more for the softness of the season. – However – I have met with a youth whose Heart, if he is to be Credited, has been less guarded – indeed it has yielded itself so suddenly, that had it been in any other month – I should not have known how to have accounted for so easy a Conquest.[24]

The 'youth' in question was the twenty-four-year-old Mr Barlow, whom she noted was of excellent character and good-tempered but, 'He has Read more than he has Conversed, & seems to know but little of the World; his Language is stiff & uncommon, he has a great desire to please, but no elegance of manners; niether, though he may be very worthy, is he at all agreeable' – which reveals more about what Fanny believed to be the requisites of a husband than about her suitor. Mr Barlow was not so disagreeable and dull as to be insensitive to Fanny's character. Indeed, he recognised that she was an unusual woman, with 'Affability, Sweetness & Sensibility'. His letter (which Fanny copied into her diary), though somewhat high-flown, is written in a style that is both elegant and lucid:

> Madam, Uninterrupted happiness we are told is of a short duration, & is quickly succeeded by Anxiety, which moral Axiom I really experienc'd on the Conclusion of May day at Mr Charles Burney's, as the singular Pleasure of your Company was so soon Eclips'd by the rapidity of ever-flying Time . . . permit me then Madam, with the greatest sincerity, to assure you, that the feelings of that Evening were the most refined I ever enjoy'd . . . Language cannot possibly depict the soft Emotions of a mind captivated by so much merit.

Fanny was unimpressed, asserting firmly – though only in secret in the pages of her diary – 'I had rather a thousand Times Die an old maid than be married, except from affection.' But she did not feel free to reject Mr Barlow's advances without first consulting her father: 'as I do not consider myself as an independent member of society, & as I knew I could depend upon my Father's kindness, I thought it incumbent upon me to act with his Concurrence'. She showed him Mr Barlow's letter and asked for advice on how she should reply. At first Dr Burney showed the 'indulgence & goodness' that she expected of him, but Mr Barlow was persistent. Fanny's maiden aunts, Becky and Ann, urged her not to refuse him; after all, she was already almost twenty-three. Did she want to remain forever dependent on her father? When she sent a curt reply to Mr Barlow – wishing him all happiness, but begging him to 'Transfer to some person better known to him a partiality which she so little merits' – her father was most displeased. Should she not become better acquainted with her suitor before refusing him outright?

Worse was to come. Hetty wrote to Mr Crisp, knowing his influence with Fanny, and hoping that he could persuade her that this was an opportunity she should not ignore. Mr Crisp's reply was such that Fanny felt her cause was lost, and on receiving his letter she retired to her room, weeping tears of bitter exasperation. Mr Crisp, after praising Mr Barlow's obvious good intentions in writing such a heartfelt and honourable letter, warned Fanny that:

> all the ill-founded Objections You make, to me appear strong & invincible marks of a violent & sincere Passion – what You take it into your head to be displeas'd with, as too great a Liberty, I mean, his presuming to write to You, & in so tender & respectful & submissive a

strain, if You knew the World, & that villainous Yahoo, call'd man, as well as I do, You would see in a very different Light ... such a disposition promises a thousand fold more happiness, more solid, lasting, home-felt happiness, than all the seducing, exterior Airs, Graces, Accomplishments, & Address of an Artful rake.

But Mr Crisp had underestimated Fanny. She was neither so innocent of the world – how surprised he must have been three years later to read her depiction of the rakes and prostitutes encountered by Evelina – nor so docile as to settle meekly for the fate normally meted out to women without means.

The 'Barlow Affair' illustrates the difficulties that she faced: she wanted to please her family, but she was torn by her inner resolve not to betray her own truth, her own sense of herself. 'And so it is all over with me!' she wrote to Crisp on 15 May:

& I am to be given up – to forfeit your blessing – to lose your good opinion – to be doomed to regret & the Horrors – *because* – I have not a mind to be married. Forgive me – my dearest Mr Crisp – forgive me – but indeed I cannot act from *Worldly motives* . . . your last Letter really made me unhappy – I am grieved that you can so earnestly espouse the Cause of a person you never saw – I heartily wish him well – he is, I believe, a worthy young man – but I have long accustomed myself to the idea of being an old maid – & the Title has lost all its terrors in my Ears.

She assured him that she had not taken a nun-like vow to remain single, but in a revealing afterthought told him that she had always 'determined never to marry without having the highest value & esteem for *the man who should be my Lord* [my italics]'. Fanny may have adopted a radical stance by asserting that 'marriage' was not the ultimate goal of any female, but at heart she was anything but a closet feminist. She believed rather that she should marry *only* where she had enough respect to subdue willingly her own personality to that of her 'Lord'. And although she evidently saw nothing to be ashamed of in remaining a spinster, she never followed this through by setting herself up in her own home. This would, of course, have been virtually impossible for her financially, and would have given rise to speculation about her moral virtue. But there were female writers in the late eighteenth century who made a living from their pen; the best-known example being Mary Wollstonecraft, who some ten years later maintained her own home in Blackfriars through her earnings as a journalist, pamphleteer and novelist.

Fortunately for Fanny, she did eventually prevail over her family – but only after an excruciatingly embarrassing interview with her erstwhile lover, and an even more painful conversation with her father. Her fortitude suggests that she had a sure sense of what she wanted to do with her life; that she already knew that self-expression through her writing was more important to her than anything else. And the result, *Evelina*, vindicated her decision; it reads with a natural ease and command. Yet, despite its success, Fanny was left with the question: what next?

Mrs Thrale evidently believed that marriage was Fanny's only option. Even Dr Johnson was led to speculate on her inevitable fate, declaring with characteristic perspicacity that she would be married for 'her Wit' but would need to marry for 'his Fortune'.[25] He was referring to the wealthy Jeremiah Crutchley, seven years older than Fanny, who owned a large estate in Sunninghill, Berkshire (he was later elected MP for Horsham in Sussex).[26] A close friend of both Mr and Mrs Thrale, he was a frequent guest at Streatham Park. At first Mrs Thrale claimed that he was a 'Ward of Mr Thrale', but in the *Thraliana* she hinted that he was Henry Thrale's 'natural' son. This may well be true – Crutchley was one of the five executors of Thrale's will – but, if so, it throws a strange light on Mrs Thrale's later suggestion that he was in love with her eldest daughter (and thereby his own half-sister) Queeney.

Fanny's first impression of him was not favourable: he may have been rich but she found it impossible to make conversation with him. Anyway, there were other candidates for her affections at Streatham Park. A distant cousin of Thrale, Harry Smith, was rich – with an estate worth £800 a year – and, according to Mrs Thrale, had the benefit of 'a Profession [he was a barrister] to keep him from Idleness'.[27] But Fanny could never take him seriously because of his name, which always reminded her of her own ridiculous 'Mr Smith' in *Evelina:* 'I could hardly bear to call him by his Name, for I felt a kind of *conscious Guilt* as if I had been taking unwarrantable liberties with it.'[28]

Both men appear frequently in Fanny's diaries at this time – particularly Crutchley, for whom Fanny evidently had strong feelings. Her portrait of him is unusually confused – as if she were too wrapped up in her emotions to distil in writing the essence of his character. She does not appear to have loved him in a romantic sense; yet she experienced all the topsy-turviness of emotion that Mr Crisp had once explained to her was the sign of true feeling. A few years earlier, in the extraordinary letter which he had written to Fanny after her stepsister's runaway marriage in 1772, accusing Maria of unbridled and ultimately superficial feelings, Mr Crisp had warned Fanny not to confuse what we would now call 'erotic' passion with real, lasting love. Of that second kind of attachment, he wrote:

> this passion is so deeply rooted as to be proof against time & absence – it takes such total, absolute possession of the enamoured bosom, as to leave no room for other considerations – Vanity, flirtation, the rage of general admiration are extinguished – Such a heart is for ever agitated by fears & hopes, & perpetual anxieties, till its peace . . . [there is a gap here] & rest are restored by a return of equal Passion from the beloved.[29]

This letter, written by the sixty-five-year-old bachelor to his twenty-year-old female friend, reads like a passionate plea for Fanny to understand the truth about Love, and is very different from the restrained epistles of Mr Crisp's fictional *alter ego*, Mr Villars. What kind of feelings did Mr Crisp have for Fanny? And why did she form such an attachment to him? Maria Allen distrusted him – forbidding Fanny to show him their correspondence, particularly where it related to her lover Martin Rishton. And later letters from Mr Crisp to the daughters of Thomas Payne, the bookseller (one of whom, Sally, married Fanny's sailor brother James) – in which he addresses them as 'the virgin pullets', and says that he longs to see 'that clear, transparent skin, & glow of health that made poor Jem's heart go pat-a-pat last summer; & would have served me the same sauce fifty years ago' – suggest a lingering interest in young women.[30]

This is not to say that it was an unhealthy obsession – the company of these vivacious young women must have cheered up Mr Crisp's declining years and reminded him of happier, more sociable times. Yet the closeness of his rapport with Fanny *did* prevent her from looking for male companionship elsewhere – she had no need of a confidant when she had Mr Crisp, who demanded to know all about her life and could always be depended on to give her deeply personal advice. His friendship also gave her a standard by which she measured the other men of her acquaintance. He was someone whom she knew would always look upon her with a glow of affection, and he was, too, 'so infinitely, so beyond comparison clever in *himself*' that she was never bored in his company.[31]

The callow Mr Barlow had scored badly when it came to sophisticated conversation and gentlemanly elegance, although his textbook manners and equable temperament were unimpeachable. Mr Crutchley, in contrast, was suave, well read and, one suspects, more intelligent than Fanny, with a keen understanding of the way the world worked. He features prominently in her diaries from 1778 until 1782 (so much so, indeed, that there are times when one might wish him to blazes), after which he suddenly disappears, never to be mentioned again. Crutchley, however, was also moody, fickle and insufferably proud – and the course of his friendship with Fanny was filled with uncertainties and huffs, which tell us much about her and her views on the married state.

What emerges from these experiences is her determination, above all else, to forge a name for herself as a writer. And, after the success of *Evelina*, it looked as if she might succeed. On 2 September 1778, she told Susan how she had spent three hours in the library at Streatham Park enjoying a most remarkable tête-à-tête with her new friend Mrs Thrale. It had begun with a discussion on Dr Johnson's tragedy *Irene*, but from this Mrs Thrale suddenly turned the subject round by suggesting to Fanny that *she* should write a play: 'I have a Notion it would hit *my* Taste in *all* things; – *do*, – you *must* write one – a *play* will be something *worth* your Time, it is the Road both to Honour & Profit, – & *why* should you have it in your power to gain these rewards & not do it?'[32]

This was exactly what Fanny wanted to hear, as it voiced her own – as yet secret – dream to write for the stage. Only a few months earlier, Hannah More had earned £400 for her latest play *Percy*, which played for nineteen nights in December 1777, and then sold over 4,000 copies of the script in a fortnight.[33] Was this not the way for Fanny to achieve her independence? After all, she had proved in *Evelina* that she could create characters and write convincing dialogue. As a frequent visitor to Drury Lane, and friend to the theatrical stars of the 1760s and 1770s, she had grown up with the theatre. She had burned several play scripts in that bonfire of 1767. She had acted in the amateur theatricals so beloved of her brothers and sisters. And she knew, almost by instinct, how to construct a drama. Indeed, by 4 May 1779, she was writing to Mr Crisp that she had 'finished a Play', which she hoped shortly to show him in person.[34]

FIVE

Good Night, Lady Smatter
1779–80

Well! – God's above all! – & there are *plays* that *are* to be
saved, & *plays* that are *not* to be saved! – so good Night
Mr Dabler! – good Night Lady Smatter!

Fanny Burney, August 1779

Mrs Thrale was not the only person to encourage Fanny to write for
the theatre. The playwright Arthur Murphy was invited to Streatham
Park especially to meet Fanny. 'He may be of *use* to you,' Mrs Thrale
told her, 'he knows stage Business so well.' Fanny duly involved him
in a long conversation after dinner one evening, during which he was
drawn to suggest that if he had written a book such as *Evelina*, then he
would next attempt a comedy. '*Comedy*,' he commented, 'is the *forte* of
that book.' He went on to promise Fanny that if she showed him what
she had written, then he would advise her on its production: 'I will
undertake to say I can tell what the sovereigns of the upper Gallery
will bear, – for they are the most formidable part of an Audience: I
have had so much experience in this sort of Work, that I believe I can
always tell what will be *Hissed* at least.'[1]

His words were thrilling confirmation of what Fanny had heard a
few weeks earlier from another successful playwright. By 1779 Richard
Brinsley Sheridan, who had taken over the management of the Drury
Lane Theatre after Garrick was taken ill in 1776, was recognised as the
chief arbiter of theatrical taste. Two years earlier, his comic farce *The
School for Scandal* had been a huge success (in the twelve years
following its première in 1777, it earned him over £15,000). Fanny
was introduced to Sheridan by Mrs Cholmondeley at a Twelfth Night
party on 6 January. She was talking to Sir Joshua Reynolds, when
Sheridan joined them and turned the conversation to ask Fanny what
she was working on at the moment. She replied, flirtatiously, 'Why –
twirling my Fan, I think!' But Sheridan persisted: 'No, no, – but what

are you about *at Home*?' When Fanny still refused to divulge whether or not she had begun a sequel to *Evelina*, Sir Joshua asked Sheridan whether *he* would be prepared to take anything by Fanny 'unsight, unseen'. Sheridan's response was unequivocal: 'Yes . . . & make her a Bow & my best Thanks into the Bargain!' Fanny was overwhelmed: 'I actually shook from Head to foot!' she told Susan. 'I felt myself already in Drury Lane, amidst the *Hub bub* of a first night.'[2]

Dr Johnson, too, had asked her, half in jest, to write a play, featuring caricatures of the Thrales's guests, which he suggested should be called 'Stretham: A Farce'. No such comedy has been found among Fanny's papers; and the reference to Dr Johnson's request was carefully deleted by her when she came to read through her journals in old age. But she may well have destroyed whatever she wrote while at Streatham, fearing that she had been too free with her pen.[3]

As early as 1769 she had begun to write her journal not as a simple narrative but as a conversation between different characters – as if she were deliberately practising her skills as a writer of dialogue. When, for instance, she described the wedding of their cook at Poland Street, Betty Langley, to a glass polisher called John Hutton, she talked of them as the Bride and Bridegroom and gave to each of them a role to play, as if they were actors in a domestic drama.[4] Some three years later, she wrote up a visit by one of her Burney cousins from Worcester according to 'the Grandison way of writing Dialogue'.[5] And, by September 1778, she had coined her own word to describe what she felt herself to be doing in writing these journal-letters: 'I think I shall occasionally *Theatricalise* my Dialogues' (one of many instances where Fanny coined words that are now cited in the *Oxford English Dictionary*).[6]

But to write professionally for the stage implied a 'dangerous' flaunting of the conventions for a woman. When Fanny let slip to Mr Crisp that she had begun work on a comedy, he fired off an immediate reply, advising her of the traps into which she might fall:

In these little, entertaining, elegant Histories [i.e. *Evelina*], the writer has his full scope . . . he may be as minute as he pleases, & the more minute the better . . . The exquisite touches such a Work is capable of (of which, Evelina is, without flattery, a glaring instance) are truly charming. – But of these great advantages, these resources, YOU are strangely curtailed, the Moment You begin a Comedy: *There* every thing passes in Dialogue, all goes on rapidly; – Narration, &

description, if not extremely Short, become intolerable ... The
Moment the Scene ceases to move on briskly, & business seems to
hang, Sighs & Groans are the Consequence.[7]

The audiences in Drury Lane, for example, were notoriously rowdy,
and Mr Crisp feared that Fanny would be humiliated. Yet the qualities
he defined as being intrinsic to good theatre – the sharpness of the
interaction between the characters *and* the breathless pace at which one
scene merges into the next – are precisely what have made *Evelina* so
enduringly popular, and he must surely have recognised this. His
letter was presumably intended as a gentle warning to Fanny not to
indulge herself with idle dreams. But a month later he sent a much
more vociferous epistle.

Mr Crisp was concerned not that Fanny might produce something
that would be hissed off the stage, but that she might inadvertently
slide into voicing opinions and attitudes that would harm her
reputation. 'Well – I have been ruminating a good deal on the
Obstacles & difficulties I mention'd in my last, that lye directly across
YOUR Path (as a Prude): in the Walk of Comedy ... I will never
allow You to sacrifice a *Grain* of female delicacy, for all the Wit of
Congreve & Vanbrugh put together.' He does admit that if anyone can
combine 'female delicacy' with the 'Spirit & Salt' essential to a
successful comedy, then Fanny is the person to do so, but the whole
tone of his letter is designed to divert her from playwriting and back to
'The Novel'.[8]

This was hardly surprising for an aesthete such as Mr Crisp. Drama
was considered by many scholars in the eighteenth century to be a
lesser art, lacking the spiritual depth and opportunities for moral
improvement provided by other literary forms. Even Shakespeare had
been criticised by writers such as Samuel Richardson. It was Garrick –
through his unforgettable performances as the great tragic heroes,
Hamlet, Lear, Macbeth and Othello – and Dr Johnson, in his Notes
on the plays, who encouraged a revival of enthusiasm for the
dramatist; this culminated in the Shakespeare Jubilee of September
1769, when three days were devoted to celebrating his life and works
in orations, concerts, pageants and fireworks.

An attempt had been made in 1737 to impose a new morality on the
London theatres, with a Licensing Act that closed down the smaller,
more unruly playhouses and limited the royal patent for public
performance to just two theatres, Drury Lane and Covent Garden.

The Act also gave the Lord Chamberlain powers to prohibit productions of plays that were deemed politically or morally unsound; and all new scripts had to be submitted to his office for approval. But in 1776 the connection between 'theatrical' and 'immoral' was still very much in evidence. When, for instance, Congreve's Restoration comedy *The Double Dealer* was staged in March, the playbill reassured prospective ticket-buyers that the text had been 'carefully revised and corrected, by expunging the exceptionable passages'.[9]

Mr Crisp knew to his cost that the theatre was fraught with disappointment and misinterpretation. Playwrights were not just exposed to the very public criticism of an audience; they were also at the mercy of the theatre managers, who wielded enormous power. The owner-managers of the patented theatres – Garrick and later Sheridan at Drury Lane, and Thomas Harris at Covent Garden – made huge profits. By the end of Garrick's reign in 1776, the Drury Lane theatre had been increased in size from 650 to 1,800 seats, while Covent Garden held over 2,000 (ticket prices ranged from five shillings for a box seat to one shilling in the gallery). It was the managers who submitted play scripts for approval to the Lord Chamberlain's office; they, too, selected the cast and directed rehearsals. Garrick, for instance, would assemble his players in the Green Room at Drury Lane for a preliminary reading of a new script, at which it was advisable for the author to be present. It was not unknown for actors to refuse to learn their lines because they were not being paid enough, or because they deemed the play unworthy of their talents (as Fanny was to discover many years later).[10]

For a male playwright, there were difficulties enough in the 1770s; for a woman it was doubly so. If Fanny had ventured backstage, she would have had to mingle with a band of performers whose moral rectitude was questionable (the intermingling of men and women in a working environment was so unusual then as to arouse suspicion). Yet, not to have done so would have meant leaving all the details of production (lighting, scenery, props) and rehearsal (especially changes that became obvious only after the script was read aloud) – details upon which the success of the play depended – to the theatre manager. This was all very different from delivering a *completed* manuscript to the printers via an agent, and then ensuring that the proofs were corrected as marked (indeed, even then, it was not until its third edition that *Evelina* appeared as written by Fanny).

There *were* female playwrights at this time, and successful ones too – women like Hannah More, Hannah Cowley, Frances Brooke, Sophia Lee and Elizabeth Inchbald – but they were all to experience setbacks. Mrs Inchbald, after spending eight years as an actress touring the provinces, arrived in London in 1780 with a trunkload of manuscripts (just like the heroine of Frances Brooke's novel, *The Excursion*). She spent years trying to get them staged, and eventually succeeded in having as many as twenty of them produced before she died in 1821. But on the way to acclaim (and profit), she had first to overcome an obstacle not uncommon to women who dare to invade a male protectorate. She appeared at Covent Garden one day 'with so wild an air, and with such evident emotion, that all present were alarmed'. She then told her colleagues how Thomas Harris had invited her to his home in Knightsbridge to discuss a new script, whereupon he had made 'untoward advances'. Mrs Inchbald, fearing rape, had the sense to respond 'by pulling on his hair most vigorously'. '"Oh! if he had wo-wo-worn a wig," she stuttered, "I had been ru-ruined."'[11]

A professional actress and widow (her husband died shortly before she travelled to London), Elizabeth Inchbald was sufficiently 'of the world' to put a comic face on what had happened. But Fanny, 'the prude', might not have reacted with such aplomb.

Fanny, however, paid no heed to Mr Crisp's objections. She was anxious to work within the boundaries set by a reproving world, but not if that meant sacrificing what she had come to believe was her vocation. Her reply to his letter was forthright:

> Every word you have urged concerning the *salt & spirit* of gay, unrestrained freedom in Comedies, carries conviction along with it, – a conviction which I feel in trembling! Should I ever venture in that walk publicly, perhaps the want of it might prove fatal to me: I do, indeed, think it most likely that such would be the Event, & my poor piece, though it might escape Cat calls & riots, would be fairly *slept off the stage*.

She continued: 'I cannot, however, attempt to *avoid* this danger, though I *see* it.' However, she was forced to admit to Mr Crisp that she would 'a thousand Times rather forfeit my character as a *Writer*, than risk ridicule or censure as a *Female*'.[12]

This was not entirely honest of Fanny for by the time she wrote this letter in early January 1779 she had almost finished her comedy, and shortly afterwards she asked Dr Johnson if he would look over the

manuscript on his way back to town. 'The Witlings' was to be no
secret enterprise, written at the dead of night in a chilly bedroom and
sent off anonymously to a bookseller for publication. In the year since
Evelina's appearance, Fanny had matured. She may have been anxious
that her next production would be so eagerly fanfared that disappointment and criticism were inevitable, but she was determined to
continue writing.

'The Witlings; A Comedy, By a Sister of the Order' did surprise
everyone. Fanny's entrance into the literary world had introduced her
to a different set of people, and her new-found confidence had
sharpened her observations. After reading the first two acts, Arthur
Murphy declared to Mrs Thrale that Fanny was 'a *sly, designing body*',
who 'looks all the people through most wickedly'.[13] Indeed, she was
not always a comfortable person to know. But Murphy was impressed
by what he read, and, according to Fanny, 'has not criticised one
Word, on the contrary; the Dialogue he has honoured with high
praise'.[14] Mrs Thrale (who read the script as it was written, during
Fanny's visits to Streatham Park) also enjoyed it, but admitted to her
diary on 1 May that 'none of the scribbling Ladies have a Right to
admire its general Tendency'. She saw too close a similarity between
Fanny's 'witlings' and the Bluestocking ladies who were among her
friends and acquaintances.[15]

Fanny was sufficiently encouraged, however, to spend the next few
months revising and extending her original script, and by 30 July 1779
she had shown Mr Crisp her final version. She told him that she
would 'dread to open' his reply, yet she demanded his '*real* opinion':

> I should like that your First reading should have nothing to do with *me*,
> that you should go quick through it, or let my Father read it to you,
> forgetting all the Time, as much as you can, that *Fannikin* is the
> Writer, or even that it is a play in manuscript, & *capable* of alterations:
> – And then, when you have done, I should like to have 3 Lines, telling
> me, as nearly as you trust my candour, its general effect. After that, –
> take it to your own Desk, & lash it at your leisure.[16]

And lash it he did – to such effect that Fanny abandoned it. 'The fatal
knell then, is knolled! & down among the Dead Men sink the poor
Witlings, – for-ever & for-ever & for-ever,' she told her father.[17]

Dr Burney had travelled to Chesington Hall, taking with him the
final version of 'The Witlings', to be read aloud by the assembled

company, which included Susan and Charlotte. Susan told Fanny afterwards that the reading had been a huge success, and that 'Charlotte laugh'd till she was almost black in the face'. Susan herself confessed to having been reduced to tears by the sentimental scenes.[18] To induce both laughter and tears in a single play was a considerable achievement for a novice playwright. But Mr Crisp and Dr Burney were unable to acknowledge this, so concerned were they that 'The Witlings' would insult the very literary ladies on whom Fanny depended for her reputation as a writer. They were shocked by the sometimes indelicate way in which Fanny had satirised Mrs Montagu and the Bluestockings, through the characters of Mrs Sapient, Lady Smatter and the other 'witlings', and they spared nothing in their criticism of what she had written.

Fanny was dashed by their combined assault – but she never destroyed or forgot her play. Five notebooks, each containing one act written out neatly in her 'printer's' handwriting, have survived, while among her papers are scraps of dialogue and new ideas for the plot, written years later on dated notepaper and envelopes.[19] They reveal a witty and fast-paced satire on the pretensions and aspirations of the literati.[20] There are *longueurs*, and scenes that in rehearsal would probably have been dropped or radically reworked, but the adventures of the heiress Cecilia, her fiancé Beaufort and the truly ghastly Lady Smatter are lively enough to entertain even a modern audience.

From the start Fanny captures the attention, as the curtain rises on the interior of a milliner's shop. 'The Witlings', she seems to be saying, is going to be very different from the usual fare at Drury Lane. This play begins not with a bunch of aristocrats conversing in a stylised drawing-room, but with a group of women gossiping in an ordinary, working environment. The hero, Beaufort, is waiting with Censor, his elderly friend and moral guardian, inside the shop, where he has arranged to meet Cecilia, an heiress worth about £40,000 per annum. The two men are ill-at-ease, uncomfortable in this women's world of flounces, trimmings, caps and bows.

Fanny's comedy has a traditional theme, focusing on the lovers, Cecilia and Beaufort, who are forbidden to marry by Lady Smatter after Cecilia loses her fortune – a topical allusion by Fanny to the fear of bankruptcy that obsessed London society in 1778–9. But her treatment is very different. The lovers are saved by Censor, who threatens to ruin Lady Smatter by publishing a cruel lampoon accusing her of ignorance and stupidity, unless she relents and allows the marriage to go ahead. Censor knows that Lady Smatter will give in because of the pride she takes in being Queen Bee of the Esprit Party. This group of scholarly dabblers pretends to a knowledge of literature – Pope, Swift, Shakespeare and Addison – but, in fact, knows very little and understands less: 'To a very little reading, they join less Understanding, & no Judgement, yet they decide upon Books & Authors with the most confirmed confidence in their abilities for the Task,' says Beaufort witheringly when condemning his aunt, Lady Smatter, and her salon at the beginning of the play.[21]

The humour of 'The Witlings' rests on Fanny's depiction of Lady Smatter, and of the poets who cluster round her in the hope of gaining her favour and patronage. The title was perhaps inspired by lines in Pope's *Essay on Criticism:*

> Some have at first for wits, then poets past,
> Turn'd critics next, and prov'd plain fools at last.
> Some neither can for wits nor critics pass,
> As heavy mules are neither horse nor ass.
> Those half-learned *witlings*, num'rous in our isle,
> As half-form'd insects on the banks of Nile;
> Unfinish'd things, one knows not what to call,
> Their generation's so equivocal:
> To tell 'em, would a hundred tongues require,
> Or one vain wit's, that might a hundred tire.[22]

The essay had been reissued in 1776 in a new edition of Pope's complete works. Fanny frequently quotes from Pope in *Evelina*, and in 'The Witlings' a miserable old misogynist, appropriately called Codger, echoes Pope's assertion that 'Most Women have no character at all'.[23]

But Dr Burney was not impressed by Fanny's allusions to Pope, and he wrote her a terse letter: 'the objections all fall on the Stocking-Club-Party . . . not only the Whole Piece, but the *plot* had best be kept secret, from every body'.[24] He was understandably concerned that the play might offend the very persons to whom he was indebted for patronage as a professional music-teacher. Mr Crisp, too, believed that Mrs Montagu and her circle of literary-minded friends would recognise themselves in the Esprit Club. Mrs Thrale noted in her diary that 'Mr Crisp advised her [Fanny] against bringing it on, for fear of displeasing the female Wits – a formidable Body, & called by those who ridicule them, the *Blue Stocking Club*.'[25] He was dismayed that

Fanny had taken too literally Dr Johnson's encouragement to do down Mrs Montagu ('Spare her not! attack her, fight her, & *down* with her at once!' he had challenged her. '*You* are a *rising* Wit – *she* is at the *Top*').[26] Indeed, Mrs Montagu was a rich widow with an adopted son, whose inheritance was dependent on him assuming her name so that it would be perpetuated after her death – just like the characters of Lady Smatter and Beaufort: it was a quite shocking and very funny character.

Dr Burney and Crisp were perhaps wise to suppress this. They were also alarmed by Fanny's attempts to subvert Pope's view of women. Through the aptly named Mrs Voluble, Fanny illustrates just how gullible and stupid women could be: 'She will consume more Words in an Hour than Ten Men will in a Year, she is infected with a rage for talking, yet has nothing to say, which is a Disease of all others the most pernicious to her fellow Creatures ... Her Tongue is as restless as Scandal, &, like that, feeds upon nothing, yet attacks & tortures every thing; & it vies, in rapidity of motion, with the circulation of the Blood in a Frog's Foot.'[27] But Fanny also depicts women who are spirited and independent: her milliners are working girls, not cloistered servants of their parents; and even Mrs Voluble is her own mistress, making money by letting out rooms to the infamously bad poet, Mr Dabler.

Cecilia, too, is no sycophantic lover: Beaufort is just as dependent on her for his happiness *and* financial well-being. 'The Witlings' ends with a powerful assertion of the need for 'self-dependance', which is defined as 'the first of Earthly Blessings; since those who rely solely on others for support & protection are not only liable to the common vicissitudes of Human Life, but exposed to the partial caprices & infirmities of Human Nature'.[28] Fanny gives this strongly worded speech to a man (Beaufort), but its message is unambiguously applicable to everyone, regardless of sex. At times, indeed, the play reads like a covert message to Dr Burney – Fanny still had to ask his permission before accepting any social invitations – and Mr Crisp, who still looked on her as his 'Fannikin', almost his child.

Both men were so horrified by the audaciousness of 'The Witlings' that they combined forces to bring a far more serious charge against it. They accused Fanny of plagiarising Molière's *Les Femmes savantes* – at least, according to a note that Fanny later pencilled on a letter she had written to her father during August, when the debate over the future of 'The Witlings' was at its height. There are similarities between the two comedies (Molière's dates from 1672): both depict a sisterhood of literary-minded women and a thwarted love affair. Fanny asserted, with no lack of irony, 'It is, however, a curious fact, & to the author a consolatory one, that she had literally never read the *Femmes Scavantes* [*sic*] when she composed The Witlings.'[29] But it was an accusation against which she had no defence: few can prove that they have not been influenced by what they have read or seen. A year later, for example, Sophia Lee described how her comedy *A Chapter of Accidents* was almost never staged, after Thomas Harris accused her of copying from Diderot's *Le Père de famille*. She wrote in her preface to the play how she 'learnt that merit merely is a very insufficient recommendation to managers in general! and as I had neither a prostituted pen or person to offer Mr Harris, I gave up all thoughts of the Drama'. George Colman the Elder, however, was more discerning and put on the play at his Haymarket Theatre, where it ran for an astonishingly successful 100 nights.[30]

Fanny was less persistent. 'You *have* finished it, now, – in *every* sense of the Word, – *partial* faults may be corrected, but what I most wished was to know the general effect of the Whole, – & as *that* has so terribly failed, all petty criticisms would be needless. I shall wipe it all from my memory, & endeavour never to recollect that I ever writ it,' she told her father bitterly in mid-August 1779. Reading the letter now, some two hundred years later, one can still sense the pain of her disappointment:

> You bid me open my Heart to you, – & so, my dearest Sir, I will, – for it is the greatest happiness of my life that I *dare* be sincere to you, – I expected many Objections to be raised, a thousand errors to be pointed out, & a million of alterations to be proposed; – but – the *suppression of the piece* were words I did *not* expect, – indeed, after the warm approbation of Mrs Thrale, & the repeated commendations & flattery of Mr Murphy, how could I?

Writing to Mr Crisp on the same day, she was no less dramatic: 'Well! – God's above all! – & there are *plays* that *are* to be saved, & *plays* that are *not* to be saved! – so good Night Mr Dabler! – good Night Lady Smatter, – Mrs Sapient, Mrs Voluble . . . Censor, – Cecilia – Beaufort . . . good Night! good Night!'[31] Both letters survive without her later obliterations – as if Fanny was determined that her future readers should know exactly why 'The Witlings' was buried for ever.

Dr Burney and Mr Crisp had some justification for over-protecting Fanny. Not only were female playwrights subject to all kinds of unwelcome overtures if they ventured backstage, they could also be vilified *on stage*. In August 1779 (the same month in which Fanny and her father were exchanging heated letters about 'The Witlings'), George Colman produced *The Separate Maintenance*, which uproari-ously lampooned the 'female playwrights'. One of the characters, Mrs Fustian, a 'strange, ranting, crazy being', was believed to be modelled on either Hannah Cowley or Hannah More. Sheridan, too, made his own stab at the 'foolish' aspirations of the opposite sex, when he accused them in his epilogue to Hannah More's *The Fatal Falsehood* (which was also staged in the summer of 1779) of neglecting their housewifely duties while indulging their pretensions to literary genius. And this view was echoed a few years later in a play by George Colman the Younger, entitled *The Female Dramatist*, in which the scribbling tendencies of the central character, Madam Melpomeme Metaphor, were made to appear quite ludicrous. She was told to 'turn her pen into a Needle, and her Tragedies into thread papers'.[32]

If Fanny had wandered into this theatrical minefield, she might have had an unpleasant time. Indeed, years later, the historian and critic Thomas Macaulay damned 'The Witlings', and asserted that 'Murphy and Sheridan thought so, though they were too polite to say so.'[33] But although she bowed under pressure when it came to staging her play, Fanny did not suppress her urge to write. In that pained letter of mid-August, she vowed to her father that 'the best way I can take of shewing that I have a true & just sense of the *spirit* of your condemnation, is not to sink, sulky & rejected, under it, but to exert myself to the utmost of my power in endeavours to produce something less reprehensible'. But she did promise not to attempt anything else until she had '*read* myself into a forgetfulness of my old Dramatis persona, – lest I should produce something else as *Witless* as the last'.[34]

Nevertheless, such discouragement inevitably led Fanny into a prolonged spell of gloom and inactivity, and for several months she makes no mention of playwriting – or indeed of writing anything. Family problems took the place of literary preoccupations. Her older sister Hetty was ill (probably suffering from a miscarriage) and Fanny spent a good deal of time with her in Charles Street, nursing her back to health with doses of 'bark' (extracted from cinchona bark, an early form of quinine). The Burneys were also worried again about Charles, who had written a series of depressed letters home to St Martin's

Street from Aberdeen, where he was studying divinity at the university. The letters are now missing, presumably destroyed by Fanny for being too revealing of her brother's misdemeanours (Mr Crisp spoke of him as 'that worthless wretch Charles'). Dr Burney hoped that his second son (who had not inherited the Burneys' musical talent) would become a clergyman, but, if he failed to gain a degree, Charles could not be ordained, let alone offered a living.

The Thrale household was also in turmoil. Mrs Thrale had almost died while giving birth to a stillborn son on 10 August 1779 (after unwillingly enduring an uncomfortably hot and bumpy coach ride from town), and was still very weak. Her husband was not in the least sympathetic. Henry Thrale had suffered a stroke in June after the shocking discovery that his brewery was threatened with bankruptcy. He soon recovered, but began to behave with even more extravagance than usual, as if all his faults had been magnified by his illness. He insisted on defying his doctors – eating, drinking and entertaining on such a lavish scale that his wife, who was unable to curb her husband's boisterous behaviour, was horrified.

At the same time, the threat of foreign invasion had become ever more real. Britain's war with the rebel American colonies (which had declared their independence in July 1776) continued until October 1781, when Lord Cornwallis finally surrendered at Yorktown. Meanwhile Spain, under the Bourbon King Charles III, joined forces with France (also ruled by a Bourbon, Louis XVI) against Britain over the colonial territories of India, Canada, Florida, Cuba and Gibraltar. By mid-August 1779, it was rumoured that the French and Spanish fleets had landed at Falmouth and were about to launch a bomb attack on Plymouth. The news was false but the fear was tangible. Mr Crisp, for example, told Fanny: 'I declare I had much rather be under Ground, than stay behind, to see the insolent Bourbon trampling under foot this once happy Island.'[35]

In the autumn, Fanny went with the Thrales on a tour of Kent and the south-coast resorts. She was not impressed by Tunbridge Wells, then a fashionable spa: 'The Houses . . . are scattered about in a strange wild manner, & look as if they had been dropt where they stand by accident, – for they form niether *streets* nor *squares*, but seem *strewed promiscussly*.' To her taste, the waters were 'mighty disagreeable', and the assembly rooms were a poor imitation of the Ranelagh Gardens: 'only *one apartment*, as there was not Company enough to make more necessary, – & a very plain, unadorned & ordinary

Apartment that was'.[36] Fanny had the snootiness of a true metropolitan; she preferred Brighton, where she was entertained by the sight of the red-coated officers of the local militia, which had rallied in readiness for an attack from the French and Spanish fleets.

Mrs Thrale kept rigidly to her daily regimen of bathing in the sea – even in November – and persuaded Fanny to join her. The 'cure' did not do Fanny much good. She succumbed to a severe attack of influenza and was nursed by Mrs Thrale, who rather acidly describes how her guest:

> has kept her Room here in my house seven Days with a Fever, or something that she called a Fever: I gave her every Medicine, and every Slop with my own hand; took away her dirty Cups, Spoons &c, moved her Tables, in short was Doctor & Nurse, & Maid – for I did not like the Servants should have additional Trouble lest they should hate her for't – and now – with the true Gratitude of a Wit, She tells me, that the *World thinks the better of me* for my Civilities to her. It does! does it?

Fanny's account of her illness was rather different: 'I took 8 grains of James' Powders [Dr James was the Dr Beecham of the late eighteenth century], – for I felt too ill to take less, & had a miserable Night, but in the morning grew more easy,' she told Susan (Fanny was ever a hypochondriac). And then continued: 'I kept my Bed all Day, & my ever sweet Mrs Thrale Nursed me most tenderly, letting me take nothing but from herself.'[37]

On this vacation with Mrs Thrale she had found herself involved in a hectic social whirl of dinner-parties, balls and sailing trips (venturing out to sea despite the threat of encountering a French or Spanish man o' war). Here we see emerging the new Fanny, the centre of attention and admired wherever she went. She told Susan how a Dr Delap, an amateur playwright and parson (rector of Kingston, near Lewes in Sussex), not only had heard from the Thrales that she was writing a play, but also had asked her to read his own work: 'There, Susy – am I not grown a grand person, – not merely looked upon as a *Writer*, but addressed as a *Critic*.'[38]

Fanny must surely have felt infuriated that her talent had been so effectively restrained by her father and Mr Crisp, particularly since she understood that *if* she wanted to build on her current popularity, then she must publish again soon. And she complained to Mr Crisp that 'The Witlings' was her *only* chance of being published within the year.

His patronising response was to come up with a feeble idea for another comedy. Fanny had given him a tragi-comic account of the Pitches family, whom she had met at Streatham Park. Abraham Pitches was a wealthy brandy merchant and later sheriff of Surrey, who had six daughters – one of whom, Sophia, died from lead or mercury poisoning, absorbed from the cosmetics she had used to whiten her complexion. (Mrs Thrale commented intriguingly on Sophia's death that it was caused by 'a Disorder common enough to young Women – the Desire of Beauty; She had I fancy taken Quack Med'cines to prevent growing fat, or perhaps to repress Appetite.')

Another daughter, Peggy, was described by Fanny as 'the greatest little Coquet in Sussex' – a comment perhaps derived from the fact that she had 'aimed her dart' at Captain Fuller, whom Fanny had met in Streatham and danced with in Brighton. In a parody that has all the acuity and acerbity of her literary successor, Jane Austen, Fanny went on to say:

> She smiled, tittered, lisped, languished, & *played pretty* all the Evening, – but the Captain was totally insensible . . . But Peggy, who thought a red Coat a certain prognostick of gallantry, was not easily to be discouraged: when she found her little graces not merely *ineffectual*, but wholly *unobserved*, she began to set down her cards, in a pretty, affected, manner, protesting she did not know how to play, & begging his advice: – nothing, however, ensued from this, but that, by his inattention & indifference, I fancy he thought her a Fool.[39]

Mr Crisp perceived in Fanny's account of the Pitches girls 'a perfect Comedy'. He suggested that she should write a drama based on them: 'the Follies of the Folks, of so general a Nature' would, he told her, 'furnish You with a profusion of what You want to make out a most spirited, witty, Moral, Useful Comedy without descending to the invidious, & cruel Practicc of pointing out Individual Characters, & holding them up to public Ridicule.'[40] Fanny did not deign to reply.

While in Brighton she had met a character who reminded her so much of her favourite 'Witling', Lady Smatter, that she was galvanised into reworking her play. In a letter to Susan dated 28 October, she mentioned a Mr Blakeney, who was 'between 60 & 70, but means to pass for about 30, – gallant, complaisant, obsequious & humble to the *Fair sex*, for whom he has an awful reverence', and who was 'as fond of Quotations as my poor Lady Smatter'. Next day Fanny carried on with her sketch of his inimitable character:

I am absolutely almost sick with Laughing, – this Mr Blakeney half Convulses me . . . His extreme pomposity, – the solemn stiffness of his Person, – the conceited twinkling of his little old Eyes, – & the quaint importance of his delivery, – are so much more like some Pragmatical old Coxcomb represented on the stage, than like any thing in real & common Life, that I think, were I a man, I should sometimes be betrayed into *Clapping* him for acting so well![41]

On her return home to St Martin's Street in December, Fanny set about revising 'The Witlings', in particular Act IV, which tells of the antics of the Esprit Party. Sheridan was still expecting the comedy for his next season at Drury Lane; and when told by Dr Burney that the play was unsatisfactory, he refused to believe it. Indeed, he was insistent upon being allowed to judge for himself whether the play would succeed. But the surviving fair copy of 'The Witlings' shows none of the corrections intended by Fanny. There are some cuts, but only in Act I where Beaufort describes his aunt's literary club – and these are scored through very lightly in pencil (rather than in the black ink she used to cover up family gossip).[42] If Fanny did rewrite the fourth act, she did not preserve her alterations.

Perhaps she was persuaded not to meddle with what she had written after talking to Arthur Murphy at a dinner-party given by the Thrales at their town house beside the brewery in Borough. He asked her whether she had finished 'The Witlings', to which she replied that she had 'quite given it up, – that I did not like it now it was done, & would not venture to try it'. His response was most gratifying to Fanny: 'What! . . . condemn in this manner! – give up such writing! – such Dialogue, such Character! – No; it must not be, – shew it me, you shall shew it me, – if it wants a few Stage Tricks, trust it with me, & I will put them in.'[43] Such was Murphy's enthusiasm for her dramatic talent.

Mr Crisp, however, was still thinking of yet more reasons why Fanny should give up 'The Witlings'. 'The Play has Wit enough, & enough,' he told her, 'but the Story & the incidents don't appear to me interesting enough to Seize & keep hold of the Attention & eager expectations of the generality of Audiences.'[44] One cannot help feeling that if this was the case, why did he not say so before? Fanny did not reply to his letter immediately; when she did, two months later, she merely thanked him for 'the openness & sincerity' of his comments.[45]

But she did take heed of his advice, and 'The Witlings' was shelved, if never actually forgotten. Fanny was too attached to Lady Smatter, and some twenty years later the character resurfaces in all her ghastly pretentiousness in a five-act comedy that is, if anything, a more virulent attack on the literati. In 'The Woman-Hater', the romantic twist is removed so that Lady Smatter can take centre-stage. She is the butt of the play's satire, exposed time and again as a sham. Though she has read all the 'right' books, she has understood none of them; her speeches are just a series of quotations from the literary classics (Pope, Swift, Dryden and Shakespeare) threaded together in a meaningless and unthinking way. Written some time in 1800 or 1801, this was an attempt by Fanny both to make some money and finally to achieve her ambition of becoming an acknowledged playwright, without the interference of Mr Crisp (who had died many years earlier in 1783) or her father (by then a crusty old man crippled with rheumatism).

'The Woman-Hater' was never brought to life, yet Fanny never gave up on her dream of having her plays performed, and among her papers when she died were fair copies of four comedies and one tragedy, with three more tragic dramas in varying stages of completion. As late as 1836 she was still reading through them, and noting down in pencil on her scripts the number of minutes it took to read aloud each act. But by the time she died in 1840, none of them had been aired in public. We do not know whether she regretted this; what can be said – now that her plays have been rescued from obscurity and made available to the general reader – is that the wit of her comic interplay still rings true.[46]

In 'A Busy Day', for example, which she also devised in 1800–1, Fanny turned her keen eye for hypocrisy and cant on the class war between the upstarts of the City (the 'vulgar Cits') and the landed gentry. The heroine of this romantic comedy – like Evelina, an orphaned heiress – falls in love with an aristocrat, only to discover that her relations are anything but noble. Fanny's preoccupations – with class, money, how to get on in the world, the relations between men and women – are set in an eighteenth-century context of gaming clubs, ballrooms and elegant drawing-rooms, but the comedy works not so much through gags and one-liners as in the way the characters interact (or fail to do so). It relies on the confusions that arise because people don't listen to each other, don't say exactly what they mean or judge people on how they appear to be, rather than how they actually behave. Fanny's sensitivity to inflection, to fleeting nuances and mood, and her understanding of the waves of feeling that often underlie what is being said, ensured that what she wrote still seems lively and original today.

One scene in particular shows her fresh approach to writing for the stage. The three leading ladies (there are at least seven lively roles for women in 'A Busy Day', one of which is the heroine's maid, Deborah) hold the stage for an entire scene – without a man or chaperone in sight. They are gossiping about the male characters in a manner not so very different from conversations now shared by women. 'What a barbarous thing it is Jemima, that one has no shelter from these odious monsters the men,' bewails the hysterical Miss Percival – a rather silly, irritating female, who suffers from an overdose of sensibility but who is redeemed by her razor-sharp wit: 'I wish one could find some inhabited Island, to which one could retreat from them in a Mass. But perhaps they would only pursue one. Men are amazing plagues.' Miss Percival is more than a little reminiscent of Fanny's rebellious stepsister, Maria, and her style of conversation could well have sprung from the early diaries.

When Fanny died, she left behind trunkloads of papers, old envelopes and notebooks on which were scribbled 'Narratives' and 'Incidents' – the discarded remnants of a writer who never stopped practising her craft. Among them are plot devices ('A strange and sudden rushing into company of *some* queer personage'; 'An anxious expectation of a beloved object; the moments linger, the Time arrives; – it passes – at length, a noise – hope revives – Joy paints success – one enters! alas! one the least wished'), character sketches, and long lists of names. These include 'Miss Embellish', 'Mrs Tant mieux pour ses amies', 'Mr Fastidio', 'Mr Snuffle', and perhaps the most tantalising, 'Sir Chrystal Astrakhan', for whom there is also a profile written on a tiny scrap of paper:

Sir Chrystal Astrakhan possessed a character free from all shadow of evil. He knew nothing of the World, & was indifferent to such ignorance. It was a circumstance not despised, but forgotten. He thought of mankind niether as of his friends or his Enemies; he thought not of them at all, but as they presented themselves before him; & then, without the smallest consideration either of what they had been, or were likely to become, he received or neglected them, according to his own immediate impulse. All this was of no effect of insensibility; it resulted simply from absence; he unaffectedly honoured merit; where-ever circumstance forced upon him its perception; he would indignantly have hated vice, could *its* idea have entered his mind.[47]

A rather vague, contradictory character (as, it has to be said, are most of Fanny's *virtuous* fictional men), Sir Chrystal never came to anything more than this sketch – at least, as far as we know. Along with Miss Hasty, Mr Punctilio and Mrs Teizer, he was a lost dramatic opportunity.

Instead, Fanny focused her energies on producing another novel. By early August 1780, she had reinvented Cecilia, the heroine of 'The Witlings', as an heiress in search of a husband. She spent the next five weeks at Chesington Hall, promising Mr Crisp: 'I will bring you the little sketch I made of the Heroine you seem to interest yourself in, & perhaps by your advice, may again take her up, – or finally let her rest.' Mr Crisp was no doubt relieved to find that Fanny had at last given up on 'The Witlings', and after reading what she had written so far, he pronounced, 'It will do! It will do!'[48] Indeed, it did: when *Cecilia; or Memoirs of an Heiress* was published in July 1782, it was to prove even more popular than *Evelina*.

SIX

Cecilia
1780–2

The whole of this unfortunate business . . . has been the result of PRIDE
and PREJUDICE.

Cecilia

'Everyone knows the concluding sentence of *Cecilia*, which determined both plot and title of *Pride and Prejudice*,' asserted a biographer
of Jane Austen in 1930.[1] One of the hot literary debates of those years
was between the relative merits of Jane Austen (whose *Pride and
Prejudice* was published in 1813) and Fanny Burney, whose *Cecilia* had
appeared in 1782. *Cecilia* ended happily for its lovers, but only after
900 or more pages of prevarication; and before it ends one of the
minor characters declares, 'The whole of this unfortunate business . . .
has been the result of PRIDE and PREJUDICE.[2]

Jane Austen herself left no explanation of why she changed the
original title of her novel from 'First Impressions' to *Pride and
Prejudice*; indeed, the whole tenor of her book is quite different from
the vast sweep and extraordinary complications of *Cecilia*. But that she
was influenced by Fanny's novels, there can surely be no doubt. She
knew them sufficiently well to quote from them often in her letters to
her sister Cassandra, writing, for example, in January 1809: 'Take care
of your precious self, do not work too hard, remember that Aunt
Cassandras are quite as scarce as Miss Beverleys' (Fanny Burney's
heroine was called Cecilia Beverley).[3] And, in *Northanger Abbey*, she
refers to *Cecilia* as being one of the fictions read by Catherine
Morland: 'Oh! it is only a novel! . . . It is only *Cecilia* . . . or, in short,
only some work in which the most thorough knowledge of human
nature, the happiest delineation of its vanities, the liveliest effusions of
wit and humour are conveyed to the world in the best chosen
language.[4] Jane Austen is here contrasting Fanny's fictions with the
gothic fantasies of Ann Radcliffe (who wrote *The Mysteries of Udolpho*

in 1794) and the dark tales of 'horror' that were popular during the 1790s. Indeed, it could be said that Jane Austen's novels would not have emerged without Fanny Burney's attempts to create realistic, if heightened, portraits in words of the society in which she lived. Later in *Northanger Abbey*, Fanny is applauded by the narrator as her 'sister author'.[5]

Jane Austen (born in 1775) was a generation younger than Fanny, but she shared Fanny's preoccupation with the plight of daughters without dowries, and her novels reflect the same obsession with money and class that beset Regency England. The two authors never met, but there was a real connection between them: in the 1790s Fanny often took tea with the Reverend Samuel Cooke of Great Bookham in Surrey, where she was then living. His wife, Cassandra (*née* Leigh), was a cousin of Jane Austen's mother.[6]

Both writers were concerned to show the cruelties of a society where appearances mattered more than moral behaviour; and to highlight the dangers of perverting one's inner instincts and feelings by blindly accepting the conventions of that world. But, whereas Jane Austen refined her fictions, delineating with precise and startling accuracy the politics of family life within a small rural community, Fanny paints on a very different, broader canvas. In *Cecilia*, she draws on all social types to create her huge cast of characters, throwing snobbish aristocrats together with low-life traders and merchants, and then observing their discomfort as they are forced to communicate with each other.

Cecilia could be said to be the true daughter of *Evelina*. But whereas that first book was primarily an entertainment, a witty portrait of a young girl's adventures in the world (with love story attached), its successor is a far more mature work. An exposé of the decadent, wayward and unequal society of late eighteenth-century England, it ends on a cryptic note in an endeavour to show that happiness is elusive and cannot be guaranteed. While Fanny's readers laughed at Evelina's mishaps and misfortunes, they found themselves weeping at the harrowing misadventures of Cecilia. Yet Cecilia is no mere victim: her experiences teach her how to get what she wants, and although by the end she has suffered too much to enjoy unalloyed bliss, she at least learns that what matters in life is not fortune or social position but true understanding between family and friends.

Cecilia is not a tedious moral fable; far from it. It is dauntingly long for a modern reader – at five (rather than three) volumes, almost three times longer than *Evelina* – but it races along. The heroine, like her namesake in 'The Witlings' and her former incarnation as Evelina, is an orphaned young girl; but she is somewhat older – with only a few months left before her twenty-first birthday – and richer: she will inherit £10,000, plus a guaranteed £3,000 per annum on reaching her maturity. She has the advantage, in eighteenth-century terms, of striking beauty (although Fanny, as usual, gives little indication of her heroine's actual appearance), but she has no family, no connections, no lineage. *And* an unfortunate proviso is tied to her inheritance: the man she marries must adopt her name or give up her fortune, which, to the class-conscious aristocrats of the time, meant that Cecilia was virtually unmarriageable.

This new Cecilia is superficially a straight copy of the original, but whereas in the play Cecilia's fate was determined by a group of literary poseurs, in the novel she has become a much more complex heroine, struggling to find her purpose in life through her own endeavours. She begins as an innocent dupe of the rakes, gamblers and spendthrifts she meets in the ballrooms of the West End, but is transformed by what she observes and experiences in the chaotic streets of an overcrowded and turbulent London. By the novel's end she has come to an understanding of those less fortunate than herself, especially the builders, traders and sewing-women who have been impoverished by the selfish greed of her feckless guardians, Mr Harrel, Mr Briggs and Mr Delvile.

In one of the most memorable scenes, the indolent and dissipated Mr Harrel commits suicide in Vauxhall Gardens, after forcing his terrified wife and a reluctant Cecilia to drink champagne with him in a candle-lit supper-box. It is Cecilia who later discovers him, covered in blood, after he has run off into the inky blackness of a moonless night and shot himself in the head with a pistol. More blood confronts the unwary reader when Cecilia's lover, Mortimer Delvile, tells his mother that he is resolved to marry Cecilia, even though this will mean taking *her* name. In a scene that shocked several critics, Mrs Delvile becomes so angry that she bursts a blood vessel and collapses, with blood gushing from her mouth and nose. (Mr Crisp, for example, was uncomfortable both with the virulence of Mrs Delvile's reaction, which he regarded as unseemly in a woman, *and* with Fanny's gruesome description of it.)

Perhaps the most extraordinary (and shocking) episode comes near the end, when Cecilia believes herself to be abandoned by Mortimer (whom she has secretly married). She tries to find him at his parents' grand house in St James's Square but is turned away, and so ends up wandering hopelessly and alone through the West End and into the more dangerous alleyways of the City. Darkness falls; the streets become more and more deserted. She is overwhelmed by exhaustion and emotional distress, and falls senseless in the doorway of a public house, where she is taken in and locked in an upstairs room. Feverish and totally cut off from her surroundings, she becomes delirious. She loses her reason, her self; and from a lady in silks and pearls becomes little different from a madwoman in Bedlam, sleeping on a straw-covered floor and tethered to the door to prevent her escape.[7]

These surreal, nightmarish pages reminded me more of Lucy Snowe's hallucinatory wanderings in Charlotte Brontë's *Villette* than the work of her closer contemporaries, such as Maria Edgeworth (1767–1849), Ann Radcliffe (1764–1823) or, indeed, the restrained and yet highly charged Jane Austen (1775–1817).[8] Fanny's lovers cannot be said to have the psychological depth of Elizabeth Bennet and Mr Darcy – although the scenes between Mortimer and Cecilia do gather momentum throughout the book and have a tearful tension all their own. But she is a superlative storyteller, rushing the reader from one dramatic episode to the next. At the same time, she exposes, to punishing effect, the unfairness of the rules that applied in late eighteenth-century society, especially where they concerned women. Cecilia, with fortune and beauty but no family, becomes the victim of all the evils of her time – suffering from the careless behaviour of supposedly well-bred aristocrats with more prejudice than common sense, just as much as from the advances of rakish, greedy, unscrupulous men with arrogant pride but no moral worth. Both abuse her and threaten her survival.

Cecilia could be described as subversive – its heroine has to learn 'self-dependance' in order to survive; and to live by her own rules of conduct rather than by those imposed by convention. In this, she echoes the final speech in 'The Witlings' in which the hero, Beaufort, declares 'That Self-dependance is the first of Earthly Blessings'. As an unmarried daughter still totally dependent on her father, this was an issue uppermost in Fanny's mind at this time, and her journals for these years are full of veiled references to the difficulties of her position. She described how she felt like a pawn, torn between the demands of her father at St Martin's Street, Mr Crisp in Chesington and Mrs Thrale in Streatham, bound by duties and circumstances beyond her control. 'I have almost been an Alien of late, – nobody in the World has such a Father, such Sisters as I have, – nobody can more fervently love them, – & yet I seem fated to Live as if I were an Orphan,' she wrote to Susan in June 1780 from Brighton, where she was staying with the Thrales. 'For the World I would not offend this dear Family the Thrales, whom I love with the utmost affection & gratitude . . . but as I shall not even wish to leave them when they are in sickness or in sorrow, if I also stay with them when they are in Health & in Spirits, I am niether Yours, nor my own, but theirs.'[9]

Fanny's response to her dependent situation was not shared by Mrs Thrale, who confided in her diary that a mutual acquaintance was 'disgusted at Miss Burney's Carriage to me, who have been such a Friend and Benefactress to her: not an Article of Dress, not a Ticket for Public Places, not a Thing in the World that She could not command from me: yet always insolent, always pining for home, always preferring the mode of life in St Martin's Street to all I could do for her.'[10] Mrs Thrale's feelings were tinged perhaps with the jealous realisation that she could never be as close to Fanny as Susan. An only child herself, she could not comprehend the depth of fellowship that existed between the sisters.

But Fanny had not been at home for almost three months, and her letter to Susan was written just after the Gordon Riots had brought such violence to the streets of London that Fanny had been afraid for her family. She had been in Bath with the Thrales when she heard news of the anti-Catholic riots that had begun in the East End of London on the evening of Sunday, 4 June. What started as a peaceful protest, led by Lord George Gordon, in reaction to the Catholic Relief Act of 1778 soon turned into a terrifying witch-hunt against anyone with papist connections. Anti-Catholic feeling had been intensified in the 1770s by the influx of Irish workers and Catholics from Holland and France, who settled in the East End, where they competed for jobs in the weaving and tanning industries; jobs that were increasingly under threat with the development of the new 'factory-based' textile technologies (using the flying shuttle and spinning jenny) and the import of cheaper foreign cloth from the East Indies. (Queen Charlotte made a point of dressing herself and her Court in Spitalfields silk in the 1780s in support of her British subjects.)

The rioters quickly moved into the West End, looting and fire-bombing houses known to belong to Catholics. The Burneys were surrounded in St Martin's Street by papist families, and, on the evening of Tuesday, 6 June, Dr Burney had to shout out to the mob crowding up the street, 'No Popery', to prevent them attacking his own house. That evening, Charlotte and Susan sat up all night, watching from the observatory at the top of the house as the night-sky was lit up by the rioters' bonfires. Next day, Dr Burney attempted to move his precious library to what he thought would be the relative security of his sisters' home in Covent Garden, but was unable to take his coach through the unruly and hostile crowd. By Friday, 9 June, Lord Gordon had been arrested, and the militia had succeeded in regaining control of the situation. But by this time anti-Catholic sentiment had spread beyond the capital, and in the early hours of that morning Fanny and Mrs Thrale watched as the new Roman Catholic chapel in Bath was burned to the ground.

Mr Thrale, though not a Catholic himself, had voted for the Catholic Relief Act (which relaxed some of the laws against Catholics entering public life or being allowed to take certain kinds of employment) and was reported in the Bath newspaper to be a papist. In panic, he rushed his family and Fanny away from Bath in an attempt to find a haven from the riots. He dared not return to London, as he had been told that his brewery in Borough had been attacked by the mob and that Streatham Park was being looted of all its furniture (the news was false). Fanny later told Susan how they had fled from Bath to Salisbury, arriving late that night with nowhere to stay. From there, they had moved on to Southampton and Portsmouth, arriving in Brighton on 19 June, where at last Fanny received letters from Susan, which reassured her that her family was safe.

Susan had experienced the full horror of the riot, and gave Fanny a graphic account. Returning to St Martin's Street on the evening of Tuesday, 6 June, after dining with her friend Lady Hales in Brook Street (between what was then Oxford Road and Piccadilly), she had been forced by the crowds to abandon her carriage and only reached the safety of home after pushing her way through the angry crowd. Dr Burney's sisters, Nancy and Becky, also had a narrow escape when the rioters daubed their front door with an 'O', as if marking them out as being sympathetic to the Catholic cause (they had not given enough to a toll levied by the mob).

The social unrest provoked by Lord Gordon's demonstration against the Catholics died away as quickly as it had erupted; and the summer of 1780 was remembered afterwards by Fanny not for that frightening journey through the South of England, but for being the time when she began serious work on *Cecilia*. She spent the rest of the summer at Chesington Hall on a long-promised visit to Mr Crisp, and by the autumn was back home in St Martin's Street, on the orders of her father, who was anxious that she should finish her new book as soon as possible.

Dr Burney had arranged for *Cecilia* to be published by an old friend, the printer and bookseller Thomas Payne; this time, Fanny was not going to be allowed to organise the publication of her novel herself. There were to be no more undercover negotiations via agents in disguise; no more manuscripts left anonymously in coffee-houses. A different publisher was thought by Dr Burney to be necessary; someone who would recognise Fanny's new status as a successful author, and pay her accordingly. Thomas Lowndes had been negligent of Fanny's best interests, rushing out the first edition of *Evelina* without her corrections; and then cashing in on its success by advertising it in December 1778 along with another anonymously printed novel, *The Sylph*, in such a way as to suggest that both books were by the same author. Fanny received little of Lowndes's profits: the artist who prepared the drawings for the illustrated fourth edition of February 1780 was paid more than Fanny, receiving £73 for three drawings, compared with Fanny's thirty guineas.[11]

Dr Burney's plan was that Fanny's novel should appear at the same time as his own new literary project, the second volume of *A General History of Music*. Fanny promised to spend the winter months working on her book; even Chesington was, it seems, out of bounds. On 18 November she wrote to Mr Crisp, 'You must know I am at this Time at Home incog. & never go out, except sometimes by 8 o'clock round the Park for a Little Exercise.'[12] (She would have reached St James's by walking down what was then Hedge Lane [now part of Trafalgar Square] and into Cockspur Street; from there turning into Spring Gardens, which led into the formal tree-lined promenades of the park.)

By December she was so burned out by this intensive régime that she let rip to Mrs Thrale: 'I am often taken with such fits of temper about it [*Cecilia*], that, but for my Father, I am sure I would throw it behind the Fire! – as, when he knew nothing of the matter, was the case with many of its Predecessors: all, indeed, but Evelina.'[13] A few days later, she wrote to Susan: 'I over harass myself, & that, instead of making me write more, bothers, & makes me write less, – yet I cannot help it, – for I know my dear Father will be disappointed, & he will expect me to have just done, when I am so behind hand as not even to see Land! – Yet I have written a great deal, – but the Work will be a long one, & I cannot without ruining it make it otherwise.'

There was not half so much pleasure in writing for her father as there had been in working in secret and for her own amusement. 'O that I could defer the publication,' she moaned to Susan a couple of weeks later, '& relieve my Mind from this vile solicitude which does but shackle it, & disturb my rest so abominably, that I cannot sleep half the Night for planning what to write next Day, – & am next Day half dead for want of rest.' She had by then been allowed to visit Mr Crisp, but on arrival at Chesington Hall she succumbed to such a high temperature and fever that she spent the next few weeks as an exhausted convalescent, wandering around the house shrouded in as many as five blankets to keep warm. Her appetite disappeared, and she would only take asses' milk for nourishment, upon hearing which Mrs Thrale sent an ass to Chesington from those she kept at Streatham.

Dr Burney could be accused of heartlessness in encouraging his daughter so to rush on with her book that she virtually collapsed with exhaustion, but his entreaties may, inadvertently, have improved it. The first three volumes of *Cecilia*, in particular, race along with an intensity derived from the way it was written – in prolonged bursts of energy while cooped up either in the observatory at St Martin's Street or in her closet at Chesington Hall. Such a tight deadline also ensured that Fanny had little time to indulge her fears that her second novel would in no way match the brilliance of her literary début. 'I go on but indifferently,' she had confided to her sister Hetty: 'I don't write as I did; the certainty of being known, the high success of Evelina, which, as Mr Crisp says, to fail in a 2 [second volume] would tarnish, – these thoughts worry & depress me.'[14]

When she wrote this at the beginning of January 1781, she had still to finish the third and final volume. Three weeks later, on 30 January, she wrote to Mrs Thrale to excuse herself yet again for failing to come to Streatham: 'My Pens,' she explained, 'as you may plainly see, – I have worn them all to stumps.' She was in despair: although the third volume was completed, she was still a long way from resolving Cecilia's difficulties: 'I have finished the 3. Tom: – but the worse is, there must be another, & that I have merely begun, – for I could not squeeze all I had to do in 3.'[15]

By the end of volume three, Mortimer has declared his love for Cecilia but, almost in the same breath, tells her that he cannot marry her because of the clause appended to her fortune, by which he would have to forfeit his name in favour of hers. Cecilia is insulted and the lovers part, with Mortimer resolving to leave immediately for Bristol and thence the Continent:

> The dye, she [Cecilia] cried, is at last thrown; and this affair is concluded for ever! Delvile himself is content to relinquish me; no father has commanded, no mother has interfered, he has required no admonition, full well enabled to act for himself by the powerful instigation of hereditary arrogance! Yet, my family and every other circumstance is unexceptionable; how feeble, then, is that regard which yields to one only objection! how potent that haughtiness which to nothing will give way! Well, let him keep his name! since so wondrous its properties, so all-sufficient its preservation.[16]

A proud speech, worthy of Fanny herself.

Cecilia takes refuge with an elderly friend in the country, far from the dangerous amusements of London. Fanny, too, retreated – to Chesington Hall – anxious that there was no way she could complete her novel in time to coincide with her father's new book. The adventures of this more mature Evelina had come to illustrate a much more ambitious theme. Cecilia, like her predecessor, arrives in London from a childhood spent in the provinces and is thrust into a hectic whirl of balls, masquerades, evenings at the opera and jaunts to the shops of Bond Street. But she soon tires of the inane chatter of the pretentious characters whom she meets – the voluble and silly Miss Larolles, for example, or the foppish Mr Meadows, who is classified as an Insensibilist because of his supercilious attitude to everything. Cecilia abandons the rustle of silks and dainty sashaying of the dancers in the ballroom and goes in search of 'real' life, finding herself in the muddy streets and cramped, unhygienic lodgings of the poor. Here, she sees the difficulties faced by other women in a world where all the best opportunities are reserved for the sons and a woman's job is to get married.

It is as if Fanny is unleashing all her own fears and resentments. Her novel is suffused with a deeply felt 'feminism', in the truest sense of the word: as a wish to see women and men on equal terms. From the beginning, Cecilia is surrounded by men who look upon her as their 'future property', who scrutinise her like a man 'on the point of making a bargain, who views with fault-seeking eyes the property he means to cheapen',[17] whose refusal to accept her *as she is* ultimately drives her from her senses. But the novel is not didactic; it teems with life, and rarely a page passes without some dramatic scene – an elaborate masquerade with Cecilia pursued by the Devil Incarnate; an execution at Tyburn; duels at dawn; the suicide at Vauxhall; a violent thunderstorm (which provokes Mortimer to reveal his feelings for Cecilia); and Cecilia's own strange wanderings through London, 'endued with supernatural speed, gliding from place to place, from street to street'.[18] Try as she might to be moral, improving, Fanny could not be anything but a dramatic writer, and the fascination of *Cecilia* is its vivid atmosphere, the sense that this is *how things were* in the 1780s.

Mrs Thrale declared that the novel was 'the Picture of Life such as the Author sees it: while therefore this Mode of Life lasts, her Book will be of value, as the Representation is astonishingly perfect: but as nothing in the Book is derived from Study, so it can have no Principle of duration – Burney's Cecilia is to Richardson's Clarissa – what a Camera Obscura in the Window of a London parlour, – is to a view of Venice by the clear Pencil of Cannaletti.'[19] In a way, she was right. Despite being championed by Dr Johnson, who remarked, 'she fills the Whole World! – a little Rogue! – A World she is in herself, with her Harrels & Hobsons',[20] the book's initial success was later contradicted by a series of criticisms from the likes of Hazlitt and Macaulay. They regarded Fanny Burney as a lesser talent than her predecessor Charlotte Lennox (whose *The Female Quixote* so impressed Dr Johnson), or her successors Maria Edgeworth (author of *Castle Rackrent* and *Belinda*, and Elizabeth Inchbald. Hazlitt echoed Mrs Thrale in his 'Lecture on the English Comic Writers', published in the *Edinburgh Review* in 1819 (while Fanny was still alive), when he said that Fanny's novels were 'quite of the old school' and that 'She is a quick, lively, and accurate observer of persons and things; but she always looks at them with a consciousness of her sex, and in that point of view in which it is the particular business and interest of women to observe them ... her *forte* is in describing the absurdities and affectations of external behaviour, or *the manners of people in company*'.

Hazlitt's view that Fanny's writing was often overblown, caricatured, dependent on surface illusion rather than on a deep exploration of personality, cannot be denied. But, if anything, his objections proved that Fanny *did* have a particular genius all her own: a talent for turning into a gripping read what Hazlitt considered 'a mere fable'. Infuriated by the exorbitant length and endless twists and wrong turnings of her later novels, he declared that 'Her ladies "stand so upon the order of their going"; that they do not go at all'.[21] But even that acerbic critic Lord Macaulay was forced to admit in 1843 that 'in spite of the lapse of years, in spite of the change of manners, in spite of the popularity deservedly obtained by some of her rivals . . . She lived to be a Classic.'[22] Indeed, her novels – *all of them* – are still in print and are read for enjoyment rather than as mere period pieces. Fanny's ability to speak directly to her readers is as true now as when her novels were fresh from the press.[23]

Fanny Burney, *c*.1778*

* see Notes on Illustrations on p.322 for details on all pictures

James Macburney

Dr Charles Burney

Esther Sleepe Burney

Elizabeth Allen Burney

Fanny's Siblings

James

Susan

Charles

Charlotte

Susan, Cousin Richard, Fanny
and Mr Crisp, by Paul Sandby

A Sunday Concert, 1782, by Charles Lorraine Smith
with Dr Burney in conversation on the right

Commerce, or the Triumph of the Thames, 1777–83, by James Barry
with Dr Burney in the water on the right surrounded by nereids

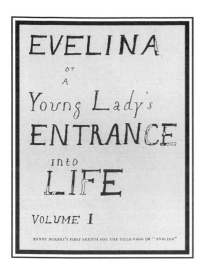

EVELINA

or

A

Young Lady's

ENTRANCE

into

LIFE

VOLUME I

FANNY BURNEY'S FIRST SKETCH FOR THE TITLE-PAGE OF "EVELINA"

Fanny Burney's first draft
for the title page of *Evelina*

A scene from *Evelina*,
by Edward Francisco Burney

Remarkable Characters at Mrs Cornelys' Masquerade,
engraving from the *Oxford Magazine*

Mr Crisp

Dr Samuel Johnson

Mrs Thrale and her daughter, Queeney

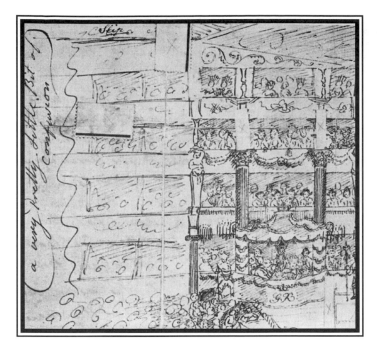

Sketch of the interior of Covent Garden Theatre by Fanny

David Garrick as Richard III in 1771

Fanny's fair copy of *The Witlings*

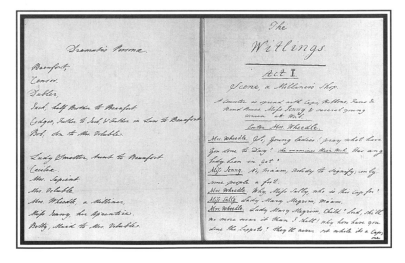

An Elegant Establishment for Young Ladies by Edward Francisco Burney

Edward Francisco
Burney

SEVEN

Misery and Men
1782–6

I am sometimes dreadfully afraid for myself, from the very different behaviour which Nature calls for on one side & the World on the other.
Fanny Burney, January 1784–1

Cecilia almost never made it into print. After finishing the third volume, Fanny found herself enmeshed in her own emotional dramas and unable to focus on her work. In May 1781, Mr Crisp warned her: 'Your slight machine is certainly not made for such rough Encounters', echoing his earlier description of her as a finely tuned timepiece which could easily be jolted out of kilter.[1] He was referring to Fanny's entanglement with the affairs of the Thrales. On 3 April, Henry Thrale had eaten such a large meal that even the servants at Grosvenor Square, where the Thrales had rented a house for the season, were frightened for him. He retired to his room and some hours later was discovered lying on the floor in a coma by sixteen-year-old Queeney. She called for help and put him to bed, but he died in the early hours of the next morning without regaining consciousness.

The Thrales had been planning a huge entertainment for that very day, 4 April; the first at their new West End address. Musicians chosen by the Italian singer and composer Gabriele Piozzi – to whom Mrs Thrale had been introduced at one of Dr Burney's Sunday-evening concerts in St Martin's Street – had been hired to entertain the guests; and an elaborate banquet of meats, pies, ices and exotic fruits had been prepared. The ridotto was cancelled, but the fact that Piozzi was invited as the star guest was later to have much significance for Mrs Thrale. (She was at first unimpressed by the Italian tenor; and at Dr Burney's had been so bored by his singing that she very rudely stood up and mimicked his extravagant gestures behind his back.)

Mrs Thrale's initial reaction to her husband's death shocked Fanny, who recalled many years later: '*Elle était froide de nature, peu demonstrative ou plutôt glaciale.*[2] Fanny dashed over to Grosvenor Square as soon as she heard the news, but arrived only to see her friend's liveried coach turn out of the square on its way to Streatham Park. She returned to St Martin's Street and waited anxiously for ten days before hearing from Mrs Thrale. The letter invited Fanny to spend the summer at Streatham, promising her freedom from family duty and the tranquillity of the countryside so that she could work on her book, in return for her conversation after dinner.

Anxious both to escape the pressures of St Martin's Street and to comfort her friend, Fanny persuaded her father to allow her to go. But she did very little work on *Cecilia*. Her journal-letters to Susan from that summer are filled instead with word-for-word accounts of her 'tête-à-tête's' with Jeremiah Crutchley who, as one of the executors of Thrale's will, was almost permanently at Streatham Park in these weeks. (Thrale had left his affairs in a muddle, but he at least had the foresight to ensure that his four surviving daughters would be well provided for if he died, referring to Queeney as his 'eldest son', and leaving each of them enough money to live independently.)[3]

Crutchley's dedication to organising the sale of the brewery led Fanny to revise her initial, rather hostile opinion of him, and by May she was declaring to Susan that she both respected and esteemed him, 'for his whole conduct manifests so much goodness of Heart & excellence of principle that he is fairly un Homme comme il y en a peu' (a quotation from *Evelina*, in which one of the characters gives her opinion of the hero, Lord Orville).[4] At the same time, Mrs Thrale wrote in her diary, 'what better could befall Miss Burney? or indeed what better could befall *him*, than to obtain a Woman of Honour; & Character, & Reputation for superior Understanding.' But, she added, 'I would be glad however that he fell honestly in Love with her; & was not tricked or trapp'd into Marriage poor Fellow: he is no Match for the Arts of a Novel-writer.'[5] Whose side was she on?

By September, Fanny had begun to believe that Crutchley's regard for her was deepening, and she told Susan: 'his civility & attentions were Daily encreasing, so that I had become very comfortable with him, & well pleased with his society'. Mrs Thrale, too, decided that her friend 'honestly loves the Man' and tried to expedite a match. But Crutchley was a man of estate and substantial means, and Fanny was sensitive to the disparities between them. One Sunday morning as they walked back from church together, Mrs Thrale teased them in such a loud voice that all her other guests could hear: 'How well those 2 names go together . . . I think they can't do better than make a match of it.' Crutchley wandered off in embarrassment, muttering about the kindness of friends, which Fanny interpreted as an insulting suggestion that she was not good enough for him. As she told Susan ruefully, 'these rich men think themselves constant prey of all portionless Girls, & are always upon their guard, & suspicious of some design to take them in'.

She was, however, constantly in his company and discovered that she could talk with him almost as freely as with Susan. (He said of her that she was 'one who sees all things & People right'.) In her journal-letters, Dr Johnson's conversation is replaced by that of Crutchley, whether it be about the *Lives of the Poets* or the 'buzzing Idiot of an insect' that Fanny had saved from the flames of a candle. Yet Fanny was unable to fathom this 'clever, odd man'. She complained to Susan of 'the utter impossibility of discovering the sentiments or meaning of this young man'. In one letter she hinted that he cared for her and vice versa, but by the next had taken offence from a supposed slight.

Perhaps she was reluctant to recognise her own feelings. As a teenager, Fanny appeared more at ease with her father's literary friends than with men of her own age. Certainly, she could not understand the behaviour of women who, like that other Streatham guest Sophia Streatfeild, were prepared to exploit their femininity. Miss S.S. was notorious for being able to weep soft tears to order – a talent that Fanny reported to Susan with some astonishment:

Now for the wonder of wonders. Two Crystal tears came into the soft eyes of the S.S., – & rolled gently down her Cheeks! – such a sight I never saw before, nor could I have believed; – she *offered* not to conceal, or dissipate them, – on the contrary, she really *contrived* to have them seen by every body. She looked, indeed, uncommonly handsome, for her *pretty Face* was not . . . *blubbered*, it was smooth & elegant, & niether her Features or complexion were at all ruffled, – nay, indeed, she was *smiling* all the Time.[6]

Fanny could not comprehend how anyone could cry *without* feeling, *and* not mind that she was the butt of everyone's 'Loud & rude bursts of Laughter'. She was bemused that, despite her learning and evident intelligence (Sophia Streatfeild was as famous for her knowledge of Greek as for her beauty), Sophia was quite happy to reduce herself to fluttering and dimpling when in the company of men. Fanny was shocked, too, by a conversation that she overheard between Crutchley and Mr Seward (the son of a brewer and another frequent visitor to Streatham Park), in which Miss S.S. was remarked upon 'with how much impertinence! as if she was at the service of any man who would make proposals to her!' She told Susan, 'From such Admirers & such Admiration Heaven Guard me.'

The 'follies & Vices of mankind' were much on her mind at this time. When in Bath with the Thrales the previous summer, she had met a Miss White, whose frank views on the opposite sex made Fanny uncomfortable. Miss White had confessed that she was miserable at home and unhappy in company, but that there was one thing that she thought might make her happy – a love affair. Unfortunately, she had no wish for an 'Intrigue' – with all its implications. She thought, however, that such unconventional relationships brought happiness, and that 'the reason the men are happier than us, is because they are more sensual'. Fanny could not agree, and told her confidante that she would not 'think such thoughts for the world'.

Hypersensitive and self-conscious, Fanny appears to have disliked physical displays of affection – except, of course, if they were from Dr Johnson. When, for instance, she was involved with her Worcester relations in an amateur production of Arthur Murphy's comic romance, *The Way to Keep Him*, she amused her stepsister Maria by adamantly refusing to kiss her cousin Richard on stage in the final reconciliation scene, even at the cost of dramatic effectiveness. All that she would grant him was a gentlemanly peck on the hand (she was twenty-five at the time). Earlier, when living in Poland Street, she had dropped out of a reading of Garrick's farce, *Miss in her Teens*, organised by their friend and neighbour Mrs Pringle, because she feared it would involve her in too much sexual innuendo. Murphy perceived Fanny's prudishness, and teased her about it after accompanying her back to London from a dinner-party with the Thrales: 'Ask her if I did not behave in the most composed manner all the way to Town, without once *touching her Knees*, & calling a Blush of Surprize.'[7]

Fanny's friendship with Crutchley appears to have plunged her into an emotional crisis, a confusion of feeling that she sublimated in *Cecilia*. Although Fanny did not set out to write an autobiographical fiction, it seems very possible that the tensions between Cecilia and Mortimer in the third volume – as he is torn between love and desire for her, and his respect for his mother – were at least a reflection of Fanny's own experience of infatuation and hurt pride. These scenes had been drafted *before* the summer of 1781, but Cecilia's humiliation at Mortimer's unwillingness to accept the conditions of her inheritance is written with such deep feeling that is difficult not to believe it came out of Fanny's own experiences at Streatham Park.

She told Susan, for example, of a conversation on the sin of pride that had been inspired by a sermon which the Streathamites had heard one Sunday. 'This Sermon is all against us!' they declared at dinner afterwards, and continued to discuss the subject throughout the week. Fanny accused Crutchley of having 'A general contempt . . . of every body & every thing . . . A total indifference . . . of what is thought of him by others, & a disdain alike of Happiness & Misery'. But there was nothing to compare with the pride of a Burney – and Crutchley was to suffer from it. Fanny, believing him to have changed his mind about her because of her lack of 'breeding', scorned him by refusing to share his umbrella while walking home from church in the rain; an incident that bears remarkable similarities to the crucial scene in *Cecilia*, where the lovers are caught in a thunderstorm and Cecilia proudly refuses to walk back to Delvile Castle under Mortimer's umbrella. Cecilia is described as being 'much provoked with the perpetual inconsistency of his [Mortimer's] behaviour, and deemed it wholly improper to suffer, without discouragement, occasional sallies of tenderness from one who, in his general conduct, behaved with the most scrupulous reserve'.[8]

This was not so very unlike Fanny's own reaction to Crutchley, who suddenly vanishes from her journals after the 'umbrella' incident, and is only rarely mentioned again. We do not know whether he turned his attentions elsewhere (Mrs Thrale began to think he was courting her daughter, Queeney), or whether he was deterred by Fanny's confusion about him. Fanny retreated to bed with another fever, writing to Mr Crisp at the beginning of October that she had been blooded and ordered 'to live wholly on Turnips, with a very little dry Bread, & what Fruit I like: *but* nothing else of any sort'.

Perhaps the thought of marriage had frightened her. Certainly, her observations on the married state would not have encouraged her: she had lived with the stifling tensions that the second Mrs Burney often created in St Martin's Street (Fanny once commented to Susan how 'the least appearance of comfort with any part of the family, she regards as *cabal*, & therefore becomes suspicious, sour & violent');[9] she had seen the difficulties of her sister Hetty (who had given up performing once she had children, because she no longer had time to practise); and she had listened while Dr Burney's friend, the agricultural reformer Arthur Young, indulged in long and secret complaints about his miserable marriage to the second Mrs Burney's irritable and irritating sister. Marriage implied being shackled to a husband and children, who would deny Fanny the time *and* space she needed to achieve her ambition of becoming a writer on a par with Richardson and Fielding.

Perhaps, also, she was shaken by the prospect of losing her beloved sister to marriage. Throughout 1781, Susan was courted assiduously by a friend of their brother James, who had sailed with him on Captain Cook's disastrous third voyage to the South Sea Islands. Captain Molesworth Phillips had returned to Britain as a hero in the autumn of 1780, after reputedly killing the islander who had murdered Captain Cook. It was said, too, that he had saved the life of a fellow sailor by turning back to help him swim to the safety of the *Resolution* after the violent fracas between the explorers and the native islanders. Other tales from that voyage suggested that Phillips had a fiery temper: he challenged a fellow officer to a duel on the way home, but his opponent refused to fight. And there were no eye-witnesses to confirm his claims to bravery. But James remained a lifelong friend: Phillips was good company, and shared the Burneys' love of music and the theatre. He often told how he had pawned his shirt to see one of Garrick's last performances.

Tall, dark, fit and adventurous, he must have appeared a glamorous figure, *and* he was promised (or so he claimed) an estate in Ireland, in County Louth to the north of Dublin. Susan was twenty-five, a third daughter with no dowry, and possibly suffering from a hopeless infatuation with a musician and friend of her father. A fine singer and harpsichordist herself, she was a keen visitor to the opera – often attending the morning rehearsals at Covent Garden – and her comments on individual singers and new compositions reveal a discerning taste. She had, too, a phenomenal musical memory, and could repeat accurately arias that she had heard just once. It has long been suggested that Gaspare Pacchierotti, the Italian castrato depicted as the tall, gangly singer in Charles Loraine Smith's caricature *A Sunday Concert*, was in love with Fanny, and possibly Susan too. He had, by all accounts, a pure, sweet voice as well as an intuitive intelligence and the kindest of temperaments. Dr Burney was amazed by his courage when he performed at Covent Garden in the week of the Gordon Riots, although he was a foreigner *and* a Catholic, reporting to a friend that the singer was 'as superior in courage to the rest as in talents'. In the same letter, he also remarked that Pacchierotti's cadenzas were 'the most learned, the most pathetic, the most original & fanciful, or the most brilliant I ever heard in my life from any Singer'.[10] Susan admired his artistry and told Fanny how she could hardly bear to attend his début at Covent Garden, so anxious was she that he should sing well. Could she have been a little in love with him and thus proved susceptible on the rebound to the undoubted (if somewhat dangerous) charm of the eligible Captain Phillips?

Her letters, unfortunately, are unlike Fanny's, in that they reveal little about her emotional life, and there is nothing tangible to suggest what she felt for Pacchierotti, although it is possible to detect something of a glow in what she writes about him. Of her feelings for Phillips, whom she was eventually to marry on 10 January 1782, she also says very little. Certainly, he was gallant enough to persuade Mr Crisp of his suitability: 'Suzette's Husband, Captain Phillips, is a noble, Brave, open, agreeable Fellow but 26; and I really believe, now he is married and settled (apparently in a high degree to his own liking) he will prove Economical, for which he Naturally has a Turn – *when not led away by high spirits of Company*.'[11] (Mr Crisp was astute enough to recognise that such charm had its dangerous aspect.) Fanny, too, thought that the couple 'could do very well' together, and looked upon Phillips as 'a sweet-blooded young man'. But even before the marriage, the Captain showed that he could be unreliable, disappearing off to Sheffield for reasons unknown; a trip that was explained away to Fanny by James with the frank admission that 'no man cares for a Girl out of sight'.[12] And, as soon as the wedding was over, Phillips took Susan away from London and her family to live what would be a peripatetic existence, in rented cottages, far from the musical and intellectual life of the capital.

Fanny does not appear to have attended the ceremony, which took place at St Martin's-in-the-Fields; rather surprisingly, the witnesses on the marriage certificate are Dr Burney and Charlotte, and there is no description of the celebration among Fanny's papers.[13] Three weeks earlier, Fanny had written a rambling, disjointed, heartfelt letter to Susan: 'there is something to me at the thought of being so near parting with you as the Inmate of the same House – Room – Bed – confidence – life, that is not very *merrifying*'. She did, however, add, 'I would by no means have things altered. Oh far from it!' But the intensity of her feelings for her sister – joyous for her happiness, yet miserably aware of the loneliness she would feel when Susan left home and transferred her loyalties to her husband – perhaps meant that Fanny was fearful of becoming too emotional if she attended the wedding. ''Tis a vile thing that I have such pitiful Brains they will never be content without keeping a correspondance with the Heart, & hanging so upon it, that they catch all its infirmities!' she told her sister.[14]

Susan's marriage, indeed, ended the sustaining rapport between the sisters upon which Fanny had depended. Charlotte, always sweethearted, generous and true, attempted to take Susan's place, but she was nine years younger than Fanny and never so in tune with her sensibilities. In March 1782, Fanny wrote:

> O my dear Susy, if I was but to tell you how I miss you at Home! – I did not know how *singularly* our two minds were blended, till you were thus removed . . . our good Charlotte, who has the truest affection for me, which warmly I return, means to supply your place but has not the *powers* – our tastes do not so naturally accord, our likings, our dislikings, are often dissimilar – we don't admire the same people, we don't read the same Books, we don't search the same amusements, we don't adore the same Pacchierotti.[15]

Never again would Fanny be able to rely on Susan as an on-the-spot editor, providing an immediate response to her work as she wrote it. Susan had herself begun writing some years before Fanny, while she was at school in France, and her letters, though less vividly characterised and less revealing of her innermost thoughts, are no less entertaining. She wrote in a smooth, flowing style of great clarity and depth of intelligence, and her manuscripts show few deletions or corrections. When Susan left home, Fanny lost not only her dearest friend but also her most valuable critic. Indeed, *Cecilia* was never given a final read-through: 'There is no wading through such stuff by oneself,' Fanny confessed afterwards.[16]

She had other excuses for her failure to finish her book. 'I am so dreadfully frightened about Charles,' she told Susan at the end of June 1781: 'Good God of Heaven preserve the poor fellow from what I fear! He is now never out of my mind.' Fanny was summoned home from Streatham by her father to await the arrival of the 'High Land Laddie'. (Charles had finished his degree in March but had not yet returned from Aberdeen.) Mrs Thrale was not amused, writing in her diary,

'What a Blockhead Dr Burney is, to be always sending for his Daughter home so! what a Monkey! is not She better and happier with me than She can be any where else? Johnson is enraged at the silliness of their Family Conduct.'[17] Dr Burney, however, was dreading his son's return and relied on Fanny to provide a calming influence. He hated scenes, yet was furious with Charles for once again threatening the family with disgrace.

All mention of Charles's troubles were later obliterated by Fanny, but it seems that 'Poor, thoughtless Charles' was not only in debt again, but had also become romantically attached to a girl called Jane Abernethie. It was a foolish liaison: she was a cousin of Lord Fife and way above Charles socially; he was a penniless student with a blemished record (the Bishop of London had refused to ordain him because he had been expelled from Cambridge). However, a letter from Fanny to Susan, written at the end of May, has now been deciphered to suggest that Charles had married Jane: 'I am now particularly interested to hear everything that relates to poor Charles . . . whose Scheme in his Letter . . . lately to *his wife*.'[18] If this were the case, then Charles had been more 'wild, giddy, thoughtless' than usual.

When he eventually returned to London at the beginning of July, having left his family in suspense as to his whereabouts for some three months, he brought with him substantial unpaid bills, but no Jane Abernethie. Instead he carried into the house a dog called Chloe, which he said was a gift from her – typically, the dog turned out to be in pup, causing yet more mayhem in St Martin's Street. Jane Abernethie was never heard of again, and Charles was sufficiently subdued by his experience to attempt a radical reform. Indeed, he became so successful a scholar and teacher that he was respected as one of Britain's leading classicists and a close friend of Hazlitt, Charles Lamb and Leigh Hunt.

As Charles arrived back home, however, so James was about to leave, anxious to take part in the naval campaign against the French and Spanish fleets. He was eventually appointed captain of the *Latona*, 'one of the best Frigates in the Navy' (according to Fanny), and was away at sea throughout the winter of 1781–2, during which time his family had no news of his whereabouts or whether his ship had been engaged in battle. On 12 February 1782, Fanny wrote a thankful letter to Susan: 'He is safe, thank God, though he has had a terrible cruise, wretched weather, much danger, infinite sickness, & no prize [a French or Spanish ship].'[19]

Fanny was still struggling to finish *Cecilia*: 'I would to Heaven it were possible for me to have a reading de suite of it with you, my Susy! – more than with any body!' she told her sister on 25 February 1782. But Susan was by then living in Ipswich, in Suffolk, where Captain Phillips was in charge of organising a recruiting party for the marines. Instead, she showed her finished manuscript to Mr Crisp, whose response was not at all what she had hoped. Warning Fanny that she had 'so much to lose, You cannot take too much Care', he advised her to make certain changes, especially to the scenes in which she had resolved the lovers' dilemma. Fanny stood firm:

> Your Letter, my dear Daddy, which I have just received has given me so much uneasiness that I may as well answer it immediately, as I can do nothing for thinking of it . . . The conflict scene for Cecilia between the mother & son to which you so warmly object, is the very scene for which I wrote the Whole Book! & so entirely does my plan hang upon it, that I must abide by its reception in the World, or put the whole behind the Fire.

In this crucial episode, Fanny shows how pride and prejudice can overset common sense. She could not change it, without blurring the focus of her book. Nor could she alter the character of Mrs Delvile – both warm-hearted and arrogant, intelligent and narrow-minded – without diminishing her. She insisted in that letter to Mr Crisp: 'I meant in Mrs Delvile to draw a great, but not a perfect character. I meant, on the contrary, to blend upon paper, as I have frequently seen blended in life, noble & rare qualities, with striking & incurable defects. I meant also, to shew how the greatest virtues & excellencies may be totally obscured by the indulgence of violent passions, & the ascendancy of favourite prejudices.'[20]

Mr Crisp urged her to end on a happier, more positive note. But Fanny was absolutely sure of her intentions: 'I think the Book, in its present conclusion, somewhat original, for the Hero & Heroine are niether plunged in the depths of misery, nor exalted to unhuman happiness, – Is not such a middle state more natural? more according to real life, & less resembling every other Book of Fiction?' Quite so. And she added, 'I am prepared to fight a good Battle here, but I have thought the matter much over, & if I am made to give up this point, my whole plan is rendered abortive, & the last page of any Novel in Mr Noble's circulating Library may serve for the last page of mine.'[21]

Fanny had not struggled for over a year to finish her novel simply to give in to the recommendations of her 'guardians'. She knew it was too long, and had 'a thousand million fears for it', but she believed in what she had done. In any case, Mrs Thrale, who had seen Fanny's fair copy of all five volumes as she prepared them for the printer, praised her for depicting 'Life itself'. *Cecilia*, declared Mrs Thrale, is 'Such a Novel! . . . indeed I am Seriously & Sensibly touched by it, & am proud of her Friendship who so knows the Human heart: – May mine long bear the inspection of so penetrating, so discriminating an Eye!'

Meanwhile, Dr Burney was busy pulling strings to ensure the success of his daughter's book, arranging for some verses to appear in the *Morning Herald* as advance publicity. The poem talks of the various 'Blue-stocking' ladies (Mrs Montagu, Mrs Boscawen, Hannah More, Elizabeth Carter and Sophia Streatfeild) and of their literary endeavours, and then refers to 'Little Burney's quick discerning'. Fanny never indicated whether she knew that the doggerel was penned by her father, who, she said, was 'so delighted, that, though he was half afraid of speaking to me at all about them at first, he carries them constantly in his pocket, and reads them to everybody!' But a draft copy has been found among his papers, in his handwriting, proving his authorship.[22] Fanny's reaction was to become even more panic-stricken that those who were looking forward to another *Evelina* would be disappointed.

Her worries were unfounded. *Cecilia; or Memoirs of an Heiress*, by 'The Author of Evelina', appeared at last on 12 July 1782 (almost two months later than Dr Burney's history of music), to great excitement and applause. The first edition of 2,000 copies (costing 12s. 6d for the five volumes) was sold out by October. Queen Charlotte approved of the novel so much that she gave it to her princesses to read, both for their entertainment and their moral improvement; and the historian Edward Gibbon said that he read all five volumes in one day (upon hearing which, Dr Burney commented: 'I suppose a Day in the new Planet – of which the year is fourscore times as long as ours, & Perhaps the days of the same proportion').[23] Even Mrs Montagu was rumoured to have wept on reaching the final page, 'because it was the conclusion'.

More flattering still was the attention Fanny received from Edmund Burke, the political writer, who asked Sir Joshua Reynolds to invite her to a dinner-party given by Reynolds at his new house on Richmond Hill so that he could meet her. Afterwards, Burke wrote

Fanny a letter full of compliments: 'You have crowded into a few small volumes an incredible variety of characters; most of them well planned, well supported, and well contrasted with each other . . . In an age distinguished by producing extraordinary women, I hardly dare to tell you where my opinion would place you amongst them.'[24]

Whereas *Evelina* received only brief mentions in the newspapers, *Cecilia* was given the full critical treatment, with a six-page review in the December edition of the *Monthly Review*: 'The great and merited success of Evelina hath encouraged the fair Author to the present undertaking – in which we are at a loss, whether to give the preference to the design or the execution: or which to admire most, the purity of the Writer's heart, or the force and extent of her understanding.' The reviewer was so certain that his readers would already know *Cecilia* that he did not summarise the plot. He criticised the novel for being too long, and was unhappy with some of the characterisation: 'We think this ingenious Writer not thoroughly successful in her attempts to ridicule the absurdity of quoting French phrases, in a silly officer; nor in exposing the rudeness of inattention in an affectedly absent man. They are both intolerable, and almost as intolerable in fiction as they would be in reality.' But the overall impression was one of glowing praise for a novel that shone with its 'own native lustre'.[25]

Mr Crisp was overjoyed that his protégée had confirmed her place in the literary establishment, and in August invited Edward Francisco to Chesington especially to paint Fanny's portrait. By 1782, Edward had been recognised by Reynolds as a painter of considerable 'genius': two years earlier, his three illustrations of scenes from *Evelina* were included in the Royal Academy exhibition. Mr Crisp believed that Edward would paint his cousin with sympathy and authority. Indeed Edward, who was quiet but keenly observant and witty, applied Fanny's talent for characterisation to drawing. Fanny, however, had to be cajoled into dressing up in her 'Vandyke' costume with its lace trimmings and slashed sleeves: 'Remonstrations were unavailing, & declarations of aversion to the design were only ridiculed; both Daddys interfered, & when I ran off, brought me back between them, & compelled my obedience.' She was not alone in thinking that the result had been painted with the 'heart's eye' rather than with a painter's objectivity; but Edward's first attempt to capture her likeness gives a clear impression of the rush of conflicting thoughts hidden behind her demure smile. Two years later she sat to him again, extravagantly attired in her new 'Lunardi' bonnet.

Fanny's success brought with it no solution to her practical problems. Although she made more money from *Cecilia* than she had earned from her first novel – it was rumoured, falsely, that she made as much as £1,500 from sales of the first edition – she ill-advisedly sold the copyright to Thomas Payne for a one-off sum of £250; £200 of which was invested on her behalf by Dr Burney, giving her an annual income of £20. This was barely enough to keep her in hats. She needed either to write something else very quickly – or, like Susan, find a husband. Yet the extraordinary effort of finishing her novel had left Fanny so drained of energy and inspiration that when she was asked by Frances Brooke to join a new periodical, written by women, Fanny declined, saying she was 'disinclined to writing at present'.

On a frosty night in December 1782, she travelled to Streatham Park from St Martin's Street for an evening of conversation and music. A 'very full assembly' had been invited, including the cultivated 'Wit' and writer, Richard Owen Cambridge, and his clergyman son George. Afterwards, what Fanny remembered most about the occasion was her meeting with the Cambridges, 'who both, though at different times, sung to me the praises of Capt Phillips, with so much energy & heartiness, that I was ready to shake hands with them, & Cry, "Gentlemen, agreed!"' She was relieved to talk about something other than *Cecilia*, and especially to make friends with people who knew her beloved Susan's husband.

When Fanny next met this seemingly inseparable father and son, at a New Year's Day gathering at St Martin's Street, 'young Mr Cambridge' engaged Fanny again by enthusing about the company he had just met at Chesington Hall (his father knew Mr Crisp from the time when they both lived at Hampton in the 1750s). To talk of her two most dear people was a sure way to win Fanny's friendship, and her first impressions of George Owen, who was four years younger than herself, were markedly favourable: 'Who, indeed, of all my new Acquaintances, has so well understood me? – the rest all talk of *Evelina* & *Cecilia*, & turn every other word into some compliment, while he talks of Chesington, or Captain Phillips . . . He niether looks at me with any curiosity, nor speaks to me with any air of expectation.'

A week later George Owen rescued Fanny from an awkward incident at the Opera, which she had attended with Mrs Thrale and Queeney. There was such a crush of theatre-goers looking for sedan-chairs afterwards that Fanny found herself separated from her friends and involved in a quarrel with a 'Gentleman' who declared that the chair which Fanny had hoped would take her back to St Martin's Street (no more than five minutes from the Haymarket, but along narrow, dark streets too dangerous for a lady to negotiate unattended) was already engaged by him. George Owen stepped out and, 'in a loud & commanding Voice, ordered the Chairmen, to take me instantly. They resisted some Time, & said they were engaged ... Mr Cambridge, however, assumed so authoritative a voice & manner, that he fairly intimidated them, & triumphantly Handed me into the Chair.' It was an action worthy of her chivalrous hero, Lord Orville; indeed, George Owen was compared to Evelina's lover by his father, in a conversation with Fanny. Fanny herself was to tell Susan, 'I like him, indeed, extremely. He is both elegant & sensible, & almost all the other folks I meet, deserve, at least, but one of these epithets.'

By February 1783, Fanny was being quizzed by Mrs Thrale: 'Is George Cambridge in love with you, or is he not?' Fanny was both 'vexed & half frightened'. Once again, she was to put herself through the endless 'Does he? Doesn't he?' ambivalence of her relations with Jeremiah Crutchley, and her diary begins to read like a bad novelette. She later rubbed out much of what she had written about the affair, so that it is impossible now to come to a complete understanding of what went on between Fanny and this tall, slim cleric, whose quiet demeanour belied the sharpness of his intellect and wit. (Nor do we have any indication from the Cambridges – father or son – as to their feelings for Miss Burney.) Suffice it to say that the friendship began as a meeting of like minds, common opinions and a shared sense of humour. Fanny was observed by her friends swapping glances with George Owen across the fireside, chatting animatedly to him on the sofa, sharing private jokes about the other guests – sometimes rather unkindly giggling about the struggles of the more elderly members of their circle, Mrs Vesey and Sir Joshua Reynolds, to keep up with the conversation via their ear trumpets.[26]

But it was not only George Owen who paid court to Fanny: his father took to calling at St Martin's Street almost daily in the spring of 1783 – often at what would seem to be most unsocial times, arriving sometimes at well past ten o'clock and staying until almost midnight. And, while Mrs Thrale noted in her diary that Fanny had an admirer in George Owen,[27] Fanny confided to Susan that the attentions of Mr Cambridge senior were such that Charlotte, Captain Phillips and even Mrs Burney had all been 'so much struck with his manner of hanging over me, as to think his amazing partiality all on *his own* account, &

more than was simply for the Book [i.e. *Cecilia*]'. Fanny was appalled, 'when I think this, – & *I think all sort of thoughts* [my italics], I am more wretched than any thing ever made me for myself in my whole life. Even independent of our notions about the son, – might not the whole Family rue the Day they ever saw me, if there is the least Ground for this dreadful suspicion?' Inevitably, her relations with the son became somewhat strained – and his with her.

At this point in their growing friendship – some time in April 1783 – George Owen failed to arrive at a gathering to which Fanny was also invited. The evening, a Friday, marked a turning-point: Fanny constantly referred back to it, as if her disappointment at his absence suddenly revealed to her just how much she felt for him. What happened, and why, was carefully covered up by her later, so that all we can be sure of now is that, from this 'fatal evening', Fanny embarked upon a slow descent into misery and ill-health. All future social concourse was spoiled, for fear of bumping into the Cambridges, father or son, and thereby having to endure the embarrassment of sensing everyone else in the room closely watching her reactions. And, when a 'fatal paragraph' appeared in one of the gossip columns, she became even more self-conscious. Fanny obliterated all mention of this so that, once again, we cannot know why the paragraph was so 'fatal'; presumably it linked her name with George Owen (or was it with his father?).

'I never before felt any real hesitation whether the married or single life would make me happiest,' she told Susan, suggesting that for the first time she had seriously contemplated marriage. But she was still not sure which path was right for her. In January 1784, she confessed to Susan that she was 'sometimes dreadfully afraid for myself, from the very different behaviour which Nature calls for on one side & the World on the other'. Her letter was short, a single sheet only, and was not edited by her later *except* for the word 'Nature', which was scrubbed out in thick black ink and can now be deciphered only with great difficulty. What does she mean by it? That for the first time she wanted a relationship with a man? That she had feelings which she sometimes feared might overwhelm her? She shied away from saying any more, as if too much had already slipped out, and ended her letter with the flip comment, 'The Evening rubbed on, – & rubbed off.'[28] But that single sentence perhaps explains why she became so confused about both Jeremiah Crutchley (who never married) and George Owen (who remained a bachelor until 1795, when he allied himself with a wealthy heiress).

Fanny was missing the companionship and wise advice of her sister – and of Mrs Thrale, who was herself experiencing the pangs of passion unrequited. In January 1783, Fanny wrote to Mrs Thrale's eldest daughter, Queeney: 'Good God of heaven how dreadful in all its circumstances is this unhappy infatuation! . . . I think with you that her rage and grief will half madden her, & I see her frame is already so shaken that who can answer for the effect of passions so violent.' Mrs Thrale had fallen victim to the charms of the Italian tenor, Gabriele Piozzi. Her friends were shocked: Piozzi was a superlative singer and interpreter of the Italian opera, but he was a foreigner, a performer *and* a Roman Catholic.

Fanny had observed as early as the previous September that Mrs Thrale was in love with Piozzi ('that little dear discerning Creature Fanny Burney says I'm in love with Piozzi – very likely! he is so amiable, so honourable, so much above his Situation by his Abilities').[29] But she refused to accept that Mrs Thrale could ever be happy with him, and her obsession with being seen to do the right thing meant that she snubbed the woman who had given her so much warmth of friendship and the confidence to face the world beyond St Martin's Street. When Mrs Thrale retired to Bath with her daughters in an attempt to forget her 'Lover', who had returned to Italy to pursue his musical career, Fanny did not visit her, despite hearing that Mrs Thrale's health was so broken there were fears she might die. Her ever-cautious father was concerned that contact with Mrs Thrale might endanger Fanny's unblemished virginal reputation, and Fanny bowed to his wishes. In July 1784 Mrs Thrale married Piozzi; Fanny did not write to congratulate her or wish her happiness, and it was many years before the former friends met again.[30]

Fanny was also to lose at this time another source of undemanding affection and worldly wisdom. Mr Crisp was very ill, but although Susan stayed with him throughout March and April 1783 (where, one might ask, was her husband, Captain Phillips?), Fanny did not join her in Chesington. Perhaps she could not face the knowledge that she could no longer expect the guidance and support that Mr Crisp had always given her. Whatever the reason, it was not until she heard from Susan of Mr Crisp's rapid deterioration that Fanny travelled to Chesington. She arrived in time to 'close the Eyes of the kindest – Wisest – most scrupulously sincere & honourable, & most deeply sagacious, and most partially affectionate of Friends ... For equal unison of Head & Heart – of mind & manners, none have come within my intimacy.' She added: 'Amongst Females I have known more.' Mr Crisp died on 26 April, aged seventy-six.[31]

Fanny was at first inconsolable; so much so that Dr Burney felt obliged to warn her against self-indulgent wallowing in emotion: 'as something is due to the living, there is perhaps a boundary at which it is right to endeavour to stop, in lamenting the dead. It is very hard, as I have found it all my Life, to exceed these bounds in our duty or attention, without its being at the expence of others.' Indeed, she needed to gird herself against the succession of 'home and bosom strokes' that afflicted her at this time. Only two months after the loss of Mr Crisp, she was shocked to hear that Dr Johnson had suffered a stroke which affected his speech. Although he was able to continue writing and translating, he was depressed by his inability to converse and troubled by this intimation of his approaching end. His visitors found him preoccupied with Death and with his disappointment in Mrs Thrale: 'She had disgraced herself, disgraced her friends & connections, disgraced her sex, & disgraced all the expectations of mankind,' he told Fanny. He burned all Mrs Thrale's letters to him, without reading them, in the vain attempt to drive this friend of nearly twenty years from his mind.

He did make an initial recovery, regaining much of his speech and asserting, 'I will be conquered; I will not capitulate.'[32] But by the beginning of December 1784, his chronic physical infirmities had so tightened their grip that he was barely able to get out of bed. When Fanny called on him at his lodgings in Bolt Court on 8 December, he refused to let her in because he was too ill. Three days later, Dr Burney visited and was asked: 'Tell Fanny to pray for me.' The following morning, a Sunday, Fanny called to find the bedroom so crowded with male well-wishers that she remained in the unheated parlour downstairs until three or four in the afternoon, when she was told that Dr Johnson was now 'too weak for such an interview'. The next day, he died.

Fanny wrote shortly afterwards, 'I was very sad within, – the loss of Dear Dr Johnson, – the flight of Mrs Thrale, – the Death of poor Miss Kitty Cambridge [George Owen's sister, with whom Fanny had become very friendly], – & the breach irreparable of my intimacy with her Brother, – all these home & bosom strokes ... were revolting in my mind the whole time.' And – she might have added – she was worried about Susan, who had been taken by the penniless Captain Phillips to live in lodgings in Boulogne-sur-Mer, where she found herself among a motley group of expatriates, many of whom were trying to escape their debts or misfortunes at home in Britain.

Fanny herself became ill with a 'nervous Night fever and cough', which suddenly worsened on 28 January 1785, when she experienced 'a total loss of strength, & nearly of sight, & of speech, which lasted about 2 hours, & frightened my dear Charlotte into frightening our dear Father to send for Sir Richard Jebb who also attended on the King'. Fanny told the royal princesses a couple of years later how she had coughed so violently during this seizure that her whalebone stays split. (It is extraordinary to imagine her wearing such apparel while so sick and confined to bed.) When, after several weeks, she left town to recuperate in Twickenham, at the invitation of Mr Cambridge senior, who owned a large, gracious house on the banks of the River Thames, she was too frail to walk and had to be dosed with valerian on arrival. (She did not have to face an encounter with George Owen, who had by this time retired to his parish in Hampshire.)

The cause of her illness was never diagnosed, but it would seem that mental anguish was part of the problem. Certainly, she was unable, or reluctant, to eat anything, and three weeks after her seizure she noted how she had eaten some turnips for dinner, her first food 'since my first attack'. It was not the only time she had starved herself. When threatened with an unwished-for engagement to Mr Barlow, she had refused food; when feverishly completing *Cecilia* against the deadline set by her father, at the same time as her sister married Captain Phillips, she lost her appetite. Dotted throughout her letters and diaries are references to how she ate only a potato for dinner, or refused anything but bread and turnips, or went on a diet of oranges and lemons. Fanny, it seems, was fussy about what she ate, had a small appetite (Mr Thrale was constantly encouraging her to eat) and took refuge in not eating when upset. For her, eating could be an ordeal, an unpleasant physical process, a fearsome necessity.

She made a joke of this in her diary for 1777:

There is something, in the part of our Daily occupation, too singular & uncommon to be passed over without some particular Notice & observation. Our method is as follows; We have certain substances of various sorts, consisting *chiefly* of Beasts, Birds, & vegetables, which, being first Roasted, Boiled or Baked . . . are put upon Dishes, either of

Pewter, or Earthen ware or China; – & then, being cut into small Divisions, every plate receives a part: after this, with the aid of a knife & fork, the Divisions are made still smaller; they are then (care being taken not to maim the mouth by the above offensive Weapons) put between the lips, where, by the aid of the Teeth, the Divisions are made yet more delicate, till, diminishing almost insensibly, they form a general *mash* or *wad*, & are then swallowed.[33]

But the ironic detachment is perhaps a mask for a *real* difficulty, an actual fear of physical, bodily functions, which could, at times of emotional trauma and confusion, become a dangerous weapon, a means of opting out of a life that had become intolerable to her.

Fanny's situation by the beginning of 1785 was lonely, uncomfortable and somehow blighted. Huge success had greeted her in 1778 and 1782 with the publication of her novels, a gratifyingly hectic and stimulating social life had followed – and an introduction into the world of the Bluestockings, provided by her membership of Mrs Thrale's Streatham salon. Fanny had always been able to rely on Mr Crisp for that special kind of unqualified love and admiration that belongs to the 'favourite'. She was the confidante of her brothers James and Charles, as well as of her sisters. Now all that was gone; and the house in St Martin's Street was beginning to feel very empty. In June 1783, Charles had married advantageously, if not happily, the daughter of a schoolmaster in Hammersmith, then a small village a few miles west of London on the River Thames. Two years later, James married Sally Payne, one of the daughters of Thomas Payne the publisher, on returning from another long voyage to the East Indies, while Charlotte was being courted by Clement Francis.

Herein lies a tale that was particularly mortifying for Fanny. In 1785 Clement Francis had returned from India (where he had acted as secretary to the Governor-General of Bengal, the infamous Warren Hastings)[34] with the ostensible intention of marrying the author of his favourite novel, *Evelina*. But on meeting the bright, bubbly, cheeky Charlotte – whom Fanny once described as 'blooming like a budding little Hebe'[35] – he had opted instead for the younger sister. They married a year later, and went to live in Aylsham, Norfolk, where Francis practised as a physician. Fanny was left at home with only her garrulous stepmother – whom she had once suggested to Mr Cambridge senior was the inspiration for the impossibly demanding and acutely embarrassing Madame Duval in *Evelina*[36] – and her teenage stepsister, Sarah Harriet, for company.

Fanny took refuge in religion; and for the first time wrote of how she found comfort in prayer and meditative reflections on the ephemerality of this world and the promise of happiness beyond. She began to compile a commonplace book of quotations from the Bible and writers on religion. She was encouraged in this by Mrs Delany, whom she had first met on 19 January 1783 at a dinner given by Hester Chapone.[37] Fanny felt an immediate rapport with this tall, dignified, well-educated and saintly eighty-five-year-old, who reminded her so much of her maternal grandmother: 'the resemblance with which she struck me to my dear Grandmother in her first appearance, grew so much stronger from all that came from her mind, which seems to contain nothing but purity & native humility, that I almost longed to Embrace her'. In August 1785, when Mrs Delany was confined to bed with a painful illness, Fanny went to stay with her as both nurse and companion. It was during this visit that Mrs Delany (whose second husband, the Revd Patrick Delany, had died in 1768 without leaving her any estate) heard that she was to receive an annual pension of £300 from Queen Charlotte, and the use of a house in Windsor.

Once installed in her new home in St Alban's Street, Windsor, Mrs Delany invited Fanny on a visit so that she could meet her patron. Dr Burney could not have been more thrilled – a daughter now mixing with the Royals. Fanny wrote to him: 'But – my dearest Padre – what shall I do for you at Court? – You know not yet how I stand there! but I think not despicably, – & so if any little thing occurs to you to wish for, pray employ me; – for that, you know, will be making some use of a Queen's kindness.'

Fanny's first meeting with Queen Charlotte took place on the evening of Friday, 16 December 1785. The day before, Mrs Delany had been in the midst of a conversation with Fanny, advising her on how to behave in the royal presence:

'I do beg of you,' said Dear Mrs Delany, 'when the Queen, or the King, speaks to you, not to answer with monosyllables. The Queen often complains to me of the difficulty with which she can get any conversation, as she not only always has to start the subjects, but commonly entirely to support them: & she says there is nothing she so much loves as conversation, & nothing she finds so hard to get . . . Now as I know she wishes to be acquainted with you, & converse with you, I do really entreat you not to draw back from Her, nor to stop conversation with only answering yes & no.'

Suddenly a 'Thunder' was heard at the door. Fanny rushed out of the room, too shy to face meeting the King or Queen so unexpectedly. The next evening, however, she was not quick enough in her retreat, and the door of the drawing-room slid open to admit a 'man, in deep mourning' (the Queen's brother, the Prince of Mecklenburg-Strelitz, had just died). When Fanny observed the bright glitter of a medal on his jacket (the star of the King's Order of the Garter), she realised it was the King and panicked: 'A Ghost could not more have scared me. O mercy! thought I, that I were but out of the Room! Which way shall I escape? & how pass him unnoticed.'

But the King had caught sight of Fanny and asked to be introduced. He was intrigued to meet the celebrated author of *Evelina*, and wanted to know how she had been discovered: 'But what? What? – how was it? – What? – What?' Fanny, too overwhelmed to reply coherently, mumbled:

> I – I only write, Sir, for my own amusement – only in some odd, idle Hours.' The King persisted. 'Your publishing – your printing?' [Fanny hesitated], 'not knowing how to tell him a long story, & growing terribly confused at these questions, besides – to say the truth, his own What? What? so reminded me of those vile probationary odes, that, in the midst of all my flutter, I was really hardly able to keep my Countenance . . . I do really flatter myself this is the silliest speech I ever made! I am quite provoked with myself for it, but a fear of laughing made me eager to utter any thing.[38]

Shortly afterwards, the Queen joined them.

In the months and years to come, Fanny's diary would be filled with accounts of life at Court, for in June 1786 she was offered a position in the Royal Household. The Second Keeper of the Robes, Madame Hagedorn (she was unmarried but, according to the convention of the time, was known by the married sobriquet), who had been with the Queen since she was a young princess in Mecklenburg-Strelitz, had decided to return to Germany, and Fanny was the obvious candidate to replace her. Since becoming Queen, Charlotte had surrounded herself with a cosmopolitan staff of educated tutors, nurses and advisers, such as the 'turbulent' clergyman, Monsieur Guiffardière, who read sermons to the Queen; Lady Charlotte Finch, appointed governess to the Prince of Wales and a fluent reader of French and Italian; and Monsieur De Luc, who was Swiss and appointed to read in French. The Queen was herself not an enthusiast for the endless card-playing beloved of the King (she forbade all playing for money), or for the nightly musical concerts that the King organised while they were at Windsor (mostly consisting of works by his favourite, Handel). She preferred instead to discuss books, often of a devotional nature (before leaving Mecklenburg-Strelitz, she had been a secular canoness of the Protestant abbey of Herford in Westphalia), or to listen while others read to her. To appoint Mrs Delany's new young friend would mean that the most talked-about writer in London was now a member of her Court.

Friends of the Burneys, who were concerned that Fanny was still living with her father (suppose he were to die suddenly), believed it was an offer she could not refuse. Fanny, however, was horrified: 'no situation of that sort was suited to my own taste, or promising to my own happiness'. But the decision was not hers alone; she was duty-bound to consult her father. And, deep down, she knew that to refuse a royal appointment was impossible. By Monday, 19 June, everything was settled, and the next day Fanny went to the Queen's Lodge in Windsor to view her future home and receive her instructions from the Queen.

EIGHT

Second Keeper of the Robes
1786–90

Sweet Queen! – She seems as fearful of employing me as I am myself of being employed.

Fanny Burney, June 1786

'I left no one behind to regret,' Fanny told Susan after leaving St Martin's Street on the morning of 17 July 1786 in a coach bound for Windsor. She was accompanied by her father and Mrs Anna Ord, one of the original Bluestockings and an honorary member of Dr Johnson's Literary Club ('the best mistress of a family I ever saw'), on whom Fanny had come to rely after her breach with Mrs Thrale.[1] Mrs Ord lent Fanny her liveried coach-and-four; behind followed Dr Burney's shabby carriage laden with Fanny's baggage. She had prepared a whole new wardrobe of clothes and undergarments, almost like a trousseau; indeed, she joked to her aunts Becky and Nancy that she had received – and accepted – a proposal from none other than the 'Sovereign of this Realm – of the united 3 Kingdoms of England, Scotland & Ireland, with France taken into the bargain, as a *blessing* – not to mention possessions in the East & West Indies, & *once*, in America'.[2]

She took no interest in the countryside through which they passed (by the market gardens of Middlesex and along the River Thames into Berkshire); and gives no hint of what she wore, or whether it was a hot, sunny, or wet day. She was filled with dread: 'all my most favourite schemes – & every dear expectation my Fancy had ever indulged of happiness . . . all was to be given up'. Her father and Mrs Ord, however, chatted gaily, believing that Fanny's future was now safeguarded.

How wrong they were. Although the post of Second Keeper of the Robes brought with it a salary of £200 per annum, Fanny still had no 'self-dependance'. When, some three and a half hours later, the two coaches finally came to a halt by the gate of Mrs Delany's house in

Windsor and Fanny stepped down to embark on her new life, Dr Burney had to assist his daughter, whose 'trepidation' was such that she could hardly breathe. As she walked the short distance from St Alban's Street to the Queen's Lodge, where the King and Queen resided when at Windsor (the state apartments in the castle were too draughty and uncomfortable for the Royal Family),[3] she knew that Fanny Burney, novelist, was about to become Miss Burney, royal servant.

At the lodge, a uniformed page escorted her to the Queen's drawing-room, where she was received by her royal mistress 'with a most gracious bow of the head, & a smile that was all sweetness'. But this did little to calm Fanny's agitation; or to prevent her spirits sinking beneath the realisation that she was now committed to nothing short of a life-sentence. 'I am married,' she told Susan. 'I look upon it in that light – I was averse to forming the union, & I endeavoured to escape it, but my friends interfered, – they prevailed – & the knot is tied.'

On this first day, however, Fanny was treated more like a visitor than a courtier, 'without even the most distant hint of business'. She was shown to her apartments – a large drawing-room on the ground floor facing the Round Tower of the castle, and an adjoining bedroom. For the first time, Fanny had her own maid and manservant (something she had never had at home) and, compared with noisy, dusty St Martin's Street, her accommodation was 'airy, pleasant, clean & healthy'. Her bedroom looked out on to the gardens; and the Queen had herself ordered new furniture and carpets, including 'a mahogany four-poster with japanned cornices; and . . . a fine white mattress made remarkably thick & full (by order)'.[4] But these were small compensations for her separation from family and friends, and for her new obligations.

From the moment Fanny said farewell to her father, who dined with Mrs Delany before returning to town, and to Mrs Ord, who continued on her way to Bath, she was swept up into a very different way of life. A bell summoned her to dinner; and thus began the dreary routine from which Fanny would not escape for five years. The Royal Household followed a tightly regulated schedule that was rarely disrupted; the Queen noting in her diary, day after day, the exact and unvarying time at which prayers were said, breakfast taken and bed reached. By the end of her first week, Fanny had already come to detest the relentless regimen by which her days were governed.

Indeed, the record she made for Susan reads like a school timetable or the Hours observed within a religious order:

> I rise at six o'clock. Dress in a Morning Gown & Cap & wait my first summons, which is at all times from 7 to near 8; but commonly in the exact half-hour between them . . . The Queen never sends for me till her Hair is Dressed . . .
>
> By 8 o'clock, or a little after, for she is extremely expeditious, she is Dressed. She then goes out, to join the King, & be joined by the Princesses,[5] & they all proceed to the King's Chapel in the Castle, to Prayers. [Fanny, meanwhile, was free to retire to her own room for her own solitary breakfast.]
>
> At 9 o'clock I send off my Breakfast things, & relinquish my Book, to make a serious & steady examination of every thing I have upon my Hands in the way of business, in which preparations for Dress are always included . . . not for the present Day alone, but for the Court Days, which require a particular Dress . . .
>
> That over, I have my time at my own disposal till a quarter before twelve, except on Wednesdays & Saturdays, when I have it only to a quarter before Eleven. The Hour advanced on the Wednesdays & Saturdays is for curling & craping the hair, which it now requires twice a Week.
>
> A quarter before one is the usual time for the Queen to begin Dressing for the Day. Mrs Schwellenberg then constantly attends; so do I . . . We help her off with her Gown, & on with her powdering things, & then the Hair Dresser is admitted. She [the Queen] generally reads the news-papers during that operation . . .
>
> It is commonly 3 o'clock when I am thus set at large And I have then two Hours quite at my own disposal . . .

Hair-dressing was an elaborate operation, piling the long tresses into intricate decorative curls, and then rigorously powdering the construction. Fanny was allowed to withdraw until this was over. But, as Second Keeper of the Robes, she was expected to assist with the Queen's daily wardrobe; to have ready her garments and accessories in the correct order for dressing, and to hook the myriad tiny buttons. For Fanny, never herself interested in dress, these tasks were irksome.

But it was not just that she had become little more than a glorified domestic servant (she was often caught by the bell and had to dash along the corridor 'half-undressed'); she was also obliged to spend hours in the company of her superior, the First Keeper of the Robes, Madame Schwellenberg. A difficult, irritable woman who had never known life outside the Court, Fanny soon nicknamed her the 'Cerbera' (the three-headed dog who, in Greek legend, guarded the entrance to Hades) and compared her bad-tempered nature with that of her stepmother. Madame S. was lampooned in the newspapers as 'the toad-eater', as she was always with the Queen and carried with her a small box containing her pet frogs. But her chief fault, as far as Fanny was concerned, was that she preferred cards to conversation:

At 5 we have Dinner. Mrs Schwellenberg and I meet in the Eating Room. We are commonly Tête à Tête: when there is any body added, it is from invitation only . . . From this time, naturally, I belong to Mrs Schwellenberg wholly . . . When we have Dined, we go upstairs to her Apartment, which is directly over mine. Here we have coffee.

Here we sit, when I behave as I ought to do, till half past 6 when the Major [Major Price, the King's Equerry] goes to attend the King to the Terrace. And here we sit, also, when also, as I behave as I ought to do, till the Terracing is over; this is at about 8 o'clock.

During the summer months, the Royal Family promenaded on the castle terrace every evening, an opportunity for the people of Windsor to see their monarch at ease with his children.

Tea follows & the Concert in the Concert Room – about 9 o'clock.

From that time, if Mrs Schwellenberg is alone, I never quit her for a minute, till I come to my little supper, at near Eleven. If she has any body to play at Cards, I steal away for 5 minutes at a time into my own Room . . .

Between Eleven & 12 my last summons usually takes place . . . Twenty minutes is the customary time then spent with the Queen: Half an Hour I believe is seldom exceeded.

I then come back, & after doing whatever I can to forward my Dress for the next morning, I go to Bed – And to sleep, too, believe me, – the early rising, & a long Day's attention to new affairs & occupations, cause a fatigue so bodily, that nothing mental stands against it, & to sleep I fall the moment I have put out my Candle & laid down my Head.

Fanny wrote this account of a royal day on 24 July: one week was sufficient to impress upon her the reality of her life at Court. But though she was appalled to discover the exact nature of her role in the Queen's household (ranking way below the ladies-in-waiting, who all came from the peerage), she did not allow herself to languish in self-pity – at least in the beginning. It was as if her arrival at Windsor reawakened her urge to write. She knew that she was privileged to be given such an intimate view of the monarchy, and, though conscious that she had a responsibility not to confide what was ultimately private to the Royal Family, was aware that this was an opportunity for her to flex her skills as a 'journalist'.

Fanny wrote her 'Court Journals' (as she later called them when she came to edit and bind them together) for Susan, who was now living with her two children (and often-absent husband) in Mickleham, a small village below Box Hill in Surrey:

> I do not see why a simple account of inoffensive actions can have no more to fear from the reader than from the listener. & while I never made the most distant allusion to politics, to the Royal Family's private transactions, or opinions, nor to any state affairs of any kind, I see not why I must be deprived of my long accustomed confidence in the Dearest & Sweetest of Sisters, whose never failing discretion, honour, & fidelity have always called for my trust from the earliest time I have had anything to communicate.

At first, she sent her journals in monthly bundles (the 'Windsor Journal') but, with the onset of the King's illness and the ensuing Regency crisis in the winter of 1788–9, Fanny wrote a separate entry for each day.

There was, as she said, something about Court life: 'something so little like common & real life, in every body's standing, while talking, in a Room full of Chairs, & standing, too, so aloof from each other, that I almost thought myself upon a Stage, assisting in the representation of a Tragedy'. Fanny also wrote her sister Hetty (after meeting the King and Queen at Mrs Delany's in December 1785, and so before she had any experience of royal service) an hilarious spoof on the ridiculous way in which the etiquette of the Court ignored normal human functions.

Under the heading 'Directions for Coughing, Sneezing or Moving Before the King and Queen', she described how:

> In the first place you must not Cough. If you find a cough tickling in your throat, you must arrest it from making any sound: if you find yourself choaking with the forbearance, you must choak: But not cough. In the 2nd place, you must not sneeze. If you have a vehement Cold, you must take no notice of it. If your nose membranes feel a great

irritation, you must hold your breath; if a sneeze still insists upon making its way, you must oppose it by keeping your teeth grinding together; if the violence of the repulse breaks some blood-vessel, you must break the blood-vessel: But not sneeze. In the 3rd place, you must not, upon any account, Stir either hand or foot. If, by chance, a black pin runs into your Head, you must not take it out . . . If the blood should gush from your head by means of the black pin, you must let it gush. If you are uneasy to think of making such an appearance, you must be uneasy but say nothing about it. If, however, the agony is very great, you may privately bite the inside of your cheek, or of your lips, for a little relief, taking care, meanwhile, to do it so cautiously as to make no apparent dent outwardly. And, with that precaution, if you even gnaw a piece out, it will not be minded, only be sure either to swallow it, or commit it to a corner of the inside of your mouth till they are gone – for, You must not spit.[6]

And yet Fanny saw, too, that behind all this formal behaviour and ceremonial, the King and Queen and their thirteen children (seven princes and six princesses) lived a domestic life that was little different from that of any family. As she was to remember in 1818 (after the Queen had died): 'When I was alone with her she discarded all royal constraint, all stiffness, all formality, all pedantry of grandeur, to lead me to speak to her with openness and ease.'[7] Fanny witnessed the affection between husband and wife while waiting on the Queen in her dressing-room: the King breaking into German whenever he wanted a private word with his wife, or giving her a fond peck on the cheek.

Queen Charlotte had arrived in Britain from Mecklenburg-Strelitz in September 1761 as a seventeen-year-old princess who spoke only German. The marriage had been arranged by her father and the Earl of Bute, whose emissary Colonel Graeme had reported that the princess was 'not a Beauty, but what is little Inferior, she is *Amiable*, And her Face rather Agreeable than Otherwise'.[8] She had never met her future husband. The wedding took place on the evening of the day after she landed in England, her gown of silver lace and pearls chosen by the King. Her only words were spoken in German: 'Ich will'.

Fanny considered it her duty to make an accurate record of all she observed, as if she understood that this was why she had been placed at Court, despite her own wishes. Her real role was soon made clear to her. On the morning of Wednesday, 2 August 1786, a woman named Margaret Nicholson waited for hours outside St James's Palace in the hope of catching a glimpse of the King. As he alighted from his carriage, she approached him with what was thought by his attendants to be a petition. Instead, she drew a knife from her bodice and thrust it towards the King's chest. He stepped backwards just in time, but she then lurched forward again, this time touching his waistcoat with the point of her knife.

Fanny was with the Queen when the King returned from town, and she overheard their conversation as he told his wife of his remarkable escape. 'You may have heard it wrong [from the newspaper reports],' she wrote afterwards to Susan. 'I will concisely tell it right.' And this she did, employing to full effect her ability to memorise *exactly* what the King had said:

> 'Has she cut my Waistcoat?' cried he [the King], in telling it – 'Look! for I have had no time to examine.' Thank Heaven, however, the poor wretch had not gone quite so far.
>
> 'Though nothing,' added the King, in giving his relation, 'could have been sooner done, for there was nothing for her to go through, but a thin Linen & Fat!'
>
> While the Guards & his own people now surrounded the King, the Assassin was seized by the populace, who were tearing her away, no doubt to fall the instant sacrifice of her murtherous purpose, when the King, the only calm & moderate person then present, called aloud to the Mob 'The poor Creature is mad! Do not hurt her! She has not hurt me!'
>
> He then came forward, & shewed himself to all the people, declaring he was perfectly safe & unhurt; & then gave positive orders that the woman should be taken care of, & went into the Palace, & to the Levée.

Fanny went on to eulogise at length the bravery of the King and the calm of the Queen in the face of such a *real* drama.

> There is something in the whole of his behaviour upon this occasion, that strikes me as proof indisputable of a true & noble courage: for in a moment so extraordinary, an attack, in this Country, unheard of before, to settle so instantly that it was the effect of insanity, to feel no apprehension of private plot or latent conspiracy, to stay out, fearlessly, among his people, & so benevolently to see himself to the safety of one, who had raised her arm against his life, – these little traits, all impulsive, & therefore to be trusted, have given me an impression of respect and reverence to the intrinsic worth of their operator that I can never forget, & never think of but with fresh admiration.

For most of her five years in the Royal Household, however, Fanny was tediously employed in a humdrum round of dressing and undressing. Although, as the King was to remark, she soon proved adept at mixing the Queen's snuff ('Miss Burney – I hear you cook Snuff very well!'),[9] the rest of her duties were not so congenial. She disliked, in particular, the manner in which she was *summoned* to the Queen's presence: 'My summons, upon all regular occasions, that is, Morning, Noon, & Night Toilettes, is niether more nor less than a Bell: upon extra-occasions, a Page is commonly sent. At first, I felt inexpressibly discomfited by this mode of Call, a Bell! – it seemed so mortifying a mark of servitude, I always felt myself blush, though alone, with conscious shame at my own strange degradation.' Worse still for Fanny, who hated sewing, was the necessity to spend hours trimming bonnets, stitching caps and repairing petticoats in preparation for the Thursday-afternoon Drawing-Room in St James's Palace, at which 'full Court dress' (huge hoops, heavy brocade overgowns and dressed hair) was required. (St James's was used only for state occasions by George III; when in town, the Royal Family resided in the Queen's House at the end of the Mall, which had been bought by George III in 1762 and was later transformed into Buckingham Palace by his son.)[10]

There were occasional interruptions to this deadening routine. Only a few weeks after Fanny became Second Keeper of the Robes, the King and Queen went on a royal visit to Oxford and Blenheim, staying on the way with Lord and Lady Harcourt at Nuneham Park. But this grand expedition impressed upon Fanny the humiliating reality of her position at Court. Assigned to the fourth coach, she travelled *behind* the ladies of the bedchamber and the maids of honour, and her companion was Miss Planta, an assistant in the royal nursery, whom Fanny regarded as being 'friendly and well disposed' but more often than not referred to as 'poor Miss Planta'. On arrival at Nuneham, Fanny was mortified by her reception. She knew the Harcourts, had socialised with them in London, but now she was ignored and treated as a domestic servant: 'I think I never remember to have felt so much shame from my situation as at that time,' she complained to Susan. 'To arrive at a House where no Mistress nor Master of it cared about receiving me; to wander about, a Guest uninvited, a visitor unthought of; without even a Room to go to, a Person to enquire for, or even a Servant to speak to.' Fanny never forgave Lady Harcourt for this slight, always referring to her afterwards as 'haughty' and 'vain'. She does not appear to have understood that Lady Harcourt had other, more pressing concerns – to feed, entertain and house not just the King and Queen but also their entire household.

However, Fanny's sense of the absurd did not entirely desert her. As she accompanied the royal party on their tour of the Oxford colleges, she was in attendance, struggling to remember that she must keep her place. Etiquette required that she should walk backwards out of the royal presence; no easy feat, especially as she was obliged to wear a sacque – a long, loose gown with a finely pleated back that fell from the shoulders to the ground to form a train.[11] First, she observed in wonder as Lady Charlotte Bertie demonstrated a perfect example of what she dubbed the 'Court-retrograde motion':

> Lady Charlotte, by chance, happened to be very high up in the Room, & near to the King: – Had I been in her situation, I had surely waited till his Majesty went first; but that would not, I saw, upon this occasion, have been etiquette; – she therefore faced the King, & began a march backwards – her ankle already sprained, & to walk forwards, & even leaning upon an Arm, was painful to her; nevertheless, back she went, perfectly upright, without one stumble, without ever looking once behind to see what she might encounter, & with as graceful a motion, & as easy an air, as I ever saw any body enter a long room, she retreated, I am sure full 20 yards backwards out of one.
>
> Such is the Mastery of very early use & practice.

Then Fanny attempted to follow suit:

> I glided near the wainscoat, – Lady Charlotte, I should mention, made her retreat along the very middle of the Room, – & having paced a few steps backwards, stopt short, to recover, &, while I seemed examining some other Portrait, disentangled my train from the Heels of my shoes, & then proceeded: a few steps only more; & then, observing the King turn another way, I slipt a yard or two at a time forwards; & hastily looked back, & then was able to go again according to rule, – & in this manner, by slow & varying means, I at length made my escape ...
>
> Since that time, however, I have come on prodigiously, by constant practice, in the power & skill of walking backwards, without tripping up my own heels, feeling my head giddy, or treading my Train out of the pleats: accidents very frequent among novices in that business: & therefore I have no doubt but that, in the course of a few months, I shall arrive at all possible perfection in the true Court-retrograde motion.

The King and Queen were entertained by the Oxford dons with a lavish luncheon, while their attendants – not invited themselves to the meal – had to stand for hours looking on. Fanny, who had been up since six o'clock so that her hair could be dressed, almost fainted with hunger, and had to be rescued by Colonel Digby, the Queen's Vice-Chamberlain. An old hand at such occasions, he magicked from his pocket some apricots and bread, which he insisted upon giving to Fanny: 'but I was not inclined to the repast, & saw he was half famished himself . . . however, hc was so persuaded I must both be as hungry & as tired as himself, that I was forced to eat an apricot to appease him'.

Colonel Digby was to become a close friend and comrade-in-arms. When Fanny first met him, he was living through the nightmare of watching as his wife, Lady Lucy, died of cancer, leaving him with four young children. After that first encounter in Oxford, she saw little of him. But by the time he returned to full attendance at Windsor after his wife's death (the children being cared for by his family), Fanny was herself in mourning for Mrs Delany – her great, and only, comfort at Court – who died on 15 April 1788.

Mrs Delany was such a friend of the King and Queen, and her house in St Alban's Street was so close to the Queen's Lodge, that Fanny had been free to visit her in the evenings after dinner. Her fireside became Fanny's refuge from the claustrophobic tensions of life with Madame Schwellenberg, and her company relieved Fanny's miserable isolation from her family and literary friends in London (courtiers did not expect, and were not granted, holidays). With Mrs Delany, she never had to suffer the stultifying boredom of an evening at piquet;[12] indeed, she was encouraged to talk freely on anything and everything, from the latest comedy at Drury Lane to the most profound matters of faith. In return, Fanny admired and respected this learned and talented woman, whose second husband had been a friend of Dean Swift, and who was also an accomplished artist, developing in her early seventies an extraordinarily effective technique for creating plant and flower impressions from cut paper, which she dyed herself.[13] At this time, Mrs Delany was also looking after her teenage seventeen-year-old great-niece, Georgiana Marianne Port, whose lively, teasing conversation reminded Fanny of her own teenage years in St Martin's Street.

When she died, Mrs Delany bequeathed to 'Miss Burney' the 'Flower in paper mosaic out of the tenth vol of the Quarto Edition of

Shakespeare'. And in her will, she asked Fanny to remember her: 'I take this liberty that my much esteemed & respected Friend may sometimes recollect a Person who was so sensible of the Honour of her Friendship & who delighted so much in her Conversation & Works.'[14]

Fanny, in turn, missed the company of this gifted and generous woman. Colonel Digby was well-placed to take over from Mrs Delany in Fanny's affections. They were both grieving, both suffocating in a Court where, Fanny at least believed, it was difficult to converse about the things that *really* mattered. Colonel Digby gave her the impression that he was deeply spiritual, and their favoured topics of conversation were the ephemerality of this life and the promise of happiness in the hereafter. But Digby, the 'Mr Fairly' of Fanny's letters (she used code-names for everyone at Court: the King was the Oak, for example, while the Queen was the Magnolia), was called 'Mr Feignwell' by Susan for reasons that will become clear.

Fanny wrote an intensely emotional explanation of what Mr Fairly/ Feignwell had come to mean to her on 20 November 1788.

> His Friendship offered me a solace without hazard; it was held out to me when all else was denied me; – banished from every Friend, confined almost to a state of captivity, harrowed to the very soul with surrounding afflictions, & without a glimpse of Light to when or how all might terminate; – it seemed to me in this ... situation, that Providence had benignly sent me in my way a character of so much worth & excellence, to soften the rigour of my condition.

This was written at the height of the King's illness. Fanny had been cooped up in the Queen's Lodge at Windsor since 5 November. No one was allowed to leave the house, and the unpredictability of the King's behaviour had plunged the Royal Household and the Government into confusion.

Intimations of the King's malady had first appeared in the summer of 1788, when he was taken ill with what at the time was thought to be a severe bilious attack. He was advised to take the waters, and the Court embarked on a five-week tour of the Cotswolds, staying in Cheltenham and Worcester. The spa waters had no beneficial effect, but it was not until the middle of October that his illness became so severe that he was unable to continue fulfilling his role as King. On Thursday, 16 October, while at Kew, he became so unwell that he was not fit to travel back to Windsor.

In the summer months, the King and Queen spent alternate Tuesdays to Fridays at Kew, where they enjoyed a much freer, simpler existence away from the rigid protocol of Windsor. Kew House, where they resided (also known as the White House or 'The Palace'), was a small, winged mansion that stood on the south side of Kew Green. The royal couple appeared at their happiest and most relaxed in this rural, village environment, living less like monarchs than as 'the simplest Country Gentlefolks'.[15]

On that Thursday, the King had risen early, as was his custom (his equerries often complained to Fanny of the inexhaustible energy of the King, with which they, as his attendants, were obliged to keep up), and had 'walked for several hours in wet grass', before travelling to St James's for the Thursday-afternoon levée, without changing his wet stockings (or so the story goes). He returned late but took no dinner, eating instead four large pears. That night he woke with severe stomach cramps and a delirious fever, alarming the Queen, who rushed out of her room in her nightshift to seek assistance.

No one knew what was wrong; except that the King was not himself. It was thought wisest to remain at Kew (where it was easier to confine the household) until he made some improvement. But Kew House was essentially a summer residence and was not equipped with the same comforts as Windsor. Fanny was without sufficient clothes – and, much more seriously, without books ('there are not 3 amongst us,' she bewailed to Susan). In desperation she began writing 'a Tragedy'.

The sad, isolated atmosphere in which she was living dictated her subject-matter: an historical tragedy set in tenth-century England, in which the doomed lovers – Edwy, King of the West Saxons, and Elgiva, his second cousin and a royal princess – were irrevocably caught up in the battle for power between Edwy, as King, and Dunstan, as head of the English Church.[16] Such historical plays were fashionable – the fourteenth-century *Richard Coeur de Lion* (in Middle English verse) was a popular success in 1786, while Richard Cumberland's *Battle of Hastings* had met with 'uncommon applause' at Drury Lane in 1778.[17] Fanny's setting – the 'magnificent gothic chambers' of Edwy's castle – came straight out of Horace Walpole's fantasy, *The Castle of Otranto*, which had appeared in 1764 and which Fanny had read avidly after meeting the author at his Strawberry Hill home in 1787 (she was on a visit with her father).

As Fanny remarked to Susan, 'I have just begun a tragedy . . . it may while away the tediousness of this unsettled, unoccupied, unpleasant period.' However, the dramatic reality of the King's illness and its paralysing effect on the Royal Household were such that Fanny was unable to continue with her imagined drama: 'misery so actual, living, and present, was knit too closely around me to allow my depressed imagination to fancy any woe beyond what my heart felt'. She realised that she was a privileged witness to a significant historical episode, and her journal comes back to life after the lethargy born of the boredom she had experienced since July 1786.

Fanny's journals to Susan had descended into a catalogue of complaints against the Cerbera, the grinding irritation of whose company can be deduced from her account of a quarrel over an open window. Madame S. was insistent whenever they travelled to and from Windsor, Kew and St James's that the coach glasses should be kept open – even in midwinter. She, however, never sat by the open window, and it was Fanny who suffered from the blasts of icy air (the journey from Windsor to London took over three hours). Fanny's eyelids eventually became so severely chapped that they streamed with blood but, when she complained, her discomfort was dismissed: 'O ver well! when you don't like it! [don't do it] – What did the poor Hagedorn bear it. – When the blood was all running down from her Eyes!' (Fanny's long-suffering predecessor had also suffered from inflammation of the eyes; and for the same reason.) Fanny was furious, but was unwilling to complain to the Queen about her most trusted attendant. Instead, she refused to speak to Madame Schwellenberg and at dinner refused all food, except for 'some Greens'.

But all such petty feuds disappeared in the face of the 'living tragedy' of the King's illness. That the King was unable – indeed, unfit – to rule was a fearful prospect. 'We are all here in a most uneasy state,' wrote Fanny; 'the King is better & worse so frequently, & changes so Daily, backwards & forwards, that every thing is to be apprehended, if his nerves are not in some way quieted. I dreadfully fear he is on the Eve of some severe Fever! – The Queen is almost over-powered with some secret terror.'

The King had initially recovered sufficiently to enable the royal party to travel back to Windsor on Saturday, 25 October, but that night Fanny had 'a sort of conference with His Majesty', which suggested to her that he was anything but well. He spoke to her 'with a manner so uncommon, that a high fever alone could account for it, – a rapidity, a hoarseness of voice, a Volubility, an earnestness, – a vehemence, rather, – it startled me inexpressibly.' Several sleepless nights followed – with the Queen refusing to leave her rooms or to see anyone – until Wednesday, 5 November, when the crisis reached its height.

That evening, 'a stillness the most uncommon reigned over the whole House. Nobody stirred; not a voice was heard; not a step, not a motion. – I could do nothing but watch, without knowing for what . . . There seemed a strangeness in the House most extraordinary.' Fanny waited in her room for the Queen's summons, wondering why, for once, she could hear no music: 'My apartment seemed wholly separated from life & motion!' When, eventually, she heard the bell and rushed along the corridors to the Queen's dressing-room, she found her 'ghastly pale' and 'disordered'. The King, Fanny was told, had broken out into 'a positive Delirium' during dinner; the Queen had collapsed in a fit of violent hysterics; and 'the Prince of Wales burst into tears'!

Fanny slept only fitfully; she woke next morning to hear men's voices in the corridor outside her room. The equerries had been up all night, along with all the King's pages. When she went to the Queen, she found her still in bed and looking 'like Death' (never before had Fanny been allowed to enter the privacy of the Queen's bedroom). Fanny burst into tears, prompting the Queen to follow suit, who would always be grateful to Fanny for enabling her to find such relief. The King, Fanny learned, had come into the Queen's room during the night and had harangued her incessantly. His eyes, the Queen said, were 'nothing but black-currant jelly, the veins in his face were swelled, the sound of his voice was dreadful; he often spoke until he was exhausted, and the moment he could recover his breath began again, while the foam ran out of his mouth.'[18] It was only with difficulty that he was persuaded to leave her and retire for the night. The physicians decided that the Queen should be kept away from the King; in future all decisions would be taken by the Prince of Wales. The Queen's fate thus lay in the hands of her eldest son. 'What will become of me! What will become of me!' she lamented to Fanny.

At first it was hoped that the King's collapse would be short-lived, but it soon became obvious that the physicians had no idea how to treat him. They began by blistering his legs, his chest, even his head, hoping to draw out the fever; and insisted on giving him increasingly large doses of an emetic, believing that the expulsion of the noxious bile would cure his delirium. All to no avail. It was therefore decided by the Prince of Wales and the Cabinet to remove the King to Kew. This was a drastic step – to move the Court *without* consulting the King was to take a constitutional and personal risk. The physicians feared for their lives if the King did not recover (they were already receiving threatening letters for failing to cure him), but also if the King did recover and accused them of usurping his authority. The Queen reluctantly agreed to 'sanctify the proceedings', but refused to cede any authority to the Prince of Wales. (Susan referred to the Prince of Wales at this time as 'Gonerillo'.)

On Saturday, 29 November, 'O dreadful day', the Queen and the two eldest princesses, Charlotte and Augusta (the others remained behind in Windsor), were quietly hurried away to Kew, followed by Fanny and the other members of the Queen's household. Once there, they waited 'in dreadful suspense', wondering whether the physicians would succeed in persuading the King to leave the castle. He eventually arrived while they were at dinner, confused as to why he was not with the Queen. He was taken to rooms on the ground floor of the mansion; the Queen was upstairs, but not above the King, for fear that the sound of her footsteps might disturb him. Fanny recalled, 'I could not sleep all night – I thought I heard the poor King . . . his indignant disappointment haunted me.'

From this time, Fanny entered into a new confidence with the Queen. She was the messenger sent by the Queen first thing each morning to find out from the King's doctors how her husband had spent the night. Fanny waited outside the King's rooms (she was not allowed to enter) throughout that ice-cold winter, freezing in the dark, unheated passage until the signed bulletin had been prepared, which was then sent post-haste to William Pitt, the Prime Minister. The Queen knew that Fanny would give her a faithful account of what the nightly report contained, without embellishing it with all the 'cruel particulars'. She knew, too, that she could rely on Fanny's discretion: Fanny dutifully refrained from committing anything to paper 'that is told me in confidence', so that her journals for these months give nothing away on the actual behaviour of the King.

We have to look elsewhere – for instance, to the diaries of Colonel 'Wellbred' Greville, one of the King's equerries[19] – for the details of how the King's illness wrought disturbing changes in his behaviour, so that he became quite violent, hitting out at his pages and swearing uncouthly at those obliged to wait on him. From being a devoted and affectionate husband to Queen Charlotte, he suddenly turned against her, calling instead for his 'Queen Esther', and making lewd comments about other ladies of the Court. Greville tells us what went on behind those doors closed to Fanny – that the royal pulse was measured as 140 on one occasion; that the King talked sometimes for nineteen hours without a pause and went without sleep for twenty-nine hours. From Greville we learn that the King was obsessed with the loss of the American colonies after the recognition of their independence in 1783; and that he would cradle his pillow, pretending it was Prince Octavius, who had died in 1783, aged just four. But it is to Fanny that we must turn for an insight into what it *felt like* to be in the midst of this personal, and national, trauma.

To read her letters to Susan in one sitting – from the onset of the King's delirium in October to its cessation some five months later – is to experience the unfolding of a dramatic tragedy.[20] As Susan commented, after reading the episode where the Queen bursts into tears, 'This dear Violetta [Fanny's code-name while at Court] carries us along with her every step – thro' all the gloomy passages – & in reading it is impossible not to share the alarm she felt in hearing men's voices at that earlier hour in the dressing room.'[21] Fanny writes with a consciousness of her audience, investing each detail with a theatrical dimension, and yet she never forgets that for the chief players this was a very human trauma. Her descriptions of those bleak, tormented months haunt the reader, so vividly does she capture the strain of living cooped-up in an icy-cold and uncomfortable house, with no knowing when it might end. The courtiers could only stand by and watch as the Queen's distress turned her soft-gold hair to grey; there was nothing they could do to relieve her anxiety.[22]

On Monday, 2 February 1789, however, there were at last signs of an improvement, and it was Fanny who was the first to witness them, in the gardens of Kew Palace:

What an adventure had I this Morning! one that has occasioned me the severest personal terror I ever experienced in my life ...

I had proceeded in my quick way, nearly half the round, when I suddenly perceived, through some Trees, two or three figures. Relying on the instructions of Dr John [Dr Willis' junior], I concluded them to be workmen, & – Gardeners; yet tried to look sharp – & in so doing, as they were less shaded, I thought I saw the Person of his Majesty.

Alarmed past all possible expression, I waited not to know more, but turning back, ran off with all my might – But what was my terror to hear myself pursued! – to hear the voice of the King himself, loudly & hoarsely calling after me, 'Miss Burney! Miss Burney!'

I protest I was ready to die. – I knew not in what state he might be at the time; I only knew the orders to keep out of his way were universal; that the Queen would highly disapprove any unauthorised meeting; & that the very action of my running away might deeply, in his present irritable state, offend him.

Nevertheless, on I ran, – too terrified to stop, & in search of some short passage . . . the Garden is full of little labyrinths, by which I might escape . . . Heavens how I ran! – I do not think I should have felt the hot lava from Vesuvius, – at least not the hot Cinders, had I so ran during its Eruption. My feet were not sensible that they even touched the Ground . . .

Only when she heard Dr Willis calling out to her that 'it hurts the King to run' did she stop and turn round:

I saw the two Doctors had got the King between them, & about 8 Attendants of Dr Willis's were hovering about . . . As they approached, some little presence of mind happily came to my command; it occurred to me that, to appease the wrath of my flight, I must now shew some confidence. I therefore faced them as undauntedly as I was able, – only charging the nearest of the Attendants to stand by my side.

When they were within a few yards of me, the King called out, 'Why did you run away?'

Shocked at a question impossible to answer, yet a little assured by the mild tone of his voice, I instantly forced myself forward, to meet him – though the internal sensation which satisfied me this was a step the most proper, to appease his suspicions & displeasure, was so violently combated by the tremor of my nerves, that I fairly think I may reckon it the greatest effort of personal courage I have ever made.

The effort answered – I looked up & met all his wonted benignity of countenance, though something still of wildness in his Eyes. Think, however, of my surprise, to feel him put both his hands round my two shoulders, & then kiss me on the Cheek! – I wonder I did not really sink, so exquisite was my affright when I saw him spread out his arms! – Involuntarily, I concluded he meant to crush me; – but the Willis's, who have never seen him till this fated illness, not knowing how very extraordinary an action this was from him, simply smiled & looked pleased, supposing, perhaps, it was his customary salutation! . . .

After this extraordinary encounter with the King, Fanny continued:

What a conversation followed! – When he saw me fearless, he grew more & more alive, & made me walk close by his side . . . What did he say? – He opened his Whole Heart to me . . . He assured me he was quite well, as well as he had ever been in his life; & then enquired how I did, & how I went on? & Whether I was more comfortable?

If these questions, in their implication, surprised me, imagine but how that surprise must increase when he proceeded to explain them! – he asked after the Coadjutrix [Madame Schwellenberg], laughing, & saying, 'Never mind her! – don't be oppressed, I am your Friend! – Don't let her cast you down! – I know you have a hard time of it – but don't mind her!'

Almost thunderstruck with astonishment, I merely courtsied to his kind, 'I will be your Friend', & said nothing . . .

The King spoke to Fanny about her father and his history of music, which brought him to his 'favourite theme, Handel':

Then he ran over most of his Oratorios, attempting to sing the subjects of several airs & choruses, but so dreadfully hoarse, that the sound was terrible . . .

What a Scene! How variously was I affected by it! – but, upon the whole, how inexpressibly thankful to see him so nearly himself! so little removed from recovery.

The story of how Fanny was chased round Kew Gardens by the King became one of the favourite episodes in her diaries on their publication in the 1840s – and is still well known to many who would not otherwise have heard of Fanny Burney. Indeed, that she intended it to be seen as a set-piece is suggested by the survival of two different sketches for what would be her later, finished account. In one of them, she described the King's appearance in very different terms from those she eventually used:

> He is muffled – wrapped & disguised
> But the indignant voice
> terrific . . . met my eye
> Clamps instantly are taken off
> approached – & salutes.[23]

She did not want posterity to know that the King had been manacled like the inmate of a lunatic asylum.

The first edition of her journals carefully altered the details of another drama in 1788–9 in which Fanny was both participant and observer. A surviving letter between Charlotte Barrett (Fanny's niece, responsible for that 1840s edition) and Charlotte's daughter and fellow editor, Julia Thomas, reveals how they scratched out sections that referred to 'Colonel Digby's jilting'. Julia wrote to her mother, 'If you can cut out a volume of Digby, it will be an improvement.'[24] A good deal of this material has now been recovered, revealing the extent of Fanny's involvement with Mr Fairly/Feignwell.[25]

While at Kew in the winter of 1788–9, the routines of the Court were so disrupted that the Queen very often did not dress all day, and the after-dinner tea-parties presided over by Madame Schwellenberg were discontinued. Fanny spent her evenings in her room, waiting for the Queen's bell. Often, however, she was not alone. The ever-attentive Mr Fairly/Feignwell had no apartment of his own at Kew; instead, he would make his way up two flights of stairs, past coal-stores and piles of laundry, and along the narrow passageway to Fanny's bedroom. At first, she was not at all comfortable with entertaining a man in such a place – 'This was very disagreeable to me, – & the more as I could not, without an appearance of affectation, or prudery, send him down again, after all he had so lately given me to understand of his admission into higher rooms of equal privacy.' But she very soon got used to the idea: surely, she reasoned to herself, there could be no harm in being closeted at night with a man whose conversation was so filled with references to the Divine and to the revered sermons of Dr John Moir, the author of *Discourses on Practical Subjects*?

Moreover, her friendship with Mr Fairly/Feignwell meant that Fanny was privy to the letters written between the Queen, the Lord Chamberlain, the Prime Minister, and the Prince of Wales concerning the condition of the King (many of which were copied by Colonel Digby in her bedroom using her pens). As the Queen's Vice-Chamberlain, Digby was responsible for protecting the Queen, which necessarily involved him in the difficult business of delaying the submission of the Regency Bill to Parliament. Fanny is too discreet to reveal to us these delicate constitutional negotiations – but they must have added spice to their conversations. It may also explain why she was willing to risk offending Madame Schwellenberg by spending so much time with him. Indeed, Madame S. did complain to the Queen that she hardly ever saw her assistant. And Fanny's maid, Goter, warned her mistress that everyone was gossiping about her and Colonel Digby. Fanny's footman, Columb, thoroughly disliked him, calling him a 'villain', and attempted to foil his visits upstairs by telling him falsely that Fanny was with the Queen.

Fanny's relationship with Mr Fairly/Feignwell was complicated by a series of huffs and misunderstandings reminiscent of her confused feelings for Jeremiah Crutchley and George Owen Cambridge, and is charted by her with as much detail. From the start, Fanny was aware that there was a difficulty, a gulf between her and the Colonel, imposed by 'his connections – his family – his high rank in office'. She tried to convince herself that his friendship meant no more to her than if he had been her brother, '& I thought it a Dream – & tried to wake from it'. But she did not listen to her instincts – or pay any attention to the rumours that reached her via Columb that Digby was to marry one of the ladies-in-waiting, Miss Charlotte Gunning, the daughter of Sir Robert Gunning and worth £10,000 a year. 'It seemed the height of improbability to suppose that any man, with an actual & serious attachment, could take such assiduous pains to cultivate every possible intercourse with another Person.'

But while arguing with herself that her feelings represented nothing more than friendship ('Is Friendship, then, unattainable, but between persons of the same sex? No, I can never believe that! – it does but require a more scrupulous attention to the Character & Disposition, – nothing more'), she was succumbing to Digby's flirtations. When he asked her whether Madame Schwellenberg had questioned her on her night absences – and made the mistake of implying to Fanny that the Cerbera might 'suspect' she was closeted in her bedroom with him – Fanny noted, suggestively: 'He stopt, – seemed dismayed at the word which escaped him unawares, & almost bit his lip through with vexation & confusion, – never looking near me, & beginning to finger the wax about the top of one of the Candles, & to put it into the flames, & draw it out, backwards, & forwards, with most fluttered motions.'

Isolated from her family and friends, and bereft of anyone with whom she could discuss her feelings, Fanny allowed herself to believe that Colonel Digby was truly attached to her: 'What times were these!' she wrote. 'I almost copy them now, as if I were copying scenes from *Evelina* or *Cecilia*, in which I had only an imaginary, though a strong interest.' Following the tortuous progress of her emotions is very like reading about the misadventures of her heroine Cecilia with her errant lover Mortimer Delvile. 'His Heart was surely Mine,' she wrote to Susan on 19 March 1789. 'His conduct, his high character, his solicitude for my confidence, his reproaches for my withholding it . . . in short, an assiduity to secure my friendship, esteem, sympathy, confidence, so unweariedly exercised for now so long a time thus concurred to satisfy me His Heart was mine.'

She wrote this on the day that the Royal Household celebrated the King's recovery with a ball at Windsor. Fanny attended, but refused to dance. The King had made steady progress since his encounter with Fanny at the beginning of February, and by Sunday, 1 March prayers were being said in all the churches of London, thanking God for the King's recovery. (It took a week for this official prayer of thanksgiving to be distributed, so that it was read to the rest of the country on the following Sunday.) By 10 March, Parliament had reconvened with the King in attendance and, four days later, the Court returned to Windsor, to be greeted by flower-decked streets and a huge fireworks display in the evening. A Royal Progress was planned through the South of England: proof that the King had recovered and was in command of the three kingdoms.

The sense of national relief was tangible. Fanny noted from Weymouth in late June: 'Not a Child could we meet, that had not a Bandeau round its Head, Cap, or Hat, of God Save the King; all the Bargemen wore it . . . & even the Bathing Women had it in large coarse Girdles round their waists. It is printed in Golden Letters upon most of the Bathing Machines, & . . . adorns every shop, & almost every House in the two Towns of Weymouth and Dorchester.' The fear that had been engendered by the King's illness was very real. Indeed, while George III was celebrating his recovery with a daily swim in the sea, serenaded by fiddlers who played 'God Save the King' from a bathing-machine, just across the Channel in France the authority of the monarchy itself was under threat.

During the winter of 1788–9, the demand for a meeting of the Estates-General, to include a Third Estate made up of representatives of the people (as opposed to the Nobility and the Church), had increased and was accompanied by sporadic outbursts of violence against the landowners and the Church. At the beginning of May 1789, the people's deputies had converged on Paris, proclaiming that 'A New Order of Things Is Born'. But, by the end of June, the three estates had still not agreed to sit down together in the same assembly, and one of the deputies, from Poitou, prophesied to his sister: 'The Estates-General of 1789 will be celebrated but by a banner of blood that will be carried to all parts of Europe.'[26]

Fanny, immured at Windsor, heard little of what was going on in the outside world, and became ever more preoccupied with her own emotional dilemma. Colonel Digby had vanished once the King's return to health resolved the constitutional crisis. When he returned, several weeks later, it was as if he were 'quite another man'. Fanny told her sister: 'Alas – the commotion within what to wish was now more forcible than ever.' Once again, Fanny's confused emotional state led her to question whether she wanted marriage or preferred to remain single. Digby's version of what passed between them does not exist; all we can surmise from Fanny's letters to Susan is that, although she found in him a meeting of minds, she was in the end not really attracted to Mr Fairly/Feignwell. He was too much the debonair officer, too practised at putting on the mask required of a courtier. And yet she had been tempted to think otherwise, and was humiliated to discover from the Court rumour-mill (though not from Mr Fairly/ Feignwell himself) that he was about to marry Miss Gunning. Fanny should have paid more attention to the warnings of her devoted servants, Columb and Goter. Ruefully, she admitted to Susan, 'if my Heart had been engaged in this affair, if my affections had been touched, beyond gratitude & esteem – the instantaneous effect of this sudden conviction, which forced its way all at once upon my mind, would infallibly have been immediate Death by an apoplectic Stroke.' Fanny was ever the dramatist.

She was relieved, no doubt, to have escaped from 'a man of double-dealing, & selfish artifice', but she could not deny the depths of her disappointment. What now was left to her but a lifetime of service in 'the Prison'? Perhaps she took comfort in re-reading one of her letters from Mr Crisp, which she had preserved carefully among her trunkloads of papers:

Dear Fanny

Though the weak knotty joints of my knuckles are somewhat tired with writing to your Mamma by this post, I cannot forbear forcing them to pay this short tribute of acknowledgement for your kind and entertaining letter. You are an exceeding good child, and I shall cherish you accordingly. You have good and grateful sentiments about you; in short you have good things in you, and I wish it was in my power to bring about, – but stop, my pen! You are going beyond your line; but there are many valuable people in this wide world of ours, that for want of rightly understanding one another, do not do what Nature seems to have intended they should do; I mean draw close together by mutual attraction. 'Tis pity; for the really valuable do not over-bound. The esteem you express for sincerity shews the world has not infected you with its contagion; but beware of too liberal a use of it, my dear Fanny; 'tis a dangerous weapon to carry about one; it is a guard that is very apt to eat into the scabbard and wound its owner. At my hour of life 'tis not worth while to change one's old habits; but, if I were to begin the world again, I should certainly carry it very much muffled up . . .

As for sincerity, Fanny, such a young, untainted, unhackneyed mind as your own may naturally enough be struck with the bright side of it; but take the word of an old sufferer; it ten times hurts the owner for once it does any good to the hearer, whom you are to thank and be highly obliged to, if he does not from that moment become your enemy. Whenever, therefore, you have heated your imagination with these glowing, generous, great sentiments, let me recommend to you by way of a cooler, to reflect on the following lines in the mouth of a more wary character –

> 'What! shall I wear my heart upon a sleeve
> For daws to peck at?'[27]

NINE

Love and Marriage
1790–3

I feel that as Such a Man could live, *I* could live, be it how it might.

Fanny Burney, June 1793

Fanny's dismay at Colonel Digby's duplicity was as nothing compared to her despair at finding herself, at the beginning of 1790, still at Court with no prospect of escape. Whether or not she had been seriously attached to Mr Fairly/Feignwell, their conversations, their shared love of books, had relieved the tedium of her evenings pent up with the irascible Madame Schwellenberg. Now all that seemed left to her was an endless round of cards, and a life dominated by 'feathers, flowers, hoop or furbelows'.[1]

In April, she wrote that she had 'involuntarily let this Month creep along unrecorded . . . I could not muster courage for a journal'. Her life in the Royal Household – with its ceaseless attendance on the Queen, and her isolation from family and friends – had broken her health and, seemingly, her spirit. She did not even bother to record the speeches that she heard while attending the trial of Warren Hastings on behalf of the Queen. The erstwhile Governor-General of Bengal had been impeached in 1787 for alleged corruption and treasonable activity against the interests of the Crown. His trial, which continued for seven years before Hastings was eventually acquitted, turned into a political battleground, with the Whig Opposition adopting the view that Hastings's alleged abuse of the royal prerogative was an example of despotic tyranny – an emotive and potentially explosive issue considering the current situation in France. (The Revolution had begun in earnest in July 1789 with the storming of the Bastille.) Fanny, like her father, was resolute in her antipathy to the Whigs.

Fanny made no mention of being ill at this time, but when she appeared in public at the trial in Westminster Hall, her father's friends were shocked by how much she had changed. William Windham, who led the case for the prosecution against Hastings, protested that her 'suffering' should be ended as soon as possible, and told her brother Charles that Fanny was being robbed of the 'use & privilege of God's best Gifts, Talents & Liberty'. Windham was even prepared, he told Charles half in jest, to move an Act of Parliament to enforce Fanny's release from Court. Charles was 'quite amazed' – and even more so when Sir Joshua Reynolds also urged upon him that Fanny should be allowed to take a 'moonlight Flight' from her captivity, and offered his own home as 'a refuge from pursuit'.[2]

Charles was probably more uncomfortable than amazed: he wanted Fanny to use her position to secure him the Bishopric of St David's. Her brother James, also, was hopeful that Fanny's favour with the King and Queen might influence the Admiralty to offer him the command of a ship – he had been land-bound on half-pay for some five years. But Fanny could no longer tolerate her life at Court, and on 29 May she seized the opportunity of an evening alone with Dr Burney at a commemorative performance of Handel's *Messiah* (she had been released from her duties while the Queen was in town) to confess the depth of her misery and her wish to resign.

To her immense relief, Dr Burney was not surprised. Fanny's decline in health and spirits – and the fact that she had not published anything since *Cecilia* in 1782 – had been much discussed by his friends and fellow members of Johnson's Literary Club. There had arisen 'a general feeling of compassion for Miss Burney' and an indignation against not only the Queen but also Dr Burney, for allowing his daughter to sacrifice her talent to his ambition. They advised him, indeed, to withdraw his daughter from Court as soon as possible, or see her carried out of Windsor in a coffin. Dr Johnson's biographer, James Boswell, 'almost forced an entrance into the palace' to see Fanny, hoping to persuade her to provide him with anecdotes from Streatham of the 'gay Sam', the 'Agreeable Sam', whom Fanny had known and loved. She refused, believing it would be a betrayal of her friendship, but Boswell took the opportunity to declare, 'It won't do, Ma'am, you must resign. We can put up with it no longer. Some very violent measures, I assure you, will be taken. We shall address Dr Burney in a body.'

By October 1790, Fanny had drawn up a 'memorial', formally asking the Queen for permission to resign. She was ill, she noted in her journal, 'the Whole of this month . . . the Day was a burthen – or rather, myself a burthen to the Day. A languor so prodigious, with so great a failure of strength & spirit, augmented almost Hourly, that I several times thought I must be compelled to excuse my constancy of attendance. But there was no one to take my place.' Dr Burney was shamed into acknowledging that Fanny's poor health was not this time the result of nerves and hypochondria, but a consequence of her unsuitability for a life at Court. Yet by the end of 'most painful 1790', Fanny had still not found the courage to submit her resignation.

On 5 January 1791, the Queen hosted a ball, which Fanny was too weak to attend. Nevertheless she was obliged to wait up until the Queen retired for the night, so that she could undress her: 'I sat up, therefore, – & I will not tell you how I wiled away the Night: it was about 5, I believe, when I came to Bed; & from this time the pain in my side ceased to consist of flying stitches, it was fixt to one spot, though I never felt it but when coughing, sneezing, or in some particular motion: & then, indeed, it cut like a Razor.' She could not sleep; she lost her appetite and suffered from dizzy spells and attacks of breathlessness. Nowadays, such symptoms would probably be diagnosed as brought on by stress and severe anxiety. The Queen's physician, Dr Gisburne, recommended that Fanny should take opium and three glasses of wine a day; a remedy that ameliorated, but did nothing to cure, her suffering.

Eventually, however, Fanny was desperate enough to ask Madame Schwellenberg to pass on her resignation to the Queen. But she refused, suggesting instead that Fanny should take leave of absence for six weeks – a response that horrified Fanny's sisters, who pleaded with Dr Burney on her behalf, adopting the slogan:

Heaven free the Encaged
And appease the Enraged.

In a letter to Charlotte, Susan advised patience and prayer: 'that our poor Sufferer's anxiety may not prove too much for her frame before the release takes place – I grieve for her unremitting fatigue, & ceaseless agitation of mind'.[3]

January, February, March, April 1791 were endured by Fanny as if she were in a long, dark tunnel of misery, She became so thin, pale and unhappy that even Madame Schwellenberg was forced to admit that Fanny was 'woefully altered' and, to Fanny's surprise, she offered to intercede with the Queen on her behalf. But it was not until the morning of Sunday, 3 July 1791, at nine o'clock precisely (Fanny, unusually, recorded both the date and time of her interview), that Fanny was informed by the Queen that a new Second Keeper of the Robes had been appointed (the daughter of a clergyman in Hanover, Mademoiselle Jacobi).

Despite her closeted life behind royal doors, the Queen was not oblivious to the difficulties that Fanny would encounter once she was living again with her father, and she offered Fanny a pension of £100, to be paid each year from the Queen's purse.[4] An unexpected relief, this provided Fanny with some small means of independence and, perhaps more importantly, the assurance that she had not incurred the Queen's displeasure by asking to leave. Indeed, Queen Charlotte insisted, 'Your Father . . . has nothing to do with it [Fanny's pension]. It is solely from me to you.'

On Tuesday, 5 July, Fanny said her goodbyes to her maid, Goter, before leaving Windsor. As she travelled for the last time in a crested carriage 'going by the name of Miss Burney's coach', she perhaps felt some regret that she was about to lose that special intimacy with royalty. But Fanny had too much independence of spirit to enjoy the rituals of monarchy, with its dressing-up and submergence of personality in archaic and often absurd codes of behaviour. And her sigh of relief as she wrote the final words in her journals for those years is tangible: 'Here, therefore, end my Court Annals. After having lived in the service of Her Majesty Five Years within Ten Days From July 17 1786 to July 7 1791.'

Fanny's departure from the Royal Household was much like her arrival: she was collected by her father from the Queen's House at the west end of the Mall and taken home. But they did not return to St Martin's Street. In the five years since Fanny's first day at Windsor, Dr Burney had been appointed as the organist of Chelsea College (originally a divinity college established by James I in 1609, it had a chapel with a fine organ), and was now living with Mrs Burney and Fanny's nineteen-year-old half-sister, Sarah Harriet, in a suite of rooms in the former college. (Her half-brother, Dick, had been sent off to India as a teenager after causing some kind of trouble, probably a romantic misalliance.) It was an uncomfortable arrangement for Fanny, who had to share a room with Sarah Harriet. Fortunately, after a couple of weeks of rest and recuperation, she was taken off by her friend Mrs Ord on a tour of the spa towns of the South-west.

Anna Ord, an independent, forthright woman who had been a widow for twenty-five years, took it upon herself to rescue Fanny. She was a worthy substitute for Mrs Thrale, whom Fanny did not contact on her release from Court although she knew that the Piozzis were back in England and living in Streatham. Yet Mrs Thrale-Piozzi had not forgotten her protégée, noting in her diary on 13 September 1791:

> Miss Burney has left the Queen's Service & Family, Ill health her pretext ... *my* Notion always was that her Majesty confided in, & loved the little cunning Creature as *I* did: while *She*, to cover her real consequence at Court, pretended disgust & weariness among her friends ... no one possesses more powers of pleasing than She does, no one *can* be more self interested, & of course more willing to employ those Powers for her own, and her Family's Benefit – & no one certainly ever enjoyed a better Opportunity – Were I as near the Queen, I'd make her love even *me*.[5]

Fanny instead allowed herself to be virtually adopted by Mrs Ord, one of whose daughters, Charlotte (who was a year younger than Fanny), was to die in a tragic accident after her muslin gown was set alight by a spark from an unguarded fire on a cold, snowy night. Charlotte was alone and had to struggle to reach the bell so that she could ring for help and, by the time their manservant reached the scene, her dress was alight. He rushed her into the street and rolled her in the snow in an attempt to dowse the flames, but the burns she suffered were so severe that she died a few days later with 'an agonising scream'. (The obituary columns of the *Gentleman's Magazine* reveal that such tragedies were not uncommon in those years of flimsy materials, open fires and candlelight.)[6]

Fanny and Mrs Ord left London on 1 August, bound first for the cathedral city of Winchester. While there, they met a group of French travellers – Fanny's first encounter with the refugees from the Revolution. 'We soon found they were Aristocrates,' she later told Susan, 'which did better for them with Mrs Ord & me, than it would have done with you Republicans of Norbury and Mickleham!'[7] Fanny may have disliked her years at Court, but she was a Royalist through and through, and was appalled to discover that she was at odds in such views with Susan. She had missed the more wide-ranging discussions of the situation in France: within the walls of Windsor, there were obvious limitations on her freedom to question the monarchy. Susan, however, had followed the newspaper reports from Paris on the debates in the Constituent Assembly; and she agreed with the demands for a constitution and equality for all before the law.

By the middle of 1791, however, the reform movement in France, led initially by enlightened aristocrats such as the Comte de Mirabeau and the Bishop of Autun, Comte de Talleyrand-Périgord, had been replaced by anarchic militancy and the demand for an end to all authority and privilege. Louis XVI and Marie-Antoinette were virtually imprisoned in the Tuileries, and when on June 20-1 they attempted to escape to the Austrian Netherlands, where Marie-Antoinette's brother, Joseph II, was Holy Roman Emperor, they were intercepted at Varennes and brought back ignominiously to Paris accompanied by 6,000 armed 'citizens' – the *sans-culottes*. The mystique of monarchy, and of hereditary privilege, had been irrevocably undermined. Those aristocrats who had the means to do so began to trickle across the Channel, foreseeing that reform was fast turning into brutal revolution.

In August 1791, Dr Burney wrote to Edmund Burke thanking him for the copy of *Reflections on the French Revolution* which Burke had sent him – a letter that Fanny later edited, correcting her father's grammar but leaving his sentiments unaltered: 'I have never had a doubt of our constitution being the best calculated for the full enjoyment of rational liberty which any nation upon Earth can boast. I have travelled through the best parts of Europe, at a period of my life when I was most likely to look around me to reflect on what I heard & saw, without ever discovering the least portion/shadow of such liberty as we enjoy.'[8]

A year later Fanny, after spending the winter 'grubbing over old books and Papers' in her father's library and reworking the tragic dramas that she had begun at Windsor, herself met Burke at a party given by Mrs Crewe (the daughter of her godmother, Frances Greville). Their conversation led to fears that the anarchy across the Channel could infect Britain: 'When he had expatiated upon the present dangers even to English Liberty & Property, from the contagion of Havock & novelty, he earnestly exclaimed, "THIS it is that has made me an abetter & supporter of Kings! Kings are necessary, & if we would preserve peace & prosperity, we must preserve THEM. We must all put our shoulders to the work! Aye, & stoutly, too!" '[9]

On the night of 20 June 1792, a crowd gathered in the gardens of the Tuileries, prepared to march on the palace and demand that Louis XVI should don the *bonnet rouge*, which had been adopted as a symbol of true patriotism. They dispersed as soon as Louis XVI appeared before them humbly wearing a red cap. But by mid-August, all semblance of government collapsed after the events of the 10th, when the King's personal regiment, the Swiss Guard, and many of his domestic attendants were massacred in an afternoon of bloody violence. France was declared a Republic, and, a week later, Dr Guillotin's invention was erected in the place de Carrousel, in front of the Tuileries, and put to use against those deemed to be traitors of the Revolution. The trickle of *émigrés* to Britain became a flood.

Two months later, while staying with Arthur Young in Suffolk, Fanny and Sarah Harriet met the Duc de Liancourt, who had fled Paris after the terrifying events of 10 August. Liancourt, who had been Louis XVI's Grand Maître de la Garde-Robe du Roi, was lucky to escape with his life. He had made his way to Rouen, where he boarded a small open boat, which arrived at Hastings on the south coast of England several days later. He looked first for a public house, where he drank several pints of ale in quick succession before falling into a deep sleep. He was fond of charming his hosts by claiming that he only realised he had reached the safety of Britain when he saw the brightly polished pewter plates and kettles in the kitchen: 'The recollection came all at once at sight of a cleanliness which, in these articles, he says, is never met with in France.' Liancourt was staying in Bury St Edmunds, where a group of French exiles had gathered around the Comtesse de Genlis and Mademoiselle d'Orléans, daughter of Philippe Egalité (the Duc d'Orléans and cousin of Louis XVI).[10]

Fanny recounted Liancourt's adventures to Susan, after they had been interpreted for her by Sarah Harriet, who unlike Fanny spoke fluent French. Susan's replies from Mickleham were also filled with news from France. At the end of September, she had heard rumours that Juniper Hall, the large house on the outskirts of Mickleham, had just been let by its owner, Mr David Jenkinson, to several French 'families'.[11] Families proved a somewhat euphemistic term: among them was Madame Anne Louise Germaine Necker de Staël, wife of the Swedish ambassador to Paris, who, though only twenty-six, was already noted for the brilliant company she had attracted to her Paris salon, and for her bravery. She had saved the lives of several of her aristocratic friends by daringly lending them her husband's diplomatic coach, with its crests and team of six thoroughbred horses, to whisk them away from Paris. One such escapee was her lover, the Comte de Narbonne, who had been appointed Minister of War by Louis XVI at the end of 1791, and was denounced for embezzling the people's taxes after the events of 10 August. On arrival in Britain, he looked for a quiet refuge, away from the glaring eyes of the conservative political establishment of London, and took out a lease on Juniper Hall, paid for by Madame de Staël.

The 'Juniper Colony', as the French exiles domiciled at Mickleham were affectionately known, included other unconventional couples, such as the middle-aged Princesse d'Hénin and her lover, the writer and scholar, the Marquis de Lally-Tollendal, and Madame de la Châtre, who arrived without her husband but accompanied by the Comte de Jaucourt, whom she was later to marry. An occasional visitor was Madame de Staël's former lover, Talleyrand, who had been forced into exile after refusing to agree to the overthrow of Louis XVI.

One arrival who received special mention by Susan was the 'open and manly' General d'Arblay, who had arrived in Surrey with his friend Narbonne some time in November. A few days later, Susan gave Fanny her first impressions of this French officer, who had been on guard with Liancourt on the night of the King's flight to Varennes, and who was later appointed second-in-command to the Marquis de Lafayette in the war against Austria that was declared in April 1792. After the events of 10 August, however, d'Arblay and Lafayette were taken prisoner by their own 'rebel' soldiers and had to be rescued by the Austrians. D'Arblay fled first to the Netherlands, and from there crossed the Channel, arriving in London at the end of September with nothing but the money in his pocket and a bag full of clothes.

D'Arblay made an immediate impression on Susan, as a person unlike any other because of his combination of aristocratic gentility and warm-hearted frankness, 'with a great share of *Gaieté de Coeur* and at the same time *naïveté* and *bonne foi*'.[12] Brought up in a château in Joigny, on the River Yonne some 75 miles south of Paris, he had been in the army since he was thirteen, and knew no other way of life. He was also a passionate reader, a published poet and an accomplished musician.[13] His name was not unknown to Fanny, for Liancourt had talked of him as a close friend while Fanny was at the Youngs, and had asked her if she knew of d'Arblay's safe arrival in Britain.

Throughout the late autumn of 1792, Susan's letters to Fanny were filled with references to 'Monsieur d'Arblay', as she described the French exiles whom she met at the home of their friends, the Locks. William Lock, a wealthy MP, and his wife Frederica were well educated, musical and artistic. Their home, Norbury Park, was, in Fanny's eyes, a 'beautiful' place. Indeed, the views across to Box Hill and the Surrey Downs from the elegant Georgian house that Lock had built on the summit of the chalk hills above Mickleham were (and still are) magnificent. But, more importantly to Fanny, the Locks were remarkably good company: 'Were I, however, in a Desert, people such as these would make it gay & cheary,' Fanny remarked to Susan after staying with them. When Susan moved to Mickleham in the summer of 1785, she came to rely on them for their friendship and the comfort of their home, where she could play music (she and Captain Phillips never had enough money to buy their own harpsichord) and read the newspapers. Her second child, Norbury, was so named because he had been born prematurely while she was staying with them.

William Lock welcomed the Juniper Hall émigrés into his home, anxious to hear at first hand the news from France. Susan, who was still fluent in French (Dr Burney's decision to send his daughters to France for their education now proved its value), was fascinated by their free-thinking ideas: 'One Sunday I walked up to Norbury and there unexpectedly I met all our Juniperians,' she told Fanny in November 1792, and she remembered the afternoon for being 'one of the best conversations I have ever heard'.[14] She was impressed by the strong bonds of friendship that drew the émigrés together, despite the fact that some had actively worked for constitutional reform while others had tried to retain their aristocratic privileges. 'They had not met since the beginning of the Revolution,' she told Fanny, '& having been of very different parties it was curious & pleasant to see them now in their mutual misfortunes meet in bons amis. They rallied each other Tu leurs disgraces good humouredly & amically.'[15]

By the middle of January 1793, Fanny herself had become acquainted with these once-wealthy but by now penniless refugees. She does not reveal the exact occasion on which she met the man who was to become 'my best of Friends', but on 28 January she wrote to her father, 'M. de Narbonne & M. d'Arblay have been almost annihilated – they are forever repining that they are French, & though two of the most accomplished & elegant men I ever saw, they break our Hearts with the humiliation they feel for their guiltless BIRTH in that guilty country.' The report of Louis XVI's execution was published in *The Times* of 25 January; but it had taken place four days earlier. Since Fanny described the way both men were affected by the news, she must have met them first, *before* 25 January, perhaps over dinner at Norbury Park (where she stayed initially, as Susan was ill): 'Poor Man! – he [Narbonne] has all the symptoms upon him of the Jaundice, – & M. d'Arblay from a very fine figure & good face, was changed as if by Magic in one night, by the receipt of this inexpiable news, into an appearance . . . black . . . meagre . . . miserable.'

Dr Burney was given a fuller impression of both men in her next letter, written a week later: 'd'Arblay is one of the most delightful characters I have ever met, for openness, probity, intellectual knowledge, & unhackneyed manners.' One senses that, at least in Fanny's eyes, he shone far and away above the Comte de Narbonne, who was 'far more a man of the World, & joins the most courtly refinement & elegance, to the quickest repartee & readiness of wit'.[16]

Alexandre-Jean-Baptiste Piochard d'Arblay was very different from the stuffy courtiers who had in recent years been Fanny's entire acquaintance. Tall, slim and fine-featured, with genial grey-blue eyes, his military bearing belied the gentleness of his temperament, which had already endeared him to Susan and her young children, who rushed to greet him whenever he called. Like Dr Burney, he was never happy unless he had a book in his pocket, preferably a volume of Petrarch or Lamartine, and he could also strum a fine tune on the mandolin. Fanny felt an instant rapport with him, while he in turn was impressed by this shy, quiet Englishwoman, whose blushes hid deep feelings and strong opinions. Fanny appeared less flashy and less brilliant than the effervescent Madame de Staël, yet she was keenly noticed by the equally withdrawn and sensitive Frenchman.

Fanny had taught herself to read French, but unlike Susan she had never lived in France and she refused to say anything in company, for fear of revealing her ineptitude. D'Arblay soon suggested that he should be her 'Master of the language', and Fanny agreed, writing to her father to *inform* him that she would be extending her stay in Surrey. A fortnight later, she wrote again: 'some circumstances are intervening that incline me to postpone it [her return to Chelsea] another week'. She refrained from telling her father what the 'circumstances' were that 'inclined' her to stay; they were not going to be easy to explain. Fanny had at last met the man of whom she had dreamed.

D'Arblay's suggestion that they should be language tutors to each other was a clever ruse to spend time alone with Fanny without arousing the suspicions of his fellow Juniperians. They began to write for each other Thèmes, or exercises in composition – d'Arblay's in broken English, Fanny's in equally stilted French – which they lovingly corrected before returning. Fanny preserved them in a bundle of papers, tied and labelled for her grandchildren as 'Some of the

Original Thèmes in French & in English that passed between General d'Arblay & F. Burney . . . to the month of April when the Thèmes were changed happily! happily! For reciprocated Letters, till F. Burney became the thrice blest Wife of the most amiable & most Honourable of Men'.[17]

At first, Fanny's essays were preoccupied with the problem of Madame de Staël, to whom she was strongly drawn as a woman very like Mrs Thrale 'in the ardour, & warmth of her temper & partialities', and whose offers of friendship Fanny found it 'impossible to resist'. Madame de Staël, too, from their first meeting liked the author of *Cecilia*, the novel that had so 'soothed and regaled' her father during the trial of Louis XVI. (Jacques Necker, the former French Finance Minister, was himself now living in exile, in Coppet just outside Geneva.) She invited Fanny to join the community of friends at Juniper Hall, and Fanny accepted with delight. But when she asked her father's permission, she was sent a horrified reply, fuelled by fears that Fanny was already becoming too intimate with this group of French exiles. Dr Burney warned Fanny that Madame de Staël was being gossiped about by the London literary community, as having abandoned her husband and children to be with Narbonne, who was much more than just a friend. Worse still, she had also been Talleyrand's mistress.

Such rumours were true: Madame de Staël had given birth to Narbonne's son just a few weeks before joining her lover in Surrey; she had left her children (another son by Narbonne and her Swedish husband's child) in Coppet with her parents. They were, however, much exaggerated. There was much distrust in Britain of these French aristocrats, many of whom had been at the forefront of the original reform movement, and who had called for a National Assembly of elected, rather than hereditary, representatives. They were regarded as responsible, at least indirectly, for unleashing the forces of anarchy that culminated in the execution of Louis XVI; and their easy morals and disregard of the more conventional English rules of social exchange were seen as confirmation of their rebellious and dangerous leanings. That they were now exiles – blacklisted in France and in danger of their lives if they returned – was not acknowledged.

Dr Burney strongly advised his daughter to break off all relations with the Juniperians, which put Fanny in a very awkward position. She refused naïvely to believe the rumours about Madame de Staël, writing to Dr Burney that 'M. de Narbonne was of her society, which contained 10 or 12 of the first people in Paris, & occasionally, almost *all Paris*; she loved him even tenderly, but so openly, so simply, so unaffectedly, & with such utter freedom from all coquetry, that if they were two Men, or two women, the affection could not, I think, be more obviously undesigning.' She added, curiously unperceptively, that while Madame de Staël was 'very very plain; – he is very handsome; – her intellectual endowments must be with him her sole attraction. M. Talleyrand was another of her society, & she seems equally attached to him.'[18] But Fanny could not risk offending the Queen. Nor did she wish to enjoy the hospitality of a woman who, as it had been pointed out to her, was living in such an unorthodox manner. How could she extricate herself *without* offending the man whom she was already addressing as 'my dear Master', and who was Narbonne's closest friend?

The courtship of Fanny and Alexandre d'Arblay is as romantic as the best of stories, and was conducted under the most difficult of circumstances. In the Thèmes, which after Fanny's return to Chelsea were delivered between London and Mickleham via the Locks' gardener, Alexandre wrote to Fanny of Madame de Staël's 'uncommon' character, but diplomatically refrained from saying anything about her relationship with Narbonne. In this first exercise, d'Arblay stumbled over his grammar but made his opinions very clear:

> Mr [corrected to Dr by Fanny] Burney can't refuse to some poor french bannished the portion of happiness which Miss Burney blesses them with. these very unfortunate gentlemen know only Mr Burney by his reputation and by chance of his charming work; they had accustomed themselves to the idea of his excellent qualities; they would be very sorry to be obliged to accuse him with so unjust selfishness.

D'Arblay began by calling Fanny 'My dear Master in gown' but soon referred to her as 'My dear Master in all'; and by his fourteenth thème (written on 28 February) he was writing with vastly improved fluency: 'I can't answer to your endearing letter. I can't indeed! My feelings are too strong.'[19]

Fanny offered to lend him £100; Alexandre responded by rushing up to London with his reply, and posting it from Westminster so that it would arrive at Chelsea the same day. He refused her offer of money, but gently; telling her that he had one reason, and one reason only, for wishing to remain in England – and that was a certain friend and language tutor. Such a sweetly disguised declaration exactly matched Fanny's shy inability to articulate her own emotions, but her initial reaction was to panic. She dashed off a letter to Susan on 4 April:

> I will be quite – quite open – & tell you that Everything upon Earth I could covet for the peculiar happiness of My peculiar Mind seems here united – were there not one scruple in the way which intimidates me from listening to the voice of my Heart – Can you guess what it is? I do not wish myself richer, grander, more powerful, or higher born, – one of his first attractions with me is his superiority to all these considerations – no – I wish myself only to be *younger!*[20]

Fanny was not even two years older than Alexandre (he was born on 13 May 1754; she on 13 June 1752). Her 'scruples' were perhaps a veil to disguise her deepening love: d'Arblay was the first man for whom she seriously contemplated giving up her single status (though still living under her father's roof, she was at least not subjected to the domineering will of a husband). But, she told Susan, 'His nobleness of character – his sweetness of disposition – his Honour, Truth, integrity with so much of softness, delicacy, & tender humanity – except my beloved Father & Mr Lock, I have never seen such a man in this World, though I have drawn such in my Imagination.' Fanny believed that she had found her own Lord Orville (or Mortimer Delvile). With such conviction, it is understandable that she ignored the *real* drawbacks to their connection.

General d'Arblay was not only French – a member of a people so depraved, in English eyes, that they were prepared to kill their own monarch – he was also Catholic. Indeed, it is probable that he was under surveillance by the Government: his friends at Juniper Hall had employed an English tutor called William Clark, who might well have been the same William Clark who in 1791 submitted a report on the Comtesse de Genlis and the French community in Bury St Edmunds.[21] When, on 31 January 1793, the new Republic of France declared war on Britain and Holland, the émigrés in the South of England found themselves in an impossible situation. Many retreated to the Continent voluntarily; others were forced to leave under the Aliens' Act newly extended to include émigrés from France. Madame de Staël made her way back to Coppet via Belgium and Holland, after running out of money; Talleyrand was asked to leave by William Pitt at the end of January 1794, and sailed for America.

Narbonne, however, stayed on; so did d'Arblay, who had nowhere else to go. Denounced as a traitor, his family estates in Joigny had been confiscated, and he did not think that he would be able to recover them for at least thirty or forty years – the length of time he reckoned it would take for the fires of rebellion to burn themselves out. Instead, he offered his military services to the British Government, dreaming up a radical and somewhat impractical scheme (given the degree of anti-French hysteria) to raise a regiment of émigré soldiers, a Corps d'Artillerie à Cheval, which would fight *with* the British against the French rebels. He sent his proposals to the Prime Minister, William Pitt, and the Earl of Clarendon, who was in charge of the British cavalry forces, but never received a reply.

These drawbacks were of no consequence to Fanny, who on 5 April confessed to Susan: 'I feel that as Such a Man could live, *I* could live, be it how it might.'[22] To d'Arblay, she replied in French that if his plans to stay in England depended on her, then she did not think he would leave the country: '*S'il tient à moi – le moindre du monde – que vous travailliez pour rester en Angleterre – Je ne crois pas que vous partir . . . Je ne suis pas maintenant dans l'état de parler – d'autre chose – ce sera, donc, un thème bien court – mais je l'expédié afin de ne pas paroître insensible à votre désir de vouloir me consulter sur vos procédés.*'[23] A prudent response, yet the General was sufficiently encouraged to set off from Juniper Hall at seven o'clock the next morning and walk the eighteen or so miles to Chelsea with a rose tree for his beloved. He did not see her – Fanny was out all morning on a round of visits to Mrs Ord and Mrs Lock, who was staying at her London house in Portland Place. Undaunted, the General continued the next half-mile to Sloane Street, where he hoped to find Fanny with her sister Charlotte. Without success. Tired, hungry and disappointed, he hired a horse to take him back to Mickleham, where he arrived in the early evening, much to the bemusement of his friends.

Yet his efforts did not go unrewarded: from that day, Fanny began a series of letters to Susan, which she would later call the 'Courtship Journal'. In them she described her growing love for d'Arblay and their difficulties as they sought to overcome the disapproval of her father and his literary friends. Three days after joyfully receiving d'Arblay's rose, Fanny was plunged into despair. Susan pointed out that £100 a year (equivalent to about £5000 now) was barely enough to live on (and might well have been withdrawn, had the Queen disliked the match), to which Fanny replied: 'I see all your objections, & I know them to be Feathers to what *every body* else will start.' Indeed, Mrs Ord believed that all the French émigrés should be deported.

Dr Burney, too, refused to meet General d'Arblay, remaining in his room when Alexandre called on Fanny in Chelsea on 13 April. Instead, he asked that d'Arblay, whom he knew was a Constitutionalist, should write for him a comprehensive analysis of all the factions in France. Little did he suspect the integrity and intelligence of his future son-in-law. D'Arblay's lengthy reply began by setting out the reasons why reform of the monarchy had been essential, but went on to castigate the 'Revolutionaires' for pursuing their own personal interests. He ended judiciously by extolling the virtues of the 'excellent . . . Constitution Anglaise', which was, he argued, the model of just and fair government.[24] Dr Burney was so mollified that, when Alexandre called again at Chelsea two days later, he invited the Frenchman into his library, where the two men found common cause in their mutual love of French and Italian poetry.

D'Arblay, however, was concerned that he had nothing to offer a wife and that, if she married him, Fanny would be forced to live as a social outcast, cut off from the literary life of London, and with very little money. He retreated to bed with a severe migraine. Fanny responded with the spirited determination that had characterised her life before her years of personal disappointment. On 9 May, she told Susan: 'If it should, indeed, be my lot to fall into the hands of one so scrupulous in integrity, how thankfully shall I hail my Fate!'[25]

Susan bore nobly all this talk of 'integrity' and 'sincerity' – and argued d'Arblay's case with their father on Fanny's behalf – at a time when her own marriage was proving less than happy. Captain Phillips, whose inheritance had not materialised, often left her on her own in Mickleham, while he chased wild schemes to make money (probably gambling). His charming manner hid a jealous, difficult temperament: on one occasion, he 'played' so violently with Norbury that the two-year-old ended up with a dislocated shoulder. By 1787, Susan had asked Fanny to send letters to her via Norbury Park so that 'the Vagabond' would not see them.[26] The arrival of the French exiles was a welcome respite and, when the Juniper Hall community disbanded at the end of May 1793, d'Arblay and Narbonne began dining each day with Susan. There have been suggestions that the reason Narbonne did not return to the Continent with Madame de Staël was because he had fallen in love with Susan. Indeed, he stayed on for another year, and did not reply to Madame de Staël's increasingly desperate letters. But Susan says nothing of her feelings for him, although it is possible that Captain Phillips's increasing (and inexplicable) hostility towards his wife could have arisen from misplaced jealousy.

Susan, certainly, admired the Frenchman and discussed with him her sister's romantic dilemma, almost as if he were part of the family. She and Narbonne were concerned that Fanny's prudishness and sensitivity meant she would suffer acutely from the gossip that connection with an émigré would arouse, and that neither Fanny nor Alexandre was accustomed to managing on the meagre finances that were all they could expect to have. Susan concluded that it was up to Fanny to write another novel: 'For my own part I can only say, & solicit, & urge to my Fanny to *print, print, print*! – Here is a resource – a certainty of removing present difficulties.'[27]

Fanny, meanwhile, retreated to her old refuge, Chesington Hall, overwhelmed by her emotional confusion. In the peaceful seclusion of its familiar surroundings, she found the courage to act on her feelings for d'Arblay, convinced that with him she could live anywhere and on almost nothing. And, as she told her father, she might yet find the inspiration for another novel: 'as to Les Muses – they are the most skittish ladies Living – one, with Bowls & Daggers, pursues – another with a Mask escapes – However, I wind round & round their Recesses, where of old I found them – or where, rather, they found *me* – & perhaps we may yet meet in some Green Retreat.'[28]

She returned to Chelsea on 1 June, from where she wrote a decisive letter to Alexandre: 'You desire to know if I have weighed well how I could support an entirely retired life &c – Here comes a great YES!' She promised to learn 'the details *du ménage*' (until now she had never needed to know the practicalities of housekeeping), and thanked him for the receipt of another bouquet of roses.[29] All that remained was for Dr Burney to bless the match. But another three weeks passed before Fanny felt strong enough to confront him with her decision. She escaped from Chelsea to stay at Norbury Park, where she and Alexandre composed a formal request (in French), encouraged by William Lock, who promised them as a wedding gift a portion of land on his estate so that they could build their own cottage.

They waited anxiously for eight days before Dr Burney grudgingly replied. He acknowledged that his daughter had been made happy by Alexandre, but he asked them to postpone all thoughts of marriage until there was some resolution of the situation in France (only a few days later, for example, the Committee of Public Safety authorised the implementation of the death penalty against anyone suspected of hoarding grain). Nothing Dr Burney said, however, could make any difference now to Fanny's resolve.

A few minutes before seven o'clock on the morning of Sunday, 28 July, she took the arm of her brother James (who had agreed to stand in for Dr Burney, after he refused to attend his daughter's 'imprudent' marriage) and walked the short distance up the lane from Susan's cottage to Mickleham Church, where General d'Arblay and the Comte de Narbonne, impressively attired in their military regalia, awaited her. The only other witnesses at this early hour were Susan and Captain Phillips and Mr and Mrs Lock, who welcomed Madame d'Arblay as she walked back down the aisle on the arm of her husband, wearing a ring engraved with the words '*Ca douçeur m'enchent*' (Your sweetness enchants me).[30] Two days later, the ceremony was repeated in the Catholic chapel of the Sardinian Embassy in Lincoln's Inn Fields in London. D'Arblay was concerned that if he did eventually recover his estates, then Fanny would need a Catholic certificate of marriage to ensure 'she may not be excluded from their participation'.

So Fanny married, much as Mrs Thrale had done, an impoverished foreigner and a Catholic. Passion had prevailed over prudence, and, while advocating reason and restraint in her fictions, in life Fanny followed the dictates of her heart. It was a decision she was never to regret, despite the shock she gave to all who knew her. Her stepsister Sarah Harriet had not suspected that d'Arblay's visits to Chelsea were anything but friendship, and after the marriage she wrote to a cousin, 'I never shall look upon any thing as being improbable, or unlikely.' And when Maria Rishton read the announcement in a newspaper, she wrote to Susan (their first communication for twenty years), 'Can you conceive any thing equal to my surprise to hearing our Vestal Sister had ventured on that stormy sea of matrimony – I am sure some friends I had with me must have thought me mad – I believe I cried – and laughed twenty times in the course of the day ... I beg you will send me a description of this Conquering Hero who has thaw'd Fanny's Ice.'[31]

As Fanny concluded in a letter to Marianne Waddington (the Marianne Port of her Windsor days): 'Happiness is the great end of all our worldly views & proceedings; & no one can judge for another in what will produce it.'[32]

TEN

Camilla
1793–9

The proper education of a female, either for use or for happiness, is still to seek, still a problem beyond human solution.

Camilla

The d'Arblays' honeymoon was shortlived: Fanny and her 'French avanturer' had to face the harsh realities of a future without estate, profession or trade. By the end of August 1793, they had moved from Phenice Farm (a rambling farmhouse on Blagden Hill just above Mickleham, where they spent the first weeks after their marriage) into a rented cottage in Great Bookham. 'M. d'A' (as Fanny now referred to her husband in her journal-letters) had grand plans to design and build their own 'Maisonette' on the land given them by William Lock, but as yet the d'Arblays had no money for such an ambitious project. Nor did they have much experience of fending for themselves. M. d'A took up gardening with more enthusiasm than knowledge, using his military sabre as a hedge-cutter and amusing their neighbours by digging up a precious asparagus bed. Fanny's letters to her father from 'The Hermitage', as she christened their first home, are filled with domestic detail as she asked for advice on how to make soup, or reported on the novel taste of freshly picked cabbages – they had 'a freshness & a goût we had never met with before'. Dr Burney's hostility to the match did not last long when he heard from Fanny of her happiness, and of the earnest attempts of his new son-in-law to provide for her.[1]

M. d'A's real concern, however, was to find some way of recovering his estates in France. When, at the end of September, news reached Britain that there had been a Royalist uprising in the French naval port of Toulon, he determined to rush across the Channel to join it. Fanny was so shocked and upset that she found herself unable to discuss with her husband what he should do and instead wrote him a letter (which she pleaded with him to destroy after reading; he kept it). She had, she says, deceived herself into 'a belief that the Profession of blood was wholly relinquished – I had understood you that you had satisfied yourself, & might now with a safe conscience, retire from public life. If this had been my belief before I belonged to you – before I had experienced that perfect felicity which I hardly thought mortal, but which you have given to my existence – Judge the bitterness of my disappointment at this juncture.'[2] She could not refuse to let him go; but nor could she bear the idea of him taking such a risk – especially after hearing of the execution of Marie-Antoinette, who on 16 October had been driven in an open cart through the streets of Paris to the guillotine in the place de la Révolution.

Fanny retreated to bed with a severe fever, tenderly nursed by Susan (the Hermitage was only a couple of miles over the hill from Mickleham). By mid-December, however, the threat of separation from her husband was removed by the collapse of the Royalist attempt to seize power in the south of France. M. d'A went back to his gardening; Fanny sought her own solution to their financial problems. On 19 November, she had published a twenty-seven-page pamphlet entitled *Brief Reflections relative to the Emigrant French Clergy; earnestly submitted to the Humane Consideration of the Ladies of Great Britain*. It was her first venture into print for eleven years, and, despite 'some loss in the play of the pen', was welcomed by the *Critical Review* as a sign that the author of *Evelina* and *Cecilia* 'will again delight and again instruct us'. Some critics, however, disliked its pompous style – a view with which modern readers are likely to agree. Fanny's attempt to rally financial and moral support for the 6,000 or more priests who had been forced to flee the French Revolution and find refuge in the south-coast towns of England reflected her conservative and sanctimonious streak: 'Come forth, then, O ye Females, blest with affluence! spare from your luxuries, diminish from your pleasures, solicit with your best powers; and hold in heart and mind that, when the awful hour of your own dissolution arrives, the wide-opening portals of heaven may present to your view these venerable sires, as the precursors of your admission.'[3] Indeed, it was difficult to believe that this overblown rhetoric was by the same writer who had produced *Evelina.*

Perhaps, though, it is unfair to criticise Fanny; she was engaged, after all, on a mission to raise £7,500 to save these destitute refugees from hunger and starvation. More significantly, she was trying to prove her credentials as an 'Establishment' figure, at a time when M. d'A did not dare show his face in London for fear that he might be deported.[4] Nevertheless, the style and content of *Brief Reflections* suggests that her years at Court had not only affected her health; she was now keenly aware that she was writing for an audience that included the Queen and the princesses.

These changes were to become even more apparent in her next literary performance. Fanny had never given up on the idea of writing for the stage and, now that she was happily married and living in the peaceful seclusion of a small village, she resurrected some of her old manuscripts. She had begun work on *Edwy and Elgiva*, her historical tragedy, during the King's illness. 'An almost spontaneous work', it now filled her with 'a secret sensation of horror' at what she had written.[5] But she was confident that, from this bare outline, she could create a successful drama. By the summer of 1794, she had sent the script to her brother Charles (now living in Greenwich as headmaster of his own school) with a view to presenting it to John Kemble, the actor-manager then in charge of the Drury Lane Theatre. In mid-November, she informed her father that Kemble had accepted her 'piece' and 'with the most flattering expressions'.[6]

No mention was made, however, of when the play would be staged, and this was now of crucial importance to Fanny. For by August, she realised she was pregnant. She had been ill throughout May and June with a 'constant bilious attack', and on 16 June began experiencing 'spasms'. At first, the doctor seems to have been unaware of her condition, but gradually it became clear that her ill-health was because she was expecting her first child – at the age of forty-two. At nine o'clock on the morning of 18 December, she gave birth to a son, named Alexander Charles Louis Piochard after Alexander, 'that tremendous warrior', his uncle Charles, Louis de Narbonne and his father's family.[7] The birthing cushion, made from white silk and decorated, in the new fashion, with steel pins that traced the words 'Long live the dear child' on one side and the initials 'F. d'Arblay' on the other, was preserved in the family for many years.[8] Fanny left no account of the birth – her journals for these years are very sparse since she saw Susan almost daily, but she later described how her 'little man' was brought into the world in the arms of Mrs Lock.

Alex, evidently, was a precocious child. When he was just two weeks old, Fanny wrote to her father that he was 'a very interesting little Creature, already, & has a thousand little promises of original intelligence'. In her absorption, *Edwy and Elgiva* was shelved; but only temporarily. On 2 February 1795, Charles reported to his sister that some of the newspapers had advertised that 'a new tragedy called *Edwy and Elgiva* is in rehearsal'. In fact, the play had received its initial reading in the Green Room at Drury Lane on 5 January, when Charles had travelled up from Greenwich to read the play to the assembled cast – which included John Kemble, Sarah Siddons, Robert Bensley and John Palmer. Charles, however, said nothing of this to his sister; an entry by Mrs Thrale-Piozzi in her diary explains why: 'the Actors dropt silently off, one by one, and left him Charles *all alone*'.[9] Once again, Charles was thoughtless, failing to alert Fanny that her play would need revising *before* presenting it to the harsh scrutiny of a boisterous audience.

Fanny knew herself that in its present form *Edwy and Elgiva* was far from perfect, and in January she asked M. d'A to tell Charles that she wanted to make 'divers corrections & alterations'. Shortly afterwards, however, she succumbed to a high fever after suffering from an abscess on her breast. (Alex was weaned very prematurely, since she refused to farm her son out to a wet nurse.) And, in the end, no changes were made to the text. On 9 March, *Edwy and Elgiva* (in the neat hand of a professional copyist) was submitted to the Lord Chamberlain's office for approval and passed for performance at the Theatre Royal, Drury Lane, by the Examiner of Plays, John Larpent (a friend of the Burneys). Rehearsals had already begun the previous week; but Fanny was too weak to lift a pen, let alone travel to London to attend.

This was a disastrous mistake. On the opening night – Saturday, 21 March – Fanny arrived at Drury Lane with M. d'A a few minutes before curtain-up, wrapped in an 'immense pelisse' and a huge bonnet to keep out the cold. From their private box, she and M. d'A (accompanied by Charles and Susan) experienced what must have been an excruciating humiliation. Despite its star-filled cast, the play was cheaply staged (no attempt had been made to recreate the 'magnificent gothic chambers' or 'forest' of Fanny's stage directions), and so badly rehearsed that some of the actors had not even bothered to learn their lines. John Palmer, who played Aldhelm, the rebel priest and supporter of Edwy, was reported afterwards by Mrs Thrale-Piozzi as only having '*but 2 lines* of his part by Heart!' Not surprisingly, the audience failed to grasp the pathos of this tragic tale, and instead collapsed into hysterical laughter as Mrs Siddons (playing the murdered heroine Elgiva) was carried across the stage on a chaiselongue, moaning from her wounds (she was supposed to be lost in a dense forest).

Over the next couple of days, no fewer than sixteen newspapers expressed their concern that the 'author of *Evelina*' could have produced such a ludicrous tragedy. The *Morning Herald*, for instance, ridiculed Elgiva's dying scene, and noted how the laughter occasioned by Mrs Siddons's appearance 'was inconceivable'.[10] The *Morning Post* suggested that the play was 'one continued monotonous scene of whining between the two lovers'.[11] Mrs Siddons, indeed, bewailed four days later to Mrs Thrale-Piozzi: 'Oh there never was so wretched a thing as Mrs D'arblaye's Tragedy ... In truth it needed no discernment to see how it would go, and I was grieved that a woman of so much merit must be so much mortified. The Audience were quite angelic and only laughed where it was *impossible* to avoid it.'[12]

One has some sympathy with the actors, who had to declaim lines such as these in the dying scene between Edwy and Elgiva:

ELGIVA O Edwy! lend me courage, – not despair –
EDWY My Brain turns round – I know not where I am –
      Nor whom – nor what – O kind Distraction seize me!
      Merciful Madness! –
ELGIVA Edwy, generous Edwy!
      Repress thy sorrow – for my sake – for me –
      Spare, spare the fleeting moments that remain. –
EDWY I will! – I feel my wrong – Canst thou forgive it?
                                    (*kneels by her side*)
      Can thy pure Spirit – see! I am calm! – forgive me?
ELGIVA Forgive? – dear to my Heart! – my noblest Edwy! –
      Ah me, I die! – O call forth all thy firmness –
EDWY I will! believe me – trust – I'll wound no more,
      Expiring Angel! thy seraphic peace! –
ELGIVA Ah – take my last farewell – my tenderest –
                                              Dies[13]

Fanny withdrew her play immediately – and it has never been performed again. But her experience that night in no way deterred her. She left the theatre buzzing with ideas, and two months later hinted to her father that she had 'thoughts of a future revise of *Edwy and Elgiva*, for which I formed a plan on the first Night, from what occurred by the representation: but then – I want Mr Palmer to be so obliging as to leave the Stage!'[14] What spirit!

Her old friend Richard Owen Cambridge suggested to Fanny that she should have the tragedy printed by subscription – there was a large market for play scripts in these years, created by the increasing popularity of amateur theatricals. When Mrs Montagu seconded the idea, Fanny was tempted not only to rescue *Edwy and Elgiva* but also to revise the other 'tragedies' in her trunkload of discarded manuscripts. She had plotted several other blank-verse dramas while at Court, three of which have survived. Indeed, 'Hubert de Vere', which is set on the Isle of Wight during the reign of King John and tells the story of the rivalry between Hubert and the evil De Mowbray against the backdrop of the Barons' Revolt (1215–16), was offered to John Kemble in July 1793, before *Edwy and Elgiva*.

At some time in 1790, Fanny also began work on 'The Siege of Pevensey', which explores the relationship between Adela and her father, the Earl of Chester, during the reign of William Rufus (1087–1100). Much crisper in construction and less ornamental in style, it was never submitted for a professional staging – at least as far as we know. Scraps of a fourth tragedy, 'Elberta', have now been reassembled (for the publication of her *Complete Plays*) to reveal another doom-laden love story that takes place just after the Norman Conquest. 'Elberta' was probably the most playable of Fanny's tragedies, with a strong central character in the heroine, Elberta, and real dramatic tension as she is chased by the evil Offa and threatened with murder. Yet none of these plays shows Fanny at her best, and it would be difficult to argue that, if she had been allowed to stage them, she would have established herself as a dramatist.

More pressing, indeed, was her need to make money, and to follow Susan's advice to '*print, print, print!*' The fiasco at Drury Lane forced upon Fanny the realisation that to write for the stage was impossible while she was tied to her son; instead, she turned back to what she knew she could accomplish, and to brilliant effect – the novel.

After her success with *Evelina*, Fanny had dreamed up a new heroine, Eugenia, whose difficulties arose from the fact that she was without fortune *and* ugly. When she mooted the idea to Mr Crisp in 1780, he had responded with enthusiasm: 'I am persuaded she'd make her own Fortune,' he told Fanny. 'The Idea is new, & striking, & presents a large Field for unhackney'd Characters, Observations, subjects for satire, & Ridicule, & numberless Advantages you'd meet with, by Walking in such an untrodden Path.'[15] 'Eugenia' was eventually abandoned in favour of *Cecilia* – perhaps because she began to prove too unsettling and challenging a heroine. She was not forgotten, however, and when, in August 1782, Mr Crisp advised Fanny to profit from the enormous success of *Cecilia* by hurrying another novel into print, Fanny reminded him that she had already begun work on her 'ugly scheme'.[16]

It was to be another fourteen years before 'Eugenia' made her first public appearance, but, by the summer of 1794, Fanny had regained sufficient purpose and determination to contemplate beginning serious work on another novel. In a letter that she wrote to her father after he had visited the d'Arblays for the first time in their Hermitage, Fanny told him, 'You spirited me on in all ways, for this week past I have taken *tightly* to the *grand ouvrage*.' She promised that when she next called on him in Chelsea, she would bring with her 'a little sample of something less in the dolorous style than what always causes your poor Shoulders a little Shrug'. (Dr Burney had read through the drafts of *Edwy and Elgiva*, and had not been impressed.)[17]

Fanny's new fiction was based on her original idea for 'Eugenia', but was recast as 'Camilla; or A Picture of Youth'.[18] When she came to flesh out her tentative outline ('The life of a whole family of different sexes – ages – Tempers – Persons – Talents – Pursuits – Education. Dispersed in various parts, & occasionally encountering – hearing of one another – various successes in life'), she transferred her focus from the plight of the pock-marked and crippled Eugenia to her elder sister, the beautiful and spirited but fortuneless Camilla.[19] Her moral focus changed, too. Fanny's original intention appears to have been to illustrate how foolish it is to set too high a value on beauty and too little on character ('The soldier who enters the field of battle requires not more courage, though of a different nature, than the faded beauty who enters an assembly room'); but in the end she attempted to create a much broader portrait of how things go wrong when the older generation abrogates its responsibilities.[20]

Her heroine, Camilla (named after Virgil's woman warrior who fought against Aeneas), is the darling of the Tyrold family, and especially of her uncle, the warm-hearted, generous, but foolish Sir Hugh, who is unmarried and without an heir. On first seeing Camilla as a sprightly nine-year-old, he is enchanted by her and, in a scene reminiscent of Mr Crisp's encounter with the young Fanny, remarks: 'I can't well make out what it is that's so catching in her; but there's something in her little mouth that quite wins me; though she looks as if she was half laughing at me.'[21] He decides not only to bestow his fortune and estate on her, but also to persuade her parents that she should live with him in his grand house.

But Sir Hugh's kindliness is no match for the evils of the world, and, without the spiritual guidance of her father and the firm hand of her mother (who fears for Camilla, because 'the ardour of her imagination, acted upon by every passing idea, shook her judgment from its yet unsteady seat, and left her at the mercy of wayward sensibility'),[22] Camilla falls under the dangerous influence of Sir Hugh's unconventional neighbour Mrs Arlbery. This frank and unconventional widow advises her protégée: 'You are made a slave in a moment by the world, if you don't begin life by defying it. Take your own way, follow your own humour, and you and the world will both go on just as well, as if you ask its will and pleasure for everything you do, and want, and think.'[23] Meanwhile Camilla's sister Eugenia first catches smallpox at a local fair, from which she recovers but at the cost of terrible disfigurement, and then falls off a seesaw, injuring herself so badly that she grows up with a twisted spine (a morbid scene that is mocked by one of the characters in *Northanger Abbey*).[24] In remorse, Sir Hugh disinherits Camilla and promises his fortune to the unfortunate Eugenia.

Like its predecessors, *Camilla* is filled with memorable incident: a hair-raising accident with a team of runaway horses in Tunbridge, a vicious dog-fight, blackmail, prostitution, attempted murder and madness. There is also an extraordinary, and unforgettably vivid, account of an orchestra of tamed monkeys, which entertains the crowds at Northwick Fair by 'dreadfully scraping a bow across the strings of a vile kit, another beating a drum, another with a fife, a fourth with a bagpipe, and the sixteen remainder striking together tongs, shovels, and pokers, by way of marrowbones and cleavers'.

Fanny also recalls her own theatrical humiliation, in her description of an amateur production of *Othello* in which she daringly burlesques Shakespeare by quoting some of the speeches in the colloquial dialects of the 'disastrous buskins' who attempt to act out the tragedy. The prompter, she says, 'was the only person from whom any single speech passed without a blunder'. And the audience burst into spontaneous roars of laughter when the actor playing Othello accidentally set fire to his long black wig as he was about to strangle Desdemona:

Othello, having quenched the fire, unconscious that half his curls had fallen a sacrifice to the flames, hastily pursued her [Desdemona had run off the stage screaming that she was about to be burned alive], and, in a violent passion, called her a fool, and brought her back to the bed; in which he assisted her to compose herself, and then went behind the scenes to light his candle; which having done, he gravely returned, and, very carefully putting it down, renewed his part with the line, 'Be thus vhen thou art dead, and I vill kill thee, And love thee after.'²⁵

Othello shadows this long, contorted novel, which runs to 913 pages in the modern paperback edition. Quotations from the play are dotted throughout all five volumes, and the main reason why it takes so long for Camilla to be reconciled with the eligible Edgar Mandlebert is Edgar's jealousy and Camilla's naïvety. While he is encouraged to distrust her by his embittered tutor, Dr Marchmont, she falls victim to the seductive Sir Sedley Clarendel (as dangerously attractive as his name). But the book is an arduous read, and was a disappointment to Fanny's fans when it eventually appeared in July 1796. Indeed, Jane Austen is thought to have commented in pencil at the end of her copy of the novel: 'Since this work went to the Press a circumstance of some Importance to the happiness of Camilla has taken place, namely that Dr Marchmont has at last died.'²⁶

Fanny knew that her novel was far too long. She told the King and Queen, to whom she presented specially bound copies on its publication: 'The work is longer by the whole fifth Volume than I had first planned: – & I am almost ashamed to look at its size – & afraid my Readers would have been much more obliged to me if I had left so much out – than for putting so much in!'²⁷ She had travelled up to Windsor from Great Bookham on 5 July, as soon as she received the presentation volumes (two sets bound in red morocco for the King and Queen, and six in white-and-gold for the princesses) from her publishers. She and M. d'A left Alex at the Hermitage at about half-past five in the evening and arrived a little after seven. It was her first visit to the Queen since her marriage; and was a momentous occasion for her husband, who ventured as far as the iron railings outside the Queen's Lodge but dared not step within, 'terrified lest French feet should contaminate the Gravel within!'²⁸

Fanny dedicated her novel to Queen Charlotte, partly in gratitude for her pension; partly no doubt to secure the royal seal of approval on her new life with M. d'A. She wrote in the Dedication:

In those to whom Your Majesty is known but by exaltation of Rank, it may raise, perhaps, some surprise, that scenes, characters, and incidents, which have reference only to common life should be brought into so august a presence; but the inhabitant of a retired cottage, who there receives the benign permission which at Your Majesty's feet casts this humble offering, bears in mind recollections which must live there while 'memory holds its seat', of a benevolence withheld from no condition, and delighting in all ways to speed the progress of Morality, through whatever channel it could flow, to whatever port it might steer.

'To speed the progress of Morality' – what high-flown intentions, and how different from Fanny's professed desire in *Evelina* 'to draw characters from nature . . . and to mark the manners of the times'.[29] The wickedly witty young woman who had set out primarily to entertain herself and her readers was now conscious of her responsibility as a writer. It is as if she had begun to censor everything she wrote, and although characters like Mrs Arlbery suggest a subversive undercurrent, and appeal to the reader by being much more richly drawn and believable, in the end *Camilla* does not come alive in the same way that her predecessors did.

At first, however, the novel was in great demand, the first edition of 4,000 copies selling out in just three months. Arthur Young told Dr Burney in December that his publisher had 'informed him there never was so great & rapid a *Sale* of a Novel before'.[30] But although the gossip among her literary friends was that Fanny had 'cleared more than three thousand guineas' on publication (which was a sum 'greater than had ever at that time been received for a novel'), such rumours were much exaggerated.[31]

Fanny, anxious to secure the 'future portion' of Alex (who could not expect to inherit anything from M. d'A), had agreed with her brother Charles, who again acted as her agent (M. d'A still feared making himself known in London), to publish by subscription. Mrs Boscawen, Mrs Crewe and Mrs Lock agreed to act as book-keepers, listing those who paid the price of one guinea to receive a copy of the novel as soon as it was printed. They included 'Miss J. Austen of Steventon Rectory' and Madame Schwellenberg; while Edmund Burke sent £20 for a single copy. From the money raised in advance, Fanny had to pay the printing costs, which Charles negotiated with William Strahan, who charged £183 6s 0d (they opted to print on cheap rather than hot-pressed, wire-woven glazed paper). But again Charles gave her bad advice by encouraging her to sell the copyright, which she did for £1,000 to Messrs Payne and Cadell of Mews-Gate and the Strand.[32]

After the initial rush to buy Madame d'Arblay's latest novel, sales began to dwindle and *Camilla* was not reprinted until 1802. William Hazlitt's recollection that as a young man he had sat up all night reading the first two volumes (despite having walked all day in the rain) was not typical.[33] Horace Walpole complained to a friend, 'I have not recovered of it enough to be loud in its praise',[34] while the reviewer in the *Scots Magazine* concluded, 'From the author of *Evelina much* was expected, but we are afraid *Camilla* will rather disappoint the generality of readers. There is in our opinion, neither character nor incident to keep up the attention through five long volumes, even with all Mrs d'Arblay's good sense and nicety of discrimination.' (Fanny was most annoyed by being referred to as 'Mrs d'Arblay' rather than 'Madame'.) The most hurtful criticisms came from the *British Critic*, which admired Fanny's 'genius' for calling up 'so great a number of distinctly characterized personages . . . and succeed[ing] so well in making them act consistently, in such a variety of situations', but pointed out the 'transgressions against grammar' and the 'Gallicisms' that peppered her prose. Other critics, too, observed that Fanny's prose was less than elegant.[35] She was not a stylish writer – which is not surprising if one considers that she was never given any formal schooling – and her marriage to a Frenchman further corrupted her use of language.

And yet, without *Camilla*, one cannot help wondering whether we would now have novels such as Maria Edgeworth's *Belinda* or even Jane Austen's *Sense and Sensibility*. Fanny was innovatory. Camilla's mother, Mrs Tyrold, always refers to her husband as her 'partner', rather than as her lord and master. Their servants are also portrayed in a refreshingly different light. Now that Fanny had actually experienced what it felt like to be at the mercy of someone else's demands (no matter how kindly a mistress), and to sit in waiting for the summons of a bell, she knew that 'servants have eyes as well as their masters', and that they, too, were vital members of the household. When, for instance, Sir Hugh assembled the family to announce (prematurely, as it turns out) Camilla and Edgar's nuptials, he insisted on including all the servants 'who have no right to be left out'.[36] Servants, too, play a pivotal role in the tortuous plot.

Fanny, however, missed the vital influence of Susan, who, no doubt, would have advised her sister that the novel needed cutting. In late 1795, Susan had been forced to leave her cottage in Mickleham after her husband resigned his commission in the Marines. Although he had not been to sea since before his marriage, Captain Phillips had been retired on half-pay, which at least provided him with some income. While Susan camped out with her brothers and sisters in London, Captain Phillips travelled to Ireland to prepare the farmhouse he had eventually inherited at Belcotton in County Louth. Susan had no wish to leave her family, only to face an uncertain and lonely future in Ireland; and her unwillingness was increased by the fear that the Irish were preparing to ally themselves with the new French Republic against Britain. (Indeed, in 1797 the United Irishmen did invite the French to land in Ireland, and in June 1798 Susan was on her own at Belcotton when houses in the countryside were being plundered by the rebels.)

Susan turned to Fanny for advice – just as Fanny had talked through with her whether or not she should marry M. d'A. But Fanny, immersed in the happiness of her life at the Hermitage, does not appear to have understood Susan's plight. She was totally absorbed in her 'bambino', describing to Susan every detail of his development (and giving us glimpses of a quite new Fanny). She played ball with her baby in bed before getting up in the morning; and watched over his cradle at night, noticing his every expression. In her contentment, she failed to recognise the distress of her sister, who was enduring the misery of a marriage that had gone damagingly sour.

Money was probably the key to Captain Phillips's hostility. In the autumn of 1795, he had asked Dr Burney for a loan so that he could extend the Belcotton estate. Dr Burney agreed, presumably because he wanted to safeguard Susan's future. But, unwisely, he lent his wayward son-in-law far more than he could afford – some £2,000. Captain Phillips promised to repay the loan annually, with interest, but failed to do so, and by 1814 (when Dr Burney died) the loan had increased to £2,917. It became a constant irritation to Dr Burney, and meant that Susan became a nagging reminder to Phillips of his indebtedness to her family.

Phillips left for Ireland at the end of 1795, taking their elder son, Norbury, with him, presumably in an attempt to remove him from the influence of the Burneys. When Fanny was at Windsor to present her novel the following July, she was embarrassed by questions she could not answer about the health of Norbury, whom the Duchess of York had rescued a couple of years earlier after a coaching accident on the Dorking road in which Norbury had been run over. Fanny had no idea of her nephew's whereabouts.

When Captain Phillips returned to England the following August, he arrived without ten-year-old Norbury, who had been left with a tutor in Dublin. And he demanded that his wife and their other children (Fanny, aged thirteen, and five-year-old Willy) should travel back to Ireland with him. Susan did not want to go, and begged her sisters for advice.

They met on 11 September at Charlotte's home in No. 9 Downing Street, although no record of the sisters' gathering survives: all mention of it was later deleted by Fanny. But it seems that Susan was persuaded to accompany her husband back to Belcotton, despite her evident unhappiness. In the letter she wrote to Fanny afterwards, she promised her sister that she would accept the obligation of 'wifely submission', and a couple of months later she left London bound for Ireland.

Fanny's advice now seems unfeeling, but in the late eighteenth century marital breakdown had to be endured (especially by the wife) rather than railed against. In the few cases where couples braved the ecclesiastical courts to secure a legal divorce, the only outcome for the wife (whether or not she was the guilty party) was social ostracism, poverty *and* total divorce from her children.[37] Susan could, perhaps, have stayed behind in London, but she risked never being allowed to see Norbury again – and it would have meant living off her brothers and sisters for the rest of her life. Susan wrote to Fanny afterwards: 'the terrible struggle is over – I think I shall be capable of submitting as you would have me'.[38]

At the same time as Susan was undergoing the painful realisation that her marriage had broken down, their stepsister Maria was also planning to leave her husband. After the excitement of their elopement, the Rishtons had soon discovered their incompatibility. But Maria did not complain until she discovered some time in 1796 that her husband had been deceiving her for years – and with her closest friend. Maria stayed in Chelsea with Dr Burney for most of 1797, while she negotiated a financial settlement with her husband. But she was lucky: she had an inheritance from her father, Mr Allen of King's Lynn, which she had brought to her marriage as a dowry. Even so, it took her almost five years to free herself from Rishton and set up her own home in Bury St Edmunds. They never formally divorced: Maria was fortunate in being able to persuade Rishton to release her from her marital vows, and to secure from him the guarantee of £300 per annum.

Susan, however, had no such financial resource. And so on Friday,

14 October 1796, she and Captain Phillips set off from James's house in Westminster, after making a brief visit to Norbury Park to say farewell to Fanny and the Locks. Fanny was too overcome to watch from the window as her 'beloved Susan' drove away from this 'seat of happiness' for what would be the last time. Dr Burney had by then disclosed to Fanny his fears about Captain Phillips (who had been promoted to Major before his resignation from the Marines):

> I am fearful that this half mad & unfeeling Major means to travel to the seaside in a strange kind of open carriage, which is constructed with a basket that is to contain the whole family! . . . If I find that his plan, I shall remonstrate, though Susan & prudence would not let me attempt to interfere about the Irish Journey: as I had no hope of working upon his wrong-headed & tyrannical spirit . . . & there was great reason to fear the making bad worse, by putting him out of humour, since we *must*, circumstanced as we are, submit.[39]

Dr Burney was desperately worried that his 'favourite girl' was now at the mercy of a husband of such 'tyrannical' temper and 'wrong-headed' plans. But his concern – especially the danger to Susan's vulnerable health from this uncomfortable 270-mile journey across bad roads in windy, wet weather – was pushed to the back of his mind when, less than a week later, his wife collapsed and died (she was sixty-eight). Dr Burney was devastated. Although Fanny could never bring herself to say anything kind about her stepmother (even criticising her for asking her daughter, Sarah Harriet, and maid Molly not to call Dr Burney during the night if anything should happen to her, to spare him the shock until the morning), he was obviously very attached to his second wife, whom he described as 'the dearest part of myself'. When she died, he was unable to deal with his grief, hiding from his friends and refusing to go out. James and Charles had to take charge of all the arrangements for her funeral, and the family took it in turns to have their father to stay, in the hope that this would stir him out of his depression.

Fanny – though she missed Susan – was so wrapped up in Alex and in M. d'A's plans to build their own home (from the money Fanny had made from *Camilla*) that she failed to take any direct action to help her. And, on the day of Susan's departure for Ireland, Fanny wrote to her father to let him know that work was to begin almost immediately on Camilla Cottage, which was to be built on the land William Lock had given them in the hamlet of West Humble. Much of the work was done by the resourceful M. d'A, who swapped his military uniform for a green leather cap and workman's overalls and dug the 100-foot well and a miniature ha-ha to protect his precious vegetable patch from their cow. Sadly, Camilla Cottage was burned down in 1919, but M. d'A's sketch of the exterior has survived, as have his plans for the interior, which show that the ground floor of the two-storey 'rough-cast stone building' was devoted to a reception room, playroom, dining-room and kitchen, while upstairs there was a book room (wisely placed between the d'Arblays' bedroom and Alex's nursery) and a spare bedroom 'in case one or the other is ill'. There was a room, too, for Alex's nurse, which, generously, was the same size as the 'Chambre de Monsieur et Madame'.[40]

It was a bad time to begin such an expensive project: by its completion, M. d'A had spent more than £1,300 in labour and materials, despite doing much of the work himself. The uncertainty caused by the war with France that had begun in 1793 meant that prices fluctuated wildly, making it impossible for M. d'A to budget the costs of his building work. (On 16 December 1796, for example, forty-five French ships, bound for Ireland, had sailed from Brest with more than 15,000 troops. The fierce gales scattered the fleet and saved the English navy from a costly engagement – but this was to be only a temporary reprieve.) The Government, desperate for money to augment the navy and the army, instituted a new system of fiscal assessment by which households were to be taxed according to their income and assets (such as male servants, carriages and 'pleasure' horses – hair-powder was already a rich source of revenue). Dr Burney reckoned he would have to pay another £80 a year, while Charles and Hetty Burney had to move out of their home in Titchfield Street (where they had lived for almost fourteen years) into cheaper lodgings in Beaumont Street, off Devonshire Place.

The d'Arblays were less affected – they had only one female servant and lived without the expense of a coach or hair-powder – but they feared they would have to pay an extra 0.9 per cent of their annual income (about £1.10s).[41] M. d'A reduced the number of windows in Camilla Cottage so that he would have to pay less duty on the glass. When he and Fanny eventually moved into their new home in October 1797, there was no furniture apart from 'a little Bench borrowed of one of the departing Carpenters', no cutlery (they cut up their bread for lunch with a garden knife), and only a single saucepan in which they boiled some eggs they had brought with them. But, Fanny told Susan,

'We dined . . . exquisitely, & drank to our new possession from a Glass of clear water out of our new Well', warmed by 'a glorious fire' lit by M. d'A to welcome Fanny and Alex.[42]

It is painful now to read these letters written by Fanny to Susan – with all their effusions of domestic happiness – knowing that Susan would have read them in the comfortless sitting-room at Belcotton, virtually deserted by her husband (who was besotted with one of their neighbours, Jane Brabazon), separated from Norbury (who was boarding with a family in Dublin) and faced by bleak views across the flat coastal plain of the River Boyne (so very different from the rolling countryside of Surrey) whenever she looked out of the window. On 8 December, she wrote to Charlotte: 'I cannot boast of Belcotton as a very beautiful spot but our sitting room is warm, & the bedrooms tolerably so – I do not complain of want of neighbours, for I bear retirement better than uninteresting society.' But by the following October she was writing:

> We have here had a summer resembling a cold autumn – scarce a day of enjoyable weather – at least to me, who loves warmth . . . This is not the land of improvement my dear Charlotte – we see & hear daily much that ought to be shunned, & little or nothing that can raise emulation, or that deserves to be copied . . . My Willy copies the tones & manners of all the little & great Paddys he meets with much too successfully – but in his *inward* self he is not I hope the worse, – it vexes me nevertheless a good deal to hear his vehement brogue.[43]

Susan kept to herself Phillips's misdeeds and her own physical decline. Hetty had some insight into Susan's distress and hinted to Fanny that all was far from well at Belcotton. She was careful, however, not to alarm the hypersensitive Fanny, who continued to write monthly epistles to Susan filled with accounts of her own happy life. Thus, in the midst of her desolation, Susan received a long twenty-page account of Alex's presentation at Court, which took place on 8 March 1798, when Fanny dressed her three-year-old son in a new white muslin frock and sash and took him to the Queen's House to spend the morning with the younger princesses – Elizabeth, Sophia and Amelia – and the Queen. Fanny displays all the usual motherly fears that her 'little Savage' will disgrace himself: Alex duly complied by first refusing to speak to anyone and then, after being given a wooden Noah's Ark by the Queen, gaining enough confidence to rush along the palace corridors like a 'wild deer', and precipitating a hasty departure by bursting into the private sanctum of the King and Queen's bedroom.

Earlier, Susan had received a gruesome description of Alex's inoculation for smallpox: an incision was made in his arm and blood was forced out to ensure that the vaccine entered his bloodstream. Fanny had witnessed the inoculation of Princess Amelia while she was at Court, and had read widely on the subject before writing the scene in *Camilla* in which Eugenia catches the pox at Northwick Fair. She knew all too well what Alex would have to suffer. But she had grown up with the fear of smallpox: there was a severe outbreak of the disease in King's Lynn in 1754 while the Burneys were living there. Five days after his inoculation, Alex became, 'pale, languid, hot & short breathed . . . his Eyes became red, dull & heavy, his breath feverish, & his limbs in almost convulsive tribulation. His starts were so violent, it was difficult to hold him during his short sleeps, & his cries from pain & nameless sufferings grew incessant'. But the fever dissipated two days later, when the spots began to appear; fortunately, these were not severe and Alex soon recovered, with only a few minor blemishes.[44]

Fanny began to think of writing another play – perhaps encouraged by Sheridan, who at the end of 1796 bought the Polesden Lacey estate and the manor of West Humble, and was therefore a close neighbour. By the autumn of 1799, 'Love and Fashion', a comedy, was finished, and a copy of the script was sent (via Charles) to the actor-manager Thomas Harris for approval (he of the unwanted advances to Elizabeth Inchbald). Harris immediately accepted it for production at Covent Garden the following March, offering Fanny £400 outright. When Charles wrote to tell his sister the good news, he mentioned that Harris had remarked that he was surprised 'you never turned your thoughts to this kind of writing before; as you appear to have really a genius for it'.[45] Fanny was not taken in by such flattery, regarding herself as engaged upon a commercial, rather than literary, trans-action – to make money for her son's future. In her correspondence with Charles, she referred to Harris as 'the upholsterer' of her bare script. Her choice of profession for Harris is intriguing, suggesting that she realised Harris's role was to take the frame of her script and furnish a successful play from it.

'Love and Fashion' was never staged, but the fact that Fanny defied her father by again attempting to write for the theatre was indicative of her new-found confidence, and of her desire to find her own way to make money. M. d'A had heard news of his family in the autumn of 1798, and was threatening to risk a return to France.

Would the comedy have been a success? The surviving manuscript shows that it was not as cleverly plotted or as witty as 'The Witlings'.[46] The storyline – two brothers, one of whom is good and kindly, the other arrogant and self-important, are both in love – is predictable and weighed down by its message: the foolishness of Fashion, and the importance of marrying for love, not personal gain. And yet there is a truly farcical element to the setting – a haunted house full of inner rooms and locked closets, from which ghosts and various 'lost' characters keep emerging. Fanny also makes some incisive comments on the credit-culture of the late eighteenth century, in which sons gambled away entire fortunes *before* inheriting them (the Prince of Wales had debts amounting to £630,000 in 1795), and makes fun of those landlords who wasted their money on foppish hats and silk waistcoats while their tenants lived in rough smocks and survived on bread and cheese. But it would be difficult to argue now that this comedy could have established Fanny's reputation as a dramatist. Her comic edge was blunted by her concern to invest her writing with a moral purpose. Thus her heroine concludes, 'Ah, if even in solitude I am thus enchanted, what must be the rural life with a chosen companion?'[47] A reflection, perhaps, on Fanny's own domestic happiness.

By the spring of 1800, however, Fanny's contentment had been 'cruelly blasted'.

ELEVEN

Paris and Pain
1799–1812

Though the Busts & Medallions I have seen are, in general, such good resemblances, that I think I should have known him untold, he has by no means the look to be expected from Bonaparte, – but rather that of a profoundly studious & contemplative Man.

Madame d'Arblay, May 1802

In September 1799 the Burneys began to realise they must rescue Susan from her unhappy exile. Fanny had already written to 'Forlorn House', as Susan called Belcotton, advising her to 'Have a *whole quire of mutilated paper* at once, my dearest, – 'tis the best way: only carefully avoid any Written marks at the cutting – & if you draw a line, it will be safer not to cut till it arrives. 'Tis the only way to be comfortable with this blasting secret business which still demands concealment, & still preys on both our minds.'[1] Major Phillips had become so suspicious of letters from the Burneys (they were, indeed, offering to send Susan money so that she could travel to England without him) that Fanny suggested Susan should slice out those sections that referred to coming home, and conceal this by pasting over the gap. Fanny feared that the Major would take out on Susan his jealousy and guilt if he discovered what was being written about him.

Fanny, however, had no idea that her sister was dangerously ill. And when she heard from Major Phillips 'that the first £50 he can command shall restore Susan to her friends', she rejoiced. But a few days later, the Major wrote again, this time to William Lock. The reason for his sudden about-turn was that he was himself 'anxious' about his wife, whose condition had evidently deteriorated suddenly.[2] Both James and Charles were so alarmed that they both wrote to Susan separately, promising to meet her when she landed at Parkgate. The shortest crossing from Dublin was to Holyhead (in Wales), but the road to London from Parkgate on the River Dee, some twelve miles north of Chester, was quicker. Parkgate was a busy port in the eighteenth century, but has since become silted up, its quayside row of houses and inns little changed from 1799. Charles promised to bear the 'whole expence of her Journey from Belcotton to Greenwich, if he [Phillips] will let her come', hiring a private coach so that Susan could travel more comfortably than by the post-chaise.

William Lock, perhaps understanding that Major Phillips was reluctant to take money from the Burneys, organised with his bank for an account of £150 to be opened in Susan's name, which she could then draw on to pay her own way to London. When Fanny heard what Lock had felt compelled to do, she realised finally the gravity of Susan's illness. 'Greatly shocked and frightened', she threatened to leave immediately for Belcotton, writing to Major Phillips that she must see and judge for herself the real state of Susan's health, and to her father that they must all make 'a desperate effort to rescue Susan from her captivity, or tremble at the risk of her passing another Winter in such a situation'.[3]

It was too little, too late. When Susan finally left Belcotton in the first week of December, she was so weak she could not endure the forty-mile journey to Dublin without stopping overnight to recuperate. Weakened by constant fever, she was also suffering from some kind of bowel disorder. That she continued on her way to London, crossing the Irish Sea in the middle of winter in an open yacht, suggests her immense courage and her determination to be with her family once more.

Charles set out from Greenwich on Christmas Eve (with his son Charles Parr), arriving at the White Lion Inn in Chester on 26 December, where he discovered from the other passengers that the boat on which the Phillips had crossed from Ireland had landed at Holyhead, ninety miles away. Concerned for Susan, he could not decide whether to wait for her in Parkgate, where they had agreed to meet, or dash to Holyhead in a hired chaise and risk missing her on the way. After receiving a letter from Susan's daughter Fanny, confirming their arrival at Holyhead, Charles set off across the snowy, mountainous roads of Wales (no small decision for a man later noted for his hatred of draughts). Four days later, on New Year's Eve, he was back in Chester – without his sister. Susan and Major Phillips with Fanny (then aged seventeen) and William (just eight) had arrived in Parkgate the day before. Norbury, who was then fourteen, had been left behind in Dublin.

Too exhausted to travel on to Parkgate that night, Charles finally met his 'poor, sweet Susey' on 1 January 1800. He wrote immediately to Dr Burney and to Fanny, reassuring them that Susan was safely arrived, but had to admit that she was too weak to travel any further and that he would stay with the Phillips in Parkgate until she had recovered sufficient strength to continue on their way. The Major added, 'We *are all very merry & comfortable* here.' Charles, however, later admitted to his father that when he first saw his sister, he knew instinctively that she could not live beyond two days.[4] He was right. Fanny did not hear that Susan was safely back in England until 7 January, by which time, with an awful irony, Charles was already making arrangements for Susan's funeral.

On the morning of 6 January (the day after her forty-fifth birthday), Susan's maid had rushed in 'with a face of alarm' while Charles was breakfasting with Major Phillips. They both went upstairs to see Susan, but did not stay with her longer than about ten minutes. She had spent a very restless night, racked by pain, and was barely conscious. Her husband said nothing and shortly afterwards left the house, taking his daughter out 'on pretence of buying shoes; but in reality to prepare her, for what he dreaded'. Charles went back to sit with Susan, 'but she knew me not: – she saw me not – she spoke to me not'. At twenty minutes to two o'clock, he felt 'the last tremor of her pulse'. 'The poor sweet soul', he would always remember, died as she had lived, 'without a murmur'.

Susan was buried in the graveyard at Neston, by Parkgate, on Friday, 10 January, her memorial stone engraved simply with the words 'In memory of Mrs Susannah Phillips, wife of Major Molesworth Phillips, and daughter of Dr Charles Burney'.[5] Her brother Charles was the 'solitary mourner'. Fanny and M. d'A did not hear the dreadful news until 9 January, when Lock told them he had heard from Phillips that Susan had died (her husband had hoped to lessen the shock by sending the news to Norbury Park rather than direct to Fanny; he was not, it seems, entirely selfish and unfeeling).[6] That afternoon M. d'A sent a messenger to Dorking, ordering a chaise to take him and Fanny from Camilla Cottage up to London, in the hope that they would arrive at Charing Cross in time to catch the night-mail to Chester (five-year-old Alex was left behind with his nursemaid). But to no avail: they missed it and were, in any case, warned that the roads to the North were impassable because of heavy snowfalls and they could not hope to reach Parkgate in time for the funeral. Too upset to return home, the d'Arblays made their way across town to Chelsea, arriving at Dr Burney's by midnight.

Fanny could not believe that 'the soul of my soul' had died without her being aware of it; indeed, for many weeks she kept thinking that 'it is not – & that she will come'.[7] Fanny refused to see anyone, remaining in Chelsea College without even visiting her sisters. M. d'A, too, was banished: there was no room for him at Dr Burney's, so he stayed with Hetty and her family in Beaumont Street. Fanny was unable to cry, retreating into a silent vigil devoted to the memory of her to whom she said she owed all the happiness of her early life, and, she confided to Mrs Lock, even her husband: 'It was SHE first made me love him.'[8]

For the rest of her life Fanny would always keep 6 January as a day of meditation: fifteen years later she wrote in her diary for that day, 'Oh day – for ever dreaded – yet for ever loved! That Gave, & took away my angel sister!'[9] She insisted on spending it alone so that she could think only of Susan, reading from the 'Consolatory Extracts' that she compiled in 1800 in an effort to overcome her 'extremity of grief'. This small pocket-book of eighty-two folios contains 'improving' passages from writers such as Miss Talbot, Mrs Chapone and Mrs Carter, copied out by Fanny in an uneven, blotchy script as if written in great distress. She even included advice to 'Imagine Those We Love Dead Whilst Yet Living' from Madame de Staël, who perforce had learned how to cope with the sudden loss of those close to her.[10]

Many of these consoling thoughts suggest ways of dealing with the anger that followed her first numbness (why Susan? why *my* best beloved sister?). There is also much on forgiveness, both for Fanny, who had failed seemingly to recognise Susan's distress in those last years, and for Major Phillips, whom Fanny blamed directly for Susan's death. One page is devoted to Miss Talbot's warning that 'The use of retirement is to fit us for moving more beneficially in the World; & mixing in the World is of use to rub off the rust which the best & ablest minds will contract in long retirement.'[11] M. d'A, indeed, had to reprove his wife gently for indulging her grief, writing to her in May an essay that was very like the Thèmes of their courtship: 'What do you speak of a mind at a loss to express itself, You who are so well gifted with all that can deck thoughts by words – Try to understand what I mean and cannot write . . . Don't forget that our beloved Sister wished all things to see you happy. Her everlasting love is the same, and your happiness is yet her imperishable wish. Why will you not gratify it!'[12]

Fanny had been reluctant to return to West Humble – with all its reminders of her 'lost darling' – and had insisted on spending a month with her father, before moving on to spend another month with Charles and his family in Greenwich. She and M. d'A eventually arrived back at Camilla Cottage at the beginning of March, but even then she refused for three weeks to go out. In despair, M. d'A secretly went to fetch Mrs Lock, who insisted that her friend should 'take an airing'. Fanny complied and was forced to admit afterwards, 'I am glad of it, for it has done me good, & broken a kind of spell that made me unwilling to stir.' On the same day, she assured Charlotte (who was now living in Brighton with her second husband, Ralph Broome; Clement Francis had died of a stroke in 1792), 'Time will wear this away – time – & more submissive reflexions upon the change that to HER must be as much happier as to me it is more wretched.' But she would forever mourn the loss of her 'darling Confidant'. She had, she told Charlotte, 'lost my power of retaining and retailing – & my recollections & ideas all run – I know not how – incoherently against one another.'[13]

Once again, Fanny collapsed physically under the strain of her extreme emotional reaction. But this time she had the support and encouragement of M. d'A, and she never lost sight of her purpose – to continue writing. 'Love and Fashion', which Fanny had been preparing for production at Covent Garden at the end of 1799, was withdrawn from rehearsal after Susan's death, but not before an advertisement appeared in the *Morning Chronicle*, which was seen by Dr Burney. He had not known that his daughter was still writing comedies and was much displeased. Fanny wrote to him to reassure him that the play would not be performed that season; her letter is very different in tone from her earlier submission to her father (and Mr Crisp) over 'The Witlings':

This release by Thomas Harris gives me present repose which indeed I much wanted – for to combat your – to me – unaccountable but most afflicting displeasure, in the midst of my own panics & disturbance, would have been ample punishment to me, had I been guilty of a crime in doing what I have all my life been urged to, & all my life intended, writing a Comedy. Your goodness, your kindness, your regard for my fame, I know have caused both your trepidation, which doomed me to *certain* failure; & your displeasure that I ran, what you thought, a wanton risk. But it is not wanton, my dearest Father. My imagination is not at my own controll, or I would always have continued in the walk you approved. The combinations for another long work did not occur to me. Incidents & effects for a Drama did. I thought the field more than open – inviting to me. The chance held out golden dreams. The risk could be only our own for – permit me to say, appear when it will, you will find nothing in the principles, the moral, or the language that will make you blush for me. A *failure*, upon these points only, can bring DISGRACE – upon mere control or want of dramatic powers, it can only cause *disappointment*.

This time Fanny had no intention of abandoning her work. She continued by comparing, rather cheekily, her literary achievements to those of her father, who was working on an essay on the planets entitled 'Astronomy: An Historical and Didactic Poem':

I hope, therefore, my dearest Father, in thinking this over, you will cease to nourish such terrors & disgust at an essay so natural, & rather say to yourself with an internal smile, 'After all – 'tis but *like Father like Child* – for to what walk do I confine myself? – She took my example in writing – She takes it in ranging – Why, then, after all, should I lock her up in one paddock, well as she has fed there, if she says she finds nothing more to nibble – while *I* find all the Earth unequal to my ambition, & mount the skies to content it? Come on then, poor Fan – The World has acknowledged you my offspring – & I will *disencourage* you no more. Leap the pales of your paddock – *let us pursue our career* – & while you frisk from novel to Comedy, I quitting Music & Prose, will try a race with Poetry & the Stars.

She hoped 'my dear Father, will not infer, from this appeal, I mean to parallel our Works – no one more truly measures their own inferiority, which with respect to yours has always been my pride: – I only mean to shew, that if my Muse loves a little variety – She has an hereditary claim to try it.' Fanny usually ended letters to her father with the words 'your most dutiful & affectionate daughter F. d'A' but on this occasion she merely initialled it, 'F.d'A.'[14]

We do not have Dr Burney's response, but that Fanny was now capable of writing such a declaration of her commitment to what she believed she *must* do suggests that her various physical and emotional crises had strengthened, rather than diminished, her self-belief. And when M. d'A began writing to his wife a series of Thèmes about his childhood in Joigny in an effort to reawaken her desire to write, and to record, Fanny was encouraged to respond (in French) by telling him stories about life at Streatham Park and her friendship with Dr Johnson. She also began work on 'A Busy Day', perhaps her most accomplished comedy.[15]

Once again, however, circumstances over which she had no control prevented her from fulfilling her ambition. In April 1800, the name of Alexandre d'Arblay was deleted from the list of émigrés and M. d'A began to think of returning to France. He had drastically over-spent on the construction of Camilla Cottage, which was still without all its curtains and carpets, and the combination of rising prices (there were bread riots in Dorking in March and April) and increased taxes meant that Fanny's income from her pension and the interest on the small profits from *Evelina* and *Cecilia*, was no longer enough to support them. (The pound had halved in value since 1780.) M. d'A could see no alternative but to return to Joigny in the hope that he could salvage the d'Arblay estates. Although France was still at war with Britain, the conflict within appeared to have burned itself out: the Directory had been overthrown at the end of November 1799, followed a fortnight later on 15 December by Napoleon's declaration as First Consul.

When M. d'A heard from his mother's brother, Jean-Baptiste-Gabriel Bazille, that £1,000 would be available to him immediately *if* he signed, sealed and witnessed the rights to his property to his nearest surviving relation in France, *in a country not at war with France* (i.e. not Britain), he immediately applied for a passport, which gave him permission to travel to Holland but not France. On Monday, 17 November 1800, he left West Humble bound for Rotterdam. A month later he was back in Gravesend, where he had to wait until an 'internal' passport was issued, allowing him as an 'alien' to travel cross-country from Kent to Camilla Cottage. His trip had been fruitless: the situation in France was still too chaotic to enable him to retrieve even a small portion of his fortune.

Throughout the following year, 1801, the d'Arblays were beset by money worries, and Fanny's letters are filled with fears for her husband. M. d'A had offered to serve Napoleon in his Garde Consulaire, just as he had earlier served in Louis XVI's Garde Nationale Parisienne. Fanny was appalled, both by the idea of her husband endangering his life in military combat, and by the potential embarrassment of being an Englishwoman married to someone who was working *for* the enemy; especially since her brother James was seeking at the same time a new command in the British navy to fight *against* Napoleon. And yet, despite Fanny's opposition to such a plan, when M. d'A heard that his friend Narbonne had returned to Paris and been awarded a pension for his years of military service before the Revolution, he decided that he, too, must go back. Further encouraged by the news that the preliminaries to the Treaty of Amiens between France and Britain had been signed, he rushed up to London in mid-October 1801 to secure passports for himself, and for his wife and son.[16]

In the end Fanny and Alex did not go with him – Alex, who had grown into a thin, sickly child, had a fever and Fanny was concerned that the journey might be too much for him. M. d'A set off alone for Paris on 26 October; he had a terrible journey. Blown off-course along the coast, his boat first took refuge in Margate, then at Deal and Dover, before limping across to France and arriving in Calais almost a fortnight later. He was lucky to survive the storms. Twenty-five French naval gunboats *en route* from Calais to Dunkirk were lost at sea, and *The Times* reported that it was 'the most heavy gale of wind ever remembered'. Fanny did not learn of her husband's safe arrival until 12 November, waiting in terrible anxiety for more than a fortnight before hearing from him. The storm swept through the South of England, lashing the windows of Camilla Cottage, so that she could well imagine the conditions at sea. When she did eventually receive a letter from her 'Partner in all', he told her of his pleasure in being back in Paris, meeting friends he had not seen since before the Revolution.

Fanny occupied herself by attempting to finish 'A Busy Day', determined that this was the way to resolve their financial troubles. She wrote to 'Citoyen Darblay' – as she began to call M. d'A just in case her letters were intercepted – to assure him that she would comply with whatever he decided, but also to remind him that she was 'not without views, as well as hopes, of ameliorating our condition!' Two days later, she wrote again to say that these 'views' and 'hopes' would 'not break into our way of life': in other words, *if* she earned enough from the production and publication of 'A Busy Day', then they could stay in their Hermitage, where, she emphasised to her husband, he would always be 'master of your own *Time, leisure, Hours, Gardening, scribbling, & reading!*' 'Weigh, weigh it well,' she pleaded with him, hoping to dissuade M. d'A from his plans to live again in France.[17]

She also wrote to her friend at Court, Miss Planta (originally employed to look after the young princesses but later a companion and reader to the Queen), in the hope that she would pass on the *true* story of M. d'A's dealings with Napoleon. Fanny's name was still 'news', and she feared that reports of her possible domicile in France would appear in the newspapers and be read by the Queen. She emphasised that M. d'A had refused to return to France while that country was at war with Britain, but confessed that he had travelled to Holland 'in order to attempt the recovery of what little might yet remain unsold of his small patrimony: but that now there was PEACE, he meant immediately to visit his Relations & friends, & take with him his wife & son'. Miss Planta's reply reassured Fanny that Her Majesty 'quite approves' of M. d'A's visit to his native country; indeed, it was 'a duty he owes to his family'.

Fanny, discreetly, had made no mention of M. d'A's intention to secure an army pension from France. Nor did she admit that, while in Paris, M. d'A had visited his former military chief, Lafayette. She would have been shocked to hear that M. d'A had also been seeking a personal audience with the First Consul. For the first time, an edge enters Fanny's letters to her husband during this three-month separation. She sensed and feared M. d'A's pleasure and relief at being able to talk French freely again and to live once more the life of a metropolitan gentleman. Perhaps, she asked him, 'the renewed public sort of life you are leading' had 'lessened your taste for retirement'?[18]

Her fears were justified. Lafayette had introduced M. d'A to Napoleon's Minister of War, General Berthier, who had offered d'Arblay the command of a brigade, *on condition* that he agreed to take part in the expedition to St Domingo (now Haiti) to crush the rebels against the French colonial government. Fanny's response when M. d'A told her of his plans was one of quiet outrage: 'This is a great surprise indeed.' She had thought her husband safely on the road back to Calais. She pleaded with him to remember his wife and child before committing himself to such a rash and dangerous enterprise: 'I dread an over-strained effort of courage, a *desire d'une blessure* more than words can say.' (More than 34,000 French troops set off for St Domingo, of which 24,000 died within a year.)[19]

M. d'A set out for England, hoping that a face-to-face discussion with Fanny would persuade her that he had no alternative. They were, he told her, running out of money while living in Camilla Cottage – which they owned and where they had striven so hard to be self-sufficient – so how could they afford to live anywhere else *unless* he found some way to make money? But he was a Frenchman whose only profession was as a soldier. How, then, could he find gainful employment in Britain? His only hope was to go to St Domingo, thereby proving his loyalty to Napoleon. Perhaps then he would receive a military pension and retrieve at least a portion of his lost estates.

By 24 January 1802, M. d'A was back in Dover, waiting for an 'internal' passport from the Aliens' Office. He spent the time reading Petrarch's sonnets on the torments of love. When permission to travel was finally granted, he did not go home to West Humble: instead, Fanny and Alex went to meet him at Charles's house in Greenwich where, reluctantly, Fanny accepted that her husband had no choice but to take this risk. While M. d'A spent a hectic few days in London buying equipment for his expedition (maps, books, instruments, weapons) and procuring another exit passport to France, Fanny and seven-year-old Alex returned forlornly to Camilla Cottage, where she packed up their belongings and arranged for it to be let. They had decided that she and Alex should look for rented rooms in Richmond, which would be cheaper than staying on in West Humble. An advertisement eventually appeared in *The Times* on 7 April, offering for rent:

> a small Modern COUNTRY RESIDENCE, fitted up in the cottage stile, with 5 acres of garden, orchard, pleasure, and meadow land, in a rural and healthy situation, between the Town of Dorking, and the beautiful Vale of Mickleham, in the centre of many romantic and extensive prospects, 22 miles from London, and a quarter of a mile from an Inn on the London Road, where horses, &c may stand at livery, there being no coach-house or stables on the Premises; for the term of 12 or 18 months.

M. d'A left for France in mid-February and, for almost a month, Fanny lived with the fear that he would be killed. Meanwhile she had to face the embarrassing duty of writing again to Miss Planta to inform the Queen that M. d'A would be fighting *under the orders of Napoleon*. After a long-winded explanation of his reasons for agreeing to re-enter the French army (his hope that he would then receive half-pay in consideration of his former military service), Fanny affirmed that 'it was his M. d'A's inalterable resolution NEVER to take up arms against the British Government'. She added as a postscript, 'I presume to hope *this little detail* may, at some convenient moment, meet Her Majesty's Eyes – with every expression of my profoundest devotion.' Fanny was concerned that her pension might be withdrawn.[20]

On 14 March, however, she at last heard from her husband; a letter that brought both good and bad news. Fanny's relief on being told by M. d'A that he had not been allowed to join the expedition to St Domingo, because of his refusal to fight against his wife's native country, was tempered by his desolation. He considered himself disgraced by Napoleon: '*La cause qu'il assigne à cette disgrace, à la quelle je n'étais rien moins que préparé, est ma declaration de ne point servir contre la patrie de ma femme, qui peut encore être armée contre la République.*'[21] Alone in Paris, he begged Fanny to hurry and join him there: he could not leave France because his exit passport had been granted on the understanding that he would not attempt to re-enter Britain for one year.

Although the First Consul assured M. d'A that he bore '*le mari de Cecilia*' no resentment, this was little consolation. From being second-in-command to Lafayette at the head of the French army in Austria, M. d'A was now a disgraced soldier with barely enough money to rent a couple of rooms in Paris. Indeed, he was reduced to suggesting to Fanny that she should ask Charles to bear the expense of her journey to France. She tactfully refused – like her father, she would never take on a debt, no matter how small. Instead, she asked her brother to find for her the cheapest ticket. On the morning of Thursday, 15 April 1802, she and Alex set out at dawn to catch the diligence to Dover, which left from the White Bear Inn on Piccadilly.[22] They took with them Adrienne de Chavagnac (a year older than Alex), who had been left at Norbury Park with the Locks when her émigré parents, who had briefly joined the Juniper Hall community, returned to France in 1795. But her mother had died shortly after returning to the Continent, and Adrienne was now travelling back home to meet her father, whom she had not seen since she was two, and her grandmother, whom she had never known.

Fanny was leaving Britain for the first time; and she did not anticipate much pleasure from the experience. She was convinced that she would be terribly seasick (she was); she could not afford to travel comfortably in her own private chaise, but had to take the cross-Channel diligence, bumping along the uneven roads in close proximity to who knows whom; and she was to travel alone, with no male escort, except for two young and excitable children. 'I cross the sea tomorrow –

FANNY BURNEY

an element I so dread – with 2 children, & not a soul that knows me, or to whom I am known!' she wrote to M. d'A from Dover that Thursday.[23]

Fanny, however, made the most of her situation, describing her fellow passengers as if they were characters in a novel. The drama of her flight to France was stimulating, if also frightening. She had left behind the peaceful retirement of her life in West Humble; she was now homeless, penniless, and journeying into an uncertain future. But she had pen and paper, and she could still enjoy noting down the tell-tale quirks that betrayed what people were *really* like beneath the masks put on each day. She began once again to write long journal-letters, now designed to entertain her father, who at seventy-eight was so crippled with arthritis that he was unable to continue teaching or playing music, and her old friend Frederica Lock.

Fanny had plenty of time to observe her companions: one day on the road to Dover, a day and a night at sea, followed by two and a half days *and* nights of non-stop travel from Calais to Paris. She was amused by the 'sulky haughtiness' of an ex-soldier who was hoping to obtain an introduction to the First Consul. He was soon nicknamed the 'Highland Chief' because of his 'burnt complexion, Scotch accent, large, bony face & Figure, & high & distant demeanour . . . I never heard his name, but I think him a Gentleman BORN, though not gently bred'. The only other male traveller – an Irishman travelling to Paris to study French – was dismissed in similar fashion. He was, she wrote, 'immensely tall, very awkward, & excessively bashful with Eyes that dared look at nobody, yet leered at every body . . . & a figure the most gawky'.

Two women filled the remaining seats in the coach. Fanny was intrigued by Madame de Raymond, who carried with her a small basket of provisions so that she could avoid the expense of dining in the inns on their way. And yet Fanny assumed she must be a 'gentlewoman' because she was accompanied by her maid (who had to travel in 'a basket' attached to the back of the coach). She caused Fanny much grief by making it very clear that she had 'a horrour of being touched by either of my Children, who, poor little Souls, restless & fatigued by confinement they endured, tried to fling themselves upon every passenger in turn'. But in truth she was, like Fanny, a victim of the Revolution, returning penniless to her home after years of exile. Their other female companion, a 'gay, voluble, good-humoured & merry' Frenchwoman, had been trapped in England for

202

ten years and was taking advantage of the newly signed peace to return home and find out if her mother was still alive.[24]

The London–Paris diligence finally rumbled into the rue Notre Dame des Victoires on Tuesday, 20 April. M. d'A was there to greet his wife and son, having waited for four hours in the chill morning air. Ever prudish, Fanny later recalled that she would have preferred not to meet him so publicly after 'so painful & eventful an absence'. But she was too overwhelmed with fatigue and relief to care greatly, and after much hugging and kissing they all scrambled into the fiacre, which took them back to the rue de Miroménil, just north of the Champs-Elysées, where M. d'A had rented an apartment at No. 1185.[25]

Paris, Fanny declared, bore no comparison with London, which was 'immensely superior' to the French capital: the streets were too narrow, the houses so much taller, the pavements little more than muddy paths. But the d'Arblays' apartment, though small and up three flights of stairs, was 'pretty', light and airy, with windows on one side looking on to the gracious gardens of a mansion and, from the other, to the countryside beyond the city. Fanny was besieged with visitors anxious to meet the English wife of M. d'A and author of Cecilia, which had been published in French translation in 1783 to such acclaim that another version appeared the following year. Old friends, too, from Juniper Hall were already back in Paris.

First among their visitors was the Princesse d'Hénin, who arrived with tea and sugar for Fanny and an urn and teapot, so that she could make tea à l'anglaise. The former princess, who had grown up in a château and had married a prince who owned several houses in Paris, had lost most of her family in the Terror and now lived in a small second-floor apartment almost opposite the d'Arblays. Narbonne, too, was a regular visitor – with rooms at No. 1200 rue de Miroménil. Fanny was soon engaged in a whirl of visits and outings. On her first weekend she was taken to the Opéra-Comique, and the following evening was at the Opéra Buffo.

The stability brought by the Peace of Amiens, which was formally announced on 25 March 1802, and the election of Napoleon as First Consul for life on 2 August 1802, encouraged a reawakening of the cultural life of Paris, as if the end of the Terror had unleashed a refreshing determination to have fun. The city filled with visitors from all over Europe, like voyeurs come to see the desolation wrought by the Revolution. They were surprised to find not a subdued, broken atmosphere, but rather a renewed optimism and ambition. Theatres such as the Théâtre Olympique and the Théâtre Mozart were opened; while the musical evenings in the Tivoli Gardens, where the rich and fashionable danced to the new waltzes of Mozart, Haydn and Pleyel, were revived. Novels like Madame de Staël's *Delphine*, with its strong, independent-minded heroine, were a huge success.

Napoleon envisioned his capital as an imperial city, and had already initiated vast building schemes based on Greek and Roman models. New bridges – the Pont des Arts and the Pont d'Austerlitz – were designed; the rue de Rivoli was opened; a huge 'temple' was planned for the place Vendôme. Even fashion was influenced by the classical style: simplicity and naturalism became the rule, in stark contrast to the elaborate flounces and bouffant hairstyles and wigs still current in England.

When Fanny first walked out on to the boulevards of Paris, she realised that her Surrey wardrobe was so behind French fashion as to appear almost as absurd as the grotesqueries of her fictional Madame Duval (Evelina's grandmother). Indeed, she was promptly told by her scandalised *femme de chambre*, Pauline: '*This* won't do! – *That* you can never wear! *This* you can never be seen in! *That* would make you stared at as a curiosity! – THREE petticoats! No one wears more than one! – STAYS? every body has left off even corsets! – Shift sleeves? not a soul now wears even a chemise!' For while the ladies of Hanoverian London still laboured under layers of restrictive undergarments, the women of Napoleon's Paris had thrown off their whalebones and had adopted the plain, high-waisted dresses later known as the 'Empire style'. Undeterred, Fanny had no intention of revealing her bare arms or of exposing a good deal of naked bosom *à la mode*, and valiantly sallied forth as 'a Gothic *anglaise*' in what she had brought with her from West Humble.[26]

Even Fanny's sixteen-year-old niece, Charlotte, found it rather difficult to adjust to this fashion revolution. On a visit to her Aunt Fanny that summer, she naturally bought a new frock in the latest style, but suffered much embarrassment on her return to England. As she wrote in a letter whose wit owes much to the influence of her aunt, it was not just that her 'light French clothing' was so unusual as to provoke comment (and not always of a complimentary nature); it was also so impractical that every time a gust of wind blew down the street she worried that her dress 'should give way & no shade be left to our complete perfections'.[27]

Fanny was also puzzled by the French rules on kissing, writing to Mrs Lock of her misadventures with the 'Female Worthies' before she learned the continental art of 'saluting' both cheeks. She could laugh about her struggles to learn the rules of etiquette in Parisian society. But she had more difficulty in adapting to the language: even after eight years of marriage to M. d'A, she was 'so little able to say what I mean, as I mean, in French that I am perpetually entangled in difficulties when I attempt a phrase of more than 5 or 6 words'.[28]

Other difficulties were presented at the rue de Miroménil when Madame de Staël left her calling-card. She had returned to Paris in 1797, and was living with a new companion, the writer and politician Benjamin Constant. Fanny, however, was more disturbed by the way that Madame de Staël had gathered round her a number of political *mécontents*, unhappy with Napoleon's increasing absolutism. She had no intention of renewing her friendship with a woman whom she now considered unprincipled, as well as recklessly impassioned. But she did not wish to offend her, both because of her initial fond impression and because of the Frenchwoman's literary influence. An absurd cat-and-mouse game followed, with Madame de Staël calling on the d'Arblays only to find that Fanny had retired to bed, and Fanny responding by visiting her at the faubourg St-Germain – but only at a time when she assumed her former friend would not be at home. They never met: shortly afterwards Madame de Staël left Paris, in part driven out by Napoleon's increasing disfavour.

Madame de Staël's former lover, Narbonne, meanwhile, had found a new friend in Madame de Laval, who was living with him in the rue de Miroménil. *His* indiscretions, however, were glossed over by Fanny, who pretended to herself that there was nothing of that nature between the flat-sharing couple. Their first meeting was filled with sadness, as they both recalled that when they had last seen each other Susan was with them. Narbonne was, if anything, even more overcome than Fanny, 'pale . . . as death, and trembling all the time'. Perhaps he had been truly in love with the gentle, French-loving Susan?

Fanny had little time to regret leaving the Hermitage. Just a fortnight after arriving in Paris, she had her first glimpse of the First Consul. She and M. d'A attended the May Review in the gardens of the Tuileries palace (in this year of peace there were grand parades of Bonaparte's army every month). As special guests of one of M. d'A's former military subordinates who was now a General, Fanny and M. d'A were escorted into the palace and to the front of the crowd in the

Audience Chamber. Fanny was amazed by the number of old friends from her husband's army days who remembered him, despite his almost unrecognisable appearance, dressed as he was in a drab civilian coat and shabby boots. She was seeing her husband in a new light, at home in his own country and among the friends and associates of his bachelor life.

The crowded company of officers in gaudy uniforms and ladies in 'light drapery' were kept waiting for what seemed like hours until Napoleon's arrival was announced by a loud crash followed by a commanding shout, 'Le Premier Consul'. Fanny could not help but admire him – fascinated not so much by his demeanour as by his expression, which suggested that he was less the brutal warrior of popular English imagination than a reflective thinker:

> I had a view so near, though so brief, of his face, as to be very much struck by it: it is of a deeply impressive cast, pale even to sallowness, while not only in the Eye, but in every feature, Care, Thought, Melancholy, & Meditation are strongly marked, with so much of character, nay, Genius, & so penetrating a seriousness – or rather sadness, as powerfully to sink into an observer's mind . . .
>
> Though the Busts & Medallions I have seen are, in general, such good resemblances, that I think I should have known him untold, he has by no means the look to be expected from Bonaparte, – but rather that of a profoundly studious & contemplative Man . . . But the look however, of the Commander who heads his own army, who fights his own Battles, who conquers every difficulty by personal exertion, who executes all he plans, who performs even all he suggests – whose ambition is of the most enterprizing, & whose bravery of the most daring cast . . .
>
> The plainness, also, of his dress, so conspicuously contrasted by the finery of all around him, conspires forcibly with his countenance, which seems 'Sicklied o'er with the pale hue *sic* of Thought', to give him far more the air of a Student than of a Warrior.[29]

When, later, Napoleon descended to the gardens to inspect his troops, Fanny was intrigued that he appeared – in the casual, almost careless manner with which he held the bridle of his rearing, prancing horse – not to be a good horseman. On reflection, she observed that he 'knew so well he could manage his Animal when he pleased, that he did not deem it worth his while to keep constantly in order what he knew – if urged or provoked – he could subdue in a moment'.

Ten years later her opinion of him was unchanged. After being taken by Baron Larrey to view David's portraits of the Emperor at the invitation of Madame David, she noted of the picture entitled '*sur un Cheval fougeux*' that it depicted Napoleon as though 'absorbed in ruminations so abstruse that they lift him up above all personal care, & give him a contempt of all personal danger, contrasted with the fiery spirit & uncontrollable vigour of the wildly unruly animal'. This, she said, 'produces an effect so striking between The Horse & the Rider, that France seems depicted as retaining all its martial ardour, while governed by a Chief who owes his power & command to his own fearless self-possession.'[30]

Fanny had experienced, by the time she viewed this portrait, the consequences of Napoleon's absolutist rule. But on that spring afternoon in 1802, the d'Arblays ambled home through the gardens of the Tuileries and along the Champs-Elysées into the rue de Miroménil, which Fanny regarded as 'one of the prettiest in Paris'. Although not elegant, the rue de Miroménil is still an attractive street, beginning in the place Beauvau with tree-lined views to the Seine and, in the other direction, leading uphill to the park at Monceau. Few of the early buildings survive, certainly not numbers 1185 or 1200, nor is it now one of the outermost streets of the city! But it is still largely residential, and surprisingly quiet.

Fanny's enjoyment of her new life was not to last. A few days after the Review, M. d'A suggested to his wife that they should stay on in France beyond the year of his enforced exile from England. Perhaps, then, he could re-establish his French citizenship, and Alex could be brought up as both French and English? Fanny left no record of what was said between them and by June she was in Joigny, where M. d'A had taken his wife and son to meet his relations. Life there was less congenial to Fanny than in the capital. 'M. d'Arblay has so many friends, & an acquaintance so extensive, that the mere common decencies of established etiquette demands, as yet, nearly all my time! – & this has been a true fatigue both to my body & my spirits,' she complained to Hetty, somewhat dismayed to find that her husband's home town was so small and provincial. She could not leave the house without being greeted by someone who knew him, and the continual round of social obligations exhausted her, reminding her of the morning calls and cardparties that she and Maria Allen had so disparaged when they were teenagers in King's Lynn. If the d'Arblays stayed in France, was this how their lives would be? Too poor to live in the capital, and instead marooned in the kind of gossipy, introverted country-town community that Fanny so despised, and in which she would be unable to find the time or peace of mind to write.[31]

What, too, would happen to their son if he grew up in France? Indulged by his devoted parents, Alex was turning into a 'wild, restless & spoiled little chap', according to his grandfather, Dr Burney. But he was bright, lively and precociously intelligent. He arrived in Paris with only a few words of French (the d'Arblays always spoke English at home), yet in a few months was fluent enough 'to express everything he wishes'.[32] While they were in Joigny, he rushed in one day to tell his mother a 'great secret': he had been kissed by none other than Napoleon's brother, Louis Bonaparte, whose regiment was stationed nearby. Alex was as proud as if he had been embraced by the Prince of Wales. Did this mean, Fanny wondered, that he would grow up to become more French than English?

On their return from Joigny, Fanny insisted on moving Alex out of the city to the cleaner atmosphere of Monceau, where she hoped his health would improve. Their new rooms were only fifteen minutes' walk from the rue de Miroménil, but were located up on the hill and beside La folie de Chartres, the large garden formerly belonging to the Duc d'Orléans. A public park with lilac walks, a river, small lakes and tea-rooms, its 'bridges & queer buildings' were described by Fanny as being 'enough to content Mr Dubster himself' – Mr Dubster being the *nouveau riche* character in *Camilla* who aspired to gentility by cramming into his small back garden a collection of summer-houses, grottoes and ponds fit for a country estate. Alex's fevers did indeed stop once they were away from the 'dreadful uncleanliness' of the city, and Fanny herself began to believe that she and M. d'A could reproduce their Surrey idyll in France. She agreed (the d'Arblays were, like the fictional Tyrolds in *Camilla*, always 'partners' when making such big decisions) that her husband should use what money he had rescued from his inheritance at Joigny to buy their own house in Passy, then a small village just two miles outside the city.

Passy, at the beginning of the nineteenth century, was a quaint cluster of cottages built on a bluff overlooking the Seine, with spectacular views across to the capital. Maria Edgeworth called it 'the Richmond of Paris'. A community of writers and artists had gathered there, because its attractive villas were small, cheap and offered peaceful conditions in which to work. The d'Arblays' house at 54 rue Basse (now the rue Raynouard) was typical, with rooms on different levels, and its front door reached by walking across the roof. It was very small and reminded Fanny of Camilla Cottage, because of its 'rustic simplicity' and lack of carpets, wallpaper, furniture and curtains. Their home has long since been destroyed, but in the 1840s Balzac lived in a house nearby, which can still be visited. A long, low building, now painted white with pale green shutters, it was described by Balzac's friend Gérard de Nerval as a curious, upside-down kind of house and it still evokes the leafy, rural atmosphere that once belonged to Passy. Below it, one can walk along the rue Berton; a cobbled passageway that dates back to the eighteenth century and which it is easy to imagine Alex dashing along on his way to school (he was the kind of absent-minded child who was always late).

Fanny still believed, however, that their residence in France would be temporary. Writing to her Windsor friend Marianne Waddington in November 1802, she insisted that 'We still adhere to our plan of residence in England, but M. d'A has many incentives to make France his place of frequent abode, &, for that purpose, & others, he deems it right to establish himself as a French Citizen before our departure.'[33]

Fanny's hopes were soon to be dealt a crushing blow. By May 1803 M. d'A had secured his army pension, which – after twenty-six years, five months and thirteen days of service to France – granted him each year the princely sum of 1,500 francs (about £62 10s.). He had also been promoted on retirement to the rank of Adjutant-Général. But that same month the rumours that Napoleon was about to renew hostilities with Britain were confirmed and, on the declaration of war, all communication between the two countries was severed. Fanny wrote to her brother Charles that she felt as if they now 'were separated by the deserts of Zaara or Arabia'. Her letter, written on 16 June, was sent to England via a friend through the diplomatic postbag, but it was still opened by the Foreign Office and passed on only after being approved. From now on, Fanny could not be sure that her letters would arrive, and, even if they did, that they would reach their destination without being scrutinised by the authorities. Dr Burney advised his family not to write to Fanny, in case she was accused by the French of spying for England.

There was no question now that the d'Arblays could leave France. In 1804, Fanny wrote just one letter – to her father – and later annotated it: 'Written while shut up from England, during the horrendous war with Buonaparte. The only letter F. d'A ventured to write this year.'[34] Fanny became a virtual prisoner in Napoleon's capital, which was to acquire imperial status with the declaration of the Empire on 18 May 1804 (28 Floréal-Primaire in Year XII of the revolutionary calendar, which Fanny took to using in her diaries while she was in France, for fear of her papers being examined and declared anti-French).

She had no access to her pension from the Queen, reducing their meagre income still further. And so, in March 1805, M. d'A took an office job at the Ministère de l'Intérieur in the department that dealt with prisons and buildings. It was low-paid (2,500 francs a year, or just over £100), dull and meant they had to move from Passy and back into the city. The roads from Passy were too muddy in the winter months for M. d'A to walk the couple of miles to his office in the rue de Grenelles, and he could not afford his own coach or to hire a fiacre. They moved first to the rue du faubourg St-Honoré, and then by March 1810 to a larger apartment at No. 13 rue d'Anjou, which was close to M. d'A's military colleague and friend, Lafayette.

There are very few letters or journals from these years. Fanny devoted herself to Alex, who had grown into a 'terribly singular' teenager. 'He is untameably wild,' she told Mrs Lock, '& averse to all the forms of society. Where he can have got such a rebel humour we conceive not; but it costs him more to make a bow than to resolve 6 different problems of algebra, or to repeat 12 pages from Euripides; and as to making a civil speech – he would sooner renounce the World.'[35] Always an indulged only child, Alex became even more the focus of the d'Arblays' thoughts and dreams. Lack of money limited them to a very quiet existence, unable to enjoy the cultural life of the city, while the fear of drawing attention to themselves as a French-English couple meant that their sole company were those friends and neighbours who did not involve themselves in political debate; women like the Princesse d'Hénin and Madame de Maisonneuve, who had known M. d'A since before the Revolution. The latter, in particular, was almost like a sister to Fanny, which is perhaps surprising since she was a single mother, with a son similar in age to Alex, who had divorced her husband, a diplomat, in 1800 – a fact either not known or overlooked by Fanny. Initially, too, Fanny also had the comfort of her niece, Hetty's daughter Maria, who had married a friend of M. d'A's from Joigny, Antoine Bourdois, after meeting him at the Hermitage in the summer of 1800. Sadly, he died in 1806 and Maria, as a penniless widow, was allowed to return to England to live with her parents.

But otherwise these years in Paris, cut off from England by the

Napoleonic wars, were a calm interlude for the d'Arblays. The city itself was under no threat, and, apart from helping her *femme de chambre* Pauline with domestic tasks, Fanny had plenty of time to write. She went back to her play scripts, sharpening up the dialogue and refining the action. She also began to sketch an outline for her new 'ouvrage'.

In the summer of 1805 M. d'A was tempted by Narbonne to join Napoleon's army for the campaign against Poland. He even went so far as to make a list of pros and cons on whether he should accept, writing in the column marked *Oui*: '*Le militaire est tout*'. The *Non* column, significantly, is empty.[36] In the end, he did not go; whether Fanny, or prudence, prevailed, we do not know; and from then on, he resigned himself to the boredom of shuffling papers round an office from nine to four-thirty every weekday. He looked to his son as his hope for the future, and gave up all thoughts of reviving his military career. Instead, he assisted Fanny in making fair copies of her manuscripts, wrote verses dedicated to her, and developed his interest in mineralogy and mining. In the Berg Collection in the New York Public Library, there are four detailed and large plans drawn by M. d'A, including one for an hydraulic ram and one for melting furnaces.

Both M. d'A and Fanny were intensely proud of Alex, and in 1807 Fanny wrote a special letter to Dr Burney to tell him of Alex's success as the top student of his year in *Excellence, Mémoire, Grammaire française, Histoire, Version* and *Thème*, and second in *Géographie*. But in her letter, smuggled out of Paris in a diplomatic bag, she also revealed that she had just recovered from her second 'breast attack'. The inflammation appeared to be nothing more than a recurrence of the painful abscesses she had experienced just after Alex's birth, and was treated by a rigid diet of asses' milk and little else. Fanny was always a great believer in the curative powers of fasting and of taking no protein except for the rich, fatty milk of the ass. But the attacks began to occur with more frequency and, by the summer of 1810, she was suffering from 'a small pain in my breast, which went on augmenting from week to week'. It was, she told Hetty, 'rather heavy than acute, without causing me any uneasiness with respect to consequences'.

By the following spring, however, the pain had become so severe that she was unable to use her right arm (the lump was in her right breast), and M. d'A insisted that she consult a physician, as did several friends 'who knew something of disease'. Fanny was taken by

Narbonne to see Monsieur Dubois, who had been the obstetrician in charge of the Empress Josephine's recent pregnancy. Dubois' verdict was that Fanny should rest, avoid anxiety of any kind, but that – if all else failed – an operation would be necessary 'to avert evil consequences'.

This last and most drastic recourse was to become an urgent necessity. Fanny described the pain as becoming 'quicker and more violent, & the hardness of the spot affected encreased'. She no longer had the strength to walk up the three flights of stairs to their rooms, and M. d'A moved his wife and son to a first-floor apartment close to their original home on the rue de Miroménil. Meanwhile, M. Dubois called in a second opinion from the surgeon Baron Larrey (who later was said to have performed 200 amputations in twenty-four hours at Borodino in September 1812).

Baron Larrey 'condemned' Fanny to the surgeon's knife. She was, she said later, 'as much astonished as disappointed – for the poor breast was nowhere discoloured, & not much larger than its healthy neighbour'. But she was forced to admit that she felt 'the evil to be deep, so deep, that I often thought if it could not be dissolved, it could only with life be extirpated'. Some modern experts have suggested that, in Fanny's case, the cancer was benign and that the removal of the whole breast was not necessary. Indeed, although suppurating abscesses are typical of the last stages of breast cancer, the stabbing pain that Fanny describes is not normally associated with malignant tumours.[37] Whether it was malign or not, Fanny was convinced that she had no alternative but to endure radical surgery – *while fully conscious*. There were several treatises in existence by 1811 on the correct way to perform a mastectomy, so that the whole of the diseased mass was removed without damage to the surrounding muscle. But the science of anaesthesia had not as yet been developed, and there was no ether or chloroform with which to mask Fanny's pain.[38]

She faced her ordeal with remarkable courage, and her description of what she experienced on 30 September 1811 is impossible to forget. Indeed, she took over nine months to complete her account of it for Hetty, so painful was it for her to recall the events of that dreadful day.[39] The impact lies in her telling details, such as the curious fact that M. d'A had to obtain permission from the local police chief for straw to be laid in the street before the door of their apartment at No. 8 rue de Miroménil 'during the period of danger & Fever to the

Invalid' (presumably to protect the house from infection as well as to soften the noise from horses' hooves ringing on the cobbles).

She begins with an explanation of how she was persuaded that the operation was essential for her very survival. Once she had given formal, signed permission to Baron Larrey, however, she was told no more about it, nor what preparations she would need to make, nor on what day the operation would take place. All she was asked to do was prepare an armchair and some towels. It was not until she received the note from Baron Larrey on the morning of 30 September, informing her of his intention to arrive with his colleagues at her apartment at one o'clock, that she discovered that M. d'A and her maid had been filling cupboards with charpie (a kind of linen used for surgical dressings) and compresses. It was an ominous indication of what she should expect.

Baron Larrey's message arrived before M. d'A had left for his office, but Fanny hid the news from her husband. She waited until he had gone before asking Alex to write a note and deliver it to M. d'A's chief of staff. The note requested that M. d'A should be kept from going home until word was sent that the operation was safely over. Fanny, meanwhile, finished her breakfast, a dry crust of bread, before preparing herself for the operation.

A two-hour wait ensued – Baron Larrey had been delayed and Fanny waited for him until three o'clock:

> I walked backwards & forwards till I quieted all emotion, & became, by degrees, nearly stupid – torpid, without sentiment or consciousness; – & thus I remained till the Clock struck three. A sudden spirit of exertion then returned – I defied my poor arm, no longer worth sparing, & took my long banished pen to write a few words to M. d'A. & a few more for Alex, in case of a fatal result.

At three, four cabriolets drew up outside the front door in quick succession; at which point, Barron Larrey's assistant, who had arrived earlier, gave Fanny a 'wine cordial', probably a mixture of wine and laudanum. Fanny rang for her maid and the two nurses who had been engaged to assist, but, before she could speak to them, '7 Men in black' entered her room 'without previous message'. Fanny was outraged:

> Why so many? & without leave? – But I could not utter a syllable. M. Dubois acted as Commander in Chief. Dr Larry [sic] kept out of sight; M. Dubois ordered a Bed stead into the middle of the room.

Astonished, I turned to Dr Larry, who had promised that an Arm Chair would suffice; but he hung his head, & would not look at me. Two *old mattrasses* M. Dubois then demanded, & an old Sheet. I now began to tremble violently, more with distaste & horrour of the preparations even than of the pain. These arranged to his liking, he desired me to mount the Bed stead. I stood suspended, for a moment, whether I should not abruptly escape – I looked at the door, the windows – I felt desperate.

She called to her maid, but M. Dubois ordered, 'Let those women all go!' Fanny resisted: 'No, I cried, let them stay! *qu'elles restent*!' And so one of the nurses was allowed to remain by her side.

M. Dubois now tried to issue his commands *en militaire*, but I resisted all that were resistable – I was compelled, however, to submit to taking off my long robe de Chambre, which I had meant to retain – Ah, then, how did I think of My Sisters! – not one, at so dreadful an instant, at hand, to protect – adjust – guard me.

M. Dubois, seeing her distress, tried to calm her. She replied, ' "Can *You* . . . feel for an operation that, to *You*, must seem so trivial?" – "Trivial?" he repeated – taking up a bit of paper, which he tore, unconsciously, into a million of pieces.'

Fanny knew then that the operation was essential for her life – and that 'this experiment could alone save me from its [Death's] jaws' – but she also understood that success was by no means certain.

I mounted, therefore, unbidden, the Bed stead – & M. Dubois placed me upon the Mattress, & spread a cambric handkerchief upon my face. It was transparent, however, & I saw, through it, that the Bed stead was instantly surrounded by the 7 men & my nurse. I refused to be held; but when, Bright through the cambric, I saw the glitter of polished Steel – I closed my Eyes. I would not trust to convulsive fear the sight of the terrible incision.

A long silence followed, 'the most profound', during which Fanny assumed they each took their orders. M. Dubois tried to find her pulse; she *imagined*, she says, the others made their examination of her breast (one assumes, therefore, that they came to their decision only from what they could *see* of Fanny's breast). When, again through the cambric, she saw M. Dubois first drawing with his forefinger a line from top to bottom of her breast, then making a cross, and then a circle, she suddenly understood that they intended to take off 'the WHOLE'.

> Excited by this idea, I started up, threw off my veil, & . . . explained the nature of my sufferings, which all sprang from one point, though they darted into every part. I was heard attentively, but in utter silence, & M. Dubois then re-placed me as before, &, as before, spread my veil over my face. How vain, alas, my representation! immediately again I saw the fatal finger describe the Cross – & the circle – Hopeless, then, desperate, & self-given up, I closed once more my Eyes, relinquishing all watching, all resistance, all interference.

Having now determined to be resolute, Fanny remained calm, 'in defiance of a terror that surpasses all description, & the most torturing pain'. When she heard Baron Larrey asking one of his assistants to hold the breast, Fanny replied that she would do this herself.

As soon as the 'dreadful steel' was 'plunged into her breast', she began, she later remembered:

> a scream that lasted intermittingly during the whole time of the incision – & I almost marvel that it rings not in my Ears still! so excruciating was the agony. When the wound was made, & the instrument was withdrawn, the pain seemed undiminished, for the air that suddenly rushed into those delicate parts felt like a mass of minute but sharp & forked poinards, that were tearing the edges of the wound – but when again I felt the instrument – describing a curve – cutting against the grain, if I may so say, while the flesh resisted in a manner so forcible as to oppose & tire the hand of the operator, who was forced to change from the right to the left – then, indeed, I thought I must have expired. I attempted no more to open my Eyes, – they felt as if hermetically shut, & so firmly closed, that the Eyelids seemed indented into the Cheeks.

Fanny thought the operation was over, but for the third time the 'terrible cutting' was renewed, as the surgeons removed 'this dreadful gland' from its foundation. Yet still her ordeal continued. Several more bouts of scraping were insisted upon by M. Dubois, removing what Fanny refers to as 'peccant attoms' – presumably diseased tissue – before he was satisfied that all of the cancer had been removed: 'Oh Heaven! – I then felt the Knife rackling against the breast bone – scraping it! – This performed, while I yet remained in utterly speechless torture.'

Twice she fainted during the operation which, she later told her brother Charles, lasted for seventeen and a half minutes. Afterwards she was so weak that her cheeks were drained of all colour and her arms hung lifeless by her side, while she was lifted from the mattress and carried to her bed: 'This removal made me open my Eyes – & I then saw my good Dr Larry, pale nearly as myself, his face streaked with blood, & its expression depicting grief, apprehension, & almost horrour.' Such operations must have been as terrifying and nightmare-inspiring for the surgeons as for the patients.

That night Fanny suffered violent spasms and was given '*des potions calmantes anti-spasmodiques*'. She was violently sick. But when Baron Larrey called next morning, her fever had gone, and by the evening she was taking a little chicken broth.

Fanny's letter to Hetty has survived without any deletions or obfuscations. The first editors of the journals, however, squeamishly omitted it, glossing over 1811 with the explanation that 'During this year Madame d'Arblay's correspondence with her English connexions was interrupted not only by the difficulty of conveying letters, but also by a dangerous illness and the menace of a cancer, from which she could only be relieved by submitting to a painful and hazardous operation.'[40]

Their unwillingness to publish the details of Fanny's operation is not surprising. M. d'A himself did not know what his wife had endured on that dreadful afternoon until he read Fanny's letter to Hetty. He added a postscript in which he admitted that he could hardly bear to read to the end:

I must own to you, that those details which were, till just now, quite unknown to me, have almost killed me, & I am only able to thank God that this more than half Angel has had the sublime courage to deny herself the comfort I might have afforded her, to spare me, not the sharing of her excruciating pains, that was impossible, but the witnessing so terrific a scene, & perhaps the remorse to have rendered it more tragic! for I don't flatter myself I could have got through it.[41]

Fanny was not alone in her ordeal. Breast cancer was by no means an unusual disease, and its implications did not go unnoticed by the movement for women's rights that emerged in the 1790s, as exemplified by Mary Wollstonecraft's *Vindication of the Rights of Woman* (1792), which was written in direct response to Thomas

Paine's *The Rights of Man* (1791–2). The mastectomy, then as now, was not seen just as an amputation but had all kinds of other connotations for women, especially since such operations were always conducted by men. In 1800, for example, Maria Edgeworth highlighted the debates by giving one of the characters in her novel *Belinda* a diseased, if not ultimately cancerous, breast. Revealingly, however, Lady Delacour's 'cancer' disappeared upon her reformation from callous libertine to caring mother. Fanny's description of how '7 men in black' burst into her bedroom and ordered out her female companions, conspiring against her to remove her breast by a series of silent communications in a sign language all their own, could have been written today – so universal are its themes, so immediate its searing honesty.

She was fortunate that she was operated on in 1811 – when Napoleon's surgeons were still in Paris – and not in 1812, by which time they were employing their expertise on the battlefields of Russia. Their thoroughness saved her life, and she was to live without a recurrence of cancer for another twenty-nine years.

TWELVE

The Wanderer
1812–14

Put aside your prejudices, and forget that you are a dawdling woman, to remember that you are an active human being, and your FEMALE DIFFICULTIES will vanish into the vapour of which they are formed.

The Wanderer

When Fanny finally arrived back in Britain on 15 August 1812 after ten years' exile in France, she was so relieved to be once again in the land of her birth that she bent down and picked up 'the nearest bright pebble' from the beach and 'pressed it to her lips'. She and Alex had been rowed to shore at Deal after a terrifying crossing from Dunkirk on a ship bound for America. M. d'A stayed behind in Paris, reluctant to leave his job at the Ministry of the Interior, but Fanny was anxious to see her father, now a reclusive eighty-five-year-old, and to reassure her family that she had completely recovered from the operation on her breast, save for a weakness in her right arm and shoulder. She was also determined to save Alex from conscription into the French army, and to prepare him for further studies at Cambridge.

She seized the opportunity of the signing of the peace alliance between France and Britain on 24 March 1812, and the consequent easing of travel restrictions between the two countries, to procure exit passports for herself and Alex. Even then, she was not allowed to go to Britain (the passports were stamped for 'Newfoundland or some coast of America'); her only hope was to smuggle herself and Alex on board a ship loaded with goods secretly intended for Britain. On Friday, 3 July, M. d'A heard rumours that an American ship, the *Mary Ann*, was preparing to sail from Dunkirk for New York but would unofficially call first at Dover. At five the next morning, Fanny and Alex waved farewell to M. d'A from the windows of the diligence that would take them from Paris to the coast.

The journey took two days non-stop, except to change horses.

Fanny left in such a rush that she forgot her precious gold repeater-watch, a gift from Queen Charlotte. Her manuscripts, too, were left behind in the rue de Miroménil: she thought that papers in English might get her into trouble with the ever-suspicious French police. She intended in any case that her visit would be short (just three months), and so taken up with seeing her family that she would have little time to devote to her new novel. On arrival in Dunkirk, Fanny was disappointed to discover that the *Mary Ann* would not be leaving for another ten days. Alex, now seventeen, sauntered away the days by wandering round the docks or playing billiards in a nearby coffee-house, but Fanny was confined to their hotel with nothing to occupy her time.

She passed the endless days of waiting in writing long letters to M. d'A. Many of these epistles to her 'Heart of Hearts' (and M. d'A's replies) have survived: '*Oh ma bonne amie, que je t'aime!*' M. d'A wrote on 8 July, with as much romance as in his first letters to Fanny some nineteen years earlier. '*Je t'aime trop peu pour ce que tu mérites, mai plus qu'assez pour mon repos.*'[1] But, ever-practical, he also sent his wife sherry to restore her after the rigours of her journey, as well as oranges and lemons to stave off influenza. Fanny, in return, gave him precise instructions on how to take James's powders to ease the exhaustion and gloom of his wakeful nights: 'divide a full paper into *four/4/* parts and from any one of these numbers to take a *fifth/5/* and put it into the skin of a raisin or a prune, or a little honey or jelly, and drink it down with tea, gruel, weak broth, sage balm, or broome tea. These last three are still better than tea.' This letter, like many of the others, was actually written by Alex; after experiencing such radical surgery, Fanny still found writing difficult.[2]

Four dreary weeks later, there was still no sign that the *Mary Ann* was about to sail. Fanny decided to risk trouble with the authorities and sent to M. d'A for '*tous les cahiers*', so that she could at least use her time by working on her 'ouvrage'. 'It is utterly unfinished,' she told M. d'A in her letter of 9 August. 'The papers *rolled* were only materials of uncertainty . . . They are placed not as they follow, but according to particular intentions of changes, revisals, &c.'[3] In fact, three of what would become *The Wanderer*'s eventual five volumes had been drafted, filling a bundle of notebooks, which M. d'A packed neatly into a small valise. Inside, too, were papers giving Fanny written clearance for her manuscripts, obtained by M. d'A from the police authorities in Paris.

Fanny began to rethink her travel plans: perhaps she should remain in England until after the winter, instead of rushing back before the onset of the bad weather, and attempt to publish her novel before she returned to France. If she made money from it, then she could pay for Alex's university education. She would also please her father: 'for it is what, I know, beyond all things in the world, he most wishes'. She never lost that childlike desire to be his 'favourite girl'. 'Oh!' she continued, 'how infinitely am I thankful to be able so to gratify one of the best & dearest of Parents!'[4]

But first she had to cross the Channel – and evade the beady-eyed customs officials at Dunkirk. No easy task. In her 'Dunkirk & Deal' journal (which she compiled 'for posterity' in 1825), she recorded her adventures as she and Alex attempted to leave France. She had scarcely opened her 'precious notebooks' before hearing that the *Mary Ann* was finally about to depart, and that she and Alex should present themselves at the Customs House to obtain permission to travel. Fanny assumed this was a mere formality and was more than a little concerned when the officer in charge demanded to look inside her baggage. As soon as he saw it was packed with books and manuscripts rather than stockings and lace collars, he began 'a rant of indignation & amazement, at a sight so unexpected & prohibited, that made him incapable to enquire or to hear the meaning of such a freight. He sputtered at the Mouth, & stamped with his feet, so forcibly & vociferously, that no endeavours I could use could palliate the supposed offence sufficiently to induce him to stop his accusations of traiterous designs.'

Fanny feared that 'this Fourth Child of my Brain had undoubtedly been destroyed ere it was Born, had I not recourse to an English Merchant, Mr Gregory, long settled at Dunkirk, to whom, happily, I had been recommended as to a person capable, in any emergence, to afford me assistance'. When Mr Gregory arrived, he succeeded in persuading the irascible bureaucrat that Fanny was not only the wife of General d'Arblay, but also a friend of Monsieur de Saulnier, the Secrétaire Général de la Police in Paris. No more was said.[5]   Only a few days earlier, Fanny had had another far more frightening encounter with Napoleon's police, his 'mental diving machine' as she referred to them. While in Dunkirk, she and Alex had befriended a group of Spanish prisoners who were labouring on the fortifications for the port. Fanny was impressed by their appearance: 'They had a look calmly intrepid, of concentrated resentment, yet inalterable patience. They were mostly strongly built & vigorous, of solemn almost stately Deportment, & with fine dark Eyes, full of meaning, rolling around them as if in watchful Expectation of insult.' Sorry for them, Fanny 'took courage to speak to them – partly in French & partly in English', asking them questions about the insurrection in Spain against Napoleon's occupation, and in particular whether they had seen the Duke of Wellington, who had led the British–Spanish alliance to victory at Vittoria in 1813. She gave them what little spare change she had.

One evening, while alone and waiting for Alex to join her on the quay, she was emptying her purse to these 'new Spanish friends' when she saw an officer of the police, 'in full gold trappings, & wearing his Badge of authority, & his head covered, & half a yard beyond it, with an enormous Gold Laced cocked Hat', running towards her. He came up to her, 'fixed upon me his Eyes, with intention to petrify me', and began 'with a Voice of Thunder! vociferating Reproach, Accusation, & Condemnation all in one. His Words I could not distinguish, they were so confused & rapid from rage.' When he discovered that Fanny was to travel on the *Mary Ann*, and realised she must therefore be English, he threatened to arrest her.

Fanny was terrified:

To enter a police office with so ferocious a Wretch; – alone, helpless, unprotected, unknown; to be probably charged with planning some conspiracy with the Enemies of the State; – my poor Alexander away, & not knowing what must have become of me; – my breath was gone, – my power of movement ceased; – my Head – or Understanding, seemed a Chaos . . . & my Feet, as if those of a Statue, felt rivetted to the Ground.

But then, perceiving his 'sneering sardonic grin that seemed anticipating the enjoyment of using compulsion', she experienced 'a revolution in my senses & feelings that brought back the use of my Judgement, which told me at the same moment the danger of betraying my fears, & the uselessness of resistance'. She straightened herself up and, in her best French, asserted that she had been issued with a passport by none other than Monsieur de Saulnier, which gave her permission to travel on the *Mary Ann*. At that moment, Alex at last turned up – only just in time to save his mother – and when he confirmed her story, she was released. Fanny, however, had thought for a moment that she was about to be carried off to a squalid French prison, convicted of being an English spy.

A few days later, on the afternoon of 13 August, the *Mary Ann* eventually set sail. Fanny's relief was shortlived: they had only just lost sight of Dunkirk when the wind dropped, leaving the boat becalmed in mid-Channel, where they remained for two days under a baking sun. When they finally started moving again and entered British waters, the boat was seized by British naval officers as an enemy ship flying an American flag (all trade between Britain and the United States had been suspended since the beginning of August after the renewal of hostilities between the two countries over trading routes). All the passengers were taken off and rowed ashore to Deal – except for Fanny, who was too exhausted to be moved (even though it was calm, she had been seasick since leaving Dunkirk).

No wonder she was so thankful next day to be safe on land at last, and at home in England – even though she and Alex found themselves at Deal, while her brother Charles was expecting to meet them at Dover. She was greeted, however, as a returning celebrity by the port commander at Deal, Sir Thomas Foley and his wife, who were friends of the Locks and knew Fanny from visits to Norbury Park. They took great pleasure in introducing the author of *Evelina* to Kent society. Fanny, who at sixty was rather different from the young woman who had written that novel, much enjoyed her first dinner of 'noble Sirloin of Beef' followed by 'Plum Pudding & Apple Pye', in such contrast to the 'dainty French *plats* we had left'. And she was amused to hear once again the 'sound of the English Language ringing in my Ears'. But she was troubled by the difficulties of her situation as the wife of a Frenchman. Anxious 'not to act the part of a returned Spy against the Land that had given birth to my Husband', she wished at the same time to show that she still had a 'faithful John-Bull Heart'.

After several days, she determined to set out for London without Charles. They met *en route*, while Fanny and Alex were waiting at an inn for their horses to be changed. Charles almost missed them; so altered was his sister by her experiences in France that at first he did not recognise her. Twice Charles rode past them before realising that the matronly, grey-haired woman with the lanky, six-foot youth beside her must be Fanny and Alex. Fanny had become very plump during her ten years in France, and now spoke with a strange accent that was neither French nor English.

Charles took them straight to Chelsea, where Fanny, foreseeing that the meeting with her father would be full of emotion, asked to see him alone. 'Fortunately, he had had the same feeling, & had charged all the family to stay away, & all the World to be denied.' She found him in his library, but so changed, 'his head almost always hanging down, & his hearing most cruelly impaired'.[6] Never good at being idle, Dr Burney found the restrictions of old age acutely depressing, and had changed from being 'the sociable Doctor' to a veritable misanthrope. But he was encouraged to make the effort to leave his sofa by the welcome parties for Fanny and Alex.

Fanny's first concern was to catch up on ten years of family gossip. She was especially anxious for news of Susan's children. Fanny, the eldest, was now thirty and married to a Mr Raper, with a daughter, Catherine Minette; sweet-natured Norbury was about to be ordained for the priesthood in Ireland; and young Willy was now a twenty-one-year-old midshipman in the British navy. All this was reported back to M. d'A in a letter that reads like a round robin of who's married to whom. It also provides insights into the difficulties faced by the next generation of Burneys, none of whom was born into money or rank.

Of Hetty's children, Henry had died as a young baby, while Charles Crisp had run away to India as a teenager, where he died of malnutrition and dysentery after a long sea voyage on board a slave trader. Her eldest son, Richard, was a talented keyboard player who had much impressed the celebrated Czech composer, Jan Dussek. But having seen the struggles of his parents to support their family on the income of a musician, he had chosen instead to become a clergyman. Now aged thirty-nine, he was rector of Rimpton in Somerset, and had recently married Elizabeth Williams, who brought with her a considerable inheritance. Maria was the only one of the five daughters to marry. She had settled in Bath after the death of her French husband and set up house with her sister Sophia; Fanny, who was thirty-six, became a governess; Cecilia had been sent as a young girl to live with her aunt, who was married but childless; and Amelia, the youngest, stayed at home with her mother.

Charlotte's children were somewhat better off because she was left money by both her first husband, Clement Francis, and her second, Ralph Broome, who had died in 1805 after causing Charlotte much grief by becoming mentally unstable and violent. Both her daughters, Charlotte (who married Henry Barrett in 1807, when she was twenty-one) and Marianne, were well educated. Marianne, in particular, was an exceptionally talented linguist, fluent in French, Italian, Spanish and German as well as Greek, Latin, Hebrew and Arabic. She had benefited from the debates of the 1790s, which sought to give girls the same educational opportunities as their brothers, and although she could not, like her younger brother Clement (who was two years older than Alex), study at university, she devoted her life to her own academic and philanthropic interests. She became a friend of the anti-slavery campaigner William Wilberforce, assisting him with his work among the poor and uneducated, and for many years supported herself by working as the secretary and amanuensis of her distant relative Arthur Young, the agricultural scientist who in old age was blinded by cataracts.

Fanny was also eager to see her brother James. When she left England in 1802 he was still very much in disgrace. On 1 September 1798, he had abandoned his wife and their two children, Martin, who was ten, and little Sarah, a two-year-old toddler. His marriage to Sarah Payne had never been happy (Susan had once remarked to Fanny that it was 'a Union truly ill assorted') but to run out on her and set up house with another woman – who happened to be his half-sister, Sarah Harriet – was, not surprisingly, quite unacceptable to the rest of his family. Dr Burney was terribly shocked, especially since (after his own somewhat improper marriage) he had always been very anxious to observe the social proprieties. Perhaps, too, he had discovered James and Sarah Harriet *in flagrante*. This at least was hinted at by Maria Rishton when she reported in a letter to Fanny that their father had fled his home, 'the wretched transaction of J and S having just happened'. Chelsea had been made 'wholly comfortless and dejecting to him', she wrote, as it was 'the scene whence it [the wretched transaction] had taken place'.[7]

For a time, the errant couple simply disappeared, but James contacted Hetty at the beginning of October and told her that he and Sarah Harriet were back in London after staying initially in Bristol. Hetty reported to her sisters that she had visited them and was horrified to discover that their rooms were in 'a dirty Lodging in a Suspicious House in Tottenham Court Road', which they dared not leave unoccupied for fear they would be robbed in their absence. By January 1799, however, they had settled in an apartment at No. 21 John Street, Fitzroy Square; the address that James eventually gave to Fanny. (The family had feared at first that the couple had run off to America to escape public censure.) Dr Burney refused to have anything to do with either of them, or even to talk about them with his other children; his antagonism made worse by Sarah Harriet's attempt to persuade his housekeeper, Molly, who had been with him for years, to go with her. His comments on the affair were later destroyed by Fanny, and it was not until Joyce Hemlow disclosed in her biography of 1958 what she had discovered from her readings of Fanny's edited papers that this unhappy family secret was unearthed.[8]

Fanny's initial reaction had been to fire off letters to James, begging him to make amends for what he had done. She told Hetty, 'My Heart aches for him often, – for alienated as he now appears from *all* his connections & absorbed only in one partial affection, his Hour will come – an hour when he will wonder at his own madness. And she – poor Girl! What a lot has she dealt herself! What has the life she has chosen that can repay her, when its novelty & wilfulness are past, for the life she relinquished?'[9] But James and Sarah Harriet remained together for five years – defying social obloquy and penury – and became such a fixture that the family was forced to accept what had happened. Charlotte invited them both to dinner just three months after the elopement; and Fanny began writing to James as if nothing had happened. They all pretended that James had left his wife on amicable terms, and that Sarah Harriet had gone to live with him as his housekeeper.

It was Sarah Harriet who bravely put an end to the affair, after James suggested that his daughter should come and live with them because he felt miserable without her. Sarah Harriet thought it a 'cruel and odious idea' to take little Sarah away from her mother, and in April 1803 she decided to leave James: 'I neither will deprive James of the satisfaction of having his child with him; nor will I take upon myself the odium that would attach to my character were I to undertake the charge of her to the exclusion of her mother,' she told Charlotte.[10] This was a very real sacrifice: while James returned to live with his family in James Street and made the best of things with his wife, Sarah Harriet spent many lonely years as a governess in Cheshire. She never married, and was always reliant thereafter on her own ability to make enough money to support herself. She wrote novels, which although now forgotten were much enjoyed by her contemporaries; her first, *Clarentine*, was published in 1796, the same year as *Camilla*.[11]

By 1812, the affair had been discreetly forgotten by the family, and James was one of Fanny's first visitors at Chelsea College. They met 'with Eyes filled with affectionate tears'. And when, a couple of weeks later, Fanny dined with him in James Street, she was relieved to discover that his wife was 'extremely improved . . . & full of marked & affectionate attentions to my Brother, who both meets & returns them with a pleased distinction I was quite happy to observe'.[12] Sarah Burney must have been a remarkably forgiving woman, for she also remained a friend of Sarah Harriet.

After the joyous meetings with family and old friends, such as George Owen Cambridge (the cause of Fanny's earlier heartache was now an Archdeacon in the Church of England, and married), Fanny turned her attention to the problem of Alex. She believed that his only hope of advancement was to prove himself as a scholar, and she hoped that he would become a classicist like Charles; perhaps, too, a literary figure like his grandfather. But Alex had other ideas. His natural enthusiasm was for mathematics, a subject in which he was undoubtedly gifted, impressing his French schoolteachers, who thought him quite a genius. Fanny, however, could not believe that a career as a mathematical scientist would provide him with sufficient income to attract a wife. Alex, too, was seriously disadvantaged when compared with his peers in England, since his education in France had not introduced him to the work of English mathematicians, such as Isaac Newton. Fanny wrote a worried letter to Charles, who had taken it upon himself to prepare Alex for the entrance examinations to Cambridge: 'I BESEECH you to make a point that our Alex be orderly, tidy, & punctual: do not spare him on those matters, dearest Charles. He will more mind you than any one, though alas – ! – his absence & carelessness grow upon him daily! . . . I beg, also, that he may not play AT ANY GAME whatever. I wish him to spend all his leisure in exercise, reading, or conversation.' Alex had been introduced to the time-wasting pleasures of chess and whist by his uncle James, a master of both games.[13]

Charles junior had accomplished much since his shady beginnings in academia: by 1812, his school in Greenwich was one of the largest, and most respected, public schools in England; he was also the vicar of the fashionable parish of St Paul's, Deptford, and Chaplain to George III.[14] Quite a change from those glum days in Aberdeen when he believed that he would never recover from the shame of being expelled from Cambridge. He shared his good fortune with his family, providing for the education of his nephews, especially Alex, for whom he organised extra tuition. He also wrote a series of letters to the governors of the Tancred scholarship to Caius College, Cambridge (worth some £100 a year), in the hope that he could persuade them to award it to Alex. (Because Alex's father was French, Fanny had to provide certified proof that her son was British-born by asking the accoucheur who had delivered Alex to sign an affidavit saying that he had personally observed the birth in Great Bookham.) Charles's letters worked – together with Fanny's own application to the Queen – and Alex was accepted at Caius College in October 1813.

With Alex's future settled, Fanny had resolved her first difficulty on returning to England, but she still had to sort out her chaotic finances. When the d'Arblays left for France in 1802, their assets were minimal: a few government bonds, which paid interest annually, and Camilla Cottage (which she continually refers to as '*my* Cottage' in letters to M. d'A). Fanny had to decide whether or not to sell it. If they continued to live in France, there was little point in keeping it. But if they sold it, what then would be left for Alex to inherit? Fanny put off her visit to Surrey for four months, fearing that she would discover her precious 'hermitage' had become a damp-ridden hovel. But on 10 December 1812 she reported to her father with relief that not a single book had been damaged: 'The few that were new, & handsomely bound, are as bright as if just bought . . . not a pamphlet has a single leaf curled at the corner; not a label of the hundreds neatly written with his own hand, has dropt off, or is effaced.'[15] Books were evidently not among the d'Arblays' economy measures.

Charles advised her – in the absence of M. d'A – to keep the cottage for the sake of Alex's future, which left Fanny free to turn her mind to what she really wanted to sort out: her new novel.[16] She spent the winter months of 1812–13 with her sister Charlotte, who had rented rooms in No. 23 Chenies Street (close to the British Museum), and apart from an obligatory attendance upon the Queen (who was still paying Fanny her pension of £100 each year), and an exceptional outing in January to a ball in honour of Hetty's husband, Charles Rousseau, on his sixty-fifth birthday, where she promised her nieces that she would dance a fandango, she rarely went out. Although Fanny had recovered from her mastectomy, she was still fragile and anxious not to catch a debilitating winter cold. In any case, she wanted to devote her time to finishing *The Wanderer*.

By 22 March 1813 she was ready to negotiate terms with a publisher, and she wrote to Charles asking him to be her agent once more. This time, she told him, she must ensure that she made the maximum profit from her novel, and she suggested that the best way to do this would be to auction her manuscript to the highest bidder. She asked Charles to send a circular letter to as many as fourteen publishers – including Longman, Hurst, Rees, Orme & Brown; John Murray; Thomas Payne (the son of James's father-in-law); Mrs Elizabeth Mathews; and John Hatchard – to advise them that a new manuscript by the author of *Evelina*, *Cecilia* and *Camilla* would be available shortly. She warned Charles to 'say nothing of *its* purposes, & all that. It *looks* like Puff. They will take it – or They Will let it alone from public expectation – be its purpose &c what it may.'[17]

Charles was not convinced that this was the best way to sell the novel and, rather than accepting the highest bid – which came from Henry Colburn, who offered £1,750 down-payment for the copyright, with further instalments to be agreed – he advised Fanny to accept the offer made by Longman & co. They wanted to pay *by editions*, so that Fanny would receive £1,500 for the first edition of 3,000 copies, and £500 for each of five future editions of 1,000 copies each. But that initial £1,500 was to be paid by instalments (i.e. £500 on delivery of the manuscript, £500 six months after publication and £500 a year after publication).

Fanny had hoped for a single one-off payment of £3,000 without conditions (judging by what she had earned from *Camilla*), but she wanted to agree terms quickly so that she could see her book into print and then hurry back to M. d'A in Paris. She did make other enquiries, consulting the novelist Maria Edgeworth, whose publisher was the radical printer, Joseph Johnson of 72 St Paul's Churchyard, who had earlier published Mary Wollstonecraft's *Vindication of the Rights of Woman*. But in the end Fanny followed Charles's advice, signing the articles of agreement with Longman & co. on 4 November 1813.

She knew it was a gamble, dependent on whether the novel sold quickly enough to necessitate several editions in rapid succession: 'My Publishers forget they do not run all the risk themselves,' she told her father. 'We *share* the hazard – for it is only the first fifteen hundred that I am to receive by instalments; the rest is payable merely by succeeding editions . . . The real win, therefore, is dependent upon success . . . If all goes well, the whole will be £3,000 – but only at the end of the sale of 8,000 copies.'[18] In the event, she lost out. For what was eagerly anticipated as the long-awaited sequel to *Evelina*, *Cecilia* and *Camilla* turned out to be rather a surprise. What her fans had hoped for was a Parisian version of 'a young lady's entrance into the world' and a lively denunciation of Napoleonic France; what they found when _The Wanderer_ appeared in the bookshops on 28 March 1814 was an astringent exposé of Regency Britain. They were not amused.

Fanny, however, had never intended to write about France. As she wrote in the preface to her novel, which was dedicated to her father: 'I held political topics to be without my sphere, or beyond my skill; who shall wonder that now, – united, alike by choice and by duty, to a member of a foreign nation, yet adhering, with primaeval enthusiasm, to the country of my birth, I should leave all discussions of national rights, and modes, or acts of government, to those whose wishes have no opposing calls.' This is not to say that she would (or could) ignore the fact of the Revolution – for, as she writes, 'to attempt to delineate, in whatever form, any picture of actual human life, without reference to the French Revolution, would be as little possible, as to give an idea of the English government, without reference to our own [the Glorious Revolution of 1688]'. On the contrary, what interested Fanny, what impelled her to write, was her belief that novels could create 'a picture of supposed, but natural and probable human existence', which could then give 'knowledge of the world, without ruin, or repentance; and the lessons of experience, without tears'. Whereas earlier she had always been chary of describing her works as 'novels', now she presented a lively defence of that branch of literature; for, after all, 'What is the species of writing that offers fairer opportunities for conveying useful precepts?'[19]

The Wanderer began, as its subtitle _or Female Difficulties_ suggests, as a study of those difficulties that were not so much about fortune or rank as about the genetic accident of being born a member of the weaker sex. But this was far from being another _Evelina_, dressed up in the new clothes of the 1800s. The French Revolution was not the subject of the novel; Paris was not its setting; but the bloody years of revolution and the ensuing dictatorship of Napoleon had such an impact on the rest of Europe that their consequences inevitably pervaded the whole book. As Fanny told Marianne Waddington, who had made the mistake of professing to Fanny her fascination with Napoleon: 'had you spent, like me, 10 years within the control of his unlimited power, & under the iron rod of its dread, how would you change your language!' Fanny understood the insidious effect that such absolute power has on 'liberty':

the safety of deliberate prudence, or of retiring timidity, is not such as would satisfy a mind glowing for freedom ... it satisfies, indeed, NO *mind*, it merely suffices for *bodily* security ... PERSONALLY ... I was always well treated, & personally I was happy: but you know me, I am sure, better than to suppose me such an Egotist as to be really happy, or contented, where Corporal Liberty could only be preserved by Mental forbearance – i.e. subjection.[20]

From the opening sentence of *The Wanderer*, Fanny makes quite clear the political setting of her novel – and yet she also tells us that this is to be a very human drama. She begins: 'During the dire reign of the terrific Robespierre, and in the dead of night, braving the cold, the darkness and the damps of December, some English passengers, in a small vessel, were preparing to glide silently from the coast of France ... '[21] *The Wanderer*, she thus indicates, will not be a polemical tome but rather an illustration of the impact of such extraordinary political change on the lives of ordinary men and women. And what follows does not disappoint. As anyone who braves the daunting size of Fanny's last novel (it is some 60,000 words longer than *Cecilia*) will discover, this is her richest and most rewarding book.

The Wanderer begins as a mystery, with a heroine who has no name, no family, no money, and whose extraordinary appearance gives no indication of whether she is male or female, black or white, French or English, rich or poor. But it becomes a critique of 'foggy Britain', with its injustices to women, its cruelties to the less fortunate, its stale obsession with custom ('how it awes our very nature itself, and bewilders and confounds even our free will!').[22] Fanny, however, was at heart a conservative, and she ends her book with a prophetic warning about the ultimate consequences of liberty. If we take freedom to mean the right to question even our very existence, she argues, then we are liable to come to the dangerous conclusion that life itself has no meaning, that 'death is an end to all? an abyss internal?'[23]

On that moonless, misty night, as the frightened passengers make their escape from turbulent France, a cry for help, in French, pierces the silence. Most of them, in their panic, want to ignore it, but a young man – the hero, Albert Harleigh – realising that this is a woman in distress, demands that she be taken on board. But who is she, with her unorthodox appearance, wrapped in an assortment of clothes and bandaged over one eye? Why is she alone? And what does she throw into the sea once they are half-way across the Channel?

Her fellow travellers can glean nothing from this strange wanderer, and because they cannot perceive whether she is rich or poor, well born or lowly, they insult and ignore her. After their arrival in Dover, however, her skin mysteriously reverts to its natural porcelain-white, and they begin to realise that this 'Unknown' is not what she seems. They discover that she is beautiful: Fanny this time reveals that her heroine's hair is 'soft, glossy, luxuriant brown' and her eyes, like Fanny's, are a soft greenish-grey.[24] Her conversation and accomplishments display an elegance and knowledge that imply an expensive education. Who, then, can she be?

The mystery is kept up for three volumes as this 'Fair Incognita' struggles to retain her independence. She agrees to become the 'humble companion' of the irascible Mrs Ireton, whose impossible behaviour calls to mind the comments made by Fanny and her sisters about their stepmother.[25] Mrs Ireton graciously condescends to allow this pauper into her home because she has by this time acquired a name and a social position as 'Miss Ellis'.

At last, at the beginning of volume four, we discover the true story of 'The Wanderer'. An orphaned daughter of an English earl, her real name is Juliet Granville, but she has had to abandon it for fear that she will be pursued from France by an evil commissar of Robespierre's secret police, who had forced her to marry him for the sake of her £6,000 inheritance. Juliet, however, made a dramatic escape *before* the marriage could be consummated and, after hiding in an upstairs attic for several days – an experience oft told to Fanny by her *ci-devant* friends (former aristocrats who before the Revolution owned land by right of inheritance) – had found her way to the French coast, where she was saved by the noble Albert's intervention.

Once she arrives in England, however, Juliet's difficulties are far from over. She is unable to reveal her identity for fear of her French kidnapper, and in consequence is regarded with suspicion. She becomes an outcast, wandering across the South of England in search of refuge. Lost in the depths of the New Forest, she runs terrified through the dark wilderness, meeting only poachers, smugglers, wild dogs and starving women and children – an opportunity for Fanny to expose the rural idyll as a sham. She is eventually rescued from this nightmare by an eccentric, gout-ridden bachelor, Sir Jaspar Herrington (an endearing *hommage* to Fanny's Mr Crisp), who takes her to see the prehistoric ruins of Stonehenge, a scene redolent with Romantic sensibility. In this 'grand, uncouth monument of ancient days', Juliet finds 'a certain, sad indefinable attraction, more congenial to her distress, than all the polish, taste, and delicacy of modern skill'.[26]

Dark ruins, ghost-like apparitions, trails of blood – in *The Wanderer*, Fanny indulges her taste for gothic effects and surreal drama. Not one, but two attempts at suicide are made by Juliet's rival for the heart of Albert, Elinor Joddrel, who, as the model of a free-thinking female, is the antithesis of Juliet's quiet common sense. First, she proposes to Albert before he has even hinted that he might care for her; then, when she is rejected by him, she dares to make an attempt on her life. In the first of these dramatic scenes, she dons a masculine disguise (a large scarlet coat, spangled waistcoat, slouched hat), to mingle unrecognised with the audience at a benefit concert given by Juliet, who is a talented harpist. Just as the music begins, Elinor walks up to the platform and, in full view of the audience, draws a poniard from beneath her cloak and stabs herself.

The incident bears remarkable similarities to the scandal of Lady Caroline Lamb, who in July 1813 (some time after Fanny must have imagined this scene) tried to wound herself with a knife in the midst of a crowded ballroom, having been rejected by Lord Byron. Indeed, Byron wrote to Caroline's mother-in-law, Lady Melbourne, two days after Fanny's novel was published, telling her that he 'thought the *coincidence* unlucky for many reasons. In the first place, everybody will read Mme d'Arblay.' He had rushed to get hold of an early copy of the novel. He didn't like it. Never one to mince his words, Byron added that he doubted whether Mme d'Arblay could be persuaded to delete the scene from future editions, 'as something like it having really occurred (and of which she must have heard) would at least prevent her from being charged with *over* colouring her portraits, as the *scene* and the assembly and the *public display* would otherwise have certainly been thrown upon as *French* and not *English* manner.'[27]

Elinor is the most richly drawn of all Fanny's fictional characters. Although it is made plain that we are not intended to agree or sympathise with her (unlike Juliet, Elinor does not get her man and live happily ever after), she comes across as a much more spirited, flesh-and-blood character than Juliet, who lacks a certain spark. When, for instance, Juliet laments the 'severe DIFFICULTIES OF A FEMALE', Elinor derides her for being weak-minded: 'Put aside your prejudices, and forget that you are a dawdling woman, to remember that you are an active human being, and your FEMALE DIFFICULTIES will vanish into the vapour of which they are formed.' Juliet's suggestion that such behaviour could lead her into impropriety is roundly denounced: 'you only fear to alarm, or offend the men – who would keep us from every office, but making puddings and pies for their own precious palates!' As Elinor crisply asserts, 'Woman is left out in the scales of human merit, only because they [the men] dare not weigh her!'[28]

Elinor is made to look ridiculous by her extravagant gestures in the name of love and women's rights, but her questioning of the *status quo* is not always so very different from ideas and thoughts expressed by Fanny in her letters and diaries. Elinor, for instance, asks Albert: 'Why has man alone, been supposed to possess . . . all the fine sensibilities which impel our happiest sympathies, in the choice of our life's partners?' Must even a woman's heart 'be circumscribed by boundaries as narrow as her sphere of action in life? Must she be taught to subdue all its native emotions? To hide them as sin, and to deny them as shame?'[29] Such troubled thoughts echo Fanny's confession to Susan, in the midst of her confusion over George Owen Cambridge, that she was 'sometimes dreadfully afraid for myself, from the very different behaviour which Nature calls for on one side, & the World on the other'.

Certainly, she was troubled by the vividness and uncontrollability of her imagination, and wished that she had discussed her 'night imaginings' with Dr Johnson while he was at Streatham. Later, when she was at Court, Fanny admitted that she was 'bewildered' by her dream world, and felt sure that therein lay the key 'to deeper knowledge of the Soul & its immortality than any thing else that comes within our Cognizance'.[30] In *The Wanderer* there is a heated discussion between Elinor and Albert about the imagination and its connection with the spirit, the soul and life after death. Albert tries to convince Elinor of the existence of a spiritual world. Who otherwise can explain, he asks the unbelieving Elinor, 'the phenomenon, by which, in the dead of night, when we are completely insulated, and left in utter darkness, we firmly believe, nay, feel ourselves shone upon by the broad beams of day; and surrounded by society, with which we act, think, and reciprocate ideas?'[31]

The Wanderer is long but it is full of such stimulating debates, which are never allowed to witter on for too long. Fanny had learned the lesson of *Camilla*, which had gone to press without a final pruning. This time she ensured that she had plenty of time to edit carefully the proofs as they were sent to her by the printers throughout January and

February 1814. She even stopped the presses for a few days so that she could attend the Queen at Windsor.

The first edition sold out three days before publication, prompting Fanny to hope that her book would be a huge success, but in the end *The Wanderer* failed badly. It was savagely criticised in almost all the reviews, more than half the second edition was never sold, and it was not reprinted until the feminist revival of the 1970s.[32] One critic memorably likened its author to an 'old coquette who endeavours, by the wild tawdriness and laborious gaiety of her attire, to compensate for the loss of the natural charms of freshness, novelty, and youth'.[33]

Later reviewers, such as Hazlitt and Macaulay, also complained that most of the novel's characters (some say caricatures) were little different from those who had first appeared in *Evelina* some thirty-six years earlier. It is true that vapid, flirtatious misses, unreformed rakes, wealthy but ignorant Cits (those who had made fortunes by trading in the City), and a quantity of cranky old bachelors and irritable widows all play minor roles in *The Wanderer*, but Fanny's last novel is a much more mature work. It is not so witty, or as 'charming' as *Evelina*, and its plot is too convoluted, but its mystery keeps the reader absorbed throughout its five volumes, and there are few, if any, lapses into the kind of sub-Johnsonese didacticism that Macaulay so deplored. He had disliked *Camilla* and condemned Fanny for taking 'a bad style to France' and then bringing back with her in *The Wanderer* 'a barbarous patois, bearing the same relation to the language of *Rasselas*, which the gibberish of the Negroes of Jamaica bears to the English of the House of Lords'. Fortunately, this adverse critique was written after Fanny had died.[34]

Fanny's choice of title is a clear sign that *The Wanderer* was a radical departure from her earlier novels. The notion of the poet-wanderer was a favourite conceit of the Romantic writers of the early nineteenth century. Wordsworth's poem 'I Wandered Lonely as a Cloud', for example, appeared in 1807, and one section of *The Excursion*, which was published a few months after Fanny's novel, was entitled 'The Wanderer' after its eponymous hero. But such ideas had been discussed years earlier by Dr Johnson, whose friend Richard Savage had in 1729 published a long poem on 'the Misfortunes of Humane Life' entitled *The Wanderer*. Savage and his poetry would have been discussed by Dr Johnson and Mrs Thrale while Fanny was staying at Streatham Park; indeed, Savage was the subject of Dr Johnson's first poet's *Life*, a pamphlet published in 1744 that is regarded as the 'first true biography'. Based on his own personal acquaintance with the controversial poet, Dr Johnson wanted to lay bare the human, moral truth at the heart of this difficult and eccentric character, who was once convicted of murder but was reprieved by Queen Caroline. Mrs Thrale refers in her diary to 'Savage the poet in his Laced Scarlet Cloke', which is, intriguingly, the very disguise in which Elinor appears on her first attempt at suicide.[35] And Savage's poem has a whole section devoted to a chilling description of Suicide, who appears as a vengeful woman, 'a Fiend', confronting the poet-wanderer with 'Death in her Hand, and Frenzy in her Eye!'[36]

Fanny was accused of producing a novel that had 'a total want of vigour, vivacity, and originality'.[37] But her critics failed to observe the 'vigour' of the subtext, which highlighted not just 'female difficulties' but also the meaning of existence for both men and women, especially in a society so full of prejudice and inequalities. Rather, *The Wanderer* contained perhaps too much 'originality', too many home truths, for the novel to be an easy read for Fanny's contemporaries.

Fanny was too preoccupied in any case to take much notice of these criticisms, and she says little about them in her letters. By the end of March 1814 she was beset by worries for M. d'A, who was trapped in a city that was about to be besieged by the allied armies of Europe. On 17 March, Napoleon had been decisively defeated at the Battle of Laon, ninety miles north-west of Paris. The report in *The Times* predicted that this would be the prelude to his total downfall. Indeed, over the next fortnight, the allied troops of Russia and Prussia advanced rapidly on the capital, and by 30 March were on the outskirts, ready to lay siege to the city. By ten o'clock the next morning Bonaparte had capitulated without a fight, and at midday the Russian Emperor, Alexander I, triumphantly entered the French capital. Fanny knew nothing of this peaceful conclusion and was frantic for news of M. d'A, from whom she had heard nothing since the middle of February.

At the same time, her father was very ill. By the beginning of April, Dr Burney had stopped eating and was too weak even to speak to his family. On 14 April, as Vauxhall Gardens were lit up by the fireworks celebrating Napoleon's abdication as Emperor, Dr Burney lay dying in his room in Chelsea College. Fanny was with him, but so peaceful were her father's last moments that it was two hours before she realised he had died. 'The final exit was so soft,' she told Marianne Waddington, 'that I had not perceived it, though I was sitting by his

Bedside! . . . I forced them to let me stay by him, & his reverend form became stiff before I could persuade myself to believe he was gone hence for ever.' But she recognised that his sufferings had by this time 'far surpassed his enjoyments', and she told Marianne, 'Be not uneasy for me, my tender friend – My affliction is heavy but not great . . . I would not have wished him to linger!'[38]

Dr Burney left £7,000 in his will (about £190,000 today), plus his library of books and music, much of which comprised rare copies that he had collected on his travels through Europe.[39] He left precise instructions on how this legacy should be divided among his children; in particular ensuring that his daughters were provided for. Fanny and her elder sister Hetty were the main beneficiaries, each receiving £1,000; Sarah Harriet, too, was given £1,000, plus £100 for a wedding garment. Charlotte, however, received only £200 because, he said, she had inherited money from both her husbands. Charles, too, was left only £200; Dr Burney knew that he had made a comfortable living from his school. But when James heard that he too would inherit only £200, he was bitterly disappointed, believing that his father had snubbed him.

Dr Burney had drawn up the will in January 1807, only a relatively short time after James had returned to his wife, and before father and son had been reconciled.[40] Maria Rishton thought it heartless of Dr Burney, remarking to Fanny, 'I think poor James hardly treated . . . You will I dare say from the present filial regard, endeavour to excuse your Father . . . but why (as it appears to me) disinherit his eldest son . . . whose decline of life is embittered by professional disappointment, broken health, and comparative Poverty!'[41]

Unlike Charles, James had never cost his father anything. He had worked his own way up through the ranks of the navy after entering the service as a 'Captain's servant', an apprentice officer, at the age of ten. He had suffered from his refusal to adapt his liberal Whig views to the Toryism of the Admiralty, and had never received the credit due to him as one of the best navigators and geographical scientists of his day (he was eventually made an Admiral, but only a few weeks before his death in 1821).[42] Now, when he could reasonably have expected to receive a competence from his father that would provide for his old age and ensure that his daughter Sarah could marry with a dowry, he was galled to find that he had been left virtually nothing. After serving with Charles as a pallbearer at his father's funeral on 20 April, he refused to have anything more to do with his family and was only mollified after much pleading by Fanny.[43]

James's hurt refusal to see his siblings meant that Fanny felt that she had to stay on in London until all her father's affairs had been settled. M. d'A, anxious that Fanny would be overcome with grief, dashed over to England to be with her, surprising her by arriving without warning at her lodgings in Chelsea on Thursday, 28 April. He was also hopeful of finding some kind of employment in England – perhaps he could become the French Consul – now that the war was over and the Bourbons had been restored to the throne of France.

Louis XVIII, brother of the beheaded monarch, was crowned in Paris on 3 May 1814. Fanny had been presented to him as the author of *Cecilia* on 22 April, while he was being entertained in London before travelling to Paris for his triumphant entry into his capital city. Queen Charlotte gave her a ticket of admission to Grillion's Hotel in Albemarle Street, off Piccadilly, where the audience took place. Fanny made a record of the event later for the benefit of Alex and her (hoped-for) grandchildren: 'An avenue had instantly been cleared from the door to the Chair, & the King moved along it slowly, slowly, slowly, rather dragging his large & weak limbs than walking: but his face was truly engaging; benignity was in every feature, & a smile beamed over them that shewed thankfulness to Providence in the happiness to which he was so suddenly arrived.'[44]

Six weeks later in June, she recorded her observations on the Emperor of Russia and the King of Prussia, who were both in London to celebrate the role they had taken in the restoration of the French monarchy. Jane Austen warned her sister Cassandra on 14 June: 'Take care of yourself, and do not be trampled to death in running after the Emperor', so big were the crowds who waited on the streets to see them pass by. Fanny was more fortunate: she was invited by the Queen to a reception at St James's. Her impressions are filled with Royalist sentiment, but she also noted that 'Her Majesty said, "What cold weather! I believe it is to complement the Russians!" – meaning that they may think our climate no better than their own. I told her that to see Europe's Pacificular [the Russian Emperor was given the credit for subduing Napoleon and bringing peace to Europe] had drawn me from my solitude.'[45]

By this time Fanny was alone again: after just four weeks, M. d'A received news from Paris that he had been offered a place in Louis XVIII's Garde du Corps and, although this meant he would have to leave London immediately, he felt he could not refuse. This, after all, was a chance for him to serve his country again, and return to the way of life he had enjoyed before the Revolution. Fanny saw things differently. At sixty, she thought her husband should retire and that 'Private life ... should be sought while it yet may be enjoyed.' And she confided to Marianne Waddington, 'M. d'Arblay has resources for retirement the most delightful both for himself & his friends. I cannot, therefore, wish for the short blaze of a transient re-instatement, that must risk his strength & health.'[46]

While M. d'A dashed back to Paris in pursuit of military glory, Fanny was left alone to deal with the worrying reality that they were about to lose their home. On 14 May, she and M. d'A had received a solicitor's letter advising them that Camilla Cottage was to be sold. William Lock's son and heir, also William, had decided that he could no longer afford to maintain both a London house and a country estate and had put Norbury Park up for sale (his father had died in 1810). Fanny and M. d'A at first assumed this could not affect them, but William had discovered that there was no legal agreement between the two families over the land on which the cottage had been built and that it would therefore have to be regarded as part of the estate and sold along with it. M. d'A was outraged, and wrote a furious letter to William. Its only effect was to cause a rift between Fanny and her old and dear friend Mrs Lock, which took many years to heal.

By November 1814, the d'Arblays had lost possession of their Hermitage, receiving just £700 as compensation. Fanny began to feel that she was homeless, 'wholly ignorant even of where I shall fix my residence! Whether in Paris, or London – at Montpellier, or at Bath – or upon the banks of the Loire, – or at the foot of a Welsh mountain!'[47] For the next year, her life curiously began to resemble that of her fictional heroine, Juliet. She was unhappy at the prospect of remaining in London without M. d'A; but she knew she would be equally miserable if she returned to Paris with him, leaving Alex behind at university in Cambridge. In the end she decided, with great difficulty, that she must stay on in Britain. 'My poor fluctuating Alex,' she told M. d'A,

requires me for his health – his principles – his happiness *à venir*, & his reputation: – YOU, on the contrary, however kindly you may wish for me, could never so facilely spare me. A new world is opened to you; honours, well merited, pour upon you; you have all the security of

Monsieur d'Arblay, *c.* 1793*

* see Notes on Illustrations on p.322 for details on all pictures

George III   Queen Charlotte

Fanny Burney,
c. 1787,

South East View of Windsor Castle, with the Royal Family on the Terrace and View of the Queen's Lodge, 1783, by James Fittler, after George Robertson

Madame de Staël

The Comte Louis de Narbonne

A sketch of Juniper Hall

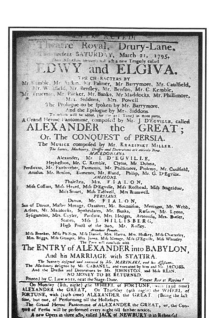

Playbill for the
only performance of
Edwy and Elgiva

*Sarah Siddons
Rehearsing in
the Green Room
with her father and
John Kemble,* by
Thomas Rowlandson

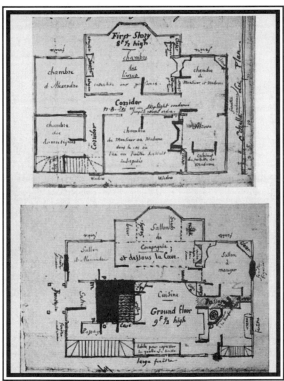

Sketches of Camilla Cottage by M. d'A

Silhouettes of Alex at three
years old, and as a young man

Pencil sketch of a retriever,
possibly by M. d'A

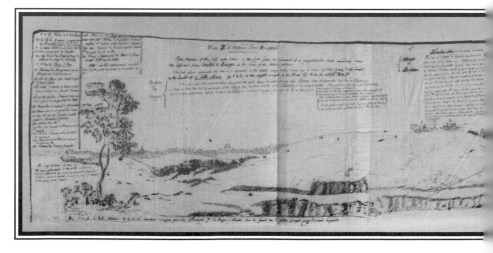

General d'Arblay in 1817, by Carle and Horace Vernet

M. d'A's sketch-plan of the decisive day of the battle at Waterloo, 18 June 1815

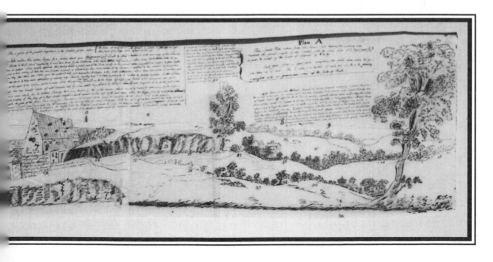

Fanny in her 'Vandyke Gown', 1782, by Edward Francisco Burney

constantly sustained, or honourably renewed connexions; Generously you may wish me at your side to share your prosperity, but 'tis to Alex alone I am essential; 'tis Alex alone I can serve.[48]

M. d'A's response did nothing to dispel Fanny's anxiety. He explained, in French (the language in which he almost always wrote to Fanny, she replying in English), that the Duc de Luxembourg had graciously offered their son a place in the Garde du Corps. It was an honour, he told her, and would mean that they could all be together in France. Fanny refused even to consider the idea of Alex embarking upon a military career: 'Is there then, *dis tu*, nothing else in France? absolutely nothing?' M. d'A could not understand Fanny's attitude. He thought Alex's obsession with science was ridiculous. In any case, what could Alex do in England? Become a priest? A lawyer?

Their discussions, conducted by letter between Paris and London, exposed their differences over Alex's future: would he settle in France and marry a Frenchwoman or become an English scholar or cleric? In the end, Fanny decided to withdraw Alex from Cambridge for a year and take him back to France, after hearing from Marianne Wadding-ton (whose husband knew one of Alex's tutors at Cambridge). The letter is indecipherable in places because of Fanny's heavy black obliterations, so we can only assume that it revealed something about Alex that forced his mother to realise that he was not perhaps as brilliant a student as she had thought: 'He never, you say, can succeed at Cambridge – unriddle to me, I beg, what that "never" means!' she replied to her friend. 'It is NOW that to know the *whole truth* may be useful; for now, just NOW the conflict is at the height which must subside by our fixing to which of his two native Countries – that of his Birth or that of his Ancestors – he will finally belong.'[49]

Alex, however, must have refused to leave, for when M. d'A (now serving his King as a General) travelled back to London to collect his family, only his wife was waiting for him.

THIRTEEN

Waterloo
1814–15

Your noble father – turned of 60 – is *at his post* in the Army – with the Maison du Roi – but *how* employed, or *where,* I am yet ignorant; – & yr wandering emigrant Mother has been forced to fly even her adopted Country.

Madame d'Arblay, March 1815

By Friday, 11 November 1814, Fanny was once more at Dover on her way back to France. In her diary for that day, just one word appears – 'Cliff' – as if she and M. d'A had taken a walk along the white cliffs above the town while waiting for the ferry that would convey them across the Channel. They had yet another stormy journey, travelling in a small, open boat, and, by the time they arrived at Calais, Fanny was so weak and dehydrated that she had to be taken off the boat in an armchair carried by a group of fishermen organised by her husband.

This was a bad beginning, especially for Fanny, who had been so reluctant to return. And her woes were compounded a few minutes later when M. d'A was involved in a near-fatal accident. He had been so preoccupied with fussing over his wife that he did not notice a horse and cart careering towards him down the street, and was hit by the wagon before he could get out of the way. The force of the blow flung him to the side of the road and he blacked out. He was thought to have been wounded fatally, but he soon regained consciousness. Nevertheless it was several days before he was sufficiently recovered from the shock and bruising pain to move on to Paris, and he was weakened by the after-effects for many months.

Fanny felt no pleasure at being back in their old home on the rue de Miroménil. She was 'frightened & incapacitated' by the realisation that M. d'A could have been killed in an instant; she disliked the fact that he was back in the army, even though as yet his duties were not arduous; she was anxious about Alex; and she suspected that the peace between France and the allies would not last and feared being trapped in Paris once more. But at least she and M. d'A were together, and they spent a quiet winter, catching up with friends and writing letters to Alex, encouraging him to make the most of his time at Cambridge. 'Our relapses have been tiresome & painful,' she wrote to James in February 1815, after a winter of almost continual illness, 'but have not robbed us of hope. Darby & Joan like, therefore, we jog on, & only wish Darby & Joan like, ultimately together to jog off.'[1]

Such domestic tranquillity was doomed: a few weeks later, rumours of Napoleon's escape from Elba reached Paris. At first no one believed that he would have the audacity to attempt to regain power after his defeat by the allies, and celebrations to mark the restoration of the Bourbon monarchy continued, partying till the early hours in what Fanny described as a veritable '*dansomanie*'. But writing with hindsight some years later, she could not believe that she and her husband's friends were so blind. For ten years she had lived in the grip of Napoleon's police state: 'I knew the Character of Buonaparte . . . the intrepidity of his Ambition, the vastness of his conceptions, & the restlessness of his spirit . . . thus aware of his own Gigantic ideas of his Destiny, how could I for a moment suppose he would re-visit France without a consciousness of success, founded upon some secret conviction that it was infallible?'[2]

She did take the precaution of obtaining a properly signed passport; while M. d'A equipped himself with firearms, ammunition and a magnificent warhorse. But right up to the day before Napoleon's triumphant arrival at the gates of the Tuileries, she remained in the city, taken each afternoon for an airing in the Bois de Boulogne in their new *calèche*, bought by M. d'A in a fit of rash enthusiasm about their future life in France. 'I have no retrospection that causes me such amazement as the unapprehensive state of mind that could urge either of us to the enjoyment of those drives when aware that Buonaparte had effected an invasion of France,' she wrote later.

On Sunday, 19 March, a week before Easter, guns were heard on the outskirts of Paris, and M. d'A rushed home from the Tuileries to tell Fanny that Napoleon's troops could be seen encamped just outside the city gates. They knelt together – 'in short but fervent prayer to Heaven for each other's preservation' – and then separated. Fanny watched from the window as her husband mounted his warhorse, laden with all the paraphernalia of warfare (helmet, bayonet, pistols, ammunition). 'Vive le Roi!' he shouted as he rode out of the courtyard, horrifying Fanny, who until that moment had not faced the fact that her husband was intending to be involved in active combat on the field of battle.

Too flustered to plan her own escape, she flung a change of linen and a pocket-book of money into a basket and rushed to the apartment of their close friend, Madame de Maisonneuve, who now lived nearby in the rue d'Aguesseau. 'The street was empty. The gay constant Gala of a Parisian Sunday was changed into fearful solitude. No sound was heard, but that of here & there some hurried footstep.'

At nine o'clock, she received a frantic note from M. d'A, telling her to leave immediately: '*Ma chère amie tout est perdu! – je ne puis entrer dans aucun détail. de grâce partez – le plutôt sera le mieux. À la vie et à la mort! Midy! Midy! – A. d'Ay.*'[3] And by eleven that night she was on her way to the Belgian border in the coach of their old friend from Juniper Hall, the Princesse d'Hénin. They travelled for two days and nights without stopping, except to change horses, taking a circuitous route on minor roads to avoid interrogation by the local police, who it was feared would be loyal to Napoleon. Fanny disguised herself as her friend's *femme de chambre*, just in case they encountered an official who was hostile to the English. By late on Tuesday night they were still only at Amiens and they did not arrive at the safety of Tournai, in Belgium, until late on Thursday.

All the way to the French border they 'were annoyed by incessant small military groups of Horsemen; but though they surveyed, or encircled us curiously, they did not yet seem authorised with powers for stopping passengers, & therefore, though suspiciously regarded, we were not stopt.' Fanny scribbled a panic-filled note to Alex: 'OH ALEXANDER! . . . Your noble father – turned of 60 – is *at his post* in the Army – with the Maison du Roi – but *how* employed, or *where*, I am yet ignorant; – & yr wandering emigrant Mother has been forced to fly even her adopted Country.'[4] Fanny began her letter on 23 March, as soon as she had crossed into Belgium and arrived in Tournai. But she and the Princesse d'Hénin hurriedly left that city when they realised that many of its inhabitants were supporters of Napoleon. They travelled on to Brussels, from where Fanny posted her letter three days later, forgetting even to frank it in her haste to give her son news of her flight from Paris.

Meanwhile, when M. d'A left the rue de Miroménil on the afternoon of Sunday, 19 March, he had gone straight to the Champs de Mars to join the general review of troops, as a member of Louis

XVIII's Garde du Corps. By the evening, however, it had become clear that there had been a wholesale desertion of the army to Bonaparte – all, that is, except for the King's personal bodyguard. Louis XVIII made secret plans to flee from Paris to Lille, in a ghastly echo of his brother's flight to Varennes. At nine o'clock, M. d'A wrote his note to Fanny, he then prepared to leave himself. But there was such confusion that, while Louis XVIII and his immediate household went straight to Lille, there were insufficient horses for all his troops to follow him. By the time M. d'A arrived at Ypres (just across the French–Belgian border, some twenty miles north of Lille), he had ridden for twenty-six hours in driving rain and was so ill with a bilious fever that he collapsed and for two days was too weak to leave his bed.

All this time, Fanny had no idea of her husband's fate. Eight days later, on 27 March, she wrote to her brother James from Brussels, where she had rented rooms in the same house on the rue de la Montagne as the Princesse d'Hénin:

> Oh James – I know not what is become of my best & dearest half! . . .
> We parted THIS DAY WEEK! – how dreadfully! – neither of us able to
> devine the destination of the other!' . . . 'A large body of English troops
> passed before my window yesterday, for the Frontieres commanded by
> Gen Clinton [who had fought under Wellington in the Peninsular
> War]. They huzza'd the whole way, & the Inhabitants huzza'd them
> from the windows.[5]

She wondered whether M. d'A was bound for the same battlefield.

Not until 2 April did she receive confirmation of her husband's whereabouts, when he walked into her room in Brussels, gratifying her wish that their first meeting after such a frightening separation should be 'without Witnesses! I ENTREAT you to contrive That. – I shall BURST if I must constrain my gratitude to Heaven & my joy & tenderness.'[6] For almost six weeks, life returned to a semblance of normality as Fanny nursed her husband back to strength after his exhausting retreat to Belgium. They promenaded each afternoon along the ramparts of the city; and drove out into the Parc de Bruxelles.

On the evening of 27 April, they attended a concert given by the great Italian soprano, Angelica Catalani. Also in the audience was the Duke of Wellington, who had rented a large house in the Belgian capital while he made his preparations for what everyone had come to believe would be the conclusive battle against Napoleon. Fanny described the evening in a letter to the Princess Elizabeth: 'the voice of Catalani charmed & astonished me – but well as she is worth looking at besides being heard, my Eyes were rivetted all the night upon The Hopes of World, the D. of W. who was just facing me. I have a faith in him so great that, at his sight, I feel all courage.'[7]

Fanny was to have need of such faith and courage: while in Brussels, M. d'A was summoned to a private audience with Louis XVIII in Ghent, at which he was given orders for 'a new and important mission'. This was to round up and interrogate deserters from Napoleon's army and persuade them (by whatever means) to fight in the service of the French King. It was a difficult enough task, made doubly dangerous by the fact that M. d'A was then seconded to the Prussian General Kleist von Nollendorf, and sent off to Trèves in the southernmost corner of the Prussian Rhineland – where there was no sympathy for the French. Alone once more, Fanny filled her days by trying to glean news of the military preparations of the allies against Napoleon, whom she called the '*tiny Tiger*'. She took the precaution of reverting to her maiden name, calling herself '*Madame* Burney'.

Throughout May, a continual procession of Prussian, Austrian, English, Scottish, Bavarian and Russian soldiers passed through Brussels on their way to the plains of Waterloo, some ten miles outside the city towards the border with France. By 30 May, the signing of the declaration of war against Napoleon by the allied forces of France, Austria, Prussia, Russia, Great Britain, Spain, Portugal, Denmark and Sweden – with the Duke of Wellington as 'Lord of All' – confirmed the rumour that the great battle to crush Napoleon now and for always would take place very soon (some said within eight days). 'How awful is this pause! How, & in what manner, will it terminate?' Fanny asked M. d'A. 'I shudder, but try vainly to run from the subject?'[8]

Fanny knew that her own future was irrevocably bound up with the fate of Napoleon at Waterloo, as she waited impatiently for news of her husband, suffering from 'fits of *morne mélancolie* as undermine, secretly & slowly, but surely, the poor harassed machine, of which the inside outworks the outside'.[9] M. d'A's letters from Trèves took six days to reach her, yet the news from Waterloo changed almost hourly. Desperation drove her to overcome her shyness, and she found herself going up to anyone she saw in the street whom she recognised as English and begging them for information.

Fanny's love of a dramatic situation gives her letters from Brussels a startling clarity that evokes all the horror, the panic, the chaos of war.

And she provides invaluable details on the run-up to Waterloo, such as the way it rained virtually every day during the fortnight preceding the battle, creating the muddy conditions that had such a disastrous effect on the morale of Napoleon's troops as they struggled to retreat from the allies.

On 9 June (just a week before the battle began) she talked to a British officer who had served throughout Spain under the Duke of Wellington and had witnessed some seventeen battles. He had just come from Waterloo, where he had seen the allies' preparations for the 'Destruction of all France'. According to him, '100,000 pieces of Cannon . . . were arrived' as well as '16 million of Congreve's Rockets! – & 16 million of Carcases [shells] with hooks! . . . The Carcases, he said, were of a fire of so noxious a nature, that no man could breathe within 20 yards of the spot on which they burst.' He went on to tell Fanny that everything was now ready for battle. 'The Duke of Wellington is completely prepared . . . He has every Horse that England could spare.' Fanny asked him, 'my voice hardly audible with the terrour he had given me', when the hostilities would begin. He replied that the Duke of Wellington wanted to defer the conflict until the harvest was over, so that there would be enough grain to feed the survivors.[10]

But a few days later, during the night of Thursday, 15 June, Fanny was awakened by confused noises in the street below. She later discovered how, earlier that evening, the Duke of Wellington, with fifty of his red-coated officers, had attended the Duchess of Richmond's ball, where he had been told that Napoleon had begun his invasion of 'les pays bas'. Wellington waited until after supper before handing each of his men a written memo ordering them to leave the ball, but discreetly, as 'they would be off tomorrow'. When Fanny looked out of her window some hours later, she could see only a few soldiers in the street. Relieved, she went back to bed, to be woken again by the sound of a bugle horn, as if troops were being mustered. She looked out; again, she could see nothing unusual, and so retreated back to bed. But after breakfast that morning, while she was walking back from the post office where she had sent off her letter to M. d'A, she heard the sound of a military band in the distance, which grew louder and louder. She watched as a complete troop of the Duke of Brunswick's regiment – infantry, cavalry, artillery, bag and baggage – marched grimly down the street in their black regalia. She realised at the time that they were destined for battle; she later discovered that they were among its first victims.

Fanny spent a terrible day. Was M. d'A still in Trèves? Was it safe to stay in Brussels? If she left, where could she go that M. d'A might find her? She scoured the streets for news – determined to find out what was happening. 'My whole character, natively reserved, fearful, & retired, was conquered', by fears for her husband and her desire 'to seek information by every means through which it might be obtained'. As she moved through the crowds who were watching the procession of soldiers marching out of the city towards Waterloo, she grew more and more uneasy. 'It was not possible for me to discern, with any solidity of conviction, whether the Belgians were at heart Bourbonites or Buonapartites'. What, then, would be her fate if Napoleon was victorious?

Her anxiety was intensified because M. d'A had signed a Proclamation of Loyalty to Louis XVIII, which, if Napoleon did succeed in regaining his Empire, would become a capital offence. Fanny was appalled that M. d'A should so have endangered his life by making a public profession of his Royalism. It was, she told him, a 'chevalresque extravagance!', which filled her with 'affright & dismay'. And she begged him, 'Oh! God! – let no rashness – no false notions precipitate *you* to mischief! To all that is *essential* to The Cause, & to Your Honour, I submit: – but Oh! go no further!'[11]

Such thoughts obsessed her as throughout the next day, Friday, 16 June, the rumours from Waterloo kept changing: one minute reporting that the battle was going in favour of Napoleon; the next, that the allies were in the ascendant. 'What a day of confusion & alarm did we all spend!' she wrote to M. d'A. 'In *my* heart the whole time was Trèves! Trèves! Trèves! That day & *This*, which is now finishing, June 17th, I passed in hearing the cannon –! – seeing the wounded & disabled return, & the ready-armed & vigourous victims march forth to the same destruction.'[12]

Fanny decided that she must wait in Brussels for M. d'A, but she had the foresight to apply for a passport that would allow her to leave at a moment's notice. She made her way to the police bureau, where she found a scene of utter confusion as a panicky crowd of Belgians, British and French, desperate to gain permission to leave the city, besieged the building. When she saw that the officer in charge (who was British) was being 'attacked, envellopped, entreated, reproached, or interrogated from all quarters; & his answers were so rough, his air was so boisterous, & his language was so harsh, that he shook off all who advanced', she realised that her only chance was somehow to find a way into the building so that she could see him in his private office. This she did, and was soon rewarded by hearing the sound of his footsteps hurrying along the corridor. He listened to her pleas, but then reproved her sharply, reminding her of her duty as an Englishwoman not to spread alarm, adding that his own wife and children were still in the city. Fanny, however, was resolute, demanding that he should at least stamp his approval on her existing passport, which, with considerable reluctance, he finally agreed to do. Now, at least, she had official authorisation to leave.

By nightfall on Saturday, 17 June, it was rumoured that victory was imminent – but to which side? Fanny's friends decided they had to make their escape, but she gambled on her faith in Wellington. She sat up all night preparing charpie (an awful reminder of her own need of surgical bandages), unable to sleep or stop thinking about M. d'A. At six o'clock she heard a sharp rapping: 'Open your door! There is not a moment to lose!' Napoleon, she was told, had seized the victory and his troops were advancing on Brussels. Fanny packed up her few belongings and hurried to join the family of a British banker, William Boyd, who had promised in an emergency to take her with them to Antwerp:

> Though the distance to the docks was short, the Walk was long, because rugged, dirty & melancholy. Now & then we heard a growling Noise, like distant Thunder . . . When we had got about a third part of the way, a heavy rumbling sound made us stop to listen. It was approaching nearer & nearer, as we soon found that we were followed by innumerable carriages, & a multitude of persons.
>
> All was evidently military; but of so gloomy, taciturn, & forbidding a description that, when we were overtaken, we had not courage to offer a question to any passer-by . . . In truth, at that period, when every other hour changed the current of Expectation, no one could be inquisitive without the risk of passing for a Spy, nor communicative, without the hazard of being suspected as a traitor.
>
> As, slowly, we now went on, we saw ourselves preceded, or succeeded by Baggage Waggons, Artillery, carts filled with women & children, & military machines of all sorts & sizes.

When they eventually reached the docks, they discovered that the barge that Mr Boyd had hoped would take them away from the city had been commandeered by Wellington (as had all other means of transport) to carry 'all the Magazines, the Artillery, warlike stores of every description, & all the Wounded, the maimed, & the Sick' immediately to Antwerp, as Bonaparte was dominating the course of the battle and was likely to win.

Fanny and the Boyds could only turn round and walk back to the city centre. All the time, the sound of the cannon seemed to be growing louder and louder, as if the battle was getting closer to Brussels. 'Yet – strange to relate! on re-entering the City, all seemed quiet & tranquil as usual! & though it was in this imminent & immediate danger of being invested, & perhaps pillaged, I saw no outward mark of distress or disturbance, or even of hurry & curiosity.'

Fanny returned to her lodgings alone, where not long afterwards she suddenly heard a 'Hurrah' in the street below, and the cry of *'Buonaparté est pris! le voilà! le voilà!'* On looking out of her window, she saw a French General in 'the full & splendid Uniform of France' and leading a 'noble War Horse' being led into the square below, where he was pillaged of all his equipment. Did this mean that Napoleon was vanquished?

Fifteen minutes later, she heard more shouts, which to her this time sounded like howls of despair. She ran to the window to see a crowd rushing through the square 'as if unconscious in what direction: while Women with Children in their arms, or clinging to their cloathes, ran screaming out of doors'. Fanny screamed out, *'Les françaises arrivent! ils sont à nos portes!'* And, throwing a shawl over her shoulders and tying on a bonnet, she rushed downstairs into the street.

Once outside, she was told that the French were indeed coming, but as *prisoners* not as vanquishers. Too alarmed now to remain by herself, Fanny went to see a neighbour who was French and who had lost her husband and three sons in the Revolution. All that day, they sat at the window watching as the wounded and dying – on foot, on horseback, on stretchers – flooded into the city. It was, she later told the Princess Elizabeth, 'a sight to break one's heart! – yet upon which the Eye, forever seeking some information, or hoping for some change, while filled with commiseration, was fixed as by Magic!'[13]

Later on, she went out in search of someone who could give her news from the battlefield, and met an Englishman:

He [the Duke of Wellington] was everywhere, he said; the Eye could turn in no direction that it did not perceive him, either at hand, or at a distance; gallopping to charge the Enemy, or darting across the Field to issue, or to change some orders . . . he seemed as impervious for safety as he was dauntless for courage: while Danger all the time relentlessly envirroned him, and Wounds, fractures, dislocations, loss of limbs, or Death continually robbed him of the services of some of the bravest & the dearest of those who were nearest to him. But he suffered nothing to check, or appal, or engage him, that belonged to personal interest or feeling: his entire concentrated attention, exclusive aim, & intense thought were devoted . . . to the WHOLE, the ALL.

But Fanny's eyewitness could not reassure her that victory for the allies was certain: 'never had he seen a Field of Battle in such excessive disorder and he had viewed many'.

Fanny spent the night with the Boyds, who had agreed to make another attempt to get out of the city early the next morning. No one went to bed, for fear of another scare that the French were coming. By morning, however, it was confirmed that Wellington was victorious and that Napoleon and his troops had been pushed into an ignominious retreat. Fanny decided not to leave Brussels, even though it meant she would be virtually alone, for fear that, if she did, she might miss M. d'A.

As she waited with increasing anxiety for news of her husband, she gathered first-hand information on this most bloody and confused of battles. The '*Piles* of Dead — heaps, Masses, *hills* of Dead! French, English, Belge & Prussian, are horrible,' she wrote to M. d'A after talking to an English soldier who had been taken prisoner by Napoleon's soldiers on the Sunday and 'carried into a Wood, with many others, where he was very ill & roughly used, stript of all his baggage, & of his shoes, & whatever did not leave him naked'. By the evening of that day, however, his captors were 'in too much trouble to watch, & he crawled upon all fours out of the wood, & crept on till he joined a party of his comrades', who took him to safety in Brussels.[14] The wounded and dying were still being brought into the city a week later, by which time it had begun to resemble 'a Walking Hospital'. Three thousand 'peasants', Fanny told M. d'A, were employed in burying the dead.

M. d'A was stuck in Trèves, some 160 miles from the scene of battle, where he expected orders to rejoin his regiment at any minute. But it was as if he had been forgotten, and it was left to Fanny to tell him of the victory of Wellington and the allies. She sent him Wellington's Proclamation of 22 June, which she had written down from memory; it is remarkably accurate: 'France must know I enter its territories at the head of an army already victorious; but not an Enemy! – I come an Enemy only to the Usurper, & his adherents.' M. d'A was devastated that France should have been so humiliated by the European allies. *'Pauvre Pauvre France! Vas tu être assez humiliée,'* he replied to his English wife.[15]

Then, on 9 July, M. d'A suffered a wound more terrible than anything inflicted upon him by Napoleon's imperial ambition. While waiting impatiently in Trèvcs, he was kicked by an ill-tempered horse. Although the injury went deep, it was not at first serious. But all the good surgeons had been called to Brussels and M. d'A was treated by an incompetent apothecary, who stitched up the gash before it had been properly cleansed. Septicaemia set in, the flesh rapidly turned black, and M. d'A became delirious with a high fever. The same 'quack' decided that the only way to save his patient's life was to inflict further pain by making three more incisions in his leg – all without any kind of anaesthetic – in an attempt to reduce the swelling and drain off the poison. As M. d'A slipped into a coma, Fanny was sent for, but she heard nothing for ten days. Then she received a visit from the Princesse d'Hénin, who came to tell her of M. d'A's accident: he had asked that the news should not be sent direct to Fanny so that she would not be alone when she heard it.

Fanny determined to set out immediately for Trèves, despite the Princesse's warning that the roads south of Brussels were dangerous, haunted by brigands taking advantage of the confused aftermath of Waterloo. Alone, and with just a little money and a basket filled with her letters from M. d'A, she booked herself a seat on the diligence to Liège, the only safe route, which was due to leave at nightfall. But she missed it by three or four minutes, arriving at the post-house just in time to see it disappearing down the street.

Frantic, she hired a fiacre to chase the coach to its next stopping-point on the outskirts of the city. She just made it, but this was only the first of many misadventures as she hurried to join M. d'A, terrified that he would die before she arrived. At every stopping-place, she encountered hostile police officers, who demanded to know whether she was French, English, Belgian or Prussian. Not knowing whether it was safer to admit that she was English, or to pretend to be French, she said the wrong thing every time.

In Liège the next morning, Fanny discovered that she was in Prussian-controlled territory where her passport (stamped in Brussels, but originally obtained in Paris) was declared invalid – even after her pleas that she was rushing to attend a sick friend. Driven by desperation, Fanny rose to the occasion: 'Brutality so unauthorized however it shocked, I would not suffer to intimidate me.'[16] She asserted proudly that her husband was serving in Trèves under the Prussian commander, General Kleist von Nollendorf, a name that sufficiently awed the obstreperous official to give permission for her to travel. However, at Juliers on the following day, she was asked by the police whether she was English, to which she admitted that she was from '*du pays du brave Wellington*'. Once again, she had said the wrong thing, and was allowed to leave only after mentioning that magic password, 'General Kleist von Nollendorf'.

Her worst fright occurred in Bonn: she later said its horror compared only with the operation on her breast. On arrival in the city, she had been told that the diligence would not be leaving for a couple of hours and so, with no money left to spend on the breakfast being enjoyed by her fellow passengers, she decided to while away the time and forget her hunger by exploring the town. In her exhaustion and anxiety about M. d'A, she became so lost and confused that she could not find her way back to the hotel. She had no word of German, and all whom she met as she rushed down side-alley after side-alley spoke no English. She knew that, if she missed the coach, there would not be another one for a week, and that 'even if I could here meet with a separate conveyance, the tales now hourly recounted of marauders, straggling Pillagers, & military Banditti, with the immense Forests, & unknown roads through which I must pass, made me tremble . . . Oh! this was, indeed, nearly, the most tortured crisis of misery I ever experienced!'

At last, she caught sight of a religious figurine set into the niche of a wall. She had noticed it earlier as being very like those 'ludicrous' statuettes described by Lady Mary Wortley Montagu in her letters from Germany of 1716. Fanny was disdainful of such a graven image, describing it later as:

a short, thick, squabby little personage, whose Wig, Hose, Sandals, Coat, Waistcoat, & trowsers were of all the colours . . . The Wig, I think, was blue; the Coat, Red; the Waistcoat, Yellow; the Sandals, Green; the Trowsers, purple, & the Hose, pink. I am not certain, at this distance of time, that I give the right colours to their right places; I am only sure that the separate parts of the dress employed, separately, those colours, and that what rendered them almost as prophane as they were risible, were some symbols – either of Golden rays round the Wig, or of a Crucifix at the back, which shewed that this hideous little Statue was meant for a young Jesus.

But this 'Unhappy divine' was her salvation, guiding her back to the hotel and the diligence that was waiting to take her on to Coblenz and thence to Trèves, where she finally arrived late on the evening of Monday, 24 July. She had been six days on the road, travelling throughout one whole night and for most of the other four across bandit country, in a jolting carriage enclosed with strangers whose language she could not understand. She scribbled a note to M. d'A, not wishing to shock him by walking into his sick-room unannounced. Five minutes later, François, her husband's servant, came running to meet her. He assured her that 'the Danger was over', before escorting the swooning, speechless Fanny to her husband.

She was at first filled with an 'exquisite felicity', but this soon changed to a terrible dismay when she realised how much her husband had suffered since his accident. Although she was anxious to move him to Paris as soon as possible, so that he could be attended by her own surgeon, Baron Larrey, a whole month passed before he was strong enough to withstand the journey.

Their slow trek across Belgium and France, in a specially converted open carriage that enabled M. d'A to travel with his leg raised so that no pressure was put on his wounds, was a miserable experience for him. Fanny recalled later how:

> the spirits of the poor worn Invalid were sunk, &, like his bodily strength, exhausted. After being always the most active, the most enterprizing; the most ingenious in difficulty & mischance; & the most vivacious in conquering evils, & combatting accidents; to find himself thus suddenly bereft not only of his useful, pleasing, delightful powers to serve & oblige all around him, but even of all means of aiding & sufficing to himself, was profoundly dejecting.

This was not all that depressed M. d'A, for as they crossed France to reach Paris, he began to realise how much the defeat at Waterloo had crushed his country's spirit: 'We re-entered France by the permission of Foreigners; & could only re-enter it at all by Passports of All the Allies! It seemed as if All Europe had freer egress to it than its Natives!'

But at least once they were back at the rue de Miroménil, Fanny could ensure that her husband received the best medical treatment. She discovered that their apartment was just as she had left it on that dreadful day in March, when she had feared that they had lost everything. Their friends had returned also, and before long the quiet social gatherings of former, happier days were resumed. On one occasion, Fanny found herself in the same room as Talleyrand, whom she had not seen since he had congratulated her upon her wedding in July 1793. He had spent several years in America after being expelled from Britain, before serving under both Napoleon and Louis XVIII as Minister for Foreign Affairs. He did not appear to remember Fanny, and so she went up to him and said, '*M. de Talleyrand m'a oublié: mais on n'oublie pas M. de Talleyrand.*' He started, and she saw 'a movement of surprize by no means unpleasant break over the habitual placidity, of the nearly imperturbable composure of his general – & certainly *made up* countenance'.

These days of summer were filled with 'conversational perfection! of Wit, ingenuity, gaiety, repartee, information, badinage, & eloquence'. But for the d'Arblays it was an illusory respite. M. d'A was still suffering from his wounds and unfit to resume his military duties. Even more painful, however, was his recognition that there would never now be a place for him and his family in post-Napoleonic France. He agreed reluctantly with Fanny that to return to Britain was their only option. On 17 October 1815, Fanny once more stepped on to British soil, after yet another long and wearisome journey, which she said was 'in full & terrible unison with our jarred & unstrung feelings'. She was never again to cross the Channel.

FOURTEEN

Bath
1815–18

Tout le monde dira à Alex qui est sa mère; mais – qu'il n'oublie pas qui a été son Père! C'est pour cela que je lui ai consacré et fait faire ce Portrait.

General d'Arblay, 1818

On 19 October 1815, Alex rushed to meet his parents as soon as he heard that they had arrived at the La Sablonière hotel in Leicester Square, where they planned to stay for a few days while sorting out their affairs in London. No record survives of his feelings on first seeing M. d'A – Alex was never a diarist. But he must have been shocked to see how 'cruelly changed' was his 'best friend'. Gaunt, weary and limping badly from his accident at Trèves, M. d'A was very different from the cheerful, confident General who had left for France less than a year earlier.

'We are terribly mangled by events of all sorts, public & private,' Fanny told her sister Charlotte.[1] Fanny was relieved to be with her family again; M. d'A, by contrast, was dispirited and anxious about the future. He had been honoured with the title of 'Comte' by Louis XVIII before being sent off to Trèves in May 1815, but this was little compensation for being permanently retired from the army. And he had little hope that he would receive any of his pension now that he was no longer living in France. Yet he had needed little persuasion from Fanny to leave: to remain in his native country was to be reminded constantly of how much he had lost – and of how the French monarchy had been shamed yet again by the defection of its own troops to Napoleon. As Fanny was later to write, he saw himself as 'a ruined Gentleman; ruined by public calamities, & therefore without possessions'.[2]

After a brief reunion with Alex, who was on vacation from Cambridge, Fanny and M. d'A travelled to Bath to try the waters, leaving behind the *calèche* in which they had travelled from Paris, and in which they had enjoyed so many carefree afternoon drives in the Bois de Boulogne and the Parc de Bruxelles, so that it could be sold for cash.[3] They lodged first in Rivers Street, in rooms arranged for them by Fanny's nieces, Maria and Sophia, but these proved too expensive for the d'Arblays, who soon moved into cheaper rooms in Great Stanhope Street, a less fashionable area beside the River Avon and away from the crowded streets near the Pump Room and Baths.

Fanny had first seen Bath in 1767 when she and her father passed through on their way to Clifton Hotwells. She thought then that it was a 'City of Palaces', but by 1815 its architectural splendours had been augmented by the completion of most of the Georgian buildings we know today, such as the Royal Crescent, the Pump Room, the New Assembly Rooms and Pulteney Bridge. Originally a medicinal resort for the elderly and infirm rich, Bath had become a kind of West-End-on-Avon, with a population of some 38,000 (of which over 23,000 were female). As Fanny remarked to Charles, 'so much Beauty I never any where saw assembled as daily parades Milsom Street & the Royal Crescent'.[4]

She and M. d'A rarely ventured beyond their fireside in those first winter months. However, by March 1816 the Comte d'Arblay had sufficiently recovered his strength to escort his wife to one of the twice-weekly balls in the Assembly Rooms, where Fanny watched the daughters of her old friend from Windsor, Marianne Waddington, dancing the new-fangled cotillion.[5]

Fanny was recognised as a 'celebrity' and was offered free tickets to the Theatre Royal whenever she wished; she graciously refused, explaining that, as it was so rare that she felt well enough to go out, 'I cannot answer my conscience not to contribute, upon such occasions, my small and well-earned mite for the Entertainment I receive.'[6] But in July she was tempted by what she had read about the new dramatic star Edmund Kean to see him in *Hamlet*. Fanny was not impressed. She remembered Garrick's mesmerising performances in the role, which had so affected her that she peppered her novels and letters with quotations from the play. 'The familiar whisper that follows the loud, heroic rant requires time, I imagine, for appreciation,' she commented to Marianne Waddington.[7] She also bought tickets to see John Kemble in his last benefit performance, a production of Shakespeare's *King John*. It was a generous gesture: the last time she and M. d'A had seen him on stage was at that disastrous first night of *Edwy and Elgiva* in March 1795.

Fanny was happy in Bath and hoped that M. d'A could be persuaded to settle there. She wrote to Queeney Thrale (now Viscountess Keith through her marriage to George Keith, Admiral of the Channel Fleet) that she believed it was an ideal retreat for them, more than a small town and yet in a beautiful rural setting:

> There is no place I have yet seen where the inconveniences of a limited income are so little felt, nor where the people at large are so civilised. As there are no manufactures, & scarcely any commerce, here, the rapacity of wealth has not infected men's minds ... Equipage, Servants, Table, Jewels, though *here*, as every where, very desirable, are not here *requisite* ... There is something nearer to independence from the shackles of fortuitous circumstances in the society of *Bath* than I have witnessed elsewhere.[8]

Many of her old 'Bluestocking' friends had retired to Bath from the noise and expense of London, in particular Mrs Thrale-Piozzi, who bought a house in Gay Street after the death of her second husband.[9] Fanny called on her old friend from Streatham in December 1815. Apart from a chance meeting in Windsor when Fanny was at Court, they had not seen each other since Mrs Thrale-Piozzi's remarriage, and their conversation was so stilted and frosty that, despite being 'not above 20 houses in a strait line' from each other until Mrs Thrale-Piozzi moved into Gay Street, they rarely met.[10] But Fanny persisted – anxious to make amends for having turned away from her friend – and was rewarded a year later when Mrs Thrale-Piozzi took her into her boudoir rather than entertaining Fanny in the chilly formality of the drawing-room.

The informal setting brought back memories of Streatham Park and soon, according to Fanny, they were talking 'our best'. But too much had changed them both in the intervening years, and Fanny was disappointed to find that they were like 'two strangers, who had no sort of knowledge or care for each other, but were willing each to fling & to accept the gauntlet, *pour faire la belle conversation*'. Anyone overhearing them 'would have supposed we had met for the first time, & without an acquaintance or one remembrance in common,' she wrote to Queeney afterwards.[11] Mrs Thrale-Piozzi still thought of Fanny as '*l'Aimable Traitresse*', and vowed that she would 'not assist her Reception in the World a Second time – "else she'll betray more Men" as Shakespear says'.[12]

M. d'A renewed his enthusiasm for gardening, renting a plot

between Great Stanhope Street and the river on which to grow his prize geraniums and vegetables. He had no friends in the city, and although he was soon very popular with Fanny's 'Bluestocking' circle (they found him very clever, and a man of perfect gentility), he missed Paris and the company of his French acquaintances. He was also anxious to settle his affairs in France, which he believed he could only do in person. By April 1816, he was planning his return. Fanny wrote to Alex, who was about to begin his final term at Cambridge: 'All depends upon our Alex! If he acquits himself well, the voyage to France will be but a preparation for this *final residence*, with only excursions in the summer months to the continent *all-together*.' But if he did not 'take such a degree as to enable you to procure Honour & Independence in this country . . . your Father will not relinquish his own. Who could ask him?'

Upon Alex's success at Cambridge, then, depended not only his own future but also that of his mother and father. 'Work, then, my Alex,' his mother warned him. 'Work – it would break my heart to be separated from *either* of you.'[13] A fearful burden was thus placed on Alex, who had discovered that he would have to take his degree in medicine, a subject in which he had no interest and in which he had attended no lectures nor made any studies. By some extraordinary oversight, both Fanny and Charles had failed to notice when they applied for the Tancred scholarship on Alex's behalf that it could only be given to students of medicine. This meant that Alex would either have to graduate in that subject, or forfeit the scholarship and repay the money. Neither option was feasible for Alex, whose only hope of leaving university with academic honours now depended on him being offered another scholarship that would allow him to stay on so that he could prepare for the BA examinations. Fortunately, Alex had never lacked friends and supporters, however much he infuriated them by his unworldliness and 'total inattention to college discipline', and one of his tutors arranged for him to transfer from Caius to Christ's College, where he was admitted to take a degree in mathematical sciences.

M. d'A left for Paris on 6 August 1816. Fanny stayed behind in Bath to keep an eye on Alex and ensure that he followed a strict régime of vacation reading. She described herself as Alex's 'Flapper', after the 'Flappers' in Swift's *Gulliver's Travels*. These servants of the absent-minded residents of Laputa carried with them 'a blown bladder fastened like a flail to the end of a short stick' in which 'was a small quantity of dried pease, or little pebbles', which they used 'to flap the mouths and ears of those who stood near them' to wake them from their 'intense speculations'.[14] Alex, indeed, had need of his Flapper: August was high season in Bath, and, at twenty-one, he was soon, according to his mother, mingling *à la mode* and dancing till midnight with the eligible daughters of her friends (having first been reminded by his mother that he must buy a razor – and use it).

Fanny despaired of her son as he wasted yet another whole day in a state of high anxiety about the evening ahead. 'He could not settle to work all day,' she reported back to M. d'A, and, before breakfast was finished, had rushed out 'to buy himself a pair of beautiful Woodstock Gloves. At luncheon, he was very thoughtful, & ran off again – & returned in an Hour, with a pair of expensive dancing Pumps! – And just as we were going to dinner, he bounced out of doors, & having kept me waiting till past 6 o'clock, returned with his Hair fresh cropt & curled, from the *perruquier's*!'[15] He had arranged to meet a Miss d'Alton at a party, and she was, according to Fanny, '*la plus belle jeune personne de Bath*'. Alex, here, is transformed by his mother into Mr Smith, the 'Holborn Beau' of *Evelina*. But, unlike Mr Smith, Alex was destined for academic success – at least in the eyes of his mother, who imposed on her son a strict timetable for study.

M. d'A, however, had other ideas for his son. In Paris, he had met again a *çi-devant* family with whom the d'Arblays had become acquainted in the summer of 1802 while they were living in Monceau. Monsieur de Reynier de Jarjayes had been a Chevalier de Saint Louis in 1789 and, like M. d'A, had also been appointed a Maréchal de Camp in 1792. His eldest daughter, Claudine-Augustine, was just two years younger than Alex. M. d'A wrote to Fanny extolling her virtues and hinting that she might make an ideal life-companion for their son. Fanny recalled that she was a very charming, but precociously vain little girl: 'Do you not remember her adjusting her hair, & then turning round her pretty figure twenty ways, before a high miroir, to see how she held her train, in a room full of company? & not from childish ignorance or thoughtlessness, but to use your own words, – *come une lilliputienne aux airs de princesse*?'

Fanny was appalled by M. d'A's suggestion that he should arrange a marriage for his son and, furthermore, that he should choose for him the pampered, coquettish daughter of an aristocratic French family. 'As complete as her Fortune & Situation are brilliant – can you – & is it possible – think Alexander *now* fit to propose to her? or that *she, now,* could make Alexander happy? Alas no! . . . He must see the world, & learn to bend his humour from his own exclusive pursuits ere he should become a husband & a Father.'

If this were not enough to discourage M. d'A, Fanny added that Alex 'always declares he NEVER will marry a *French Girl* – for his Father, *who would know how to manage one so much better than him*, always said he never thought of a wife till he came to England.' More significantly, Alex recognised that he could never live in France, for 'All men abroad that are not *military*, are insignificant.'[16]

M. d'A, however, ignored his wife's pleas and wrote to his old friend, proposing that their families should be united by the marriage of their children. Fanny could not believe that her 'Partner in all' could have been so thoughtless: 'OH MON AMI! how was it possible you could thus enter into a negociation for the marriage of our only child . . . was it kind – was it right – not to communicate with me first, & to hear, & to weigh what I might have to offer?' She had always regarded their marriage as a partnership, even if she recognised that M. d'A should have the final say in such important matters: 'The power of Decision is yours,' she told him, 'but the equal right of representation is mine.' She was upset that he had so completely ignored what she might have wanted for Alex: 'Est-ce Vous – bien vous – who return thus to *l'ancien régime* in a point upon which I have so often heard you condemn it?' Worse still, M. d'A had shown Fanny's letter expressing her disapproval of Augustine to her parents. 'How will they dislike me!' she bewailed.[17]

This separation was indeed an unhappy one for both M. d'A and Fanny, and their letters are full of misunderstandings, mostly over Alex. M. d'A was 'demolished' by Fanny's reaction; he was, he told her, incapacitated by *'un battement de coeur'*. Fanny had been unjust. Was not marriage into an ultra-respectable French family the best and only way for him to secure Alex's future? Fanny was adamant: she could see no future for any of them in France, and she wrote another long letter to M. d'A, this time mostly in French so that she could be sure her meaning would be understood. She pleaded with him to withdraw his offer, assuring him that 'to lead Alex so early & unformed to the Altar, would be offering up, in all human probability, Two victims to *ennui* & regret'.[18] M. d'A could not argue with such common sense and so abandoned all hope of sorting out a future for his son in France. Three weeks later he was back in Bath, 'harrassed to death, & after a passage the most dangerous & painful'.[19]

He took refuge in digging over his vegetable plot, while Fanny sorted through her father's papers, a task that she had begun during M. d'A's absence. At some point he prepared a sketch-plan outlining the course of the Battle at Waterloo on Sunday, 18 June, with annotations from Fanny's record. Alex came home for the Christmas vacation and surprised his mother by making a real effort to prepare himself for the oral examination he must take before readmission as a BA student. This meant that he would have to dispute with his tutor for three hours – in Latin – on English mathematicians and their theories. Fanny feared that her undisciplined son would never prepare himself adequately for such a rigorous test. But Alex's performance was a triumph. 'Hourray! Hourray! Hourray! Hou-r-r-r-rray! I have acquitted myself as well as the most sanguine expectations could have anticipated,' he wrote to his mother on 7 March 1817, adding, somewhat poignantly, 'The only difficulty now is to restrain Papa – for there is no knowing what he will expect next.'[20]

But M. d'A was by this time too ill to share in his son's delight. The trials he had endured in 1815 had left him with a depressing languor and digestive problems, and by the middle of February this had developed into a serious bout of jaundice. (This explains, perhaps, his uncharacteristic irritation over the question of Alex's future.) When Alex came home to celebrate his success, M. d'A was still feverish and in pain. But his son's arrival – bright, carefree and now enthusing over Byron's poems, which he read to his parents 'with congenial warmth & Fire' – seemed to revive M. d'A, and he began to venture out again and to contemplate yet another return to France. Fanny decided after much agonising not to go with him. Although she feared for her husband's health (which was far from 're-established') if he stayed in Paris without her, her brother Charles had warned her that it was *essential* for her 'not to quit the kingdom while A's degree is pending'. Alex had been invited to join a summer reading-party in Ilfracombe, which would be supervised by one of his tutors; nevertheless, Fanny thought she should go too, as his 'Flapper'.

M. d'A left for Paris on 12 June 1817, having arranged to meet Alex in London on his way to Dover. Alex arrived at M. d'A's hotel, La Sablonière, in time to dine with his father but, after the meal, wandered off and did not return until after M. d'A had left for Dover at five o'clock the next morning. In Alex's version of what happened, his father became so absorbed in reading his newspaper that he appeared to be ignoring his son. Only then, Alex told his mother, did he leave the hotel and call on his Uncle James, who tempted him into a game of chess that went on into the early hours. M. d'A, however, was not just hurt that Alex had failed to turn up to say farewell; he had also been worried about him, having had to leave London with no idea where his son had spent the night. M. d'A was convinced that Alex had 'an UNFEELING Heart', and was not consoled by Fanny's philosophical riposte that at least they could be thankful Alex's dissipations were not more dangerous to his reputation or his meagre finances.

Perhaps because he was still far from recovered from the jaundice, M. d'A viewed Alex's behaviour as a bad omen. His Parisian friends – Madame de Maisonneuve and her brother General Victor de Latour-Maubourg, the Princesse d'Hénin, the Comte de Lally-Tollendal and the Prince and Princesse de Beauvau – welcomed him back, and did all they could to raise his spirits. But he spent many of his evenings alone, seeking entertainment at the theatre because he felt too miserable for company. He commissioned a portrait of himself from Carle Vernet and his son Horace, so that Alex would never forget him: '*Tout le monde dira à Alex qui est sa mère; mais – qu'il n'oublie pas qui a été son Père! C'est pour cela que je lui ai consacré et fait faire ce Portrait.*'[21]

In this moderately sized oil painting, he appears not as M. d'A but as the Chevalier, resplendent in his uniform and seated in front of a scene of battle, with guns firing and a handsome warhorse (Horace Vernet was renowned as a fine painter of horses). He is wearing his three military medals – the St Louis, la Fidelité and the Légion d'honneur – showing how he fought for France both before and after the Revolution. The portrait can now be seen in the Long Gallery at Parham Park in Sussex, where it hangs opposite Edward Francisco's painting of Fanny as a girlish thirty-year-old in her 'Vandyke' dress. In a glass cabinet below are the silver epaulettes and collar worn by the General in his picture.

While in Paris, M. d'A heard that Madame de Staël had died on 14 July 1817 after suffering a cerebral stroke; she was fifty-one and only five years earlier had given birth to a son fathered by her new consort, a Swiss–Italian soldier some twenty-two years her junior (the scandal reached all the European papers). The news was a further jolt to M. d'A's weary and dejected mood, reminding him of the absence of his close friend Narbonne, who had died in November 1813 while serving under Napoleon as the military governor of Torgau in Saxony. (Narbonne was said to have bravely chosen to visit his troops who were dying from an epidemic fever, which he then caught himself.)

The divided loyalties during those years of Revolution and Empire were far from healed: M. d'A's brother had died fighting for the Republic in 1795 after starting out as a Constitutional Monarchist like M. d'A. In his letters to Fanny, M. d'A told her of the duels being fought in the Bois de Boulogne between former supporters of Bonaparte and the ultra-Royalists.

M. d'A fretted away his wakeful nights, worrying about Alex, whom he now believed would inherit nothing except spiritual guidance (and even in that M. d'A felt he had failed). This only increased his physical discomfort: he was unable to sleep, to breathe easily or to eat without suffering afterwards. His letters to Fanny chart his search for a remedy – carrot tea, magnesian tea (ordinary tea dosed with magnesium), Sirop de Scille (a kind of onion), which had such a drastic effect that it left M. d'A trembling and weak. Nothing worked, and in August he asked Baron Larrey to examine him. Fanny was so worried that she threatened to abandon Alex and rush over to Paris to look after her husband. She waited for over a fortnight in ever-increasing anxiety, before hearing that Baron Larrey had decided not to operate and that M. d'A was feeling better. He would, he promised, be with her soon in Ilfracombe.

She and Alex left Bath on 30 June travelling overnight by postchaise. It was a hot, sticky and tiring journey, yet Fanny was able to recall vividly several years later how she had passed the time by listening to the adventures of their battle-wounded fellow traveller. A twenty-nine-year-old Irish captain, he had fought in America, Spain, Portugal and at Waterloo, where he had been lamed for life by a bullet wound that had fractured his hip. He impressed Fanny by being 'happy enough . . . for the wonder of being alive, the surgeons having all given him over, both on the Field of Battle, where he was first dressed, many hours after passing for dead; & at Brussels'. He must have felt a certain surprise when the elderly woman who listened so attentively to his tales of battle revealed that she, too, had been in Brussels in June 1815 and might well have prepared the bandages that were used to bind his wounds.[22]

Their destination, Ilfracombe, was a small fishing-port on the coast of north Devon, which also served the ferries to Bristol, Cardiff and Dublin. It was by no means a fashionable seaside town, but suited Fanny's purpose by being much cheaper than other resorts like Lyme Regis, with none of the distractions of Bath. While Alex spent much of the day studying, Fanny went for long walks with Diane, a young terrier that M. d'A had given his wife before leaving for France. On one blustery afternoon she went further than usual into the caves below the cliffs of Capstone, hoping to find some unusual pebbles to add to her husband's geological collection. A storm threatened, but by the time Fanny reached the entrance to the caves, the sea was 'clear, smooth, & immoveable as a lake'. She decided the tide must be receding, as she had noticed a young woman walking in front of her and clasping a book, as if intent on finding somewhere to sit and read, so she wandered further into the caves than she had ever been before, in the hope of finding some 'splendid treasure for my Bag'.

Fanny was so affected by the grandeur of the setting – 'The whole was alltogether strikingly picturesque, wild, & original. There was not one trace of Art, or even of any previous entrance into it of Man. Almost, I could imagine myself its first Human Inmate' – that she lost all sense of time. It was not until Diane began to whine and whimper and to tug at her gown that she looked back to the sea, and was horrified to realise that the tide had come in so quietly and quickly that there was no longer any way out of the cavern.

At first she remained reasonably calm, believing there must be another exit, since the young woman she had seen earlier was still in the vicinity. But when Fanny went to look for her, she was gone. 'I now rushed down to the Sea,' she remembered later.[23] But she was too late: 'Billows, mounted one after the other, as if with enraged pursuit of what they could seize and swallow.' She ran from side to side, looking desperately for an opening between the rocks that was wide enough for her to squeeze through. But there was none. When Diane found a gap far too narrow for a human, Fanny was left quite alone and surrounded by a threatening sea:

Now, indeed, I comprehended the fullness of my danger. If a Wave once reached my feet, while coming upon me with the tumultuous vehemence of this stormy moment, I had nothing I could hold by to sustain me from becoming its prey – and must inevitably be carried away into the ocean, & sunk to its bottomless Pit: – & while the prospect of this terrific premature Death struck me with dread, the idea of my poor desolate Alexander – of my many, many affectionate Relations & deeply attached Friends – and – Oh more than all! of the piercing agonies of the tenderest of Husbands . . . I flew that thought, & darted about in search of some place of safety.

The only thing she could do was clamber up to find a ledge on which to sit until the tide receded. So, notwithstanding her stiff limbs (she was now sixty-five), long skirts and flimsy cloth shoes laced with ribbon, she began to climb. 'The roughness of the Rocks tore my cloaths; its sharp points cut now my feet, & now my Fingers.' But she carried on, climbing on all fours and forcing her feet into 'such nooks or crevices as they could dig for themselves'. But then disaster struck again – one of her shoes got stuck and she left it behind as she struggled to reach the next ledge. Undaunted, she used the curved handle of her parasol to wrestle the slipper free.

At last she reached a ledge where she could stand easy and rest, but when she turned again to look at the sea, she discovered that it was still rushing in. Soon 'an immense breaker attacked my rock, & impeded in its height from going straight forward, was dashed in two directions, & foamed against each side'. Fanny felt giddy, she felt faint, she even felt seasick:

> What a situation for a Female Alone – without power to make known her danger – without any resource for escaping its tremendous menace, but by painfully, laboriously, & perilously standing upright, & immoveably on the same spot, till it should be passed – without any human being knowing where to find her, or suspecting where she might be – a Female, & past 60 years of age!

Fanny was never one to minimise a drama, and her 'Adventures at Ilfracombe', which she wrote up in 1823 in a specially sewn booklet, reads like a gripping short story – with a suitably happy ending. It was almost dark before the tide had receded sufficiently for her to be able to clamber down, and even then she was too scared of smugglers and brigands, or of losing her way, to move. She resigned herself to a long, chilly wait until dawn, when she could find her way back to the town, but then heard a shout and moments later saw a light in the distance. Alex had come to find her with one of his student friends and a local fisherman. 'Oh thank God!' he exclaimed, collapsing with exhaustion in her arms.

When they finally arrived back at their boarding-house, Alex was so overcome that the doctors wanted to bleed him, rather than Fanny. She heard later how he had spent the afternoon rushing around Ilfracombe, clutching his head in his arms in despair that his mother had been captured by bandits and murdered. Fanny herself enjoyed a hearty roast-beef supper before going to bed.

Many years later, the son of one of Alex's fellow students claimed that Madame d'Arblay had never been in such danger, and that she had in fact been found sitting on the sands at the entrance to the caves rather than half-way up a rock. Perhaps Fanny did exaggerate a little. But Macaulay noted in his review of Fanny's published diaries that the Ilfracombe Journal was an illustration of Fanny at her best. Certainly, the picture she creates of the 65-year-old matron scrambling up the steep, crumbling rockface, parasol aloft, is inimitable.

A couple of days later, Fanny heard from M. d'A that he would be returning soon, having failed to achieve anything by his trip.[24] Before he left Paris, he took an English doctor friend, George Hay (who had promised to accompany M. d'A back to England in case he fell ill while travelling), on a walking tour of the grandiose building projects commissioned by Napoleon – the arcades of the rue de Rivoli, the Palais d'Orsay, the Galérie Napoléon, which linked the Tuileries and the Louvre, and the Pont d'Austerlitz – which had so transformed the French capital. He would not see them again.

Fanny and Alex went back to Bath in time to welcome him home, and were alarmed to see that M. d'A, who had to spend three days in bed to recover from his journey, appeared thinner and weaker than ever. A month later, on 3 November 1817, Queen Charlotte, accompanied by the Princess Elizabeth, arrived in Bath on her first royal progress without the King, who was now blind, senile and never moved from his suite of rooms at Windsor. M. d'A took his wife 'under his protecting arm' to see the illuminations and decorations in the town. She noted later that this was the last time 'that Arm would ever, in public, have strength to protect me!'[25]

When the Queen returned to the city at the end of December (she had curtailed her previous visit after only a few days when her beloved grand-daughter, Princess Charlotte, died in childbirth on 6 November to a great outburst of national mourning), M. d'A and Fanny went early one morning to the Pump Room for an audience, but M. d'A was in such pain that he had to withdraw after a few minutes so that he could sit down. Fanny wrote to her sister Charlotte that 'the sight of his sufferings is truly afflicting, & it requires all the courage I can muster to support both my own spirits & his: for dreadfully, indeed, at times, are *his* sunk by the length of his illness, & the severity of his torments'. She added that 'M. d'A has reaped no sort of advantage from his Continental tour . . . This has been a direful disappointment indeed!'[26] On a scrap of paper in the Berg Collection is preserved a

'Rhubarb prescription', which is dated 23 December 1817 and labelled 'For Spasms': 'One large teaspoonful of the Tincture of Rhubarb to be taken each day before dinner in two or three tablespoonfuls of Peppermint Water. When the spasm comes on, a small teaspoonful of sal volatile to be taken in a wineglass of water.'[27]

On the night of Saturday, 24 January 1818, M. d'A woke up in terrible pain and became so fearful that the next morning he called for another doctor, William Tudor, Surgeon-Extraordinary to the Queen, to come and see him and give a second opinion. Tudor came straight away on that Sunday, and after M. d'A explained his symptoms – chronic constipation, severe haemorrhoids, pain, weakness, fever and weight loss, indicating that he was suffering from cancer of the rectum – Tudor told him that an operation was necessary but that his condition was such that it was now too late. M. d'A accepted his verdict, but Fanny refused to lose hope, believing that her husband was 'tormented with false apprehensions' and that he was 'persuaded he was worse than appeared to be the case'.

A brief respite arrived in the person of Alex, who rushed back to Bath on 28 January with the news that he had been awarded his degree and that he was tenth on the list of twenty-eight Wranglers (those mathematicians graduating with First Class Honours). It was a creditable performance, which Fanny was sure would lead to further academic honours. She wrote to her old friend, George Owen Cambridge, who as an Archdeacon and friend of Bishops had offered to put in a good word for Alex: 'My Alexander is blyth as a lark at the event which has lately terminated so many anxious fears & flattering hopes.'[28] A fortnight later Alex was elected a Scholar of Christ's College, and by March had been made a Fellow. His future seemed assured.

Three days later, however, his father began confiding in a 'Private Diary' the fears that he dared not share with Fanny. '*Je sais que je m'affaiblis horriblement,*' he wrote on 19 February. '*Je ne crois pas que ceci puisse encore bien long. Chère Fanny – Cher Alex!* God bless you! & unite us for ever! Amen!'[29] Fanny refused to leave her husband's side through day and night. But still she would not accept the fate to which M. d'A had resigned himself, writing to Charlotte at the end of March: 'The opening spring & soft weather will greet him – I think – I hope – I trust – I pray! with returning ease & comfort!'[30]

M. d'A tried to take his mind off his constant and at times excruciating pain by putting his own papers in order and writing his will. 'I have not other knowledge of the occupation than a remembrance of his demanding many pins, by which I now know he affixed written labels to the several instructions,' Fanny recalled later. He copied old letters into pocket-books, and read with his wife from the works of Byron, Southey and Hannah More, whose most recent novel, *Coelebs*, Fanny dismissed as being 'filled with Reflexions, Maxims, Moral lessons, acute observations, & admirable strokes, of cleverness of every sort – though all so ill & unskilfully combined . . . as to make a *whole* that is the quintessence of solid Lead, while the *parts* frequently deserve setting in Gold'.[31]

On 5 April, M. d'A wrote his last words – '*Patienza! Patienza!*' – after which he was too weak to hold a pen. Yet that same day, Fanny wrote to Charlotte that she believed her 'poor Invalid' was about to recover. M. d'A tried to warn his wife, but each time he began to talk of the future she changed the subject. For two days, he spoke to no one – not even Fanny – wishing to prepare himself for what must come. 'In that frame of his Mind, & Will, one word that was not essential, disturbed him! so concentrated in himself he desired to be!' wrote Fanny later. But he was 'always as free from irritation as from despondence – always gentle & kind, even when taciturn – & even when in torture'.[32] He was, he assured his wife, ready for death. Indeed, Hetty remarked as she left his sick-room: 'How serene he looks! – What serenity is in his countenance!'

During the night of 21 April, M. d'A suffered a sudden relapse, finally convincing Fanny that 'the dreadful blow was impending over us'. She scribbled a distraught letter to Alex, begging him to 'come instantly – *coûte qui coûte* – If he sees you again he may yet have the divine feeling after which I fear to aspire – I have a stupour upon me inconceivable – I am Numbed – insensible – I don't shed a tear.' The letter was sealed with black wax.[33] But Alex, worried by the news of his father, had already left Cambridge for Bath and arrived the next morning as M. d'A was being given the Last Sacrament – against Fanny's wishes, who believed that this Catholic rite was an admission of hopelessness.

M. d'A rallied on Alex's arrival. Throughout the following night, he talked to Fanny and Alex of his 'approaching dissolution' and of what he wished for them both, while they wept quietly beside him. He pleaded with his wife that she would not seal herself off from the world and not talk about him (after Susan's death in 1800, she had been unable – even with M. d'A – to mention her sister's name).

'*Parles de moi! Parles et souvent – surtout à Alexandre; qu'il ne m'oublie pas!*' he begged her, anxious that Alex would forget him and his French heritage.

As morning dawned on Thursday, 30 April, M. d'A appeared calm. He had, Fanny wrote later, 'imparted all he could suggest for our Good . . . and quietly, therefore, he awaited his doom'. That evening, he slumped into unconsciousness until Fanny managed to revive him with sal volatile. She began to hope again that perhaps he would recover. But M. d'A's doctor expressed 'something like censure that I could desire his life in such sufferings'. She became too distraught to mix her husband's medicines – chiefly saline draughts and opium – and Alex took over, surprising his mother by his calm efficiency.

On Sunday, 3 May, M. d'A was still cheerful, and at about noon called for a drink. He was too weak to hold the cup himself, but afterwards he leaned forward, took Fanny's hand, and, holding it between both his hands, spoke softly to her, '*Je ne sais si ce sera le dernier mot – mais, ce sera la dernière pensée – Notre Réunion!*' Once more only did he speak to her – to ask for his pillows to be moved – before sliding peacefully into a sleep from which he never awoke:

> The sleep was so calm that an hour passed, in which I indulged the softest – though the least tranquil hope, that a favourable crisis was arriving – that a turn would take place, by which his vital powers would be restored . . . but when the hour was succeeded by another hour – when I saw a universal stillness in the whole frame such as seemed to stagnate – if I so can be understood – all around – I began to be strangely moved . . .
> Another Hour passed – the concentrated feelings, the breathless dread in which I existed . . . His Face had still its unruffled serenity – but methought the hands were turning cold . . . the stillness grew more awful – the skin became colder.[34]

Alex ran to fetch Mr Tudor, who finally pronounced that 'All was over'.

In the winter months of 1819–20, when Fanny wrote her detailed account of her husband's last illness, she had no memory of the hours and days that followed: 'I had certainly a partial derangement. My Memory paints things that were necessarily real, joined to others that could not possibly have happened, yet amalgamates the whole so together, as to render it impossible for me to separate Truth from indefinable, unaccountable Fiction.'

M. d'A was buried on 9 May, in the Walcot Street cemetery in
Bath. A simple, black marble stone was placed over the grave, as
directed in his will, and a memorial tablet was erected in the gallery of
the church of St Swithin's nearby, bearing a lengthy inscription
composed by his wife, which can still be seen:

Sacred to the revered Memory
of Comte Alexandre Jean Baptiste
PIOCHARD D ARBLAY;
Chevalier de St Louis; de la Légion d'Honneur;
du Lys; et de la Fidélité:
Lieutenant General des Armées
et Officier Superieur des Gardes du Corps
de S. M. Louis XVIII, Roi de France.
These Honours, Sole Rewards of his faithful Services,
It is easy to Name, and grateful to Record;
But who shall delineate his noble Character?
The Spirit of his Valour, or the Softness of his Heart?
His feeling of Reluctance to leave his weeping Family,
Yet pious Resignation to relinquish this vain World?
His Kindness on the Bed of Torture;
The PURITY of his INTEGRITY: the TRANSPARENCY of his HONOUR;
or the indiscribable charm of his Social Virtues!
His shadowy, faded Form
Is deposited in WALCOT Church Yard.
His devoted Wife, and darling Son
Consecrate This poor Tablet to his loved Remembrance;
With devout Aspiration that his own tender Last prayer
For their Eternal RE-UNION in the blest Abode
of Immortal Spirits
May mercifully be accorded
By the ever-living GOD.
Through the mediation of our Lord Jesus Christ. *Amen!*
Died 3d May, 1818. Aged 65.[35]

FIFTEEN

Last Thoughts in Mayfair
1818–40

An elderly lady, with no remains of personal beauty, but with a simple and gentle manner, a pleasing expression of countenance, and apparently quick feelings.

Sir Walter Scott, November 1826

Fanny refused to go out for several months after her husband's death, except on Sundays when she attended morning service at the Octagon Chapel on Milsom Street. Alex stayed with his mother, and tried to comfort her by reading with her from the Gospels (after her mother had died, Fanny had read the Bible through from Genesis to Revelation three times). Her sisters and friends feared for her sanity, knowing how in the past she had given herself over utterly to grief. 'God help her! no one else can!' said Charlotte Cambridge, George Owen's sister. But by the middle of July 1818 she began to emerge from her despair, writing a memorandum to herself: 'To force Exertion from Inertion For the remnant of my saddened Existence Let me keep a Register from this day 12 July of fatal 1818 of 4 Things necessarily to be performed.' She promised to work through M. d'A's papers so that Alex would have them as a personal history of his father; to destroy those manuscripts too private for anyone else to see; to record 'all his diversified studies'; and to sort through all his letters.[1]

She began to think of leaving Bath, now filled with painful memories. She saw nothing of Mrs Thrale-Piozzi who, on 27 January 1820, gave a grand party in the Lower Rooms for 600 'friends' to celebrate her eightieth birthday (she was actually seventy-nine, but considered that she was entering her eightieth year). After a concert and supper, the guests danced till the early hours, led by their gallant hostess, who then amazed them all by being just as lively the next morning at breakfast. The following evening, she danced again at the party given for her servants. (Fanny was by then living in London and did not attend.)

The cost of her celebrations almost bankrupted Mrs Thrale-Piozzi and soon afterwards she was forced to leave Gay Street – in an echo of the last days of her extravagant first husband. Thereafter she led a peripatetic existence in the resort towns of south-west England – Penzance, Exeter and Clifton – but fell one night in her hotel room as she was struggling to get into bed. She never recovered from the ordeal of lying there without help and she died on 3 May 1821.

Fanny, meanwhile, settled in London after her brother James promised to help her find rooms and ensure that she would never be without company when she needed it. She was deeply touched: 'An idea of comfort begins to steal its way to my mind, in renewing my intercourse with this worthy Brother – who feels for me, I see, with sincerity & affection.'[2] By the end of September, she was ready to leave Bath, and on 30 September she arrived at James's house in Westminster, where she stayed for a few days before moving into her own apartment at No. 11 Bolton Street, just off Piccadilly. The elegant, five-storey terraced house now bears a plaque marking Madame d'Arblay's residence from 8 October 1818 to 1 November 1828, when she moved to Half Moon Street nearby.

Alex did not travel with Fanny to London but returned to Cambridge, so for the first time since 3 May she was alone – apart from her dog Diane and her maid, Elizabeth Ramsay, daughter of the family with whom she and Alex had boarded in Ilfracombe, who had asked to come and work for her. For Fanny, the nights were feverish and restless and the ensuing days passed very slowly: 'Life seems to linger as if Time travelled with leaden feet.' But in London, where she had never lived with M. d'A, she could at least go out without being constantly reminded of him, and she resumed her habit of walking each day, either in the tree-lined paths of Green Park or the more open meadows of Hyde Park beyond.

A whole year passed during which Fanny could only bear the company of her close family – James, Charlotte, and her cousin Edward Francisco, who would call most Sunday evenings for tea ('silent & elegant, yet observant & penetrating as usual'). Sarah Harriet, too, visited her stepsister whenever she was in London with Lord and Lady Crewe, for whose children she was now governess. Their brother Charles had died five months before M. d'A, after suffering a stroke on Christmas morning; while Hetty and Charles Rousseau had moved to Bath to be near their daughters.

Fanny spent the first anniversary of her husband's death – that 'piercing month' – in 'irrepressible sorrow'. This was, however, a turning-point. Shocked by the intensity of her morbid feelings, she began at last to look beyond them, to the possibility of peace of mind without M. d'A. She wrote to Hetty on 20 June 1819 confessing that 'A lowness – utterly unconquerable, of spirits, has kept me from writing sooner', but she assured her sister that she was now over the worst. She also mentioned the birth on 24 May of Alexandrina Victoria, daughter of Edward, Duke of Kent, and Victoria-Maria-Louisa of Saxe-Coburg-Saalfeld, the 'New born presumptive Queen', whom Fanny saw as a babe in arms two months later on a visit to Queen Charlotte at Kew Palace.[3]

In August 1819 Fanny was at last tempted away from home by George Owen Cambridge and his wife (Cornelia, née Mierop), who invited Fanny to spend a few days with them at Twickenham Meadows on the banks of the River Thames. From there, she went on to join her sister Charlotte, who was staying with her daughter Charlotte Barrett and family in Richmond. 'We have . . . had my Aunt d'Arblay & her son Alexander on a visit with us in the house for some weeks,' wrote Charlotte's daughter, the clever Marianne, who was also in Richmond at the time. 'She is a most gentle & pleasant visitor, is quiet, & kind, & easily pleased – So is her son, who is a person of fine abilities, & very amiable, poor dear fellow. He has an astonishing memory, so has his Mother; but it is impaired by trouble, for she is very low, & has by no means recovered the loss of her husband.'[4]

Fanny took with her a trunk filled with her father's papers, which she had promised to sort through and edit, with a view to publishing a volume of Dr Burney's memoirs and correspondence, along the lines of his own history of music. She hoped both to confirm her father's reputation as a scholar and friend of the great and the good, and to make some much-needed money for herself and Hetty, the joint legatees of Dr Burney's estate. Hetty, indeed, agreed that their father had 'designed & wished & bespoke Fanny for his Editor', as did James, Charlotte and Sarah Harriet.[5]

Fanny began work on her new project in the summer of 1817 while she and Alex were in Ilfracombe. At first she assumed her task would simply be to select and revise what her father had written (when he died in 1814 he left some twelve notebooks of unfinished memoirs);

the rest she would burn. But three years later she was still struggling to read through everything, and yet had collected very little material that she considered worth publishing. She had been surprised to find that Dr Burney's memoirs did not provide a portrait of the society musician whose salon at St Martin's Street would be described later by Macaulay in such complimentary terms: 'few nobles could assemble in the most stately mansions of Grosvenor Square or Saint James's Square, a society so various and so brilliant as was sometime to be found in Dr Burney's cabin'.[6] She decided, on the contrary, that his papers 'were so unlike all that honoured writer had ever produced to the Publick, that not only they would not have kept up his Credit & fair Name in the literary World, if brought to light, but would certainly have left a cloud upon its parting ray'.

Of his childhood years, Fanny had discovered the details that shocked her: 'The dissipated facility & negligence of his Witty & accomplished, but careless Father; the niggardly unfeelingness of his nearly unnatural Mother'. And she believed the name of Burney would be shamed if these details were made public. She was disappointed to find nothing about her own 'dear & lovely Mother' and, when she came to the years in St Martin's Street (1774–87), all she could find were long lists of dinners eaten and concerts attended. Dr Burney was too preoccupied with making money or writing to have the time or the inclination to record his own life for posterity.

Fanny took it upon herself to remove and burn 'all that appeared to me peccant parts, that might have bred fevers, caused infectious ill-will, or have excited morbid criticism or ridicule'.[7] She then spent the next twelve years writing her own account of his life, based loosely on what was left of the memoirs and the correspondence. Her *Memoirs of Doctor Burney, Arranged from his Own Manuscripts, from Family Papers, and from Personal Recollections. By His Daughter, Madame d'Arblay* was published by Edward Moxon (the poets' publisher, whose list of authors included Wordsworth, Southey and Tennyson) in November 1832 (just after the passing of the great Reform Act, which gave the vote to all male householders worth £10 per annum), priced £1 11s. 6d. for the three volumes. The first reviews were favourable, welcoming a history of the life of such a key figure in London's cultural life, with its references to Dr Johnson, David Garrick, Mrs Thrale, Burke, Sheridan, Reynolds and James Bruce, explorer of the Nile. But in April 1833 the acerbic critic John Croker wrote a twenty-nine-page article in the *Quarterly Review*, damning the *Memoirs* and their author.

Croker, who had earlier savaged *The Wanderer*, lambasted Fanny for destroying her father's papers. He asserted, 'The habit of *novel-writing* has led her to colour and, as she may suppose, embellish her anecdotes', and he suggested that her intention was not to memorialise her father, but to glorify her own name. Fanny should have allowed her father to speak for himself, and should have published separately '*her own* story and her contemporaneous notes and *bona fide* recollections of that brilliant society in which she moved, from 1778 to 1794'.[8]

Indeed, it is difficult not to agree that Fanny's editing of her father's papers was ruthless. The scraps that have survived – such as the story that he once borrowed a nightcap from Lord Nelson after setting his own on fire while working late by candlelight – would suggest that his autobiography would have been much livelier and more revealing than the memoirs produced by his over-zealous daughter.

In 1833, however, Fanny was too worried about Alex to be much concerned by Croker's attack. Since his father's death, Alex had led a wandering, purposeless life. He had been ordained on Trinity Sunday 1818, just weeks after the funeral, so that he could take up his appointment as a Fellow of Christ's College (all Cambridge dons had to be at least deacons in the Church of England). But he took no interest in his students, was not suited to teaching, and spent more and more time away from college. And yet he had no intention either of settling down as a country cleric. Instead, he spent his summers roaming the Continent, usually on his own, and often leaving his mother with no idea of his whereabouts.

In July 1821, he set out for Switzerland with two friends from Cambridge – Charles Babbage (whose mechanical calculator is now regarded as the first step towards modern computing) and William Herschel (son of the Astronomer-Royal who discovered Uranus). But Alex abandoned them after only a few days to wander off on his own, extending his original six-week tour to a nine-month expedition. From time to time, he sent his mother a brief note, giving her his impressions of the magnificent scenery of the Jura Mountains, or describing his meeting with Sarah Siddons, who was visiting her brother John Kemble in Lausanne after retiring from the stage (she was by now sixty-six). But one letter, rather than reassuring, alarmed Fanny, when she read that he had circumnavigated Lake Geneva in only seven days, which meant that he must have walked more than thirty miles a day: 'But how could you suggest so dangerous a plan as walking round the Lake in so short a time: It was enough to Kill your body, & to starve your Mind.'[9]

She added, 'I am really not quite easy at your Wandering thus alone': a theme that was to recur in Fanny's letters to her son over the next decade. Year after year, she worried about him, her concern heightened because she so rarely heard from him and did not trust him to look after his own poor health. On one occasion, she sent him a blank sheet with just the cryptic remark 'I regret not having sent this Answer to your promised Letter sooner'. In October 1829, for example, Hetty told Charlotte that she had glimpsed Alex before he set out for Dover, 'and *to you* I must say – how sorry I was to see how *old* he looked, his poor Mother is in a most anxious state about him & his affairs, – for a fortnight she was expecting news from him – at last comes a witty letter in doggerel Verse without a word of business in it ... nothing seems done – *or* in my opinion *very* likely to be done except indeed requisitions for fresh supplies of *money*'. Alex was then thirty-five.[10]

Whether from his inability to fit in – he had never grown out of his 'rebel humour' – or perhaps because he felt suffocated by his mother's finicky concern for his well-being, Alex continued to disappear, often for several months at a time, either to Paris or to the south-coast towns, especially Dover, where in the early 1830s a salon of fashionable literati had gathered round the exotic Clara Bolton. The former mistress of Disraeli was reputed to be besotted with the new recruit to her clique, the versifying Reverend d'Arblay. Her feelings were perhaps reciprocated: in May 1835 Alex drafted a letter to her, which implied that their 'friendship' was something more. And when he first kissed her, he wrote, 'I was so *overwhelmed* that the only relief I could find to save me from the threat of *insanity* was to give out, as I did, my *whole soul* upon paper.' Now he wished to apply some kind of 'sedative', alarmed by the 'excessive agitation' of her response to his letter.[11]

Alex was by this time in deep trouble. In 1824, he had accepted with great reluctance the curacy of the new Camden Chapel in the parish of St Pancras, part of the evangelical mission to the fast-growing communities on the edge of the capital. It was not a very profitable living, worth just £200 per annum, but both Fanny and George Owen Cambridge saw it as a challenge, and an opportunity for Alex to make his mark in the Church. Indeed, Alex was a fine preacher, whose declamatory manner (derived most probably from his frequent visits to the theatre) much impressed his clerical colleagues (he was on several occasions invited to preach in St Paul's Cathedral). But he was hardly a model parish priest. As Hetty remarked to Fanny, 'I feel convinced that in heart & soul he possesses every noble and endearing Quality requisite to make a good & respectable divine – and Heaven forbid I should ever suppose him capable of any greater sin than that of Occasionally reading the Marriage Service over a new-born infant, or perhaps leaving out the Ten Commandments in the Service.'[12] He was good-hearted, but he was also chronically ill-disciplined, forever chasing after his latest obsession, whether it be chess, Byron, his desire to become a famous poet (he always regretted not taking a better degree and dreamed of achieving 'national fame') – or women.[13]

The soft-hearted and eligible Alex (whom Jane Austen once teasingly told her sister Cassandra she might marry; he was, after all, the son of the celebrated 'Miss Burney')[14] was not averse to finding a wife, providing she was English. His first romantic attachment seems to have been to Cecilia Lock, grand-daughter of the Locks of Norbury Park, whom Fanny called 'the new Evelina'. But he was soon deterred by his mother, who with commendable common sense warned him that Cecilia, like Augustine de Reynier de Jarjayes, would need a husband with enough capital to keep her in the manner to which she had been brought up. In late 1823, however, he became infatuated with another grand-daughter of the Locks, Caroline Angerstein.

She was the daughter of an MP and wealthy art-dealer, and therefore, as Sarah Harriet would have said, of a quite 'different cast' from Alex. Nevertheless he persisted, asking his mother to write a letter on his behalf to Caroline's parents: 'My dear Mother, I solemnly request you to be so kind as to make known to Mrs A———n the state of my feelings with respect to Miss A———n, together with my present hopes and chances of rising in my profession.' He added:

I pledge myself to bear as manfully as I can any disappointment, and at all events not to make you chargeable with that which, in all human probability, is already decided . . . At the same time, my feelings at this moment are in a state of ungovernable anxiety, which may make me talk a great deal of nonsense backwards and forwards; but of this I beg you *to make no account*, only bearing in mind that the whole is *at my peril*, as you will only be acting *by my express desire* and earnest request.

276

A letter that reveals all of Alex's excitable temperament.[15]

At the beginning of 1824, Caroline became ill with an undiagnosed fever, which from Fanny's account would appear to have been largely nervous in origin – Caroline could not eat and believed herself to be on the brink of death. Alex remained at her parents' home throughout her illness, but a marriage between Caroline and Alex was never mentioned, and we can only assume that Fanny did nothing to further Alex's hopes. Charlotte Barrett indicated later, however, that she thought Alex would have been accepted, had his intentions been made known. Certainly Caroline did not marry until 1841 and, when she did, she chose a cleric.

Perhaps Alex's disappointment over Caroline persuaded him to accept the living of Camden. If so, it was a mistake, and it was not long before he began to disappear, leaving his parishioners in Camden Chapel increasingly resentful that they arrived for a service to find no one in the pulpit. By October 1834, Fanny was driven to write to him in Brighton, where she thought he was staying, after hearing rumours that a group of his Camden parishioners was plotting to have him removed by the Bishop. She sent him an obtuse, coded warning: 'O be careful for *watch* is the word. Let nothing strange occur – Doubt & inquiry are on foot.'[16] Alex returned to London and spent the winter dutifully fulfilling his obligations, but by the spring he was tempted to wander off again – to Dover and the company of Clara Bolton and her friends.

A few weeks later, Alex wrote that emotion-filled letter to Clara Bolton, ending their 'relationship'. But not long afterwards Fanny received a letter from him asking for her benediction: at the beginning of May 1835 he had proposed marriage to a young teacher whom he had met through Clara, and she had accepted. Fanny's initial reaction was concern that her son, who was now almost forty, had been too precipitate, and she replied by return of post advising him to 'closely, honorably, & openly consult, & discuss with her, your feelings & your Situation ere your ties become indissoluble'.[17] Two months later, however, after meeting Alex's 'intended partner', she told Charlotte that she was 'in Heaven! so much I like her! – so much – much – that *love* is the only proper word! . . . *This* is a balm to all *worldly* evils.'[18]

Mary Ann Smith appears to have been a remarkably kind and understanding person, with a genuine affection for Alex. Charlotte Barrett thought her 'very kind, gentle & pleasing – not *really* pretty, but nothing *unpretty* – a very nice, sensible, engaging creature.'[19]

Fanny declared that Alex had at last found his own Flapper, and that Mary Ann was the 'amiable, prudent & softly wise, yet deeply wise Companion', whom she had always wanted Alex to marry.

Alex, however, could not afford a wife, and he had made little effort to impress the Church authorities and achieve promotion to a more prosperous benefice than Camden. Unsure how to resolve his difficulties, he retreated from everyone, seemingly paralysed by his own fears for his future, and by despair that he had failed his mother and had nothing to offer Mary Ann. On 16 December 1835 he sent a note to Fanny by special messenger:

> O I am very unhappy. I know not what to say . . . A deep deep Gloom has laid hold of me & God knows if I shall ever shake it off – The more I pine in solitude the worse it grows. Poor generous noble May! Her fresh heart her happiness ought not to be put at stake upon one whose spirit is broken whose soul is fled. How I admire her, & the more I admire her how I feel wretched at the impossibility of *now* doing her justice as she deserves.

The single sheet, written in thick black ink, is almost illegible, with very little punctuation – as if written in great despair.[20]

Mary Ann stood by Alex, but they never married. On 20 March 1836, he preached his last sermon in Camden, then wandered off again; this time to Cambridge where he hoped to be offered a lectureship, having abandoned all hope of furthering his career in the Church. He left Fanny to sort out his unpaid bills, which were presented to her by his landlady, verger and bookseller. Mary Ann wrote to Fanny: '*daily & deeply* do I deplore an influence that has sunk into apathy so fine, so noble a mind – but he will recover dearest Madame d'Arblay & be again the comfort to you he has been & to me will ever be *all & every* thing'.[21]

Her optimism was misplaced. In the autumn of 1836 Alex was given the charge of St Ethelreda's in Ely Place, Holborn; once again, through the recommendations of his mother's old friend George Owen Cambridge. The chapel itself was a damp, semi-derelict building that had been closed for many years; Alex's appointment was intended to bring new life to a redundant parish. His inaugural sermon was filled with hope, and with a very real sense of his renewed dedication:

> To the Venerable G. O. Cambridge, Archdeacon of Middlesex . . .
> When you proposed to me to take the charge of ELY CHAPEL, I was well

aware of the arduousness of the undertaking. I knew that, lost in a recess, it attracted no notice from passers by, and was unknown to many in its immediate neighbourhood. I knew that, since it had been closed, other places of worship had sprung up, and had drawn off those who formerly attended there. But I knew also that, while large subscriptions were collecting for building new temples to the Lord, this ancient house of prayer [which dated back to the thirteenth century] could not long remain neglected, without furnishing a handle to the enemies of the church. I did not think myself at liberty to shrink from a possible chance of being useful.[22]

But to preach every Sunday to a dwindling congregation who could not understand his high-flown language and literary allusions, to survive on the meagre income that such a run-down parish offered, and to be so far outside the clerical limelight proved too difficult for Alex. Only a few weeks after the vigorous optimism of that first sermon, he caught a chill while taking a service in the unheated chapel. Never strong, he soon succumbed to influenza from which he did not recover. He died in his mother's home at Half Moon Street on 19 January 1837, aged forty-two. But Fanny was not by his side. Alex had expressly forbidden his mother to enter his sick-room, and he died alone and without her benediction.[23] He did, however, ask Mary Ann in the event of his death to take care of Fanny, a charge that she devotedly fulfilled.

Alex was buried in Bath beside his father in the Walcot Street cemetery.[24] At first Fanny bore up surprisingly well, sustained by the company of Mary Ann and by the consolatory letters she received from George Owen Cambridge's wife, Cornelia, praising Alex's 'pure and unoffending spirit'; from Charlotte Barrett, who spoke of his 'sweet and guileless temper'; and from Charlotte, who left perhaps the most astute explanation of Alex's difficulties: 'noble minded as he was in *reality*, he was so artless, so unsuspicious – so unable to cope with the World, & its ways – that – for a moment at a time – when only meditating on that poor darling – *exclusively* – I regard it as a mercy in the almighty to have taken him to Heaven, while watch'd & cherished as he continued to be by his precious mother, who understood him better than all the world besides.'[25]

When left alone, however, Fanny broke down: 'My Heart is of lead,' she wrote to her nephew Charles Parr (Charles's son) on 15 March. 'I cannot describe the chasm of my present existence – so lost in grief – so awake to Resignation – so inert to all that is proffered – so ever & ever retrograding to all that is desolate! – I am a non–entity!'[26] More than two years later, in March 1839, she wrote to Charlotte Barrett: 'I have been very ill . . . with nights of consuming restlessness and Tears. I have now called in Dr Holland who understands me marvellously – & I am now much as usual. – No – not that; – still tormented by nights without repose.'[27]

After Alex's death, Fanny, who in January 1837 was in her eighty-fifth year, was left with only one close relative, Charlotte. James had died, like their brother Charles, from a heart-attack or stroke at the end of 1821. The hospitable Admiral, memorialised by Leigh Hunt as the 'first man who planted a pun in Otaheite', was much mourned by his friends. Charles Lamb, for example, wrote to Wordsworth: 'There's Captain Burney gone! What fun has whist now?'[28] Major Phillips, who was by then back in London and living in Lambeth, commissioned a bust of his fellow adventurer in the South Seas and then had the cheek to ask Fanny and James's son Martin to pay for it.[29] Hetty, too, had died in February 1832, thirteen years after her husband Charles Rousseau.

Fanny herself was very deaf and almost blind from cataracts in both eyes. But she had spirit enough to 'fight against the Windmills' of fate, moving away from the home where Alex had died to start afresh in a new apartment at 112 Mount Street (off Park Lane). On 2 September 1837, she wrote cheerfully to Charlotte, 'what a chaos I live in! Trunks – Boxes – Hampers – Baskets – are to tread over or between every step. You cannot figure to yourself such a confusion. Yet all is better – my amiable *Child* [Mary Ann] only lives to watch & indulge me – only survives her promised expected betrothed Companion for life to soothe his Mother! My Charlotte be happy for me.'[30]

Charlotte, too, had watched helplessly as both her sons, Clement and Ralph, suffered long, lingering deaths, literally wasting away with consumption. And her daughter Marianne had died suddenly in 1832 while with her mother (her funeral was attended by 'great numbers' of the poor). Fanny wrote to her sister every Sunday: 'I hope you do not neglect the brandy my love. Dr Holland said "Take the Yoke for nourishment – 'tis the purest I know for convalescence – & add the brandy for *strength*" – brandy, at 7s a bottle, is cheaper than any medicine at 3s a vial, & a large spoonful will serve the purpose, taken regularly!' And she included the recipe for her own favourite night-time noggin of sherry and egg yolks: 'The Egg should be taken in after mixing like a Saline draught. I find it, with sugar & lemon *peal* juice, the pleasantest beverage I know.'[31]

Fanny promised to brave the journey to Brighton to visit Charlotte, who in the autumn of 1837 was staying with the Barretts. On a chilly morning in November, she boarded the 'Red Rover' to the coast, travelling alone (Mary Ann was visiting her own family in Greenwich). She stayed for a month, and on her return to Mount Street began to welcome visitors again, sending Charlotte a witty report on James's daughter Sarah and her husband John Payne (grandson of the bookseller and printer Thomas Payne, who had published *Cecilia*), who had called on their great-aunt: 'the Paynes have been here, in such evident surprize they were at a loss for words, & could do little else but stare from me to each other with a wonder that expressed, "She is really alive!" '[32]

But only a few days later Charlotte suffered a fall while on her own. She was not badly injured but the shock seemed to weaken her. Fanny wrote an emotional letter to Charlotte's daughter marked 'Read privately':

> I wrote to this effect to my dear sister Esther – that from this time we must hold ourselves prepared to give or to receive from each other one of the bitterest afflictions that remained to our lots – but that, unless we were together at the time, we must bear it in absence! . . . Not such was my preparation for my Alex! – alas! I had no premonition – nor even a thought had crossed my mind that he would go first![33]

Charlotte did eventually recover, valiantly travelling alone from Brighton for one last meeting with Fanny, and renting her own apartment in Mount Street. But she collapsed with a fever while in London and died of 'a sporadic & bilious cholera' on 12 September 1838. She was buried in St Martin's-in-the-Fields, the church in which as the young 'Charlottina' she had married Clement Francis.

Fanny was now left quite alone. But she never lost her faith or her spirited outlook on life. She was sustained every week by a visit from Archdeacon Cambridge, who came to share a private communion service with his old friend. When her stepsister Sarah Harriett – who had settled in Bath after spending several years in Italy, where she had been befriended by writers such as Henry Crabb Robinson and Walter Savage Landor – wrote to Fanny in February 1839 for advice concerning her latest novel, *The Romance of Private Life*, Fanny sent a typically witty reply: 'Be better, my dearest old & young Girl for I must not have you slip thro' my fingers.' Sarah Harriet had evidently asked Fanny for suggestions for her chapter-headings: 'I will tell you a short cut to getting mottos – Beg – Borrow – or the other thing – Dr Johnsons Dictionary – & you will find with ease & facility a word for every chapter & no trouble but great pleasure & *délaissement*.'[34] A letter that she could have written from Streatham fifty years earlier.

Another regular visitor was the poet Samuel Rogers (1763–1855), who had first met Fanny at his home in St James's Square in June 1813. He and his sister Sarah would come for tea and to bring Fanny up-to-date with the newest literary sensations, such as Tennyson, Southey, Harriet Martineau and Frances Trollope. Some years earlier, in November 1826, he had introduced her to Sir Walter Scott, who had been anxious to meet the 'celebrated authoress' of *Evelina* and *Cecilia*. In his diary, Scott has left a vivid picture of Fanny in her Mayfair years: 'an elderly lady, with no remains of personal beauty, but with a simple and gentle manner, a pleasing expression of countenance, and apparently quick feelings'. He was gratified to be told by her that there were two persons she wished to meet, 'myself, of course, being one, the other George Canning', adding, 'This was really a compliment to be pleased with – a nice little handsome pat of butter made up by a "neat-handed Phillis" of a dairy maid.'[35]

Scott was impressed by the amount of money Fanny had earned from the publication of *Camilla* – some 3,000 guineas – which was rather different from the £700 that Scott had been paid for his most successful novel, *Waverley*, which was published in the same year as *The Wanderer*. He did not mention Fanny's last novel and probably had not read it. By 1826, it was out of print.

In the winter of 1839, Samuel Rogers was among Fanny's last visitors in the weeks before she died. She had moved yet again, into a cheaper apartment at 29 Lower Grosvenor Street (she still lived alone, though Mary Ann often stayed with her), and had also braved the mournful task of rewriting her will for the third time. After the death of her sole remaining sibling Charlotte, she left her money to Charlotte Barrett's son, Richard (the income from her French and English investments was worth some £400 per annum, or £14,000 in 1990s terms). His promising career as an academic had been blighted by a deterioration in his eyesight and Fanny hoped to provide him with financial security.

She disposed of her papers: those written by her or by M. d'A and

Alex were given to Charlotte Barrett, while all her father's remaining letters and memoranda were left to Charles's son, Charles Parr Burney. With her will, which she signed on 6 March 1839, she enclosed a letter to be sent after her death to the princesses: 'I cannot resist in these solemn preparations, for my last moments, – inserting a tenderly posthumous Farewell to my revered and dear Princesses, Their Royal Highnesses The Princess Augusta; The Princess Elizabeth, Landgravine of Hesse Homburg; The Princess Mary, Duchess of Gloucester; and the Princess Sophia – though I have nothing I dare venture to offer, save my dying Benediction.' She signed herself, 'Frances d'Arblay, otherwise La Comtesse Veuve Piochard d'Arblay'.[36]

By 1839, her health was so poor that she spent every other day in bed, and she was unable to read for more than a few minutes at a time. But she still took an interest in the world beyond her rooms, writing to Charlotte Barrett in the summer about the 'poor young innocent & inexperienced Queen', whom she had seen as a young baby twenty years earlier. Queen Victoria, who inherited the throne on the death of her uncle, William IV, on 20 June 1837, had been criticised in the papers for summarily dismissing one of her ladies-in-waiting, who had been accused (falsely) of being pregnant. 'I am convinced,' Fanny told her niece, 'she has been betrayed into a wrong measure from being deluded into a wrong opinion, & therefore, though not blameless, is extremely to be pitied; for her hasty order of exile from her presence was a mere unweighed impulse of *Virtue*. How could she disbelieve a medical man? How credit him, without the deepest indignation at such a disgrace to her virgin Court?'[37]

This is Fanny's last known letter. In November she collapsed with an illness 'which showed itself at first in sleepless nights and nervous imaginations'. She had constant fever, was unable to eat, and was distressed by 'spectral delusions'. Mary Ann sat with her, and Charlotte Barrett came often to visit, anxious that the last words of someone who had been so famous should not be forgotten. She read to her aunt from the Gospel of St John until Fanny became too weak to listen with any understanding: 'My dear,' she told her niece, 'I cannot understand a word – not a syllable!'

At last, on 6 January 1840, she died, in peace and with resignation, her last moments recorded by Charlotte:

> At another moment she charged the same person with affectionate farewells and blessings to several friends, and with thanks for all their

kindness to her. Soon after she said, 'I have had some sleep.' 'That is well,' was the reply; 'you wanted rest.' *'I shall have it soon, my dear,'* she answered emphatically: and thus, aware that death was approaching, in peace with all the world, and in holy trust and reliance on her Redeemer, she breathed her last on the 6th of January, 1840; the anniversary of that day she had long consecrated to prayer, and to the memory of her beloved sister Susanna.[38]

On Wednesday, 15 January her remaining family gathered in Bath for her funeral. Mary Ann Smith and Fanny Raper (Susan's daughter) travelled together from London in the old-fashioned post-chaise, taking two days, while Charlotte Barrett was encouraged by her son Richard to brave the 'railroad', which took two hours. Sarah Harriet was already in Bath, living in a boarding-house in Henrietta Street. Perhaps, too, her cousin Edward Francisco and nephew Martin (James's son) made the trek from London to pay their last respects.

After a simple service taken by Charles Parr Burney's son, the fourth Charles Burney, her coffin was carried the short distance to the Walcot Road cemetery, where she was buried beside her husband and son. At last she was together again in spirit with her 'Partner in all' and their *'petit sauvage'*.[39]

When Fanny died in January 1840, she had outlived not only most of her family but also her literary success. Her reputation as a writer depended by then on just two novels, *Evelina* and *Cecilia*, so that when Thackeray came to write a review of her *Diary and Letters* in 1846, he wondered why 'we had not many hundreds of volumes of novels from her', as if she had written nothing else. Those readers who had been charmed by *Evelina* had mostly died; its new fans enjoyed it for different reasons. The world had moved on from Evelina and her education in the ways of Georgian society.

Charlotte Barrett was so concerned that Fanny's literary reputation had been damaged by the virulence of John Croker's attack on her *Memoirs of Doctor Burney* in the *Quarterly Review* that she wrote to Macaulay asking him to write a refutation; he declined. Undaunted, she determined to memorialise her aunt by publishing a selection from the voluminous diaries and letters that had been left in her care. It was a mammoth task, in which she was assisted by her daughter Julia and Minette Raper (Susan's grand-daughter), made more difficult by the way Fanny had spent the last lonely years of her life sorting through her papers and editing out all that she did not want posterity to know. But the seven volumes that eventually appeared between 1842 and 1846 brought Fanny a host of devoted Victorian readers, who were entertained by the diaries just as their Georgian predecessors had been by the novels. As Thackeray said in his review:

> You get portraits sketched from the life of many famous personages, who, though they figured but fifty years back, belong to a society as different and remote from ours, as that of Queen Anne or the Restoration – as different as a minuet is from a polka, or the Calais packet, which was four-and-twenty hours on its journey to Calais from Dover, to the iron steamer that can rush hither and thither and back half a dozen times in the day.[1]

Without *The Diary and Letters of Madame d'Arblay*, it is possible that

Fanny Burney would be known to us only as one of those minor lady novelists who were so numerous during the Georgian period. But her real skill was as a reporter, a witness, and in her diaries she has left an extraordinary historical document. Her phenomenal memory, her gift for writing dialogue enabled her to recreate, on the page, conversations that are so sharply real you feel that you are there with her in the room. Rarely, too, can anyone have been in so many places at *the* significant moment – whether it was the drawing-room at Streatham Park as Mrs Thrale teased Dr Johnson; the Drury Lane Theatre as Garrick thrilled his audience as King Lear and Abel Drugger; the corridors of Kew Palace as George III was put in a strait-jacket; or inside the Tuileries palace, watching from the window as Napoleon took the salute as Emperor . . .

Now, at last, Fanny's own contribution to literature and to our understanding of the past is being recognised, belatedly, with the decision to erect a memorial tablet to her in Westminster Abbey, alongside those dedicated to her father and her brother Charles. At the same time, her novels – even *The Wanderer* – are being closely scrutinised by a new generation of scholars, intrigued to discover Fanny's insights into ideas that are little different from those advocated by modern feminists. Even Fanny's comic plays are being rescued from oblivion, with successful stagings of 'A Busy Day' in Bristol and London in 1993 and readings from 'The Witlings'; in November 1997 in universities and among groups of actors interested in Georgian drama *The Writings* played for two nights in a small London theatre, to packed houses and much applause and laughter. Whether Fanny would herself approve of *Camilla* being examined in the light of its 'body language', or of 'sexual imagery' being discovered in *Evelina*, is a matter for debate. But that her novels are still being read – and not just by women of a certain age or by academics – is a tribute to her ability to engage and inspire her readers with her enthusiasm, her spirit and, above all, her gift for life and friendship.

ACKNOWLEDGEMENTS

I must first acknowledge my gratitude to Professor Lars Troide and McGill University, Montreal, for their hospitality, and for allowing me to read through the Burney papers, in particular the editorial annotations to *The Early Journals and Letters*, which are being prepared for publication. Without such scholarly good will, this book could not have been written. All quotations from the unpublished material are from my readings and any errors are, of course, my own.

I must also thank the Society of Authors for a grant of £500 from the Authors' Foundation.

Quotations from the papers of Queen Charlotte are with the gracious permission of HM The Queen. Those from the Henry W. and Albert A. Berg Collection are used with the kind permission of the New York Public Library.

No biographer of Fanny Burney can hope to replace the pioneering work of Professor Joyce Hemlow, whose 1958 *The History of Fanny Burney* first inspired me. Without her scholarship, my own book would not have been possible. She went on to lead the editorial team at McGill University, Montreal, whose patient deciphering of Fanny's deliberate obliterations and obfuscations is now available to all readers in the revised edition of the later journals and letters. Joyce Hemlow's enthusiasm ensured the completion of the twelve volumes, which take us from Fanny's release from Court in the summer of 1791 to her death in January 1840. Her work is now being continued under the auspices of Professor Lars Troide; and three of the prospective twelve volumes of *The Early Journals and Letters*, beginning in March 1768, have already been published.

I am very grateful to Joyce Hemlow for being so encouraging to me in my attempt to write about Fanny, and I shall always remember taking tea with her, and the afternoon we spent laughing together over our struggles to read through Fanny's voluminous and much-scattered correspondence.

Without Jenny Uglow of Chatto & Windus, this book would never have materialised. I am indebted to her scrupulous editing, her empathetic ear and the never-failing arrival of an inspiring postcard whenever despair loomed.

My colleagues at the *Sunday Telegraph* have heard a good deal more about the Burneys than they would have wished; I am particularly grateful to Miriam Gross, the Literary Editor, who both suggested I should write a book and then made it possible for me to do so. My thanks are also due to Jane Mays and Heather Neill for their professional encouragement.

Dr Alvaro Ribeiro, SJ (the editor of Dr Burney's letters), first suggested that

I should examine the Burney papers at McGill University, for which I am very grateful. I would also like to thank: Mr and Mrs John Comyn, for their generous hospitality and assistance in looking through the Burney family papers in their possession; Bill Fraser, for lending me his copy of the 'Worcester Journal'; Professor Roger Lonsdale, for his enthusiastic life of Dr Burney; Dr Stewart Cooke at McGill University and Dr Nancy Johnson, for their scholarly encouragement and friendship; Olwen Hedley, for her instructive biography of Queen Charlotte and for many afternoons spent discussing life at the eighteenth-century Court; Karin Fernald, whose entertaining readings from the diaries have provided many insights and much stimulating conversation; Alan Coveney, for his production of 'A Busy Day' and for guiding me through the eighteenth-century theatre; Peter Sabor, editor of Fanny's plays, for an enlightening correspondence; Ray Desmond, former archivist at Kew Gardens, who gave me an informative tour of the walks that Fanny would have taken in 1786–91; the Bebbingtons of the Juniper Hall Field Centre in Mickleham, Surrey, for their hospitality; Flora Fraser, for her insights into the Royal Household of King George III and Queen Charlotte; Susan Bennett at the Royal Society of Arts; Penelope and Anthea Lynex, for miraculously finding a picture; Patricia Crown, for helpful insights into Edward Francisco Burney; and Jean Bowden, for her efficient stewardship of the Burney Society.

The librarians at the Berg Collection in the New York Public Library were unfailingly helpful in supplying me with 'boxes' as soon as requested. My thanks must also go to the curators at the Robinson Library, Armagh, the Cheshire Record Office, the Essex Record Office, the Norfolk Record Office, the King's Lynn Museum, the Theatre Museum in Covent Garden, the library at Westminster Abbey, the Royal Hospital, Chelsea, the London Borough of Richmond, the National Portrait Gallery, the Guildhall Library and the Royal Archives at Windsor. Special thanks must be given to the Librarian and staff of the London Library.

Alison Lyon bravely took on the task of reading the text in its raw condition; her comments were of invaluable assistance. Vivien Cripps accompanied me without complaint in my search for Fanny's Paris life; and the Cameron family provided respite care whenever required. Without the faith of Mary Harron and Gloria and Stephen Vizinczey, I would never have embarked on such an ambitious project. I am also grateful to Philippe Savoy, Ian Everall, Paul Korytko (for help with French translations), Jean and Douglas Gibson, Julie Friedeberger, and the Barcelonans for their patience.

Finally, to my family I owe the inspiration and determination to continue.

NOTES

Abbreviations used in the Notes

ED The Early Diary of Frances Burney, 1768–1778, edited by Annie Raine Ellis, two vols

EJL The Early Journals and Letters of Fanny Burney, 1768–91, edited by Lars Troide *et al.*, twelve vols

JL The Journals and Letters of Fanny Burney (Madame d'Arblay), 1791–1840, edited by Joyce Hemlow *et al.*, twelve vols

Memoirs (Klima) *Memoirs of Dr Charles Burney, 1728–1769*, edited by Slava Klima, Garry Bowers and Kerry S. Grant.

1. A MOST FEELING GIRL: 1752–68

1 In her novel *Evelina*, published six years earlier, Fanny had suggested (through the character of the rakish Sir Clement Willoughby) that hats could be worn for flirtatious effect: 'Indeed,' cried Sir Clement, 'I must own myself no advocate for hats; I am sorry the ladies ever invented or adopted so tantalizing a fashion; for, where there is beauty, they only serve to shade it, and where there is none, to excite a most unavailing curiosity. I fancy they were originally worn by some young and whimsical coquet.' From *Evelina*, vol. i, letter xvi, p. 59. Richard Walker, in his book *Regency Portraits*, identifies Fanny's hat as a 'Lunardi'.

2 From a letter written by Fanny to her sister Susan at the beginning of September 1782 (from the unpublished material at McGill University). The spelling in quotations from original sources has been modernised where appropriate; but the original punctuation has been retained, except where it might cause confusion.

3 Fanny recorded in her diary for Saturday, 28 June 1783 that she had sat for John Bogle, the miniaturist, and there is a miniature (now in private possession) of a young woman surrounded by books, signed and dated by him, which many believe to be of Fanny. Richard Walker in his *Regency Portraits*, however, says that *only* Edward's portraits can definitely be said to be of Fanny, and, looking at the Bogle miniature, it is difficult to believe it is Fanny – the features are too small, the expression too dull, the set of the mouth and brow too different. There is dispute about one other portrait, by Daniel Gardner, which shows a young woman with long, dark hair coiled casually into a loose coiffure, large eyes and mouth, and an intense, abstracted expression, as if she is dreaming of her fictional world. It is dated to the early 1770s, when Daniel Gardner lived close to the Burneys in Leicester Fields, and when he is known to have painted Dr Burney. But, although there is a close likeness between the sitter and Edward's Fanny, there can be no certainty that this is the same young woman. There is, too, a silhouette by Thomas Wheeler (dating from either 1786 or 1787) in The Royal Collection at Windsor Castle, which was formerly thought to be of either Madame de Genlis or Queen Charlotte, but which is now regarded as being of Fanny. Annie Raine Ellis mentions in her Preface to *The Early Diary of Frances Burney* that 'Fanny never sat to Sir Joshua, who had had two strokes of paralysis before she knew him. Höppner painted a portrait of her, and her cousin Edward two.' There are no other surviving references to the Höppner portrait, and it is probable that she was referring to his portrait of Fanny's half-sister, Sarah Harriet.

4 Mrs Arlbery in *Camilla*.

5 From a letter to his friend Mrs Thrale, quoted in the obituary of Fanny's elder brother James, which appeared in the *Morning Chronicle*, 19 November 1821. From a family scrapbook, 'Fanny Burney and Family, 1653–1890', in the Berg Collection; with kind permission of the New York Public Library.

6 There is fierce debate among certain Burney scholars as to how we should name the author of *Evelina*, *Cecilia*, *Camilla* and *The Wanderer*, who was christened 'Frances' but was always known to her family as 'Fanny' or 'Fannikin'. One school believes that to use her nickname diminishes her stature as a writer and insists on 'Frances'. Libraries usually catalogue her works under her married name, Madame d'Arblay; but her four novels are all available in paperback as being by 'Fanny Burney'. Fanny herself published her first novel anonymously, and the rest as being 'By the author of *Evelina* . . . ' When her diaries were published after her death in 1840, they were attributed to 'Madame d'Arblay', but by 1889 when Annie Raine Ellis came to edit the previously unpublished early diaries (from 1768 to 1778), she reverted to 'Frances Burney'. How then did Madame d'Arblay become better known as Fanny Burney? I think because anyone reading the diaries and letters cannot help but come away with the feeling that you know her, just like her family and friends, and so she becomes for you not 'Frances' but 'Fanny'. This is the conclusion drawn by Joyce Hemlow in her comprehensive and revelatory *The History of Fanny Burney*, which first appeared in 1958, and I have chosen to follow her guidance. Fanny's elder sister, Hetty, was christened 'Esther' but was always called 'Hetty' or 'Hettina', while Susan was baptised as 'Susanna Elizabeth'.

7 Quoted by Annie Raine Ellis in her 1889 edition of *The Early Diary of Frances Burney*, i, p. lxxix n.

8 From Austin Dobson's introduction to his six-volume 1904 edition of the *Diary & Letters of Madame d'Arblay (1778–1840)*, i, p. 3. The fragment has since been lost.

9 From a letter to Hetty dated 25–8 November 1820. Quoted in volume xi of *The Journals and Letters of Fanny Burney (Madame d'Arblay)*, edited by Joyce Henlow *et al* (*JL*) pp. 183–97.

10 A page of family portraits in the first volume of F. Leverton Harris's 'grangerized' edition of the *Early Diary of Frances Burney: 1768–1778* in the National Portrait Gallery archive in London has miniatures of the Macburneys, father and son. James junior was painted by Michael Dahl, the Swedish portraitist, who was later to teach him. These portraits reveal a remarkable family likeness, which can also be seen in Dr Burney and later in James, Fanny and Susan (Hetty, Charles and Charlotte took after their mother). The details of family history were collected together in 1845 to form the 'Memoranda of the Burney Family, 1603–1845' (ninety-eight pages of typescript often known as the 'Worcester Journal') by a descendant of Dr Burney's brother Richard (who settled in Worcester), a copy of which was very kindly shown to me by Bill Fraser, himself descended from Fanny's sister Hetty.

11 The information on Fleetwood comes from the new scholarly edition of Dr Burney's memoirs compiled from the fragments left after Fanny's careful editing (and burning) of her father's papers, *Memoirs*, (Klima), Fragment 20, p. 39 n. 2, Fragment 27, p. 46 n. 2; and from Thomas Davies's *Memoirs of the Life of David Garrick, Esq.*, i, pp. 67–73.

12 From Fanny's account of her father's early life in the *Memoirs of Doctor Burney*, which she published in three volumes in 1832, i, p. 5.

13 From the *Memoirs* (Klima), Fragments 1–2, p. 14.

14 Ibid., Fragment 13, p. 30.

15 Ibid., Fragment 20, p. 38. My italics.

16 Ibid., Fragment 10, pp. 24–5.

17 'Rule, Britannia!' was included in *The Masque of Alfred*, a musical entertainment given by the Prince of Wales, Frederick Louis, at Cliveden, the country house that he rented in Buckinghamshire in August 1740.

18 Fielding's description, quoted by M. Dorothy George in her *London Life in the Eighteenth Century*, p. 91, was written in 1751. George's book gives a vivid account of what it must have been like to live in the capital at this time.

19 Richard Holmes's *Dr Johnson & Mr Savage* re-creates the London of the late 1730s, when the penniless poet and journalist befriended the luckless Richard Savage, who was convicted and then acquitted of murder. Savage died in a debtors' jail in 1743.

20 Fanny's version of this story can be read in volume i of her *Memoirs of Doctor Burney*, pp. 26–33.
21 From *Memoirs* (Klima), Fragment 31, p. 50.
22 According to Charles's brother, Richard. Ibid., Fragment 49, p. 83 n. 2.
23 This miniature was commissioned by Charles from the portraitist Gervase Spencer. It was in the possession of the Burney family until the 1970s. The fact that Charles had such a painting made of his future wife suggests that he originally hoped to travel with the Grevilles but had to change his plans when Esther became pregnant.
24 Joyce Hemlow discovered the marriage certificate in the registers of St George's, Hyde Park and surmised 'for the laws of nature and arithmetic will admit of no other year' that since James was born in 1750, Hetty must have been born at least a year earlier, and not in 1750, as had previously been supposed and as indicated in the 'Worcester Journal'. Hemlow, *The History of Fanny Burney*, p. 6 and n. 2.
25 *Memoirs of Doctor Burney*, i, pp. 67–8.
26 Dr Scholes gives more details of these and other concerts organised by Charles in chapter 5 of the first volume of his *The Great Dr Burney: His Life, His Travels, His Works, His Family and His Friends*.
27 As a jobbing musician at the theatre, Charles was able to watch performances from behind the scenes. *Memoirs* (Klima), Fragment 40, pp. 61–3.
28 From Thomas Davies, *Memoirs of the Life of David Garrick, Esq.*, i, p. 129 (quoted in Roger Lonsdale's *Dr Charles Burney: A Literary Biography*, p. 33). Theatrical runs were much shorter at this time and just fourteen consecutive performances would have been regarded then as a resounding success.
29 In her notoriously unreliable *Memoirs* of her father, Fanny claimed that Charles's salary was £100, but Dr Scholes included in his *The Great Dr Burney* items from the Vestry Minutes of St Margaret's, which suggested that Charles received only £30 a year. Perhaps the truth lies in the fact that by 1755 Charles was writing to the Vestry offering his resignation as organist because: 'The subscription being expired which first induced me to reside in this Town ... the organ salary is too inconsiderable to retain me in your service' (quoted by Roger Lonsdale in *Dr Charles Burney*, p. 45). This is now confirmed by a fragment from Charles's own memoir, in which he says: 'a proposal from Sir John Turner, member [for] Lynn Regis to accept of the place of Organist at St Margaret's Church in that Borough at a Salary of £100 a year, encreased to that sum from £20 a year as an encouragement to a regular bred musician of some character to come down from the Capital to instruct the children of the principal families in the town & neighbourhood in Music'. *Memoirs* (Klima), Fragment 65, p. 106.
30 From *The Letters of Dr Charles Burney, Volume I: 1751–1784*, edited by Alvaro Ribeiro, SJ, pp. 1–2. Fanny also quotes from the letter in the *Memoirs of Doctor Burney*, i, pp. 88–90.
31 Much of old King's Lynn has been bulldozed and replaced by 1960s shopping arcades and pedestrianised precincts, and there is uncertainty as to the precise house in which the Burneys stayed on their arrival in the town in 1751. Dr Scholes wrote in *The Great Dr Burney* that he had been informed by a local solicitor that the Burneys' first home was in a house called St Augustine's in Chapel Street, which still then existed. He describes it as 'a pleasant and dignified building, with a good garden behind it. In Burney's day it must have been nearly new' (p. 68 n.).
32 One of sixteen children to appear in the baptismal register of the Chapel of St Nicholas for the month of July, the entry reads: '7. Frances, d. Mr Charles & Esther Burney'. (The Burneys' lodgings in Chapel Street were closer to St Nicholas than to the Parish Church of St Margaret's by the Town Hall.)
33 From *Memoirs* (Klima), Fragment 69, p. 115. Fanny's bowdlerised version appears in the *Memoirs of Doctor Burney*, i, pp. 129–30.
34 *Memoirs of Doctor Burney*, i, pp. 131–3.
35 From Dr Scholes's *The Great Dr Burney*, i, p. 80.
36 The photograph in Dr Scholes's *The Great Dr Burney* is opposite p. 68 and the details appear as a note on p. 86.
37 *Memoirs* (Klima), Fragment 67, pp. 111–12. Sir Andrew Fountaine had been a friend of Swift and lived near Swaffham; by Halcombe, Charles means Holkham, near Wells,

which was the seat of Viscount Coke; Blickling was near Aylsham and was owned by the 1st Earl of Buckingham; Wolterton, the home of Horace Walpole's uncle, Horatio, 1st Baron of Wolterton, was also near Aylsham; and Sir Henry L'Estrange lived in Hunstanton.

38 Charles devised a new technique for striking the keys of the harpsichord, which enabled him to play with greater dexterity, impressing audiences with his superior virtuosity. It was a method of playing that distinguished his pupils, and brought him much success as a teacher.

39 The *Dizionario portativo Italiano ed Inglese, compilato da Carlo Burney*, dated 1756, along with the French dictionary, is now in the Osborn Collection at Yale University. Peggy was treated like a household pet by the Burneys and, when he left Lynn, Charles arranged for her to live out the years of her retirement in the lush green pastures of the Houghton estate. *Memoirs of Doctor Burney*, i, p. 133.

40 According to Dr Scholes's *The Great Dr Burney*, the epidemic was so serious that the hours of burial at St Margaret's were extended from eight in the morning to nine at night (i, p. 84).

41 *Memoirs of Doctor Burney*, i, p. 99.

42 The comment was made by Pacchierotti in 1781; he was loved by all the Burneys, who were loved in turn by him. From the unpublished letters and diaries of Fanny Burney, kindly shown to me by Professor Lars Troide at McGill University.

43 Fanny was preparing the memoirs of her father when she wrote to Hetty on 21 October 1821. *JL*, xi, p. 286.

44 Quoted in *Memoirs* (Klima), pp. 128–9.

45 *Ibid*. Fragment 83, pp. 130–1. The year of this performance is much debated. Dr Burney himself recorded that it took place in 1769, but this must have been an error, as he also says he did not attend it because of his commitments in Norfolk. John Beard was an actor and singer; Charles Brent was a tenor who sang for Handel; and Skeggs performed at Covent Garden.

46 In the eighteenth century, doors at the theatre opened at least two hours before performances began; those with servants would send them on ahead to reserve seats, which were always in great demand. On this occasion the doors opened at five o'clock, with the concert due to begin at seven (according to the *Public Advertiser*, quoted in Dr Scholes's *The Great Dr Burney*, i, p. 98).

47 The original row of houses in Poland Street has long since disappeared, but there is now a D'Arblay Street running at right-angles off the west side of Poland Street about half-way down, which was so renamed in April 1909 to commemorate Fanny's residence at No. 50 Poland Street from 1760 until 1770. The Westminster councillors had wanted to call the street 'Burney Street' but were unable to do so because a 'Burney Street' already existed in Greenwich (named after Fanny's brother Charles, who founded a school there in the 1790s). Information from the *Survey of London*, xxxi (1963) (*The Parish of St James, Westminster, North of Piccadilly*) and the *City of Westminster: Minutes of Proceedings of the Mayor Aldermen & Councillors, 1909*. The quote from Fanny comes from the *Memoirs of Doctor Burney*, i, p. 134.

48 Charles preserved the story in his memoirs, now Fragment 90 in *Memoirs* (Klima), pp. 142–3; and Fanny included it in her *Memoirs of Doctor Burney*, ii, pp. 168–71.

49 Fanny eulogized her father's industry in the *Memoirs of Doctor Burney*, ii, pp. 211–12. Charles's account of his professional success is now preserved in *Memoirs* (Klima), Fragment 86, p. 136.

50 *Memoirs* (Klima), Fragment 92, p. 144.

51 Ibid., Fragment 88, pp. 139–41. At this time, with England and France engaged in almost perpetual conflict, a naval career was considered both glamorous and financially beneficial. James was later accepted at the naval academy in Portsmouth to train as an officer.

52 From Joyce Hemlow's *The History of Fanny Burney*, p. 11.

53 *EJL*, i, p. 6.

54 From the *Memoirs of Doctor Burney*, i, p. 141.

55 Quoted by Hemlow, *The History of Fanny Burney*, p. 5.

56 Charles eventually went to Charterhouse in February 1768, aged ten, sponsored by the

Duke of Marlborough.

57 *Memoirs* (Klima), Fragment 103, pp. 156–7.

58 From Joyce Hemlow's suggestion in *The History of Fanny Burney*, p. 15.

59 *Memoirs* (Klima), Fragment 104, pp. 157–8.

60 In volume i of the *Memoirs of Doctor Burney* (pp. 197–8), she recalled that she 'was the only one of Mr Burney's family who never was placed in any seminary, and never was put under any governess or instructor whatsoever. Merely and literally self-educated, her sole emulation for improvement, and sole spur for exertion, were her unbounded veneration for the character, and affection for the person, of her father; who, nevertheless, had not, at the time, a moment to spare for giving her any personal lessons; or even for directing her pursuits.' Joyce Hemlow gives lists of the books mentioned by Fanny in *The History of Fanny Burney*, pp. 18–21.

61 From a box of 417 miscellaneous scraps belonging to Fanny and dated from 1772 to 1828 (Berg Collection, 19830oB), with kind permission of the New York Public Library.

62 Quoted by Dr Scholes in *The Great Dr Burney*, i, p. 82; the full letter can be found in the *Memoirs*, i, pp. 128–9.

63 The wild wood has long since disappeared, as has Chesington Hall – though the twelfth-century church with its quaint tower peeping above the trees dotted among the suburban culs-de-sac of modern Chessington may still be visited. On the north-east wall is a large memorial plaque dedicated to Samuel Crisp, with a eulogy signed by C. Burney. Charles's description of Chesington is in the *Memoirs* (Klima), Fragment 105, p. 160.

64 From a letter dated April 1774, now in the Berg Collection: 'Scrapbook: Fanny d'Arblay and Friends. England. 1759–99' (60B7137), with the kind permission of the New York Public Library. Crisp's allusion is to Shylock's daughter Jessica in *The Merchant of Venice*, in which the metaphors are all to do with flesh and feasting.

65 From *EJL*, i, p. 8; Fanny's accounts of Mr Crisp are in the *Memoirs of Doctor Burney*, i, pp. 48–54, 174; his description of her is from a letter quoted by Annie Raine Ellis in her Preface (it has since been lost) *ED*, i, p. xxxiii.

66 The marriage took place in great secrecy on 2 October 1767 by special licence from the Archbishop of Canterbury at St James's, Westminster. (Mrs Allen's mother did not welcome her daughter's relationship with Charles because of his unpredictable and 'bohemian' career. They were married by the curate Mr Pugh, a family friend; witnessed by Richard Fuller, a wealthy banker who had helped Charles secure the organist's position at St Dionis Backchurch in 1749, and Isabella Strange, wife of Robert Strange, the engraver. Charles had taught her daughter, and then became friends with the family.

67 Quoted by Dr Scholes in *The Great Dr Burney*, i, p. 75.

68 *Memoirs of Doctor Burney*, i, p. 97. My italics.

69 *Memoirs* (Klima), Fragment 113, pp. 174–5.

70 *Memoirs of Doctor Burney*, i, pp. 197–9.

71 From a letter she wrote to Susan after hearing about Fanny's marriage in July 1793. The letter, from the 'Scrapbook: Fanny Burney and Family, 1653–1890', is now in the Berg Collection (213048B); with the kind permission of the New York Public Library.

72 *Memoirs of Doctor Burney*, ii, pp. 123–6.

2. TO NOBODY: 1768–78

1 From the first page of the 'Juvenile Journal No. 1', now in the Berg Collection; with the kind permission of the New York Public Library. The sewn exercise book, covered in a blue folder, is annotated 'Begun at 15 years' and 'This strange medley of Thoughts & Facts was written at the age of 15 for my Genuine & most private amusement.' Fanny signed the first volume 'Fanny Burney, Poland Street, London, March 27'.

2 What began as a private journal became, as the family went off to live their separate lives, a means of keeping in touch. Fanny would write long monthly journals to Susan, which Susan sewed together in carefully paginated notebooks. Earlier Fanny had developed the art of writing letter-journals when describing to her father's friend and her own 'second daddy', Mr Crisp, her life among the London literati. Shorter letters were referred to as 'alives' (merely to let the recipient know that the writer was still 'alive') or as 'a few pleasing words', which gave slightly more information as to what the writer had been up to.

3 From the 'Juvenile Journal No. 1'; with the kind permission of the Berg Collection at the New York Public Library.

4 From Austin Dobson's six-volume edition of *The Diary & Letters of Madame d'Arblay (1778–1840)*, i, p. 9. This fragment of Susan's early journal has since been lost.

5 Fanny had another connection with *Robinson Crusoe*: the Chapel of St Nicholas, in which she was baptised, contains a number of memorials to the 'Cruso' family, two of which are to 'Robinson Cruso'. Defoe visited King's Lynn on several occasions, most particularly on his way north to Halifax in August 1712, where it is thought he began the novel. The memorials are dated after this visit, but the Cruso family is known to have been resident in the town from 1610 until the death of Miss Cruso in about 1905.

6 From the 'Juvenile Journal No. 1'; with the kind permission of the Berg Collection at the New York Public Library. Also *EJL*, i, pp. 1–2.

7 The letter is dated 22 January 1780. From the unpublished material at McGill University.

8 *EJL*, i, p. 14.

9 Ibid., i, pp. 57–8. Here Fanny provides an intriguing observation on the lot of women, and their need for independence, some 180 years before that other great diarist Virginia Woolf wrote her essay on 'a room of my own' based on an income of £500 p.a.

10 Ibid., i, p. 11.

11 The letter is dated 13 October 1768 and was published for the first time in the *EJL*, i, p. 50.

12 From a letter from Maria to Fanny dated 3 September 1798 and quoted in Joyce Hemlow's *The History of Fanny Burney*, p.xxxv.

13 Fanny noted in her journal that on one occasion David Garrick teased her by noticing how 'Sukey' had grown. He asked Fanny who was the older sister. She replied indignantly, 'I am, Sir, & ought to be Tallest, only she has been so wicked as to out grow me.' *EJL*, ii, p. 95.

14 Spectacles as we know them, with hinged side-pieces, were first worn in London in the 1750s.

15 *EJL*, i, pp. 10, 15.

16 The wedding, which is recorded in the parish registers of St Margaret's, took place at ten o'clock on the morning of Wednesday, 20 July 1768, and was between a Thomas Bagge and Pleasance Case. It obviously made quite an impression on Fanny for, unusually for her, she records the bridal regalia: the bride was all in white, while the bridegroom was in a dashing light-blue suit with silver and purple trimmings.

17 *EJL*, i, p. 37.

18 Ibid., i, pp. 72–3.

19 Ibid., i, p. 166.

20 The much crossed-out letter was discovered among the Burney family papers in the Berg Collection by Professor Lars Troide and is included and deciphered as an Appendix to volume i of the *EJL*, pp. 331–2. Maria's suggestion would perhaps have been appreciated by the 1960s radical Valerie Solanas, who invented the Society for Cutting Up Men. Her *SCUM Manifesto* (1968) opens with the statement that 'Life in this society being, at best, an utter bore and no aspect of society being at all relevant to women, there remains to civic-minded, responsible, thrill-seeking females only to overthrow the government, eliminate the money system, institute complete automation and destroy the male sex' (reprinted in *I Shot Andy Warhol*, by Mary Harron and Daniel Minahan (London, 1996), pp. 157–90.

21 After the passing of the Marriage Act in 1753, couples under the age of twenty-one were required to obtain the consent of their parents. The result was to vastly increase the number of elopements, Gretna Green just over the border in Scotland and Ypres in Flanders being the favourite destinations for runaways' marriages.

22 *EJL*, i, pp. 100–7. It is worth reading Fanny's account in its entirety for its vividness and sharp insights.

23 The domino – originally a plain black silk gown – was a popular choice of outfit at the eighteenth-century masquerade for those too inhibited to play a character part.

24 From the 'Scrapbook: Fanny Burney and Family, 1653–1890' in the Berg Collection

(213048B); with kind permission of the New York Public Library. Later annotated by Fanny: 'From my dear Father when I was 10 years old. Sent by post from Wood Hay in Berkshire, 1763.'

25 *EJL*, i, pp. 125–6.

26 I am very grateful to John Comyn, a descendant of Fanny's brother Charles, for the opportunity to see this painting.

27 The suggestion was made to me by Professor Lars Troide, editor of the *EJL*.

28 From *Music, Men and Manners in France and Italy 1770, Being the Journal Written by Charles Burney, Mus. D., During a Tour Through Those Countries Undertaken to Collect Material for A General History of Music*, transcribed from the original manuscript in the British Museum and edited with an introduction by H. Edmund Poole (London, 1969), p. 179. Dr Burney's journal was a huge success when it first appeared in May 1771; Dr Johnson is said to have used it as a model for his *A Journey to the Western Islands of Scotland* (1775).

29 Fanny recalled the impression Charles Rousseau made on her at his wedding in a letter to her younger sister Charlotte, dated 5–15 October 1819 (*JL*, xi, p. 140); her opinion of the marriage is given in the first volume of the *EJL*, p. 243.

30 The tragic story of Charles Crisp, and his parents' anguished attempts to find him, is told at length in the 'Worcester Journal', which was compiled by Charles Rousseau's great-grandson, Henry Edward Burney with grateful thanks to Bill Fraser.

31 The obituary, which appeared in the *New Monthly Magazine* on 1 December 1819, is quoted in the 'Worcester Journal'. (With thanks to Bill Fraser.)

32 Quoted by Alvaro Ribeiro, SJ, in his Introduction to *The Letters of Dr Charles Burney*, i, p.xxv.

33 *EJL*, i, p. 146.

34 Ibid., i, p. 151.

35 Ibid., i, p. 146.

36 Ibid., i, p. 216.

37 From a letter sent to Fanny in December 1773, ibid., i, p. 320.

38 Ibid., i, pp. 20–2.

39 Ibid., ii, p. 232.

40 The house was pulled down in 1913, but was still standing when Constance Hill wrote the first volume of her life of the Burneys, *The House in St Martin's Street*, (1907). She described it in vivid detail, while her sister Ellen G. Hill provided sketches of the observatory and the attic bedroom where, it is supposed, Fanny wrote *Evelina*. The site, on the corner of St Martin's Street and Orange Street, just behind Trafalgar Square, is now part of the Central Library, Westminster. The chapel next door, constructed in 1693, was also demolished but rebuilt to a similar design in 1929.

41 In one of her essays in *The Common Reader* (second series, 1986 edn, pp. 108–25), Virginia Woolf memorably evokes 'Dr Burney's Evening Party', based on her readings of Fanny's early diary. She talks of Fanny's 'half-suppressed, uneasy passion for writing' and of how the author makes her own impression, so that 'One seems to remember, for she paints herself while she paints the others, Fanny herself slipping eagerly and lightly in and out of all this company, with her rather prominent gnat-like eyes, and her shy, awkward manner. But the gnat-like eyes, the awkward manners, concealed the quickest observation, the most retentive memory.'

42 This account appears in *EJL*, i, p. 265.

43 Quoted by Fanny in the *Memoirs of Doctor Burney*, ii, p. 168.

44 *EJL*, i, p. 225. Of his performance of Lear, she says 'he was exquisitely Great – every idea which I had formed of his talents, although I have ever idolized him, was exceeded' (ibid., p. 242).

45 From an 'Ode to Garrick' written on the back of a bill from Twinings, the tea merchants, among the 417 scraps of dialogue, character-sketches and notebooks in the Berg Collection (198300B); with the kind permission of the New York Public Library.

46 *EJL*, ii, pp. 60–2. Fanny's description brings to vivid life the huge, full-length portrait of Omai painted by Sir Joshua Reynolds, which is now at Parham Park in Sussex, and of which there are many copies.

47 Aleksei's brother, Grigory, was the Empress's lover and father of her illegitimate son.

The Emperor Peter III died in July 1762, allegedly of haemorrhoids, but, unofficially, he was thought to have been murdered by Aleksei in a stage-managed drunken brawl.
48 *EJL*, ii, p. 181.
49 The title on Fanny's original draft manuscript (now in the Berg Collection: 196064B) is 'Eveline, or Memoirs of a Young Lady In a Series of Letters'. Written on coarse paper, folded in half, it is a very rough draft with many crossings-out.
50 The letter was addressed 'To Thomas Lowndes' and sent from St Martin's Street on 26 December 1776. The Burneys do not seem to have celebrated Christmas as we do now, and Fanny was on her own that day. *EJL*, ii, p. 215.
51 She dedicated this Preface 'To the Authors of the Monthly and Critical Reviews', *Evelina*, p. 3. All quotations from *Evelina* are taken from The World's Classics edition which uses the first edition of the novel (29 January 1778), now in the Bodleian Library, Oxford.
52 Thirteen years earlier, in 1764, Thomas Lowndes had published Horace Walpole's *The Castle of Otranto*.
53 It is now thought by the scholars at McGill University that this coffee-house was Gregg's Coffee House in Covent Garden (also spelt Grigg's), which they believe was part-owned by Dr Burney and managed by his two sisters, Becky and Ann (also called Nancy). In 1763, Dr Burney is listed in Thomas Mortimer's *The Universal Director* as having a business address at 'Grigg's' in York Street ('Charles Burney, Organist. Enquire at Grigg's Coffee House, York Street, Covent Garden'). But when she came to edit her diaries, Fanny scrubbed out Gregg's and replaced it with the 'Orange Coffee House in the Haymarket' – except for one occasion in June 1778, when she mistakenly left in a mention to 'Gregg's', alerting the suspicions of the McGill scholars. If Gregg's did belong to the Burneys, it would perhaps explain how Charles Burney junior managed to acquire his extensive newspaper collection – presumably from copies originally bought for the customers of the coffee-house. *EJL*, iii, pp. 457–9.
54 Both the draft and the final version are to be found in *EJL*, ii, pp. 213, 291.
55 *Memoirs of Doctor Burney*, ii, pp. 128–9.
56 *EJL*, ii, p. 215.
57 Ibid., ii, pp. 216–18.
58 Ibid., ii, pp. 231–2.
59 Ibid.
60 Ibid., ii, pp. 233–4.
61 Ibid., ii, pp. 285–7.
62 Ibid., ii, pp. 287–8. I am indebted to Mr John Comyn for allowing me to see his copy of F. Leverton Harris's grangerized edition of *The Diary & Letters of Madame d'Arblay* (*1778–1840*), which contains the original of Fanny's letter.

3. *EVELINA*: 1778

1 *EJL*, iii, p. 5.
2 Edward Francisco was the son of Dr Burney's brother Richard, and as a talented draughtsman and painter had been sent to London from Worcester to study at the Royal Academy. During this time he lodged with his Burney cousins, endearing himself to them all because of his quiet, unassuming personality and kindly nature. He was always to remain a favourite with Fanny. In 1780 he entered three drawings, illustrations of scenes from *Evelina* (of a disconsolate Evelina reading a letter from Mr Villars, Madame Duval after her accident on the way home from Ranelagh and the reconciliation scene between Evelina and her father), in the Royal Academy show. He is entered in the catalogue for that year as living in 'York Street, Covent Garden' – further evidence of the link between the Burney aunts and 'Gregg's'? See *The Royal Academy of Arts: A Complete Dictionary of Contributors and Their Work from its Foundation in 1769 to 1904* by Algernon Graves (London, 1905).
3 This concert took place on 12 March at the Freemasons' Hall in Great Queen Street, Lincoln's Inn Fields. *EJL*, iii, p. 8 n.
4 Mrs Draper, who was a friend of the second Mrs Burney and of the Stranges (who had witnessed the Burneys' secret marriage), wrote to the Stranges' daughter, Mary

Bruce, of the affair, who then reported what she had said to Mrs Burney (see *EJL*, ii, p. 289).

5 We know details of the elopement only from Mrs Thrale's correspondence with Dr Johnson, in which Mrs Thrale indicates her surprise that the second Mrs Burney had sent both her daughters, Maria and Bessy, abroad at a vulnerable age (their mid-teens), where, without proper guidance, they had both acted rashly and disastrously. The story is confirmed by the letters of Mrs Draper to Mary Bruce Strange (who was just a few years older than Fanny and a frequent visitor to St Martin's Street). This information comes from a note in the *EJL*, ii, pp. 289–90.

6 *EJL*, i, p. 222; and an unpublished letter from Samuel Crisp to Fanny, dated 11 August 1772, now in a bundle of eight letters by Samuel Crisp in the Essex Record Office (catalogue reference D/DL C65).

7 *EJL*, iii, p. 1.

8 Fanny says in 1796 that 800 copies were printed for the first edition, but Lowndes wrote in a letter of 1782 that he had printed 500 copies. I am assuming that Lowndes is more likely to be correct.

9 *Evelina*, Preface, pp. 7–8.

10 The original title-page (roughed out in black ink by Fanny), as sent to Thomas Lowndes with her manuscript, reads; 'Evelina, or a Young Lady's Entrance into Life, Volume I'. It can be seen in the grangerized edition of *The Diary & Letters of Madame d'Arblay (1778–1840)*, from a family collection now in the possession of John Comyn (with whose kind permission I was able to look through these original Burney papers). By the third edition of 1779, Fanny had changed the sub-title again to 'The History of a Young Lady's Entrance into the World'.

11 *Evelina*, vol. i, letter viii, p. 24. 'Anville' was presumably the name Evelina had adopted, but she felt she could not use it to Mr Villars, who knew that her real name was Belmont – a name that she could not use in society because of her father's refusal to acknowledge her existence. Margaret Anne Doody in her *Frances Burney: The Life in the Works* suggests that Fanny's choice of name 'Evelina Anville' is a feminist anagram – 'Eve in a Veil' – which seems, to me, to be taking Fanny's awareness of the inequalities and prejudices of eighteenth-century society too far. Fanny, who delighted in wordplay, was deliberate in her choice of names (the box of 417 scraps in the Berg Collection (198300B) contains lists of names to avoid, and ones to use in future works). But the difficulty of now discovering the meaning of Fanny's fictional names is illustrated by the fact that she chose to designate the French boyfriend of Evelina's dreadful grandmother Monsieur Du Bois, which was the family name of her beloved maternal grand-mother.

12 *Evelina*, vol. i, letter xii, pp. 29–36.

13 Ibid., vol. i, letter xxiv, p. 116.

14 Ibid., vol. iii, letter iii, p. 289.

15 Ibid., vol. ii, letter iii, p. 155.

16 The 'Holborn Beau' was Dr Johnson's favourite character in *Evelina*, or so he once claimed in conversation with Mrs Thrale.

17 In fact, the Hampstead museum was called 'New Georgia'.

18 *Evelina*, vol. i, letter x, p. 27.

19 Ibid., vol. i, letter xi, pp. 28–9.

20 Ibid., vol. i, letter xix, pp. 73–4.

21 In another letter, Evelina describes how Captain Mirvan has arranged for Madame Duval to be kidnapped and thrown into a ditch, where she is virtually tied hand and foot. To Fanny, this was the kind of practical joke her brothers would have played on her; to us, it appears quite needlessly cruel, and some feminist writers have suggested that Fanny is here using sexual imagery to illustrate the plight of women in the patriarchal society of eighteenth-century Britain. Madame Duval in the ditch supposedly illustrates her falling by way of her sexual organs into denigration and misuse by men. For a detailed examination of this, and other such interpretations of Fanny's fictions, see Margaret Anne Doody's *Frances Burney: The Life in the Works*, pp. 35–65.

22 *EJL*, iii, pp. 95–7.

23 This dramatic scene can be found in *Evelina*, vol. ii, letter xii, pp. 181–4.

24 *Thraliana*, i, p. 360. The conversation took place in January 1779.

FANNY BURNEY

25 *Evelina*, vol. ii, letter xii, pp. 181–2.

26 *EJL*, iii, p. 13.

27 The first quotation comes from a short, one-paragraph notice in the *Monthly Review; or, Literary Journal*, vol. lviii, article xlix, p. 316. Reviews of books by established authors could run to as many as five pages. Only a few months earlier, a novel on a similar theme – *The Excursion* by Frances Brooke (which tells of Maria Villars, who sets out for London with beauty, a little money and several manuscripts in her portmanteau, to seek her fortune, and who unlike Evelina comes to a sticky end because of her indiscretions) – had been given five pages. It has to be said that this extended space was used thoroughly to attack (rather than praise) Mrs Brooke for what it claimed was the libellous content of her novel, which accuses the actor-manager David Garrick of exploiting the writers who wrote plays for his theatre. (Mrs Brooke was paying off old scores; in 1756 she had tried and failed to have her tragedy *Virginia* staged.)

28 *EJL*, iii, p. 39.

29 Ibid., iii, p. 27. There is some confusion as to who told Dr Burney that Fanny had written *Evelina*. In a surviving fragment of his memoir, he says that Susan was his informant. But in her diary Fanny says that Charlotte brought him the copy of the *Monthly Review* containing the brief mention of *Evelina*, and he guessed that it was the 'book' that Fanny had told him about the previous year. The most likely version of what happened seems to me to be the one I have given here.

30 Ibid., iii, pp. 28–9.

31 Ibid., iii, pp. 55–6. By 'Leaf' she means Fanny's 'Dedication' to 'the author of my being'.

32 *Thraliana*, i, p. 137.

33 *EJL*, iii, p. 50.

34 The original of Mrs Thrale's letter to Dr Burney is in the grangerized edition of *The Diary Letters of Madame d'Arblay (1778–1840)* now in the possession of John Comyn. Her comments in the *Thraliana* are from July 1778, i, pp. 328–9.

35 From a journal-letter to Susan of 15 September, in which Fanny describes in great detail the reception of *Evelina*. *EJL*, iii, pp. 136–47.

36 Ibid., iii, pp. 51–2.

37 The letter is dated 8 February 1807, and is included in *Jane Austen's Letters to Her Sister Cassandra and Others*, collected and edited by R.W. Chapman, p. 180.

38 Fortunately, several sketches of the house and its spacious grounds, specially planted with cedars and oaks, have survived. It was pulled down in 1873, but the site in Colson Way, Streatham, off the Tooting Bec Road in south London, is marked by a plaque attached to a modern terraced house. Fanny's account of 27 July was written up in her journal when she got back to London, and was later sent to Mr Crisp for his perusal. *EJL*, iii, pp. 66–78.

39 The meeting took place on the morning of Thursday, 20 March 1777, when Mrs Thrale brought Dr Johnson to St Martin's Street to look at Dr Burney's library and meet his family. Fanny's account was written for Mr Crisp. Ibid., ii, pp. 223–9.

40 From letters sent to Susan from Streatham Park, where Fanny stayed throughout August and September 1778. Ibid., iii, pp. 90, 92–3, 118, 109–10.

41 This comment by Mrs Thrale is to be found in a letter from her to Dr Johnson, now in the collection of the John Rylands Library (Eng MS 541.83) and quoted in W. Wright Roberts's, 'Charles and Fanny Burney in the Light of the New Thrale Correspondence in the John Rylands Library', *Bulletin of the John Rylands Library*, 16, 1 (January 1932), p. 12.

42 Both Mrs Thrale's comment and Dr Johnson's reply are noted in *EJL*, iii, p. 162 n.

43 *Thraliana*, i, p. 430. The 'peccary' was a pig-like mammal found in the forests of Central and South America.

44 *Monthly Review*, lviii (April 1778), p. 316.

45 The other scenes depicted were Fanny's dedication to the 'author of my being'; and Madame Duval falling into the ditch and losing her wig. Dr Burney's comments are taken from a letter to Fanny written by Susan from St Martin's Street on 16 June 1778, in which Susan told her sister all that had been said by the family about the novel while Fanny was away, staying with Mr Crisp at Chesington Hall.

46 Indeed, a recent television comedy series included an episode in which two old grannies were shown running a race in slippers and hair-nets. It was embarrassing to watch, but gales of laughter could be heard from the studio audience.

47 Years later it was rumoured that Dr Johnson never read *Evelina*, or at most only half of it. In one of Lord Northcote's 'Conversations', published in the *New Monthly Magazine* in 1826, Northcote reports that he had been told by John Opie, the portraitist, that while Dr Johnson was sitting for him 'for his picture, on his first coming to town, he asked him if it was true that he had sat up all night to read Miss Burney's new novel, as it had been reported? And he made answer, "I never read it through at all, though I don't wish this to be known." ' (*The Collected Works of William Hazlitt*, edited by A.R. Waller and Arnold Glover, with an introduction by W.E. Henley, vi, p. 411.) This can be explained: first, Dr Johnson is reputed never to have finished a book; second, that whether or not he did read *Evelina*, he knew of its content and appreciated Fanny's satirical observations on society.

48 *The Letters of Samuel Johnson*, edited by R.W. Chapman, ii, p. 259.

49 This story is quoted in a letter from Dr Quinn to Dr Burney written in 1788 and now in the grangerized edition of *The Diary Letters of Madame d'Arblay (1778–1840)* owned by Mr John Comyn, to whom I am again grateful.

50 Fanny wrote this in her diary for 23 June 1778. *EJL*, iii, p. 32.

51 From a letter written by Jane Austen, dated Sunday, 2 June 1799: 'We had a Miss North & a Mr Gould of our party; the latter walked home with me after tea. He is a very young man, just entered of Oxford, wears spectacles, & has heard that "Evelina" was written by Dr Johnson.' *Jane Austen's Letters to Her Sister Cassandra and Others*, pp. 62–5.

52 *EJL*, iii, pp. 36–7.

4. MY DEAR LITTLE BURNEY: 1778–9

1 This was how Mr Seton, Hetty's fickle lover, had once described her.

2 From an exercise book of memoirs that Fanny compiled in 1804 while living in Paris. *EJL*, vii, pp. 521–46.

3 Fanny copied this letter from Mr Crisp into her diary for 16 August 1778. She had stayed in Teignmouth ('Tinmouth') in 1773, where the ever-adventurous Maria had tempted Fanny to venture into the sea. Ibid., iii, p. 82.

4 Fanny wrote this while back home in St Martin's Street, sometime between 3 and 12 September. After that first meeting with Mrs Thrale on 27 July, Fanny was invited back to stay on 21 August and did not leave until sometime after 3 September. By 12 September she was again at Streatham Park, where she stayed for several weeks. Ibid., iii, pp. 134–6.

5 Fanny was actually twenty-six, while Mrs Thrale was thirty-seven. Fanny copied the letter into her journal at the end of 1778. Ibid., iii, pp. 205–7.

6 She wrote this in May 1778 shortly before meeting Fanny. *Thraliana*, i, pp. 321–2.

7 Quoted by James L. Clifford in his biography of Mrs Thrale, *Hester Lynch Piozzi (Mrs Thrale)*, p. 9.

8 Tobias Smollett's description of Dr Johnson; in reply, Dr Johnson referred to Smollett as 'a scholarly man, though a Scot'. From *The Samuel Johnson Encyclopedia*, edited by Pat Rogers.

9 From Clifford's *Hester Lynch Piozzi (Mrs Thrale)*, p. 192.

10 *Thraliana*, i, pp. 366–8.

11 Ibid., i, p. 356.

12 In late August 1778, Fanny wrote a long, 16-sheet journal-letter to Susan, describing every detail of her stay at Streatham Park. *EJL*, iii, p. 91–122.

13 This letter to Mrs Gast (*née*) Crisp is dated 28 March 1779 and can be found in the *Burford Papers: Being Letters of Samuel Crisp to his Sister at Burford*, edited by William Holden Hutton, p. 29. It is also noted in *EJL*, iii, p. 261.

14 *EJL*, iii, pp. 255–6.

15 Ibid., iii, p. 100.

16 Ibid., iii, pp. 126–8.

17 This evening is recorded in a letter sent to Susan in February 1779. Ibid., iii, p. 251.

18 Ibid., iii, pp. 98–9.
19 Fanny's original MS, dated 14–15 August 1781, is now in the Berg Collection. The verse is quoted by Joyce Hemlow in *The History of Fanny Burney*, pp. 114–15, and will be published in volume iv of the *EJL*.
20 From *Thraliana*, 24 March 1779, pp. 375–6.
21 Written on the back of a printed sheet advertising the subscription for her third novel, *Camilla*, from June to July 1796. From the 417 scraps of manuscript in the Berg Collection (19830oB), with kind permission of the New York Public Library.
22 From 10 February 1779 and December 1778. *Thraliana*, i, pp. 366–7, 347–8.
23 *EJL*, iii, pp. 168–9.
24 The 'Barlow Affair' is recorded in detail in Fanny's journal for 1775: Ibid., ii, pp. 115–29, 135–49.
25 Fanny recorded Mrs Thrale and Dr Johnson's conversation word-for-word in her letter to Susan of 26 September 1778, suggesting that it resonated strongly with her own fears for her future. Ibid., iii, pp. 168–73.
26 Sunninghill Park was demolished in 1947. In 1990 the Duke of York's new ranch-style mansion was built on the site.
27 She made this comment in early 1781; Fanny was still without a suitor and Mrs Thrale offered her Harry Smith as a presentable match. It is taken from a letter sent by Mrs Thrale to Fanny at Chesington Hall, now in the Barrett Collection at the British Museum and to be published in volume iv of the *EJL*.
28 Fanny mentions her embarrassment in her letter to Susan of 26 September 1778. *EJL*, iii, pp. 168–73.
29 This letter is with seven others written by Mr Crisp that were collected together and pasted in a volume by a descendant of Thomas Payne, the bookseller, one of whose daughters married Fanny's brother James. Only one of them is addressed to Fanny; it is also the only letter to have been torn, cut away in places and to contain Fanny's highly effective obliterations. It can be seen at the Essex Record Office (D/DL C65).
30 The letter is dated 1 July 1781 and is addressed to 'My dear Chickens both'. It gives them news of James ('Captain Jem') Burney. Ibid.
31 From the beginning of her journal for 1777. *EJL*, ii, p. 232.
32 Mrs Thrale went on to say that if Fanny did not write a play that was better than Hannah More's *Percy*, then she deserved 'to be *whipped*'. And, she added, 'Your Father, I know, thinks the same.' Ibid., iii, pp. 132–4.
33 This information comes from a note in the *EJL*, iii, p. 133 n.
34 Ibid., iii, pp. 262–4.

5. GOOD NIGHT, LADY SMATTER: 1779–80

1 Fanny's account of Murphy's conversation with her was written to Susan from Streatham Park sometime after 16 February 1779. *EJL*, iii, pp. 243–8. Nothing of the evening appears in Mrs Thrale's *Thraliana*, though on 10 February she had noted that 'Our Miss Burney is big with a Comedy for next Season; I have not yet seen the *Ebauche*, but I wish it well.' *Thraliana*, i, p. 368.
2 *EJL*, iii, pp. 225–37.
3 Dr Johnson's comment has been rescued by the team at McGill University from a letter to Susan dated 23–30 August 1778. Ibid., iii, pp. 110–17.
4 She goes on to describe the occasion, which took place on 15 May, again revealing her somewhat cynical views on marriage. Ibid., i, pp. 65–7.
5 Fanny and Susan appear to have been on their own at St Martin's Street when their cousin Richard called. Fanny was so inspired by the extravagance of his foppish behaviour that she wrote up the evening as a comic farce and sent it to Mr Crisp. The reference is presumably to the hero of Richardson's novel *Sir Charles Grandison*, which was published in 1754. Jane Austen later dramatised episodes from the novel for a family performance. Ibid., i, pp. 201–14.
6 Ibid., iii, p. 146.
7 This long admonitory letter, dated 8 December 1778, was sewn by Fanny into her journal, suggesting that it was of more than usual importance to her. Ibid., iii,

pp. 186–90.

8 This letter, sent from Chesington, was again sewn into the journal. Ibid., iii, pp. 237–40.

9 Quoted in the introduction to volume iv (1747–76) of *The London Stage, 1660–1800*, edited by George Winchester Stone, Jr.

10 See Chapter 10 for a discussion of the fatal production of Fanny's tragedy *Edwy and Elgiva* in March 1795.

11 This episode is described by her friend, the diarist John Taylor, and is quoted by Ellen Donkin in her *Getting into the Act: Women Playwrights in London, 1776–1829*, p. 112.

12 *EJL*, iii, pp. 210–12.

13 Fanny reported this conversation, dated Friday, 28 May 1779, from West Street, Brighton, where she was staying with the Thrales. Despite herself, she was thoroughly enjoying the sensation of being a celebrity, with everyone talking about – and buying – *Evelina*. Ibid., iii, pp. 286–7.

14 Arthur Murphy was given the first act to read by Mrs Thrale on his arrival at Streatham Park on Friday, 21 May. Ibid., iii, pp. 267–8.

15 *Thraliana*, i, p. 381.

16 It was her first letter to Mr Crisp for almost two months. *EJL*, iii, pp. 339–43.

17 The letter is dated around 13 August, and was written from St Martin's Street to Dr Burney in Chesington. Ibid., iii, p. 345.

18 Quoted by Clayton J. Delery in his introduction to his edited text of *The Witlings*, p. 9.

19 Among the 417 scraps in the Berg Collection is an envelope addressed to Fanny's husband at 'West Hamble, near Dorking' (and therefore dating from the late 1790s), on which are scribbled notes about Lady Smatter. There is, too, a section of dialogue from the play, written on an envelope stamped with 'Queen's Lodge, Kew' (i.e. from 1786–91). From 'Miscellaneous; About 417 pieces of MS, 1772–1828' (198300B); with kind permission of the New York Public Library.

20 In recent years, Fanny has been rediscovered as a playwright with Clayton J. Delery's scholarly edition of *The Witlings*; and, more significantly, the first edition in 1995 of *The Complete Plays of Frances Burney*, edited by Peter Sabor.

21 Act I, lines 233–7 (Delery, p. 8).

22 From the 1776 (Alexander Donaldson) edition of *The Works of Alexander Pope: Volume the First, containing his Juvenile Poems, Translations and Imitations*, p. 83. My italics.

23 Pope's views were evidently a sore point with all women, for we find even Queen Charlotte – never likely to be regarded as a feminist – referring to them in a letter (dated 11 July 1784) to her eldest son, George, the Prince of Wales, when she says jokily, 'Alas! You know Pope says, We Women have no character at all, to which I subscribe only *so far* as concerns the little Heads, for my unsteadiness was only occasioned by delicacy and want of inclination.' The Prince had just given her an extravagant gift of exotic animals (the letter does not mention what his present was, but the Queen's menagerie at Kew included cattle from Algeria and India, 'curious birds', a 'hog like a porcupine in skin, with navel on back', and a prize collection of kangaroos). RA 36363; with the gracious permission of Her Majesty The Queen.

24 The letter was sent from Chesington on 29 August. From *The Letters of Dr Charles Burney*, (Ribeiro), i, pp. 279–81.

25 This damning comment from Mr Crisp is quoted by Mrs Thrale in a marginal gloss to her diary entry for 1 May 1779. *Thraliana*, i, p. 381 n.

26 Dr Johnson gave Fanny this advice after being told by Mrs Thrale that she had invited Mrs Montagu to dine at Streatham Park. The evening took place some time in the middle of September and was a great success for Fanny, who was told by the leading Bluestocking and hostess of Portman Square that she was '*proud* that a work *so* commended [i.e. *Evelina*] should be a *woman's*'. *EJL*, iii, pp. 150–63.

27 Act I, lines 179–89 (Delery, pp. 36–7).

28 Act V, lines 1082–6 (Delery, p. 155).

29 *EJL*, iii, p. 345.

30 From Ellen Donkin's *Getting into the Act*, pp. 77–109. I am also grateful to the library

staff at the Theatre Museum in Covent Garden, London, for this and other detailed information on theatrical stagings in the late eighteenth century.

31 *EJL*, iii, pp. 345–50.

32 From Ellen Donkin's chapter on Hannah Cowley and Hannah More. *Getting into the Act*, pp. 57–76.

33 From Macaulay's review of Charlotte Barrett's edition of Fanny's diaries, published in the *Edinburgh Review* for January 1843 and collected in *The Works of Lord Macaulay*, iv, p. 25.

34 *EJL*, iii, pp. 345–8.

35 The letter, dated 21 June 1779, survives only as a fragment and is quoted by Annie Raine Ellis in *ED*, ii, pp. 261–2.

36 She wrote an immensely long account of their journey to Tunbridge Wells, via Sevenoaks and Knole Park, for Susan on 12 October. *EJL*, iii, pp. 368–71.

37 Mrs Thrale wrote this on 1 December, 1779. *Thraliana*, i, p. 413. Fanny's report of her illness to Susan was written the next day. *EJL*, iii, p. 453.

38 Dr Delap was a dining friend of the Thrales, who had met them in Brighthelmstone, as Brighton was then known. *EJL*, iii, pp. 285, 389–91.

39 As close neighbours of the Thrales, the Pitches often dined at Streatham Park. The encounter described here took place in Brighton. Ibid., iii, p. 293. Mrs Thrale's comment on Sophia appears in the *Thraliana*, i, p. 393.

40 *EJL*, iii, pp. 353.

41 Ibid., iii, pp. 400–1, 407–8.

42 The five notebooks contain one act each, and are in Fanny's usual handwriting (unlike *Evelina*). The first two are neatly sewn, the others have been cut and appear more aged. There are some square brackets in pencil in Act IV, which indicate a possible cut, and a slight change to Act V – but nothing to diminish or cut the satire.

43 She describes this meeting with Arthur Murphy in her letter to Mr Crisp of 22 January 1780, presumably as an assertion of what other people thought of her ability to write for the stage. (From the unpublished material at McGill University; with grateful thanks to Professor Lars Troide.)

44 From a letter from Mr Crisp, dated 23 February. Ibid.

45 The letter was dated 13 April 1780. Ibid.

46 In September 1993, 'A Busy Day' a comedy first drafted by Fanny in 1800–1, was staged for the *very first* time in a theatre above a pub in Bristol. The production – by the Show of Strength Theatre Company, directed by Alan Coveney – was a sell-out and eventually transferred to London, where the critics also praised it warmly, one remarking that some of its wit was 'astonishingly Wildean'. My thanks to Alan Coveney for ideas and discussions on Fanny Burney as a dramatist.

47 These scraps have been collected together and are now in the box labelled 'Miscellaneous; About 417 pieces of MS, 1772–1828' (198300B) in the Berg Collection; with permission of the New York Public Library.

48 From Betty Rizzo's notes to the forthcoming volume iv of the *EJL*; with kind permission of Professor Lars Troide.

6. CECILIA, 1780–2

1 The biographer, R. Brimley Johnson, also edited a selection from the journals of Fanny. His entertaining, if brief, *Jane Austen: Her Life, Her Work, Her Family and Her Critics* was one of a series he wrote on eighteenth-century women, also including Maria Edgeworth and Mrs Delany. His remark on the title of *Pride and Prejudice* appears on p. 133. The argument resurfaced recently in the letters columns of several newspapers with the huge success of the television adaptation of *Pride and Prejudice*, in which it was claimed that the source of the sentiment lies in Gibbon's *The Decline and Fall of the Roman Empire*, the first volume of which was published in 1776. Fanny had read Gibbon, so it is quite possible that she was quoting from him, especially since she gives the quote to the scholarly Dr Lyster.

2 This, in fact, is not the 'concluding sentence' of the novel, but comes half-way through the final chapter. *Cecilia*, vol. v, book x, chapter x, p. 930.

3 The letter to Cassandra is dated 24 January. From *Jane Austen's Letters to Her Sister Cassandra and Others*, p. 254. Information kindly provided by Ken Thomas, archivist at Courage Ltd.

4 Catherine's comment comes in chapter v. Catherine Morland refers also to *Camilla*, which Fanny wrote in 1796, and *Belinda*, which was published by Maria Edgeworth in 1801.

5 Dr Johnson's *Rambler* essay No. 4 (Saturday, 31 March 1750) contrasts the new fashion for fictions that 'exhibit life in its true state', by Fielding and Smollett in particular, to the 'heroic romances' of the past, and would, no doubt, have been familiar to both Fanny and Jane Austen.

6 For further illustrations of this connection, see Pat Rogers's article in the *TLS*, 23 August 1996, pp. 14–15: 'Sposi in Surrey: Links Between Jane Austen and Fanny Burney'.

7 In these passages one wonders whether Fanny was recalling her father's friend Christopher Smart, a poet who spent much of his adult life in and out of either the madhouse or the debtors' prison. The Burneys were always fond of him, and Dr Burney organised several subscriptions among his theatrical and musical friends to rescue Smart from the King's Bench prison in the late 1750s and early 1760s. He died in 1771.

8 Maria Edgeworth's novels include *Castle Rackrent*, *Belinda* and *The Absentee*; Anne Radcliffe was the author of *The Romance of the Forest* as well as *The Mysteries of Udolpho*.

9 From the unpublished diaries and letters at McGill University; with grateful thanks to Professor Lars Troide.

10 From 1 July 1780. *Thraliana*, i, p. 443.

11 John Hamilton Mortimer was the artist; his drawings were engraved by Francesco Bartolozzi, John Hall and Walker (presumably William).

12 She went on to say that she had become a 'Princess in Disguise': 'I live now entirely with "dear" him in the study [presumably her father], – only stumping out, muffled up & early, now & then of a frosty & dry morning into the Park.'

13 Fanny wrote a long and grateful letter to Mrs Thrale sometime after 16 December 1780, on receiving a parcel of some dress silk from her friend.

14 Written to Hetty from Chesington on 8 January 1781.

15 From a letter written to Mrs Thrale from Chesington.

16 *Cecilia*, vol. iii, book vi, chapter ix, pp. 514–15.

17 Ibid., vol. i, book i, chapter iv, p. 34.

18 Ibid., vol. v, book x, chapter vii, p. 897.

19 Mrs Thrale, who read the proofs as Fanny rushed to revise them before sending them to the printers, wrote this on 19 May 1782. *Thraliana*, i, p. 536.

20 Dr Johnson's comment on the novel was recorded by Fanny in her journal for 10 November 1782.

21 From *The Collected Works of William Hazlitt*, pp. 122–6.

22 From Macaulay's 1843 review of the *Diary & Letters of Madame D'Arblay; The Works of Lord Macaulay*, iv, p. 2.

23 All four novels are available in paperback in the Oxford World's Classics edition. *Evelina* is by far the most popular, selling three times as many copies as *Camilla* and five times as many as *Cecilia*. *Evelina* is also published in paperback by Penguin, and a new scholarly edition by W.W. Norton is in the press. *The Wanderer*, too, is also available in other editions by Virago and Pandora Press (the latter with an introduction by Margaret Drabble).

7. MISERY AND MEN: 1782–6

1 Mr Crisp wrote to her in Streatham on 15 May 1781, and enquired after 'Albina' – the original name of Fanny's heroine – presumably out of concern that she had stopped work on her book. From the unpublished material at McGill University with the kind permission of Professor Lars Troide.

2 'She was cold by nature, undemonstrative and even icy in her reaction to his death.' The comment was written by Fanny while she was living in France between 1802 and 1812, in a fragmentary notebook now in the Berg Collection. I am grateful to Betty Rizzo for her note in the unpublished material at McGill University.

3 The Thrale brewery – with the portrait of Dr Johnson by John Opie as its trademark – survived as an independent company, Barclay, Perkins & Co., after Mrs Thrale sold it in May 1781 until 1955, when it was merged with Courage Ltd. The brewery buildings (close to Borough Market in Southwark on the south bank of the Thames) were demolished in 1986, when Courage sold the site to Southwark Borough Council. A plaque now marks the site, listing the owners of the former brewery, including Ralph Thrale 1729–58, Henry Thrale 1758–81, Barclay, Perkins & Co. 1781–1955, Courage Ltd 1955–86. There is a Thrale Street nearby.

4 The comment is made by a Mrs Beaumont, a snobbish widow to whom Evelina had been introduced in Bristol Hot Wells by her travelling companion, the worldly wise Mrs Selwyn. It is a misquote from a short story by Jean François Marmontel entitled 'La Femme comme il y en a peu' (A woman without compare); the first English edition of which appeared in 1771. *Evelina*, vol. iii, letter iii, p. 285 and n.

5 From 17 May 1781. *Thraliana*, i, pp. 496–7.

6 *EJL*, iii, pp. 313–18.

7 Arthur Murphy reported back to Mrs Thrale. *EJL*, iii, p. 297 n.

8 The scene in *Cecilia* occurs in the grounds of the gothic monstrosity that is Mortimer's ancestral home, volume iii, book vi, chapter v, pp. 471–8. Comparisons with Fanny's own emotional life can be found in her letters to Susan of 26–30 May ('This is the first quarrel I ever had with any man in my life'), 31 May ('I had new Specimens to Day of the oddities of Mr Crutchley, who I do not yet quite understand'), 14 June ('Mr Crutchley, whose solid & fixed Character I am at this moment unable to fathom'), 2–3 July ('Mr Crutchley, by the way, has been the Cause of all this illness') and 3–4 July ('for though, in the strange composition of his Character, there is a diffidence of himself the most unaffected I ever, except in Edward Burney [her cousin Edward Francisco], saw, – a diffidence which makes the misery of his life, by inclining him to believe himself always de trop, – he has yet a contempt of always all others which, however free from vanity, can possibly have no other spring than pride').

9 From a letter dated Saturday, 14 December 1782, in which she describes her stepmother as 'The Lady'. The letter, with faint crossings-out but no black obliterations, is now in the Berg Collection (from a box containing odd scraps from the Diary and Letters); with kind permission of the New York Public Library.

10 From *The Letters of Dr Charles Burney* (Ribeiro), i, pp. 310–12.

11 My italics. From a letter written to Mrs Gast after the marriage, and quoted in the *Burford Papers: Being Letters of Samuel Crisp to His Sister at Burford*, edited by William Holden Hutton, pp. 74–5.

12 Fanny had apparently quizzed James about his friend. In this letter, dated as early in the courtship as 14 January 1781, she reassured Susan that despite James's 'not very refined' explanation of Captain Phillips's behaviour, they were 'good, honest friends'.

13 The service was taken by the Revd Walter Shirley, who was married to Phillips's sister and was Rector of Loughrea in Ireland. Of course, Fanny may have destroyed all mention of the wedding because of Susan's later tragic history.

14 This letter is in terrible handwriting which changes all the time, as if written with great emotion. From the Berg Collection (3 ALS and 3 AL to her sister Susannah Burney Phillips: 196351B, 196356B); with kind permission of the New York Public Library.

15 Fanny was writing in June 1782, six months after the wedding. From a letter in the Berg Collection (3 ALS and 3 AL to her sister Susannah Burney Phillips: 196351B, 196356B); with kind permission of the New York Public Library.

16 Ibid.

17 *Thraliana*, i, p. 502.

18 My italics. The letter was dated 26–30 May 1781. Once again, I am thankful to Betty Rizzo and Lars Troide for permission to read this before publication.

19 From a letter in the Berg Collection (3 ALS and 3 AL to her sister Susannah Burney Phillips: 196351B, 196356B); with kind permission of the New York Public Library.

20 From a letter dated 14 March 1782.

21 Her letter was written on 6 April 1782.

22 The verses appeared on the morning of 12 March, and are quoted in Charlotte

Barrett's edition of the *Diary & Letters*, ii, pp. 73–8. Professor Roger Lonsdale noted in his *Dr Charles Burney* how the draft copy in Dr Burney's hand had been discovered among his papers (pp. 266–7).

23 From *The Letters of Dr Charles Burney* (Ribeiro), i, p. 344.

24 I am grateful to John Comyn for permission to read this letter, which is in the grangerized edition of the *Diary & Letters of Madame d'Arblay (1778–1840)*, now in his possession.

25 *Monthly Review; or, Literary Journal*, lxvii (December 1782), pp. 453–8.

26 The 78-year-old Mrs Elizabeth Vesey (*c.* 1715–91), married to an Irish MP, was a recognised Bluestocking and a friend of Mrs Thrale. Fanny once described her as having 'the most wrinkled, sallow, Time-beaten face I ever saw. She is an exceeding well bred woman, & of agreeable manners – but all her Name in the *World* must, I think, have been acquired by her dexterity & skill in selecting Parties, & by her address in rendering them easy with one another. – An art, however, that seems to imply no mean understanding.' From a letter to Susan from Streatham, dated 20 July 1779. *EJL*, iii, p. 338.

27 On 14 April, she wrote in her diary that 'My dearest Miss Burney has apparently got an Admirer in Mr George Cambridge'. *Thraliana*, i, pp. 562–3.

28 The letter is in the Berg Collection (from a box containing odd scraps from the Diary and Letters); with kind permission of the New York Public Library.

29 Noted by Mrs Thrale in her diary for 20 September 1782. *Thraliana*, i, p. 544.

30 The couple were married in London on 23 July 1784 at the Roman Catholic chapel in the French embassy, witnessed by the French ambassador, Count d'Adhémar de Montfalcon, and the Italian friends of Piozzi, Francesco Mecci and the Borghi brothers; followed by a Protestant ceremony in Bath two days later. Mrs Thrale's daughters and friends did not attend on either occasion.

31 Mr Crisp was buried in the parish church at Chesington. Dr Burney wrote an epitaph to his friend, which can still be seen engraved on a large memorial tablet on the north-east wall of the medieval building (which could be seen from Chesington Hall):

> Reader, this cold and humble spot contains
> The much lamented, much revered, remains
> Of One whose Wisdom, Learning, Taste and Sense,
> Good-humour'd Wit, and wide Benevolence,
> Cheer'd and enlighten'd all this Hamlet round,
> Wherever Genius, Worth, or Want was found.
> To few it is that courteous Heav'n imparts
> Such depth of Knowledge and such Taste in Arts;
> Such Penetration and enchanting Pow'rs
> Of brightening Social and Convivial Hours.
> Had he, through Life, been blest by Nature kind
> With health robust of Body as of Mind;
> With skill to serve and charm Mankind so great,
> In Arts, in Science, Letters, Church or State;
> His Name the Nation's Annals had enroll'd,
> And Virtues to remotest Ages told.

Chesington Hall was leased to a Colonel Dalrymple, aide-de-camp to Prince William, who then gave the Prince the use of the house for his assignations with the actress, Mrs Jordan.

32 Quoted by Robert DeMaria, in his *The Life of Samuel Johnson*, p. 307.

33 This is taken from a conversation that Fanny had at Chesington with Mr Crisp in the spring of 1777, in which she poked fun at the way we spend our days walking, talking, reading, writing – as if she was looking down on this strange race of mortals from far away. *EJL*, ii, p. 222.

34 Three years later, Warren Hastings was impeached and put on trial for betraying the Government and the East India Company by squeezing money out of the native Indians and using them to finance his own extravagant lifestyle. The trial lasted for eight years –

and became a battleground for the rival Whig and Tory politicians. Hastings was eventually acquitted. Fanny always supported him, believing him to have been an honest and just Governor.

35 Fanny recalled the impression made by Charlotte on the company assembled in the drawing-room at St Martin's Street for the evening concert attended by the Russian Prince Orlov in November 1775. Charlotte was then an irresistibly cheerful 14-year-old – and much the prettiest of the Burney girls. From Fanny's *Memoirs of Doctor Burney*, ii, p. 55.

36 On 22 February 1783, she wrote to Susan and described how she had travelled back to London from visiting the Cambridges at Twickenham, with Mr Cambridge senior and his daughter, Charlotte. He insisted on coming into No. 10, St Martin's Street with Fanny: 'I would fain have dispensed with Miss Cambridge's coming in, & so would she; but Mr Cambridge said she ought to make her courtsie to Mrs Burney. I believe . . . that he only wanted her to see how like Mme Duval she was.'

37 Mrs Hester Chapone (1727–1801) was a friend of Mrs Montagu and Dr Johnson; a contributor to the *Rambler* and the *Gentleman's Magazine*, she was described by another of her friends, the writer Samuel Richardson, as the 'little spit-fire'.

38 Fanny was referring here to the *Probationary Odes for the Laureatship*, which appeared throughout 1785, prompted by the death of the Poet Laureate, William Whitehead, on 14 April. They included the lines, 'What? – what? – what?/Scott! – Scott! – Scott'; a reference to Major John Scott, MP. From Austin Dobson's edition of the *Diary & Letters of Madame d'Arblay 1778–1840*, ii, p. 320 n.

8. SECOND KEEPER OF THE ROBES: 1786–90

1 Mrs Anna Ord (1726–1808), the wealthy widow of William Ord, had first met the Burneys in the mid-1770s through the Sunday-evening concerts held at St Martin's Street. She was at first a particular friend of Hetty, but adopted Fanny as her protégée after the publication of *Cecilia*. Her daughter Charlotte was just a year younger than Fanny, and Mrs Ord was a useful chaperone to them both, escorting them to the evening parties held by Mrs Boscawen, Hannah More, Mrs Montagu and Hester Chapone. Once again, all quotations from Fanny for the Court years are taken from material kindly shown to me by Professor Lars Troide at McGill University.

2 From a letter dated 28 June 1786, now in the Berg Collection (from the 'Scrapbook: Fanny Burney and family, 1653–1890': 213048B); with kind permission of the New York Public Library.

3 The elaborate improvements to the castle planned by George III and his architect James Wyatt were not completed until 1804, when the Royal Family celebrated with a house-warming ball. Until then, they lived in the Queen's Lodge, a comfortable family home opposite the south front of the Upper Ward of the castle. A long, two-storey building, it was pulled down in the autumn of 1823 (during the reign of George IV). Mrs Delany's house (also no longer standing) was at No. 14, St Alban's Street. Her garden adjoined that belonging to the Queen's Lodge and occupied land that is now part of the Royal Mews in St Alban's Street. (Olwen Hedley says in her article 'Mrs Delany's Windsor Home' for the *Berkshire Archaeological Journal* [59, 1961–2], pp. 51–5, that 'the outer foundations [of Mrs Delany's house] lie buried beneath the Mews wall where it curves under a screen of trees into St Alban's Street'.) For all details on life at Windsor and with the Royal Family, I am grateful to Olwen Hedley, whose authoritative biography of Queen Charlotte was published (by John Murray) in 1975 and has not been surpassed.

4 Quoted by Olwen Hedley in *Queen Charlotte*, p. 134.

5 By 1786, there were six royal princesses: Charlotte, the Princess Royal (born in 1766), Augusta (1768), Elizabeth (1770), Mary (1776), Sophia (1777) and Amelia (1783); of the nine princes, seven had survived infancy (Octavius, born in 1779, died suddenly aged four; and Alfred (1780) was only two when he died): George, Prince of Wales (born in 1762, the future George IV), Frederick, Duke of York (1763), William, Duke of Clarence (1765, the future William IV), Edward, Duke of Kent (1767, the father of Queen Victoria), Ernest, Duke of Cumberland and future King of Hanover (1771), Augustus, Duke of Sussex (1773) and Adolphus, Duke of Cambridge (1774).

6 Fanny's description of Court etiquette has been much quoted by her biographers since it first appeared in the diaries of 1842-6. It will be published in full in the new edition of the Court Journals being prepared at McGill University.

7 From the 'Sketch of Queen Charlotte's Character, from a Memorandum Book of Madame d'Arblay', an appendix to volume vii of the *Diary & Letters of Madame d'Arblay* (*1778–1840*), edited by Charlotte Barrett, p. 339.

8 From Olwen Hedley's *Queen Charlotte*, p. 13.

9 Snuff – finely ground, dried tobacco leaf – was a kind of eighteenth-century aromatherapy, containing properties both refreshing and remedial. Fanny would have prepared the Queen's special blend by tipping the snuff (obtained from Fribourg & Treyer, tobacconists and snuff vendors of No. 34, St James's, Haymarket, whose bow-windowed shop-front still survives, with a pane of glass advertising their services as 'Purveyors of Foreign Snuffs to the Royal Family', though the shop now sells souvenirs) on to a sheet of vellum, adding a little water – or, more likely, a perfume of some kind – and then blending it with a small ivory spatula. She would then have tipped it into the Queen's miniature snuff-box, from which the Queen would have applied the snuff to her nostrils. Queen Charlotte could be described as a snuff addict. From Olwen Hedley's *Queen Charlotte*, pp. 46, 57, 335 n.

10 Hampton Court and Kensington Palace had been the royal residences of George II; but his son, George III, disliked both, with their memories of his quarrelsome and unhappy childhood. Shortly after becoming King, therefore, he bought Buckingham House (which forms the kernel of the present Buckingham Palace) at the end of the Mall for £28,000. On 22 May 1762, he and Queen Charlotte, then expecting their first child (the future George IV), moved into their new home, leaving St James's Palace as the official seat of sovereignty. George III renamed his new palace – built in 1702–5, on land that had been part of the mulberry garden in St James's Park – the Queen's House after his new and beloved Queen. By the 1780s, however, Windsor had become their preferred home, with Kew as their summer residence. From Olwen Hedley's *Queen Charlotte*, as well as from personal conversations with her.

11 Information again derived from Olwen Hedley.

12 A card game requiring two players, using a reduced pack of thirty-two cards, and for which the players aimed to acquire card combinations (tricks), upon which the scoring depended.

13 These remarkably naturalistic pictures, the flowers dramatically set against a black background, can be seen at the British Museum.

14 From the Berg Collection (from a box containing seven folders labelled 'Miscellaneous material by or relating to members of the Burney Family and connections'); with kind permission of the New York Public Library.

15 The present Kew Palace, which stands opposite the site where the White House once stood, was formerly called the Dutch House, and from 1765 was known as the Prince of Wales's House on Kew Green, as it was the house in which the royal princes lived while at Kew. (Kew House itself was too small for the ever-increasing royal brood and their nurses, governesses and tutors.) It was pulled down in 1801, and its site is now marked by a sundial on the north lawn of the Royal Botanic Gardens at Kew. For these details, I am once again indebted to Olwen Hedley and to her book *Queen Charlotte*. For information on the precise location of the palace at Kew, I am grateful to Ray Desmond, former archivist of the Royal Botanic Gardens at Kew, and to his book, *Kew: The History of the Royal Botanic Garden*.

16 Fanny's historical source was probably Hume's *History of England*, which she had read in her teens. The text is now available in Peter Sabor's two-volume edition of Fanny's plays: *The Complete Plays of Frances Burney*, ii.

17 Ellen Donkin discusses the success of Cumberland's play in her chapter on *Edwy and Elgiva* in *Getting into the Act: Women Playwrights in London*, pp. 132–58.

18 Quoted by Olwen Hedley, *Queen Charlotte*, p. 146.

19 The Hon. Robert Fulke Greville was appointed Equerry to the King on 1 August 1781, aged thirty. From 5 November 1788 to 4 March 1789 he kept a daily record of the King's illness, recognising the importance to posterity of his witness. Too 'sensitive' to be made public in the lifetime of King George, these papers remained unpublished until

1930, when they appeared as *The Diaries of Colonel the Hon. Robert Fulke Greville, Equerry to His Majesty King George III*. Fanny nicknamed Greville 'Colonel Wellbred', saying of him: 'There is something in Colonel Wellbred, so equal and so pleasing, it is impossible not to see him with approbation and to speak of him with praise.' He was just a year older than Fanny.

20 The edition prepared by Austin Dobson in 1904 from that first published by Charlotte Barrett in 1842 had all the digressions and interruptions removed, so that it reads with mounting intensity.

21 From the Berg Collection (from 'Susan's Holograph Diary, incomplete, for 1786–92, Sent to her sister Fanny Burney d'Arblay'; 198988B); with kind permission of the New York Public Library.

22 Mrs Papendiek, daughter of Frederick Albert (who was one of three attendants to accompany the Queen from Mecklenburg-Strelitz in 1761 and who served as her hairdresser), provides this detail in her *Court and Private Life in the Time of Queen Charlotte*, ii, p. 13.

23 From the box of 417 miscellaneous scraps in the Berg Collection (198300B); with kind permission of the New York Public Library.

24 Joyce Hemlow discusses this in her *The History of Fanny Burney*, p. 493.

25 This laborious work of recovery has been undertaken by the scholars at McGill University, and will be published in the new edition of the Court Journals currently under preparation. My thanks to Professor Lars Troide for permission to read this material before publication.

26 From Mirabeau's *Journal of the Estates-General*, quoted by Simon Schama in *Citizens: A Chronicle of the French Revolution*.

27 The letter is undated and appears only in Annie Raine Ellis: *ED*, ii, pp. 194–5.

9. LOVE AND MARRIAGE, 1790–3

1 Fanny was relieved that when she attended the King's official Birthday Drawing-Room at St James's on 4 June 1792, she was able to turn up in 'more simple dressed undress'. *JL* i, p. 187.

2 From Fanny's journal-letter to Susan dated 26/7 April 1790. From the unpublished material at McGill University; with kind permission of Professor Lars Troide.

3 From a letter in the Berg Collection (196076B–196085B); with kind permission of the New York Public Library.

4 Queen Charlotte's offer to Fanny was remarkably generous for just five years' service, especially since the Queen had been vastly overdrawn on her Household Account every year from 1786, to such an extent (over £11,000, equivalent to £550,000 now) that her Lord Chamberlain, Thomas Brudenell-Bruce, the Earl of Ailesbury, repeatedly warned her that she needed to make drastic economies in her personal expenditure. Information from Olwen Hedley's *Queen Charlotte*.

5 *Thraliana*, ii, p. 821.

6 Charlotte Ord's death was reported in the *St James's Chronicle* on 19 February 1795. Dr Burney included an account of the tragedy in his 'Memoirs and Character of the Late Mrs Ord', which appeared in the *Gentleman's Magazine*, lxxviii (new series, July 1808), pp. 581–3.

7 *JL*, i, p. 17.

8 The letter is now in the Berg Collection (from the 'Scrapbook: Fanny Burney and Family, 1653–1890': 213048B), with kind permission of the New York Public Library.

9 *JL*, i, p. 196.

10 Ibid., i, pp. 238–48.

11 Juniper Hall still stands on the edge of the tiny village of Mickleham, nestling beneath Box Hill, its lawns edged by the yews planted in Mr Jenkinson's time. Only eighteen miles or so from London, it is now used by the Field Studies Council as a centre for courses in botany, environmental studies and local history. A blue plaque on the wall beside the entrance to the drive proudly announces that in 1792 the house was the refuge of exiles from the French Revolution, including Talleyrand, Madame de Staël and Narbonne, and was the place where 'Fanny Burney, the novelist, as a visitor to her sister

Susanna Phillips of Mickleham met Alexandre d'Arblay to whom she was subsequently married at Mickleham Church'.

12 Quoted by the Duchess of Sermoneta in *The Locks of Norbury: The Story of a Remarkable Family in the XVIIIth and XIXth Centuries*, p. 61.

13 D'Arblay's poems were published under the pseudonym of the Chevalier d'Anceny, a collection of which later appeared under the title *Opuscules du Chevalier d'Anceny, ou anecdotes en vers, recueilliés et publiées par M. d'A.*

14 Quoted by the Duchess of Sermoneta in *The Locks of Norbury*, p. 61.

15 From the Berg Collection ('F.B. d'Arblay, Diary and Letters'); with kind permission of the New York Public Library.

16 *JL*, ii, pp. 8–9, 11.

17 Fanny's *Thèmes* in French are printed in Appendix II of *JL*, ii, pp. 188–205.

18 From a letter to her father dated 22 February. Ibid., ii, pp. 22–3.

19 From the folder of *Thèmes* in the Berg Collection (208119B, 208134B); with kind permission of the New York Public Library.

20 From a letter in the Berg Collection (7 AL incomplete from Fanny to Susan, 211135B–211141B); with kind permission of the New York Public Library.

21 In 1797, Coleridge was hounded out of the village of Nether Stowey in Somerset, because of fears (based on his friendship with *émigrés* from France) that he was a spy, in the pay of the French Republic, fuelled by the familiar hostility against 'artists', poets and those living an unconventional lifestyle. The suggestion that the two William Clarks were one and the same is made in the introduction to volume ii of *JL* (p.xvii).

22 From the Berg Collection (7 AL incomplete from Fanny to Susan, 211135B–211141B); with kind permission of the New York Public Library.

23 'If it were up to me – in spite of the opinion of the world – whether or not you should remain in England – I do not think that you will leave ... I know not how else to say this – this, therefore, will be a very short Thème – but I will make every effort not to appear insensible to your desire that I should be consulted on what you should do.' *JL*, ii, p. 43.

24 In his definition of the 'Revolutionaires', d'Arblay displayed his abhorrence for their proposed usurpation of the monarchy, comparing them with the 'Constitutionels', who wanted to see in their country a government that followed the will of the people, based on law and the interests of all, but which was still under monarchical rule. These, again, were compared to the 'Constitutionels Anglais', who were among the best, because their 'excellente' English constitution was based on justice: '*C'est que les premiers, en rendant justice à l'excellente CONSTITUTION ANGLAISE, n'avaient pas cru devoir abandonner le désir de voir leurs pays libres, parce que cette constitution n'avait pu lui être donnée, et que ne renonçant point à l'espoir de le voir jouir d'un bon gouvernement, ils croyaient devoir laisser à l'expérience le soin de rectifier ce que la constitution établie par la première assemblée avait de défectueux.*' Ibid., ii, pp. xii–xiv.

25 Ibid., ii, p. 117.

26 Evidence of the unhappiness that Susan was already experiencing in her marriage can be detected in letters written by Susan to Fanny, which were preserved by Captain Phillips after Susan's death in January 1800. Now owned by the Robinson Library at Armagh (some sixty miles from Phillips's estates in County Louth), the first volume contains twenty-seven letters written between 15 January 1787 and 6 December 1789; the second has fifty-two letters dating from some time in 1795 to 4 December 1799. I am grateful to Mr Carson, the Librarian, for permission to read them.

27 From a letter to Fanny dated Sunday, 9 June, in which Susan wrote of her discussions with Narbonne and Monsieur d'Arblay, who added a PS after spending the day with Susan. *JL*, ii, pp. 146–8.

28 From a letter to her father in the Berg Collection (208566B, 208571B); with kind permission of the New York Public Library.

29 *JL*, ii, pp. 140–1.

30 With grateful thanks to Karin Fernald for this detail.

31 Sarah Harriet's letter (to her cousin Mary, daughter of her Aunt Martha and Arthur Young) is quoted in Appendix I of *JL*, ii, p. 183–6. Maria Rishton's letter to Susan is in the Berg Collection (from the 'Scrapbook: Fanny Burney and Family, 1653–1890': 213048B); with kind permission of the New York Public Library.

FANNY BURNEY

32 *JL*, ii, p. 179.

10. *CAMILLA*: 1793–9

1 The d'Arblays had visited the Burneys in Chelsea just a fortnight after their marriage and stayed for several days – a diplomatic mission by Fanny, which proved most effective in persuading Dr Burney that his daughter had married wisely.
2 From *JL*, iii, p. 12.
3 From *Brief Reflections relative to the Emigrant French Clergy: earnestly submitted to the Humane Consideration of the Ladies of Great Britain* (London, 1793), p. 26. Two thousand copies of the pamphlet were sold, at one shilling and sixpence each, raising valuable funds for the Emigrant Clergy Contribution Fund, of which Fanny's godmother's daughter, Mrs Crewe, was the founder and Dr Burney, the secretary.
4 Narbonne was 'asked' to leave Britain by the Prime Minister William Pitt in June 1794.
5 She made these comments on her play in a letter to Mrs Waddington (Marianne Port) written in August 1790. From the unpublished material at McGill University with kind permission of Professor Lars Troide.
6 The letter is dated 17 November 1794. *JL*, iii, p. 85.
7 From a letter from Fanny to Marianne Waddington on 23 March 1799. *JL*, iv, p. 260. Charles was so anxious to be godfather to Fanny's son that first he tried to persuade Narbonne to step down in his favour, who refused, then his father, who complied.
8 It is illustrated with other 'maternity pincushions' in *Pins and Pincushions*, by E.D. Longman and S. Lock (London, 1911), pp. 174–5. They mention that it could still be seen at the d'Arblays' former home in West Humble, near Dorking, Surrey, where a room was devoted to Burney memorabilia. But it was probably destroyed in the fire there of 1919.
9 From 17 March 1795. *Thraliana*, ii, p. 916.
10 *Morning Herald*, 23 March 1795. Quoted in *The London Stage 1660–1800: A Calendar of Plays, Entertainments & Afterpieces. Part V: 1776–1800*, edited by Charles Beecher Hogan pp. 1738–9.
11 From Peter Sabor's introduction to *The Complete Plays of Frances Burney*, i, p.xiv.
12 From a letter dated 25 March 1795, reproduced by W. Wright Roberts in 'Charles and Fanny Burney in the Light of the New Thrale Correspondence in the John Rylands Library', *Bulletin of the John Rylands Library*, vol. 16, 1 (January 1932).
13 *Edwy and Elgiva*, Act V, scene xi. *The Complete Plays of Frances Burney*, ii, pp. 77–9.
14 The letter is dated 13 May 1795. *JL*, iii, pp. 107–8.
15 From a letter written by Mr Crisp to Fanny on 27 April 1780. From the unpublished papers at McGill University; with kind permission of Professor Lars Troide.
16 She wrote to Mr Crisp from Ipswich, where she was staying with Susan and Captain Phillips, on 5 August 1782. From the unpublished material at McGill University; with kind permission of Professor Lars Troide.
17 *JL*, iii, p. 73.
18 In the first draft of this 'ugly scheme', Camilla, the eponymous heroine, was called 'Ariella' or 'Clarinda'; but in the end Fanny abandoned both of these unusual and striking names for the more conventional 'Camilla'.
19 The sketch for a novel is on a tiny scrap of paper in the Berg Collection ('Miscellaneous; About 417 pieces of MS', 198300B); with kind permission of the New York Public Library.
20 From *Camilla*, vol. ii, book iv, chapter vi, p. 308.
21 Ibid., vol., i, book i, chapter i, p. 11.
22 Ibid., vol., iv, book viii, chapter xi, p. 680.
23 Ibid., vol., ii, book iii, chapter xi, p. 246.
24 John Thorpe, Isabella's pompous brother, is trying to impress Catherine Morland with his manliness by his dislike of such 'stupid books' as *Camilla*, written by 'that woman they make such a fuss about; she who married the French emigrant'. From *Northanger Abbey*, vol. 1, chapter vii.
25 *Camilla*, vol. iii, book vi, chapter vi, pp. 427–30; vol. iii, book iv, chapter viii,

pp. 317–24.

26 This suggestion was first made by Elizabeth Jenkins in her *Jane Austen: A Biography*, and is also made by Margaret Anne Doody in her incisive *Frances Burney: The Life in the Works*, p. 272. The comment could, of course, have been made by other readers of Jane Austen's copy of *Camilla*.

27 *JL*, iii, p. 177.

28 Fanny sent her father a full account of their visit, later collating it as 'The Windsoriana'. Ibid., iii, pp. 172–96.

29 From the Preface to *Evelina*, p. 7.

30 Dr Burney wrote to Fanny to tell her of this on 2 December 1796. The letter is now in the Berg Collection (in the 'Scrapbook: Fanny Burney and Family, 1653–1890': 213048B); with kind permission of the New York Public Library.

31 Or so Lord Macaulay claimed in his lengthy review of the *Diary & Letters of Madame d'Arblay (1778–1840)* in the *Edinburgh Review* (January 1843), collected in *The Works of Lord Macaulay*, iv, p. 52.

32 *JL*, iii, p. 227.

33 From 'On Going a Journey', in *Table Talk; or Original Essays*, vol. vi of *The Collected Works of William Hazlitt*, p. 186.

34 Quoted by Edward A. and Lillian D. Bloom in their Introduction to the Oxford World's Classics edition of *Camilla*, p. xx.

35 *Scots Magazine*, lviii (October 1796), pp. 691–7; *British Critic*, viii (November 1796), pp. 527–36; Ralph Griffiths was the critic who also pointed out Fanny's solecisms in the *Monthly Review*, xxi (December 1796), pp. 452–6.

36 *Camilla*, vol. iv, book vii, chapter vi, p. 549.

37 In his study of divorce in England, *Broken Lives: Separation and Divorce in England, 1660–1857*, Lawrence Stone charts the painful and tragic stories of several families where the breakdown of the marriage became irrevocable. It is questionable, in all these families, whether the price of separation was worth it. No matter how violent and cruel their husbands had become, it was not until the first Divorce Act of 1857 that women were sufficiently protected legally to make it worth their while to seek divorce.

38 *JL*, iii, p. 200 n.

39 Ibid., iii, p. 201 n.

40 The building of the cottage is described by John Middleton in his article 'Camilla Cottage, West Humble' in *The Georgian Group Journal* (1993), pp. 94–8, which also illustrates M. d'A's plans.

41 The first *income* tax was levied by Act of Parliament on 4 December 1798 and given the royal assent on 21 March 1799. Those with incomes of between £60 and £65 had to pay 0.83 per cent, a figure that increased proportionally up to 10 per cent for those with incomes of £200-plus.

42 From Fanny's December 1797 journal to Susan (Fanny had resumed her habit of writing monthly diaries to her sister once they were separated). *JL*, iv, pp. 51–2.

43 From letters in the Berg Collection ('10 ALS from Susan Burney Phillips to Charlotte Burney Francis Broome': 196076B–196085B); with kind permission of the New York Public Library.

44 *JL*, iii, pp. 282–5.

45 Ibid., iv, p. 361 n.

46 The full text of 'Love and Fashion' is now available in *The Complete Plays of Frances Burney*, vol. i. The manuscript (236 pages neatly copied into a notebook), together with twenty-nine fragments of a first draft, is in the Berg Collection at the New York Public Library. A Memorandum Book from 1801 contains hasty revisions to the manuscript copy of the play.

47 'Love and Fashion', act iv, scene iii.

11. PARIS AND PAIN: 1799–1812

1 From a letter written by Fanny to Susan from Camilla Cottage on 29 June, in which Fanny begs Susan to let her know if there is anything any of them can do to hurry Susan home to England. *JL*, iv, pp. 304–8.

2 Fanny's letter from Captain Phillips is now missing, but she refers to it in a letter to Hetty dated 14 September 1799. His letter to William Lock is also missing, but Fanny mentioned it in a letter to her father. Ibid., iv, pp. 327, 334.

3 The message to Captain Phillips was added to her letter to Susan of 12 October. Three days later she wrote to Dr Burney, a letter that she later annotated, 'dreadful First account of the dangerous state of SUSANNA ELIZABETH PHILLIPS! & her wish to return to our Bosoms'. Ibid., iv, pp. 341–4, 345–7.

4 Ibid., iv, pp. 380–2.

5 The stone was moved when the Church of St Mary & St Helen was rebuilt in 1875. It was replaced in 1964. From Mary Ryan's article, 'A Stone for Susanna', in *Cheshire Life*, xxx, 12 (December 1964), pp. 84–5.

6 Indeed, James was always to remain friends with him, and, much to Fanny's disgust, James's son Martin went to his funeral in 1832. Major Phillips was by then living in London, and was buried at St Margaret's, Westminster, beside James (he died of cholera).

7 She confided to Mrs Lock that the depth of her grief had almost sent her mad. *JL*, iv, pp. 385–6.

8 Ibid., iv, pp. 388–90.

9 From the Berg Collection ('Memoranda, Notes, etc. Taken from Diaries and Blank-Books Comprising 63 pieces': 208269B); with kind permission of the New York Public Library.

10 'Madame d'Arblay: Her Commonplace Book of "Consolatory Extracts" occasioned by the Tragic Death of Her Sister Susan Phillips in January 1800' is now in the Henry E. Huntington Library & Art Gallery, San Marino, California.

11 Catherine Talbot (1721–70) was the daughter of a cleric who died before she was born, leaving her to be brought up in the household of his friend, Thomas Secker, the Bishop of Durham and later Archbishop of Canterbury. A friend of Mrs Montagu and Elizabeth Carter, she wrote for the *Rambler*, the *Adventurer* and the *Athenian*; after her death (from cancer), friends published her *Reflections on the Seven Days of the Week* and *Essays on Various Subjects*. She was close friends for thirty years with Elizabeth Carter (1717–1806), a prodigious linguist who taught herself Latin, Greek, Hebrew, Portuguese and Arabic, as well as French, German and Italian. Elizabeth Carter contributed regularly to Edward Cave's *Gentleman's Magazine*, and in 1752 published her *Remarks on the Athanasian Creed*. Hester Chapone (1727–1801) was part of the same Bluestocking circle, and a great friend of Samuel Richardson; indeed, it was thought that she influenced the moral outcome of his novel *Clarissa*, while Mrs Delany asserted that Hester Chapone was the model for one or two of his heroines. Dr Johnson quoted from her in his *Dictionary*; her *Letters on the Improvement of the Mind* were published in 1773. She was said to have 'mourned intensely' when her husband died in 1760 after only nine months of marriage.

12 From a tiny sewn notebook (some three and a half inches square) in M. d'A's exquisitely neat handwriting now in the Berg Collection ('Miscellaneous; About 417 pieces of MS': 198300B); with kind permission of the New York Public Library.

13 From letters dated 22 March 1800. *JL*, iv, pp. 406–7, 408.

14 The letter is dated 10 February 1800. Ibid., iv, pp. 394–5.

15 For a discussion of the play and its belated première in September 1993, see chapter 5.

16 The treaty was not officially declared until 25 March 1802.

17 The letter, written on 15 December, was sent to M. d'A at his uncle's house on the rue de l'Etape at Joigny, where he had gone after spending just a few days in Paris. *JL*, v, p. 91.

18 The amnesty for all those on the list of *émigrés* was not introduced until 26 April 1802, but many, like M. d'A, had been removed from the list before then.

19 Fanny's letter was written on receipt of M. d'A's letter setting out his plans to join the St Domingo expedition on 12 January 1802. After writing it, she and Alex left immediately to stay with the Locks at Norbury Park, too upset to stay alone in Camilla Cottage. *JL*, v, pp. 132–3.

20 The letter, written on 11 February 1802, was later annotated by Fanny, 'Letter written for Her Majesty but addressed to Miss Planta'. Ibid., v, pp. 145–8.

21 'The reason given for this disgrace, for which I was totally unprepared, is my

insistence that I will never serve against the country of my wife, if it should arm itself against the Republic.' From M. d'A's letter to Fanny written from Paris on 8 March. Ibid., v, pp. 168–70.

22 The cost of the journey for each passenger was £4 13s.

23 *JL*, v, p. 215.

24 Fanny began her letter to her father from Dover and finished it on arrival in Paris at the end of April, finally posting it to Chelsea in early May. M. d'A copied this letter and many other of his wife's letters to England into what later became the 'Paris Letter Book'. This was destroyed in the fire at Camilla Cottage in 1919, but, fortunately, other copies have survived. Ibid., v, pp. 216–20.

25 Napoleon instituted the renumbering of the streets of Paris in 1804–5, so that numbers in those streets running parallel to the Seine would follow the course of the river (i.e. from west to east); while those running perpendicular to the river began their numbering at the end of the street closest to the river. Houses on the right-hand side of the street, as one moved away from the river, were given even numbers; those on the left, odd numbers. The Hotel Marengo at No. 1185 is no more, but it would have been close to where the rue de Penthièvre now crosses the rue de Miroménil.

26 Fanny's wry account of her wardrobe crisis was given to her Court friend, Miss Planta, in the hope that it would be retailed to the Princess Augusta, whom she had always teased for her love of fashion. *JL*, v, p. 290.

27 The daughter of Charlotte and Clement Francis, Charlotte was later to marry Henry Barrett and take on the responsibility of editing and publishing her aunt's diaries after her death.

28 *JL*, v, p. 286.

29 Fanny sent a detailed account of the Review to Dr Burney in her 'Paris Journal' for May 1802. The quotation comes from *Hamlet* (act iii, scene i). *JL*, v, pp. 308–19.

30 From a section in a notebook for 1812 entitled by Fanny 'David's Studio'. Ibid., vi, pp. 622–5.

31 Ibid., v, pp. 353–6.

32 Ibid., v, pp. 529 n, 433.

33 Ibid., v, pp. 384–8.

34 Ibid. vi, pp. 472–4, 475–6.

35 From a letter to Mrs Lock, written in 1810, in which Fanny pines to be back in England. Ibid., vi, p. 591.

36 From a notebook in the Berg Collection (202962B); with kind permission of the New York Public Library.

37 Conversations with women who have experienced breast cancer would seem to confirm this theory that Fanny may well not have had a malignant tumour, for they all confirmed that they did not feel any pain before the operation.

38 Baron Larrey was later to observe the effects of cold in numbing his patients and making them less sensitive to pain while working on the battlefields of Russia during Napoleon's advance on Moscow. His observations and on-the-field experiments were to lead to the development of ether and chloral inhalations in the late 1840s. Too late for Fanny!

39 Fanny began her letter to Hetty in March 1812 (the copy that survives is in the handwriting of both M. d'A and Alex), but she did not finish it until June, by which time she was anxious that her family should have a true account of the operation, since news of it and of her bravery had, she says, 'reached Seville to the South, and Constantinople to the East'. It runs to twelve pages and was intended for all the family, and for all time. 'Respect this & beware not to injure it!!!' she wrote on the covering sheet. Attached to it was the medical report written up by Baron Larrey's chief pupil, who had sat with Fanny during the night after the operation. *JL*, vi, pp. 596–616.

40 From the *Diary & Letters of Madame d'Arblay, Volume VI: 1793–1812*, edited by her niece Charlotte Barrett, p. 347. Charlotte added: 'The fortitude with which she bore this suffering, and her generous solicitude for Monsieur d'Arblay and those around her, excited the warmest sympathy in all who heard of her trial, and her French friends universally gave her the name of *L'Ange*; so touched were they by her tenderness and magnanimity.'

41 From the fine copy of Fanny's letter to Hetty of 22 March 1812 now in the Berg Collection (209896B); with kind permission of the New York Public Library.

12. *THE WANDERER*: 1812–14

1 'O my dear friend, how I love thee! I love you too much for my peace of mind, but not as much as your worth deserves.' *JL*, vi, p. 633.

2 The letter is dated 27 July. Ibid., vi, p. 661.

3 Ibid., vi, p. 693.

4 Ibid., vi, p. 690.

5 The 'Dunkirk and Deal' notebooks, three of them, were neatly copied and edited versions of Fanny's memoranda of her journey home to England, from 4 July to 20 August 1812. Ibid., vi, pp. 702–34.

6 From her first letter to M. d'A sent from England, dated 12–22 August 1812. Ibid., vii, p. 10.

7 Fanny reported to Susan in her journal-letter of June–November 1798 what Maria had told her. Ibid., iv, p. 191.

8 Joyce Hemlow, *The History of Fanny Burney*, pp. 281–5.

9 From a letter dated 22 November 1798, which deals exclusively with the subject of James and Sarah Harriet. *JL*, iv, pp. 208–9.

10 The letter makes painful reading, and begins with a request that Charlotte should look out for a family that 'would like to give me a good fat salary as governess to her brats'. Ibid., vi, p. 521n.

11 *Clarentine* was favourably reviewed, commended in the *Monthly Review* (December 1796) for the 'vivacity of its dialogue and morality of sentiment'. It convinced Sarah Harriet that writing could be her financial salvation; she told her cousin Charlotte Barrett that 'I must scribble, or *I cannot live*' (quoted by Joyce Hemlow in *The History of Fanny Burney*, p. 321). In 1808 *Geraldine Fauconberg* was published; when *Traits of Nature* appeared in 1812, it sold out within three months and was greeted by the Princess Elizabeth 'in high terms . . . & with much praise, though not equal, of *Clarentine*' (according to Fanny in a letter to Dr Burney, 10 December 1812, *JL*, vii, p. 61). *Country Neighbours* appeared in 1820 and received a tribute from Charles Lamb, who wrote a sonnet dedicated to its heroine, Blanche, that was published in the *Morning Chronicle* (it is reproduced by R. Brimley Johnson in *Fanny Burney and the Burneys*, p. 352). She also wrote a novella, revealingly called *The Shipwreck*.

12 From Fanny's letter to Dr Burney of 10 September, written from 23 Chenies Street, where Fanny was staying with her sister Charlotte. *JL*, vii, pp. 17–18. Indeed, Charles Lamb memorialised the home of his old friend 'Captain B' in his essay 'The Wedding', describing it as an endearingly shambolic but happy place in which to while away an evening. 'My friend the Admiral was in fine wig and buckle on this occasion [the wedding of James's daughter Sarah to her cousin John Payne in April 1821],' he writes, before recalling the many hours he had spent with the Burneys: 'I do not know a visiting place where every guest is so perfectly at his ease; nowhere, where harmony is so strangely the result of confusion. Everybody is at cross-purposes, yet the effect is so much better than uniformity. Contradictory orders; servants pulling one way; master and mistress driving some other, yet both diverse; visitors huddled up in corners; chairs unsymmetrized; candles disposed by chance; meals at odd hours, tea and supper at once, or the latter preceding the former; the host and the guest conferring, yet each upon a different topic, each understanding himself, neither trying to understand or hear the other; draughts and politics, chess and political economy, cards and conversation on nautical matters, going on at once, without the hope, or indeed the wish, of distinguishing them, make it altogether the most perfect *concordia discors* you shall meet with.' From *The Essays of Elia*, with introduction and notes by Alfred Ainger, pp. 315–21.

13 James's pamphlet *An Essay By way of Lecture on the Game of Whist* appeared in 1821. *JL*, vii, p. 92. James's amiability compared to Charles's was noted by Southey in a letter to Coleridge in 1804. While bored by Charles's 'discourse upon the properties of the conjugation QUAM', he was relieved to find James 'smoking after supper, letting out puffs at one corner of his mouth and puns at the other'. R. Brimley Johnson, *Fanny Burney*

and the Burneys.

14 The school was attended in the 1830s by G.H. Lewes, George Eliot's partner. Charles had died by that time and the school was being run by his son, Charles Parr Burney.

15 *JL*, vii, pp. 60–1. Fanny's letter began with the momentous news that Napoleon had been defeated at Moscow.

16 Fanny thoroughly disliked all financial business. As she told her husband in May 1813: 'How unpleasant is all that belongs to Money! how constantly to me, wearying, wearying, wearying, & perplexing'. Ibid., vii, p. 134. Unfortunately, M. d'A seems to have been equally vague when it came to money matters.

17 The full list of publishers named by Fanny (which she had gleaned from just one week's newspapers and hoped would be added to by Charles) was: Longman, Hurst, Rees, Orme & Brown (of Paternoster Row); John Murray (at The Ship, Fleet Street); Henry Colburn (in Conduit Street); Thomas Payne, the son of 'Honest Tom Payne' (in Pall Mall); Wright, Cochrane & Co. (at Horace's Head, Fleet Street); Francis and Charles Rivington (of St Paul's Churchyard and Paternoster Row); John Robinson (also of Paternoster Row); Edward Williams (of the Strand); James Richardson (at 23 Cornhill); E.T. and Thomas Hookham Jr (at 15 Old Bond Street); Samuel Leigh (of the Strand); Mrs Elizabeth Mathews (also of the Strand); Joseph Booker (in New Bond Street); and John Hatchard, 'Bookseller to the King' (in Piccadilly). Ibid., vii, pp. 103–5, 567–8.

18 Ibid., vii, p. 195. (Fanny wrote from Richmond Hill in October 1813, where she was staying with her niece, Charlotte Barrett, whose husband was away fighting against France.) By comparison, Jane Austen received £450 for the copyright of *Mansfield Park* (published in May 1814), together with the rights for the already published *Sense and Sensibility* and *Pride and Prejudice*. The first edition of *Mansfield Park* (1,500 copies) was sold out by November; a second edition followed in 1816. Also published in 1814 was *Waverley*, which earned Sir Walter Scott some £700.

19 From the Dedication to *The Wanderer*, pp. 3–10.

20 From a letter written after the events of Waterloo, and which begins, 'How is it that my ever dear Mary [Marianne Waddington] can thus on one side be fascinated by the very thing that, on the other, revolts her? how be a professed & ardent detester of Tyranny: yet an open & intrepid admirer of a Tyrant?' *JL*, viii, pp. 282–6. Napoleon, meanwhile, had taken a copy of *Camilla* to Elba.

21 *The Wanderer*, vol. i, book i, chapter 1, p. 11.

22 Ibid., vol. i, book ii, p. 174. Fanny gives this speech to Elinor, her anti-heroine, an example of unbridled self-will. Over forty years earlier, in her diary for 15 June 1769, she had written: 'O how I hate this vile custom which obliges us to make slaves of ourselves!' She was referring to the tiresome duty of morning calls, where she endured hours of tedious conversation when she would much rather have spent her time working on her novels. 'Custom,' she continued, 'which is so woven around us – which so universally commands us – which we all blame – and all obey, without knowing why or wherefore – which keeps our better Reason.' *EJL*, i, pp. 72–3.

23 Once again, Fanny's anti-heroine Elinor gets all the best lines in a discussion that begins with the justification – or not – for taking one's own life and ends with a debate that questions the validity of faith itself. *The Wanderer*, vol. v, book ix, chapter lxxxv, p. 782.

24 Ibid., vol. iii, book v, chapter xliv, p. 411. Sophia Streatfeild's mother had nicknamed Fanny 'the Dove' in 1779 because of the colour of her eyes, which were a 'greenish-grey'. The Wanderer's eyes are described as having 'the softness of the Dove's' (a quotation from *The Song of Songs*).

25 Mrs Ireton's sarcastic wit and bitter recriminations against those unwise enough to find themselves in her company could be compared with Mr Crisp's comments on the second Mrs Burney. 'So I am to be left to myself, am I?' says Mrs Ireton, in a characteristically grumpy speech. 'In this feeble and alarming state to which I am reduced, incapable to withstand a gust of wind, or to baffle the fall of a leaf, I may take care of myself, may I? I am too stout to require any attention? too robust, too obstreperous to need any help? If I fall down, I may get up again, I suppose? If I faint, I may come to myself again, I imagine? You will have the goodness to permit that, I presume? I may be mistaken, to be sure, but I should presume so. Don't you hear me, Mistress Ellis? But you are deaf may be?' *The Wanderer*, vol. iii, book vi, chapter liv, p. 498. In the *Burford Papers: Being*

Letters of Samuel Crisp to his Sister at Burford, we find a letter in which Mr Crisp quotes from some 'treasonable correspondence' about 'Precious' (i.e. Mrs Burney) from Fanny: 'Nothing is said that she does not fly in a Passion at and Contradict! Whatever is, is wrong! that's her Maxim! I think she ought to be indicted for Living; for she is a Nuisance to Society' (p. 82). Mrs Ireton's impossible temper is also reminiscent of Madame Schwellenberg (a link suggested by the comment that Juliet/Miss Ellis has become a 'toad-eater', the appellation given to Queen Charlotte's First Keeper of the Robes).

26 *The Wanderer*, vol. v, book ix, chapter lxxxiii, pp. 763–73.

27 *Byron's Letters and Journals*, edited by Leslie A. Marchand, iv, pp. 86–7. Fanny was to make her own rather acid observations on Lady Caroline after glimpsing her in Brussels in July 1815 just after the Battle of Waterloo (Lady Caroline's brother was one of the injured). Fanny remembered later how she was 'dressed, or rather not dressed, so as to excite universal attention, & authorize every boldness from the General to the lowest soldier, among the military Groups then constantly parading the Place, – for she had one shoulder, half her back, & all her throat & Neck, displayed as if at the call of some statuary for modelling a heathen Goddess. A slight scarf hung over the other shoulder, & the rest of the attire was of accordant lightness.' *JL*, viii, p. 416.

28 *The Wanderer*, vol. iii, book v, chapter xviii, pp. 397–400.

29 Ibid., vol. i, book ii, chapter xviii, p. 177.

30 From her Windsor journal for 16 August 1787 (from the as yet unpublished material at McGill University, with kind permission of Professor Lars Troide). The discussion on dreams in *The Wanderer* is in vol. v, book ix, chapter lxxxv, pp. 780–94. Many years earlier, Fanny had confided to her diary how her worries for James's safety gave her nightmares: 'my rest is very much disturbed – I Dream confused things of my Brother for ever'. From September 1769. *EJL*, i, p. 93.

31 Such questions were much written about in the revolutionary fervour of these years. Madame de Staël, for instance, published her essay *Réflexions sur le suicide* in 1813, which Fanny had rushed to read as soon as it appeared.

32 Reviews appeared in the *British Critic* (new series), i (June 1814), pp. 374–86 ('Could the whole work have been compressed into three volumes, we should have thought that much more entertainment would have been provided for the reader'); *Quarterly Review*, xi (April 1814), pp. 123–30; *Monthly Review; or, Literary Journal*, lxxvi (April 1815), pp. 412–19 ('When a new edition of this novel is undertaken, we should recommend something of abridgement'); *Gentleman's Magazine*, lxxxiv (June 1814), pp. 579–81 ('we trust "The Wanderer" will have its use, and serve as an historical antidote to any lurking remnants of poisonous doctrines that still make their appearance at intervals'). In a letter to Longman & Co., dated 1 February 1826 (only the draft survives), Fanny asked her publisher what numbers had been sold since 1824 and noted their reply: 461 copies had been sold before Midsummer 1814, a further 23 copies were sold by Midsummer 1815, but in the following nine years only 51 copies were sold, making a final total of 535 copies. The rest of the second edition was rumoured to have been pulped. Fanny never discovered the truth, but in any case never received the £500 due her for that edition.

33 John Croker writing in the *Quarterly Review*, xi (April 1814), pp. 123–30.

34 Macaulay's criticism appeared in his review of the *Diary & Letters* in the *Edinburgh Review* of 1843. *The Works of Lord Macaulay*, iv, p. 64.

35 From her diary for 18 March 1790. *Thraliana*, ii, p. 764.

36 The quotation from Savage's *The Wanderer* comes from Richard Holmes's discussion of the poem in *Dr Johnson & Mr Savage*, pp. 88–9, 146–54. I am grateful to Karin Fernald for drawing my attention to this possible connection.

37 From the *Quarterly Review*, xi (April 1814).

38 Fanny was writing from 63 Lower Sloane Street, Chelsea, sometime before M. d'A's arrival on 28 April. *JL*, vii, pp. 322–3.

39 Most of the music was bought by the British Museum for £253, and still forms one of its most valuable collections. The total raised by the auction was £2,353 19s (about £63,550 now).

40 Percy Scholes in volume ii of his *The Great Dr Burney* includes a copy of the will (pp. 261–75).

41 *JL*, vii, p. 292.

42 James Burney, Esq., appears in the Navy List for July 1821 as appointed to the rank of 'Super-annuated Rear-Admiral' on 19 July (the day of George IV's coronation).

43 Dr Burney was buried with his second wife in the cemetery at Chelsea College. A permanent memorial was erected in Westminster Abbey in August 1817 at a cost of thirty-five guineas. It can be seen in a corner of the north choir aisle devoted to musicians (Dr Burney's plaque is immediately below that of the composer, John Blow). Fanny wrote the epitaph:

> Sacred to the Memory of Charles Burney, Mus. D., F.R.S.
> Who, full of years, and full of virtues,
> The pride of his family, and the delight of society,
> The unrivalled chief, and scientifick Historian,
> Of his tuneful art! Beloved, revered, regretted,
> Breathed, in Chelsea College, his last sigh!
> Leaving to posterity a fame unblemished,
> Built on the noble basis of intellectual attainments.
> High principles and pure benevolence,
> Goodness with gaiety, talents with taste,
> Were of his gifted mind the blended attributes;
> While the genial hilarity of his airy spirits
> Animated, or softened, his every earthly toil;
> And a conscience without reproach
> Prepared in the whole tenour of his mortal life,
> Through the mediation of our Lord Jesus Christ,
> His soul for heaven. Amen.
> Born April 7. O.S. 1726. Died April 12. 1814.

44 *JL*, vii, pp. 295–317.

45 From *Jane Austen's Letters to Her Sister Cassandra and Others*, p. 389. Fanny's account of her audience with Alexander I is in a notebook in the Berg Collection (208269B); with kind permission of the New York Public Library.

46 The letter is dated 3 June. *JL*, vii, p. 359.

47 From that same letter to Marianne Waddington of 3 June. Ibid.

48 Ibid., vii, pp. 426–7.

49 Ibid., vii, pp. 477–9.

13. WATERLOO: 1814–15

1 *JL*, viii, p. 29. The letter was sent sometime before 22 February.

2 Many years later, while living in Bolton Street, Piccadilly, Fanny composed the 'Waterloo Journal', which covered the events of that momentous period from 11 February until July 1815. It is reprinted in *JL*, viii, pp. 339–456. Thackeray is said to have used it as a source for his account of the Duchess of Richmond's ball and the chaotic aftermath of Waterloo in *Vanity Fair*.

3 'My dear friend all is lost! – I cannot go into any more detail. Leave immediately – the sooner the better. In life and in death! Midy! Midy! – A. d'Ay.' *JL*, viii, p. 58. 'Midy!' (midday) was the time they had agreed that every day they would devote to thinking of each other.

4 Ibid., viii, pp. 58–9.

5 Ibid., viii, pp. 63–4.

6 From a letter Fanny addressed to the Chevalier d'Arblay at Ghent (where she had heard the King's troops were stationed). Ibid., viii, pp. 65–6.

7 The letter has survived in a draft version made on 29 May. Ibid., viii, pp. 146–51.

8 Ibid., viii, p. 175.

9 From a letter to M. d'A, dated 9–11 June and addressed to 'Monsieur le Général d'Arblay, Officier Supérieur des armées de sa Majestie Le Roi de France, Chevalier de St

Louis'. Ibid., viii, pp. 181–7.

10 From a letter to M. d'A. Ibid., viii, pp. 183–5.

11 From letters to M. d'A dated 9–11 June and 11–13 June. Ibid., viii, pp. 187, 198–204.

12 She finished her letter two days later, on 19 June, when Wellington's victory was confirmed, although there was still no certainty that Napoleon had been finally and completely defeated. Ibid., viii, pp. 211–16.

13 It was to the Princess (now married to the Landgrave of Hesse-Homburg) that Fanny sent her first detailed account of what she had witnessed in Brussels during the weekend of the Battle of Waterloo. Only a draft has survived, dated 19–20 June. Ibid., viii, pp. 218–22. Fanny's correspondence with the Princess had begun in December 1814. In that first letter the Princess had referred to herself as 'Nobody' and to Fanny as 'somebody', in an unconscious allusion to Fanny's own nickname for herself. The Princess writes, 'I look upon myself as *Nobody*, & as *Nobody* shall I write – tho when you come to consider my *fat figure* you may be inclined to say I think there is *some Body*' (Ibid., viii, p. 7 n). The letters were never signed – for reasons of state. Fanny's 'Waterloo Journal' was based on these drafts, which contain details not included in the journal.

14 Ibid., viii, pp. 237–41.

15 Fanny's letter is dated 29–30 June; M. d'A began his heartfelt reply on 4 July. Ibid., viii, pp. 262–8, 298–300.

16 Once again, Fanny wrote up her experiences on the road from Brussels to Trèves years later, for the benefit of Alex. Ibid., pp. 474–541.

14. BATH: 1815–18

1 The letter is dated 20 October 1815. *JL*, ix, pp. 2–4.

2 From the journal that Fanny wrote after her husband's death in May 1818. Ibid., x, p. 895.

3 In July 1817, Fanny wrote to M. d'A, who was then in France, that their agent, Stephen Bonnet, a coach-builder of Leicester Square, had sold the *calèche* for £25. They received £18 1s from the sale (£6 19s was deducted as tax). Ibid. x, p. 572.

4 From a letter dated 8 April, in which she tells Charles how she met Hetty, who was staying with her daughters Maria and Sophia, as well as her old friends from Bookham, the Revd Cooke and his wife Cassandra, who were related to Jane Austen. Ibid., ix pp. 94–7.

5 Introduced from France after the Restoration, the cotillion was originally a country dance that had been adopted by the rich and fashionable.

6 From a letter to the owner of the Theatre Royal, William Dimond. *JL*, ix, pp. 118–20.

7 Alex had gone with them to the performance – in July 1816 – and had, in contrast to his mother, been bowled over by the theatricality of Kean's performance. Fanny reported to Marianne Waddington that Alex was 'almost ready for the strait waistcoat', so wildly enthusiastic was his admiration for Kean. Ibid. ix, p. 167.

8 From a letter written on 25 April. Ibid. ix, pp. 102–3. It was a view of Bath not shared by Jane Austen, who on 30 June 1808 had written to Cassandra that she had left Bath for Clifton 'with what happy feelings of Escape'. From *Jane Austen's Letters to Her Sister Cassandra and Others*, p. 208.

9 Mrs Thrale-Piozzi never regretted defying the opinion of her friends and of society by marrying the Italian singer, who had died at Brynbella, their home in north Wales, on 30 March 1809. On the day of his death, she ended the diary she had begun in 1776 on the day that her first husband presented her with six calf-bound notebooks, each with a gold-imprinted label, *Thraliana*, on the cover. The last words in that volume, now published, were: 'Every thing most dreaded *has* ensued, – all is over; & my second Husbands Death is the last Thing recorded in my first husband's Present! Cruel Death!' *Thraliana*, ii, p. 1099. And Mary Hyde's *The Thrales of Streatham Park*, p. 167.

10 In December 1815 Mrs Piozzi was still living in what she described as 'her dingy lodgings' in New King Street (a continuation of Great Stanhope Street) but by the following November she had moved into No. 8 Gay Street, distinguished by its elaborately decorated stone façade, after which it is now named the 'Carved House'. She

could only afford to move into such a fashionable street by selling all her rights to Streatham Park, according to James L. Clifford in his *Hester Lynch Piozzi (Mrs Thrale)*.
11 From a letter sent to Mrs Thrale-Piozzi's eldest daughter, Queeney, on 7 November 1816. *JL*, ix, pp. 275–8.
12 Quoted by James L. Clifford in *Hester Lynch Piozzi*, p. 447.
13 From her letter written jointly with M. d'A on or about 8 March 1816. *JL*, ix, pp. 78–82.
14 Part iii, chapter ii of Swift's *Gulliver's Travels*.
15 *JL*, ix, pp. 216–17.
16 Fanny added these strong words to a letter that began with a copy of the 'Brevet' that M. d'A had received in March 1814, awarding him the Ordre du Lys. M. d'A had asked Fanny to make a copy for him in the hope that it might persuade the military authorities to settle his arrears of pay. Ibid. ix, pp. 223–8.
17 Fanny's letter was written on 20 October 1816. Ibid., ix, pp. 246–8.
18 Ibid., ix, pp. 266–71.
19 From a letter to Charles of 30 November 1816, which was mostly concerned with Alex's future at Cambridge. Ibid., ix, p. 289.
20 Alex wrote separately to each of his parents on the day after his triumph, which took place on 6 March 1817. Ibid., ix, p. 341 n.
21 'All the world will tell Alex who his mother is, but so that he shall not forget who his father was, I have had this portrait painted, which I dedicate to him.' Fanny reminded Alex what his father had said in a letter dated 17 October 1818. Ibid., xi, p. 14.
22 From Fanny's long letter to M. d'A describing their journey to Ilfracombe. Ibid., x, pp. 530–8.
23 She wrote up the dramatic tale in French in 1823 to send to Madame de Maisonneuve in Paris. She then translated what she had written into English in a notebook of seventeen double-sheets of notepaper. It is included in volume x of the *JL*, pp. 690–714. She talked of her other two 'death experiences' as being her operation in 1811 and her terrifying journey from Brussels to Trèves through bandit country after the Battle of Waterloo in July 1815, not knowing whether M. d'A was still alive.
24 Although he did eventually receive most of the back-pay (the *retraite*) due to him from his active service in the army from 1789 until 1792 and from 1814 to 1815, M. d'A was penalised for living abroad and one-third was deducted from its value. Furthermore, he never recovered the expenses he had incurred before leaving for France in 1814 or for Waterloo in 1815 (uniforms, arms and ammunition, maps, compasses and horses). M. d'A detailed the amounts in memoranda that he left for his wife, but she suppressed most of the detail. That he was prepared to risk his health in a last attempt to retrieve such relatively small amounts of money indicates just how concerned he was for the future of his family, and just how penurious was the d'Arblays' existence. (In 1816–18, for instance, Fanny drew just £7 10s a quarter from their account at Messrs Hoare & Co. for her personal expenses.) M. d'A's campaign for compensation is detailed in an Appendix to volume x of the *JL*, pp. 960–70.
25 From the 'Narrative of the Last Illness and Death of General d'Arblay' written by Fanny from November 1819 to March 1820 to 'unburthen the loaded heart from the weight of suppression of her grief'. Ibid., x, pp. 842–912.
26 From a letter that is almost like one of her old journal-letters to Susan, written over a period of several weeks from 14 November 1817 to 4 January 1818: a time when Fanny was preoccupied with her husband's illness and her own requirement to wait daily on the Queen (who stayed in a house in New Sydney Place) while she was in Bath. Ibid, x, pp. 759–75.
27 From the 417 scraps in the Berg Collection (198300B); with kind permission of the New York Public Library.
28 The Archdeacon was now married and living in a gracious new house built in the grounds of his father's home at Twickenham Meadows. The letter is dated 12–13 February 1818. *JL*, x, pp. 787–9.
29 'I am terribly weak. I do not believe that I will have strength to go on for much longer. Dear Fanny – Dear Alex! God bless you! & unite us for ever! Amen!' He wrote nothing more until 1 March. Ibid., x, p. 803 n.

30 Ibid., x, p. 829.

31 From a memorandum book in the Berg Collection (208269B); with kind permission of the New York Public Library.

32 From Fanny's 'Narrative of the Last Illness and Death of General d'Arblay: *JL*, x, pp. 907–9.

33 The letter is in the Berg Collection ('8 AL to her son Alexander d'Arblay': 207538B, 207545B); with kind permission of the New York Public Library.

34 *JL*, x, pp. 907–8.

35 M. d'A (born on 13 May 1754) was actually sixty-three when he died, not sixty-five.

15. LAST THOUGHTS IN MAYFAIR: 1818–40

1 Written on a scrap of paper now in the Berg Collection (208269B); with kind permission of the New York Public Library.

2 From an entry in her pocket-book diary for 1818, dated 30 August. *JL*, x, p. 957. These yearly diaries were more like memoranda, usually containing little more than details of letters written, visits made and books read. But in her distress of 1817–18, when she wrote fewer and fewer letters, Fanny tended to add more to her diary.

3 Ibid., xi, pp. 102–8.

4 Ibid., xi, p. 119 n.

5 From Fanny's long letter to Hetty of 25–8 November 1820, in which she explains her problems with Dr Burney's papers and her new intentions for the memoirs. Ibid., xi, pp.183–97.

6 From Macaulay's review of the first five volumes of the *Diary & Letters of Madame d'Arblay*, reprinted in *The Works of Lord Macaulay*, iv, p. 7.

7 From her letter to Hetty of 25–8 November 1820, *JL*, xi, pp. 183–97.

8 *Quarterly Review*, xlix (April 1833), pp. 97–125. Croker's article follows a review of Tennyson's poems, bringing Fanny right into the nineteenth-century literary world.

9 From a letter dated 3 September 1821 and sent to Alex at Yverdon in Switzerland. *JL*, xi, pp. 261–5.

10 The letter, dated 25 October 1829, is now in the Berg Collection (in the 'Scrapbook: Fanny Burney and Family, 1653–1890': 213048B); with kind permission of the New York Public Library.

11 The draft is in the Berg Collection, ('Miscellaneous; About 144 MS pieces'), addressed to 'Mrs Bolton At W.F. Greville's Esq Stationbury House, near Sandwich, Kent'. One torn sheet only remains. With kind permission of the New York Public Library.

12 From a letter to Fanny dated 30 July 1817 before Alex's ordination. *JL*, x, p. 523 n.

13 Among Alexander's papers in the Berg Collection are verse translations of Lamartine and Victor Hugo, and essays on the brilliance of Napoleon. He had several of his sermons and a long ode in heptameters printed by 'private impression', with kind permission of the New York Public Library.

14 The letter to her sister Cassandra is dated 3 November 1813, when Jane would have been thirty-eight and Alex almost twenty. She had just published *Pride and Prejudice*. 'I am read & admired in Ireland too ... I do not despair of having my picture in the Exhibition at last – all white & red, with my Head on one side; – *or perhaps I may marry young Mr D'arblay* – I suppose in the meantime I shall owe dear Henry a great deal of money for Printing &c'. *Jane Austen's Letters to Her Sister Cassandra and Others*, pp. 36–8.

15 The letter is dated 24 May 1824. *JL*, xi, p. 473 n.

16 Fanny wrote her letter on 20 October 1834. Alex had dined with the Barretts who were also in Brighton, but they suspected that he was not staying at the White Horse, where he had told his mother her letters would find him. Ibid., xii, pp. 840–2.

17 Ibid., xii, pp. 866–7.

18 Ibid., xii, p. 873.

19 Ibid., xii, p. 873 n.

20 The letter is among Alex's papers in the Berg Collection; reading it in the original is to enter a mind in deep pain and confusion (198097B–198134B; with kind permission of the New York Public Library). Alex wrote in response to Fanny's 'I am Sick! Sick! Sick! – Sick at Heart! ... Never to come! never even to Write!' which she had sent by

cab to Camden Town on the night of Tuesday, 15 December 1835. *JL*, xii, pp. 884–6.
21 Ibid., xii, p. 886 n.
22 Ibid., xii, p. 910 n. The chapel was reopened for services on 27 November 1836.
23 We do not know why, though it has been suggested that Alex was suffering from syphilis, or some other disease about which he did not want his mother to know.
24 With Alex's death, the d'Arblay name, or at least M. d'A's branch of the Piochards de la Brulerie, died out.
25 *JL*, xii, pp. 15–16 n.
26 From a letter to her nephew Charles Parr Burney, who helped Fanny to revise her will, now that her son and heir had died. Ibid., xii, pp. 916–17.
27 From a letter of sympathy to Charlotte Barrett written on 5 March 1839 after the death of her mother, Fanny's sister Charlotte. Ibid., xii, pp. 963–4.
28 Quoted by G.E. Manwaring from Leigh Hunt's essay in *The Examiner*, in his biography of James, *My Friend the Admiral*. Lamb's essay on *A Game of Whist*, also quoted by Manwaring, was based on many happy evenings in James Street, presided over by the 'old Captain' and his wife 'Mrs Battle': 'who loved a good game of whist. She was none of your lukewarm gamesters, your half-and-half players ... who affirm that they have no pleasure in winning; that they like to win one game and lose another; that they can while away an hour very agreeably at a card-table, but are indifferent whether they play or no ... These insufferable triflers are the curse of the table ... Sarah Battle was none of that breed. She detested them, as I do, from her heart and soul, and would not, save upon a striking emergency, willingly seat herself at the same table with them. She loved a thorough-paced partner, a determined enemy. She took and gave no concessions ... She sate bolt upright; and neither showed you her cards, nor desired to see yours ... I never in my life – and I knew Sarah Battle many of the best years of it – saw her take out her snuff-box when it was her turn to play; or snuff a candle in the middle of the game; or ring for a servant till it was fairly over ... As she emphatically observed, cards were cards.'
29 Major Phillips had by this time abandoned his second wife, Ann Maturin, and their children. There is a story that he once went into hiding in James's house when the bailiffs came after him for unpaid debts.
30 *JL*, xii, p. 933.
31 Ibid., xii, pp. 926–7.
32 Ibid., xii, p. 942.
33 Written sometime after 10 January 1838. Ibid., xii, pp. 947–8.
34 Ibid., xii, pp. 61–2.
35 The visit took place on 18 November 1826. Scott's account of the afternoon appears in his *Journal* as edited by J. G. Tait (Edinburgh, 1939), i, pp. 277–8.
36 *JL*, xii, pp. 974–5. A copy of Fanny's will is included in an Appendix to volume xii of the *JL*, pp. 973–81.
37 Ibid., xii, pp. 966–7.
38 From Charlotte Barrett's account of her aunt's last days in the final volume of her edition of the *Diary & Letters of Madame d'Arblay*, vii, p. 382. On Friday, 10 January, an obituary notice appeared in *The Times*: 'In Lower Grosvenor Street, on Monday, the 6th instant, in her 88th year, Madame d'Arblay, the author of *Evelina* and *Cecilia*, widow of the late Lieutenant General A. Piochard, Comte d'Arblay, and second daughter of the late Charles Burney, Mus D.'
39 The memorial tablet was in St Swithin's in 1905, when a photograph was taken. But it is there no longer. It read:

Sacred to the Memory of
FRANCES D'ARBLAY
Second Daughter of CHARLES BURNEY, Mus. D:
 And Widow of
GENL. COUNT ALEXANDRE JEAN BAPTISTE PIOCHARD D'ARBLAY
The Friend of JOHNSON and BURKE
Who by her Talents has Obtained a Name
Far more Durable than Marble can Confer.

By the Public She Was Admired for her Writings;
By Those who knew her Best
For her Sweet and Noble Disposition
And the Bright Example She Displayed
Of Self-Denial and Every Christian Virtue
But Her Trust was Placed in God
And Her Hope Rested
on the Mercy and Merits of her Redeemer
Through Whom Alone she Looked
For an Inheritance Incorruptible Undefiled
And that Fadeth not Away
She Died in London on the 6th Day of January 1840:
Aged 88.

Her Remains are Deposited in the Adjoining Church-yard
Near those of her Beloved Husband, and in the Same Vault
With Those of her Only Son
THE REVD ALEXANDER CHARLES LOUIS PIOCHARD D'ARBLAY,
Who Departed This Life January 18th 1837:
Aged 42.

(Fanny was actually eighty-seven when she died.)
The Sarcophagus, too, was moved in 1955 from the cemetery to a grass enclosure beside the church. The faint engraving marks it as the grave of Frances d'Arblay and her son Alexander – but the actual site of burial is not known.

AFTERWORD

1 From Thackeray's review in the *Morning Chronicle*, 25 September 1846 (reproduced in *Thackeray's Contributions to the Morning Chronicle*, edited by Gordon N. Ray, Urbana, 1955), pp. 183–6.

NOTES ON ILLUSTRATIONS

Section 1

1 Fanny reading, by her cousin Edward Francisco Burney. Some scholars have suggested that the informal pencil and crayon drawing is of her sister Charlotte, but her casual dress and stylish bonnet all favour Fanny – as does the approximate date, 1778, the year of *Evelina*.

2 Fanny's family:
Her grandfather, the 'witty & accomplished, but careless' James Macburney (1678–1749), by the Swedish portraitist Michael Dahl.

Her father, Dr Charles Burney (1726–1814), by Edward Francisco Burney after Sir Joshua Reynolds's portrait of 1781, which was commissioned by Henry Thrale as one of the fourteen portraits of his friends (including Edmund Burke, David Garrick, Oliver Goldsmith, Dr Johnson and Arthur Murphy) for his gallery in the dining-room at Streatham Park.

Her mother, Esther Sleepe Burney (1725–62), by Edward Francisco Burney after the miniature by Gervase Spencer of 1748. The pencil and crayon drawing is one of two attempts to capture her likeness, which were later annotated by Dr Burney, 'by my nephew Ed. Burney. Drawings from a miniature picture of my 1st wife, by Spencer',

Her stepmother, the 'celebrated beauty of Lynn' Elizabeth Allen Burney (1728–96), by an unknown artist, dating from the late 1750s before her marriage to Dr Burney.

3 Fanny's siblings:
James ('Jem the tar') Burney (1750–1821), the bust commissioned after his death in 1821 by his old seafaring friend, Molesworth Phillips,

Susan Burney (1755–1800), by Edward Francisco Burney – a watercolour miniature from c. 1788, in which Susan's simple dress is trimmed dashingly with a bright lemon sash and cuffs,

Charles ('the scholar') Burney (1757–1817), by Thomas Lawrence, in about 1795, by which time Charles was a celebrated classical scholar and headmaster of his own school in Greenwich,

Charlotte ('the Dumpling Queen') Burney (1761–1838), miniature by an unknown artist dating from c. 1794 (when Charlotte was affectionately known as 'the merry widow').

Susan Burney, Richard Burney, Fanny Burney and Mr Crisp, 1780, by Paul Sandby, the Windsor watercolourist. Fanny and her sister Susan are shown with their 'Worcester' cousin Richard and Mr Crisp, which suggests they were sketched while staying at Chesington Hall.

4 *A Sunday Concert, 1782*: etching from an aquatint by Charles Loraine Smith. The drawing depicts an evening concert at Dr Burney's house in St Martin's Street on 4 June. Dr Burney is lampooned on the right, gossiping to John Wilkes's daughter. The tall, gangly figure beside the harpsichord is the castrato Pacchierotti, who is being adoringly admired by the statuesque Lady Mary Duncan, facetiously shown seated on the left. (In 1818, Loraine Smith, an honorary exhibitor at the Royal Academy, drew a monkey band – perhaps influenced by Fanny's account of the Northwick Fair orchestra in *Camilla?*)

Commerce, or The Triumph of the Thames by James Barry. In this panel, from the series of pictures painted by Barry in the Great Room of the Royal Society of Arts at the Adelphi from 1777 to 1783, Dr Burney is half-submerged in the river and surrounded rather curiously by naked nereids. Barry explained that he wished to celebrate the new 'manufactures and commerce' by representing Father Thames, 'carried along by our great navigators, Sir Francis Drake, Sir Walter Raleigh, Sebastian Cabot and the late Captain Cook', together with a musician 'as music is naturally connected with matters of joy and triumph'. His choice fell on Dr Burney, both for his 'admirable History of Music' and because of his 'useful and practicable' plan to establish a national school of music at the Foundling Hospital, of which Dr Burney was a governor.

5 Fanny's first draft for the title-page of *Evelina*; as sent by her to the printer and bookseller Thomas Lowndes in September 1777.

A scene from *Evelina* by Edward Francisco Burney; the watercolour miniature, one of three submitted by Edward to the Royal Academy exhibition in the summer of 1780, depicts the sentimental scene where Evelina meets her long-lost father, Sir John Belmont, and presents him with the letter written by her mother just before she died.

Remarkable Characters at Mrs Cornelys' Masquerade; an engraving from the *Oxford Magazine* showing a Harlequin, Friar, Nun, Green Man, and a character playing a Hurdy-Gurdy. Mrs Cornelys was a singer who in the 1760s and 1770s rented Carlisle House in Soho Square as a fashionable venue for balls and concerts. By 1778, however, her 'midnight masquerades' were thought to encourage immorality and she was forced to close down by Sir John Fielding. After some years running a shop for asses' milk in Knightsbridge, she died a pauper in the Fleet Prison. Fanny recorded in her diary for 20 April 1770 how she had been disappointed to find the rooms too crowded for dancing.

6 *Mr Crisp of Chesington Hall* by Edward Francisco Burney; painted in 1782 at the same time as Fanny's 'Vandyke' portrait.

Dr Johnson by Theophila Palmer after the portrait of 1781 which Sir Joshua Reynolds painted for Henry Thrale's gallery at Streatham Park. The 'Miss Palmer' of Fanny's letters to Susan was Reynolds's niece; an amateur painter whose portrait shows the scholar in a more approachable light and very much the kind of man who would tease Fanny that she was a 'saucy rogue'.

Mrs Thrale and her daughter Queeney in 1781, by Sir Joshua Reynolds. The portrait was hung alongside those of Dr Johnson and Dr Burney in the dining-room at Streatham Park.

7 Fanny's sketch of the Royal Box at Covent Garden Theatre on the evening of 16 October 1776, when Arthur Murphy's comedy, *All in the Wrong*, was given a Royal Command Performance. Fanny noted on her drawing how she 'sneaked out' at the end of the play just after the Royal party, 'very Glad' that she was not obliged to curtsey before them.

'The Witlings' by a 'Sister of the Order': Fanny's fair copy of the Dramatis Personae and opening scene in the milliner's shop. Although the comedy was not performed in public, Fanny never 'committed it to the flames', ensuring its survival by copying the text carefully onto thick, high-quality paper in an uncharacteristically neat hand.

David Garrick as Richard III, 1771, by Nathaniel Dance; Fanny recorded her impressions of Garrick in the role of Shakespeare's wicked King after seeing his performance in May 1772: 'Good Heavens – how he made me shudder whenever he appeared! . . . he seemed so truly the monster he performed, that I felt myself glow with indignation every time I saw him.'

8 *An Elegant Establishment for Young Ladies* by Edward Franciso Burney; Edward's risqué spoof on boarding-schools for girls dates from *c.* 1820 and is typical of his humorous and characterful style, which owed much to Hogarth.

Edward Francisco Burney (1760–1848), by Henry Edridge; Edward was praised by both James Barry and Sir Joshua Reynolds while he was a student at the Royal Academy in the late 1770s, but he never achieved the recognition he deserved. Fanny said of him in 1826: 'Dear & excellent Edward – Can it be possible such [his penurious existence] should be the result of a Life, of Talents, & of Virtues like his!'

Section 2

1 'One of the most delightful characters I have ever met, for openness, probity, intellectual knowledge, & unhackneyed manners' is how Fanny described Alexandre Jean-Baptiste Piochard d'Arblay when she met him in January 1793. This engraving from a crayon drawing by an unknown artist possible dates from that time.

2 Fanny is portrayed in silhouette (by Thomas Wheeler) in about 1787 while she was at Court. On her left is George III, and on her right is Queen Charlotte, both copied by Edward Francisco Burney from Thomas Gainsborough's formal portraits of 1783.

South East View of Windsor Castle, with the Royal Family on the Terrace and View of the Queen's Lodge, engraved by James Fittler, after George Robertson, 1783. In the summer months, George III and Queen Charlotte went 'walkabout' on the Terrace every evening so that the people of Windsor could see their King and his family.

3 Madame de Staël, from an engraving after the portrait by François Gérard. Fanny could not believe that Narbonne was de Staël's lover because she was so 'very very plain'; she failed to appreciate what others noticed – that the wife of the Swedish ambassador to Paris had very fine arms, as well as a brilliant mind.

The Comte Louis de Narbonne, by an unknown artist. Monsieur d'Arblay's closest friend from his military days in France, Narbonne was thought by Fanny to be 'far more a man of the World'.

Juniper Hall, *c.* 1793, in a watercolour sketch possibly by William Lock junior. The house, originally an old brewhouse, had by the time the French émigrés arrived been extended into a gracious mansion. Fanny is thought by some to have first seen her 'French Chevalier' in the drawing-room, which was decorated by Lady Templeton, who worked with the Wedgwoods.

4 *Edwy and Elgiva*: the playbill for that disastrous first and only performance on 21 March 1795 at the Theatre Royal, Drury Lane.

Sarah Siddons Rehearsing in the Green Room at Drury Lane with her father and John Kemble, 1789, facsimile of an old print by Thomas Rowlandson. Mrs Siddons played the female lead, Elgiva, in *Edwy and Elgiva,* and commented afterwards: 'Oh there never was so wretched a thing as Mrs D'arblaye's Tragedy.'

5 The 'Surrey Hermitage': M, d'A's drawings for the construction of Camilla Cottage and his watercolour painted on its completion in 1797. Alex was given his own playroom, the 'Sallon d'Alexander', while upstairs the biggest room was devoted to books – the 'Chambre des Livres'. Special provision was made for the storage of wine, beer and the seeds for M. d'A's precious garden.

6 Alexander d'Arblay at three years old; and as a young man in about 1815. When Fanny presented her 'little Savage' to Court in March 1798, she dressed him in a new white muslin frock and sash. This page of silhouettes must have been cut by 'sweet lovely dear Amine [Amelia] Lock' (daughter of William and Frederica Lock of Norbury Park) on Alex's third birthday three months' earlier.

The unsigned pencil sketch of a retriever is now to be found in a bundle of letters and drawings in the Berg Collection at the New York Public Library, catalogued as once belonging to Monsieur d'Arblay.

6 & 7 *Waterloo: 18 June 1815;* M. d'A must have drawn this detailed sketch-plan of the decisive day of battle while living in Bath in 1815–18. The annotations explain how 'The two plates [A and B] join together at each end . . . forming a complete circle or panorama of the field of Battle' and give details of the ebb and flow of battle, presumably based on Fanny's memories of what she had been told by the soldiers whom she met in Brussels; M. d'A was in Trèves throughout May and June 1815.

7 *'Tout le monde dira à Alex qui est sa mère; mais – qu'il n'oublie pas qui a été son Père! C'est pour çela que je lui ai consacré et fait faire ce Portrait,'* is the reason given by M. d'A for commissioning his portrait from Carle and Horace Vernet while he was in Paris in 1817. He knew then that he was suffering from a mortal disease, and feared that Fanny would be too devastated after his death even to mention his name. The epaulettes, cuffs and huge collar of his uniform as the Chevalier Lieutenant-Général d'Arblay, together with his medals (the Chevalier de St Louis, the Ordre de la Fidelité, and the Légion d'Honneur), can be seen at Parham Park in West Sussex, displayed beneath the portrait in a glass cabinet.

8 Fanny Burney in her 'Vandyke Gown', 1782, commissioned by Mr Crisp and painted at Chesington Hall by Edward Francisco Burney. Afterwards Fanny reported to Susan: 'Never was Portrait so violently flattered. I have taken pains incredible to make him [Edward] *magnify* the Features, and darken the complexion, but he is impenetrable in action, though fair & docile in promise.' The portrait now hangs opposite General d'Arblay in an alcove of the Long Gallery at Parham Park in Sussex.

SOURCES AND SELECT BIBLIOGRAPHY

Long gone are the days when you could take tea with an elderly descendant of Fanny Burney and be shown her letters, still folded in the shapes in which, a century earlier, they had been posted – as did Professor Joyce Hemlow when she was researching her biography. Since 1952 these letters, more than 2,000 of them, have been deposited in the British Museum as part of the Barrett Collection of Burney Papers. The original edition of the diaries and letters prepared by Fanny's niece, Charlotte Barrett, includes just 200, with only two letters from the last forty-five years of Fanny's life. Hence Professor Hemlow's decision to produce a new, comprehensive edition of the later journals, including much that had never before been available to the general reader. Added to these, Professor Hemlow and her team of scholars at McGill University sought to include the letters and journals bought by the Berg Collection at the New York Public Library from the descendants of Charles Parr Burney in 1924, *and* the papers of Dr Burney in the Osborn Collection at Yale University. In all, these number some 10,000 letters, with over 1,000 named correspondents.

When she came to edit the letters and journals, Professor Hemlow discovered just how much editing had already been done, first by Fanny herself, and then by Charlotte Barrett, who often changed words and phrases that she thought were ungrammatical or too colloquial, and who also cut and pasted letters together to remove anything she deemed too trivial or private for public view. Fanny's heavy black-ink obliterations were penetrated by the McGill scholars using infra-red techniques; Charlotte Barrett's scissors-and-glue compilations were steamed free and floated off, so that the letters could be returned to their original state. (In some cases, pieces of letters that had been divided between the collections of Burney papers in London, New York and Yale were put back together so that they can now be read as they were written.) These same laborious techniques are now being applied by the editorial team at McGill University to the earlier journals up to 1791, replacing Annie Raine Ellis's two-volume *The Early Diary of Frances Burney* of 1889.

Fanny did not write her journal as a diary of daily happenings; rather, she wrote monthly epistles for the entertainment first of Mr Crisp and then of Susan, as well as for Dr Burney, Mrs Lock, Hetty, Marianne Waddington, the Princess Elizabeth and, when rarely separated, M. d'A (including the Teignmouth, Streatham and, most importantly, the Court journals). In later life, after she realised that she had become a person of public significance, she also composed literary set-pieces (Ilfracombe, Dunkirk, Waterloo, Trèves), which were based on memoranda written at the time, but which she wrote up several years later for the benefit of Alex and her hoped-for grandchildren. Her letters, and those of her family, were quite different in tone: these were written as personal 'alives' or 'a few pleasing words', sent to reassure each other that all was well, and to entertain the reader with details of books read and people seen and heard. They have been comprehensively listed by Professor Hemlow in *A Catalogue of the Burney Family Correspondence, 1749–1878*.

Fanny's novels are all available in paperback; her plays can now be read in a two-volume scholarly edition; and a one-volume selection from the letters and journals is still in print (a new edition is being prepared for publication by Professor Lars Troide *et al.*).

Unpublished Burney Family Papers

The Barrett Collection of Burney Papers in the British Museum (Egerton 3690–708) (including fragments from the 'Court Journals' and the journal-letters of Susan Burney Phillips)
The Henry W. and Albert A. Berg Collection of the New York Public Library (including the manuscripts of *Evelina*, *Cecilia* and *Camilla*; 'The Witlings' and 'A Busy Day'; the 'Mastectomy', the 'Adventures at Ilfracombe' and 'The Illness and Death of General

d'Arblay'; as well as the family scrapbooks and the 417 scraps from Fanny's papers)

'The Diary of Queen Charlotte: 1789, 1794': unpublished manuscript in the Royal Archives, Windsor Castle

Essex Record Office (eight letters from Samuel Crisp – D/DL C65)

The grangerized *Diary Letters of Madame d'Arblay: 1778–1840*, with additional illustrations collected by F. Leverton Harris (of Camilla Lacy): one version of twenty volumes in the archives of the National Portrait Gallery, London; the other in the possession of John Comyn, Esq.

The grangerized *Early Diary of Frances Burney: 1768–1778*, with additional illustrations collected by F. Leverton Harris (of Camilla Lacy): five volumes in the archives of the National Portrait Gallery, London

King's Lynn Museum (one letter from Fanny Burney to Jeremy Bentham; one letter by Dr Burney)

'Madame d'Arblay: Her Commonplace Book of "Consolatory Extracts" Occasioned by the Tragic Death of Her Sister Susan Phillips in January 1800': unpublished manuscript in the Henry E. Huntington Library and Art Gallery, San Marino, California

The Public Library, Armagh (copies of letters from Susan Burney Phillips to Fanny Burney d'Arblay, in two notebooks)

The 'Worcester Journal: Memoranda of the Burney Family, 1603–1845': ninety-eight typewritten pages of family history, now in the possession of Bill Fraser

Published works by Fanny Burney

Evelina; or The History of a Young Lady's Entrance into the World (1778). The World's Classics, edited with an introduction by Edward A. Bloom with the assistance of Lillian D. Bloom (Oxford, 1982)

Cecilia; or Memoirs of an Heiress (1782). The World's Classics, edited by Peter Sabor and Margaret Anne Doody (Oxford, 1988)

Brief Reflections relative to the Emigrant French Clergy; earnestly submitted to the humane consideration of the Ladies of Great Britain (1793)

Camilla; or A Picture of Youth (1796). The World's Classics, edited by Edward A. Bloom and Lillian D. Bloom (Oxford, 1983)

The Wanderer; or Female Difficulties (1814). The World's Classics, edited by Margaret Anne Doody, Robert L. Mack and Peter Sabor (Oxford, 1991)

Memoirs of Doctor Burney, arranged from his own manuscripts, from family papers and from personal recollections by his daughter, Madame d'Arblay (three vols, 1832)

Published Burney Family Papers

A Busy Day, edited by Tara Ghoshal Wallace (New Brunswick, 1984)

A Catalogue of the Burney Family Correspondence, 1749–1878, compiled by Joyce Hemlow, with Jeanne M.M. Burgess and Althea Douglas (New York, 1971)

Catalogue of Drawings by E.F. Burney in the Huntington Collection, edited by Patricia Crown (San Marino, California, 1982)

The Complete Plays of Frances Burney, Volume I: Comedies, Volume II: Tragedies, edited by Peter Sabor, Stewart. J. Cooke *et al.* (London, 1995)

Diary & Letters of Madame d'Arblay (1778–1840), edited by her niece Charlotte Barrett (seven vols, London, 1842–6)

Diary & Letters of Madame d'Arblay (1778–1840), as edited by her niece Charlotte Barrett, with preface and notes by Austin Dobson (six vols, London, 1904)

The Early Diary of Frances Burney, 1768–1778, edited by Annie Raine Ellis (two vols, London, 1889)

The Early Journals and Letters of Fanny Burney, 1768–91, edited by Lars E. Troide *et al.* (twelve vols, of which only three are as yet published, Oxford, 1988–94)

The Journals and Letters of Fanny Burney (Madame d'Arblay), 1791–1840, edited by Joyce Hemlow *et al.* (twelve vols, Oxford, 1972–84)

The Letters of Dr Charles Burney, Volume I: 1751–1784, edited by Alvaro Ribeiro, SJ (Oxford, 1991)

Memoirs of Dr Charles Burney, 1726–1769, edited from autograph fragments by Slava Klima,

Garry Bowers, and Kerry S. Grant (Lincoln, Nebraska, 1988)
Music, Men and Manners in France and Italy 1770, Being the Journal Written by *Charles Burney,*
Mus. D., During a Tour Through Those Countries Undertaken to Collect Material for A General
History of Music, transcribed from the original manuscript in the British Museum and edited
with an introduction by H. Edmund Poole (London, 1969)
Selected Letters and Journals of Fanny Burney, edited by Joyce Hemlow (Oxford, 1986)
The Witlings, edited by Clayton J. Delery (East Lansing, Michigan, 1995)

Contemporary Sources

Austen, Jane: *Pride and Prejudice* (1813). Penguin Classics, edited by Tony Tanner (London,
1985)
——*Northanger Abbey* (1818). Penguin Classics, edited by Marilyn Butler (London, 1995)
Jane Austen's Letters to Her Sister Cassandra and Others, collected and edited by R.W. Chapman
(second edition, Oxford, 1952)
Boswell, James: *The Life of Johnson* (1791). The World's Classics, edited by R.W. Chapman
and introduced by Pat Rogers (Oxford, 1980)
Boswell's London Journal, 1762–1763, edited by Frederick A. Pottle (Edinburgh, 1991)
Burford Papers: Being Letters of Samuel Crisp to His Sister at Burford; and Other Sundries of a
Century, 1745–1845, edited by William Holden Hutton (London, 1905)
Byron's Letters and Journals, edited by Leslie A. Marchand (twelve vols, London, 1972–82)
Lord Byron: Selected Letters and Journals, edited by Leslie A. Marchand (London, 1982)
Davies, Thomas: *Memoirs of the Life of David Garrick, Esq, Interspersed with Characters and*
Anecdotes of His Theatrical Contemporaries (1780)
Letters from Mrs Delany to Mrs Frances Hamilton from the Year 1779, to the Year 1788;
Comprising Many Unpublished and Interesting Anecdotes of Their Late Majesties and the Royal
Family (London, 1820)
Edgeworth, Maria: *Belinda* (1801). The World's Classics, edited by Kathryn J. Kirkpatrick
(Oxford, 1994)
Maria Edgeworth: Chosen Letters, edited by F.V. Barry (London, 1931)
Maria Edgeworth in France and Switzerland: Selections from the Edgeworth Family Letters, edited
by Christina Colvin (Oxford, 1979)
Fielding, Henry: *Amelia* (1751). Penguin Classics, edited by David Blewett (London, 1987)
Genest, John: *Some Account of the English Stage from the Restoration in 1660 to 1830, Volume*
VII: 1790–1806 (1832)
The Diaries of Colonel the Hon. Robert Fulke Greville, Equerry to His Majesty King George III,
edited with notes by F. McKno Bladon (London, 1930)
The Collected Works of William Hazlitt, edited by A.R. Waller & Arnold Glover, with an
introduction by W.E. Henley (London, 1902)
The Letters of Samuel Johnson, edited by R.W. Chapman (three vols, Oxford, 1952)
Lamb, Charles: *The Essays of Elia,* edited with introduction and notes by Alfred Ainger
(London, 1910)
Lennox, Charlotte: *The Female Quixote* (1752). The World's Classics, edited by Margaret
Dalziel and introduced by Margaret Anne Doody (Oxford, 1989)
The London Stage: A Collection of the Most Repeated Tragedies, Comedies, Operas, Melo-dramas,
Farces and Interludes, Accurately Printed from Acting Copies, As Performed at the Theatres
Royal and Carefully Collated and Revised (three vols, London, 1825)
The Works of Lord Macaulay, Volume IV: Essays and Biographies (London, 1898)
Court and Private Life in the Time of Queen Charlotte: Being the Journals of Mrs Papendiek,
Assistant Keeper of the Wardrobe and Reader to Her Majesty, edited by her grand-daughter,
Mrs Vernon Delves Broughton (two vols, London, 1887)
Radcliffe, Ann: *The Mysteries of Udolpho* (1794). The World's Classics, edited by Bonamy
Dobrée (Oxford, 1980)
The Journal of Sir Walter Scott, the text revised from a photostat in the National Library of
Scotland, edited by J.G. Tait (Edinburgh, 1939)
An Extraordinary Woman: Selected Writings of Germaine de Staël, translated and with an
introduction by Vivian Folkenflik (New York, 1987)
Sterne, Laurence: *A Sentimental Journey,* with *The Journal to Eliza* and *A Political Romance*

(1768). The World's Classics, edited by Ian Jack (Oxford, 1984)

Thoms, William J.: *The Book of the Court; Exhibiting the Origin, Peculiar Duties, and Privileges of the Several Ranks of the Nobility and Gentry, More Particularly of the Great Officers of State, and Members of the Royal Household* (1838)

Thraliana: The Diary of Mrs Hester Lynch Thrale (later Mrs Piozzi) 1776–1809, edited by Katharine C. Balderston (two vols, Oxford, 1942)

Walpole, Horace: *The Castle of Otranto* (1764). The World's Classics, edited by E.J. Clery (Oxford, 1996)

Watkins, John: *Memoirs of Her Most Excellent Majesty Sophia-Charlotte, Queen of Great Britain from Authentic Documents* (1819)

Wollstonecraft, Mary: *Vindication of the Rights of Woman* (1792). Penguin Classics, edited by Miriam Brody (Harmondsworth, 1983)

——*Maria, or The Wrongs of Woman* (1798), edited by Anne K. Mellor (New York, 1994)

Secondary Sources: The Burneys

Brimley Johnson, R.: *Fanny Burney and the Burneys* (London, 1926)

Cooke, Stewart J.: 'The "Fortune" of Elizabeth Allen Burney', *Notes and Queries*, 39 (new series), 1 (March 1992), p. 61

——'How Much Was Fanny Burney Paid for *Cecilia?*', *Notes and Queries*, 39 (new series), 4 (December 1992), pp. 484–6.

Dobson, Austin: *Fanny Burney (Madame d'Arblay)* (English Men of Letters series, London, 1904)

Doody, Margaret Anne: *Frances Burney: The Life in the Works* (Cambridge, 1988)

Eaves, T.C. Duncan: 'Edward Burney's Illustrations to "Evelina"', *Proceedings of the Modern Language Association of America*, LXII (1947), pp. 994–9

Edwards, Averyl: *Fanny Burney, 1752–1840: A Biography* (London, 1948)

Farr, Evelyn: *The World of Fanny Burney* (London, 1993)

Gérin, Winifred E.: *The Young Fanny Burney* (London, 1961)

Grau, Joseph A.: *Fanny Burney: An Annotated Bibliography* (New York, 1981)

Hanh, Emily: *A Degree of Prudery: A Biography of Fanny Burney* (London, 1951)

Hammelmann, H.A.: 'Edward Burney's Drawings', *Country Life*, cxliii (6 June 1968), pp. 1504–6

Hemlow, Joyce: 'Fanny Burney: Playwright', *University of Toronto Quarterly*, XIX, 2 (January 1950), pp. 170–89

——'Fanny Burney and the Courtesy Books', *Proceedings of the Modern Language Association of America*, LXV (1950), pp. 732–61

——*The History of Fanny Burney* (Oxford, 1958)

——'Letters and Journals of Fanny Burney: Establishing the Text', *Editing Eighteenth-Century Texts*, edited by D.I.B. Smith (Toronto, 1968), pp. 25–43

Hill, Constance: *Juniper Hall*, with illustrations by Ellen G. Hill (London, 1904)

——*The House in St Martin's Street, Being Chronicles of the Burney Family*, with illustrations by Ellen G. Hill (London, 1907)

——*Fanny Burney at the Court of Queen Charlotte*, with illustrations by Ellen G. Hill (London, 1914)

Kilpatrick, Sarah: *Fanny Burney* (Newton Abbot, 1980)

Lonsdale, Roger: *Dr Charles Burney: A Literary Biography* (Oxford, 1965)

Manwaring, G.E.: *My Friend the Admiral: The Life, Letters, and Journals of Rear-Admiral James Burney, FRS, The Companion of Captain Cook and Friend of Charles Lamb* (London, 1931)

Middleton, John: 'Camilla Cottage, West Humble', *The Georgian Group Journal* (1993), pp. 94–8.

Morley, Edith J.: 'Sarah Harriet Burney', *Modern Philology*, XXXIX, 2 (November 1941), pp. 123–58

Roberts, W. Wright: 'Charles and Fanny Burney in the Light of the New Thrale Correspondence in the John Rylands Library', *Bulletin of the John Rylands Library*, vol. 16, no. 1 (January 1932)

Scholes, Dr Percy A.: *The Great Dr Burney: His Life, His Travels, His Works, His Family and His Friends* (two vols, Oxford, 1948)

Seeley, L.B.: *Fanny Burney and Her Friends* (London, 1890)

Other Secondary Sources

Altick, Richard D.: *Richard Owen Cambridge: Belated Augustan* (Philadelphia, 1941)

Barton Baker, Henry: *History of the London Stage and its Famous Players (1576–1903)* (London, 1904)

Brayley, Edward Wedlake: *A Topographical History of Surrey: Volume V* (London, 1850)

Brimley Johnson, R.: *Life of Jane Austen* (London, 1930)

——*Jane Austen: Her Life, Her Work, Her Family and Her Critics* (London, 1930)

Campbell, D. Alastair: *The Dress of the Royal Artillery* (London, 1971)

Cecil, Lord David: *Jane Austen* (Cambridge, 1935)

Clifford, James, L.: *Hester Lynch Piozzi (Mrs Thrale)* (Oxford, 1941)

Cunnington, C. Willett and Phyllis: *Handbook of English Costume in the Eighteenth Century* (Boston, 1972)

DeMaria, Robert: *The Life of Samuel Johnson: A Critical Biography* (Oxford, 1993)

Desmond, Ray: *Kew: The History of the Royal Botanic Garden* (London, 1995)

Deutsch, Otto Erich: *Handel: A Documentary Biography* (London, 1955)

Donkin, Ellen: *Getting into the Act: Women Playwrights in London, 1776–1829* (London, 1995)

Fitzgerald, Penelope: *The Blue Flower* (London, 1995): a novelisation of the life of the German philosopher, Novalis (1772–1801), which uses as a source Fanny Burney's account of her mastectomy

Friedeberger, Julie: *A Visible Wound: A Healing Journey Through Breast Cancer* (Shaftesbury, 1996)

George, M. Dorothy: *London Life in the Eighteenth Century* (London, 1925; now also a Penguin paperback, 1992)

Haythornthwaite, Philip J.: *Uniforms of the French Revolutionary Wars, 1789–1802* with illustrations by Christopher Warner (Poole, Dorset, 1981)

Hedley, Olwen: 'Mrs Delany's Windsor Home', *Berkshire Archaeological Journal*, 59 (1961–2), pp. 51–5.

——*Queen Charlotte* (London, 1975)

——'Queen Charlotte: Queen of Patrons', unpublished paper given at the symposium 'The Lady Patrons: Women, Culture and Patronage in Britain, 1700–1875', held at the V&A in London in July 1994

Hogan, Charles Beecher (editor): *The London Stage, 1660–1800: A Calendar of Plays, Entertainments & Afterpieces, Together with Casts, Box-Receipts and Contemporary Comment, Compiled from the Playbills, Newspapers and Theatrical Diaries of the Period, Part V: 1776–1800* (Carbondale, Illinois, 1968)

Holmes, Richard: *Dr Johnson & Mr Savage* (London, 1993)

Hough, Richard: *Captain James Cook: A Biography* (London, 1994)

Hyde, Mary: *The Thrales of Streatham Park: Journal of an Eighteenth-Century Family* (Cambridge, Massachusetts, 1977)

Ison, Walter: *The Georgian Buildings of Bath from 1700 to 1830* (London, 1948)

Jenkins, Elizabeth: *Jane Austen: A Biography* (London, 1958)

Kelly, Linda: *Juniper Hall: An English Refuge from the French Revolution* (London, 1991)

——*Richard Brinsley Sheridan: A Life* (London, 1997)

Kendall, Alan: *David Garrick* (London, 1985)

Kennedy, Gavin: *The Death of Captain Cook* (London, 1978)

McKechnie, Sue: *British Silhouette Artists and their Work* (London, 1978)

Mander, Raymond and Mitchenson, Joe: *The Artist and the Theatre* (London, 1955)

Morgan, Fidelis: *The Female Wits: Women Playwrights of the Restoration* (London, 1981)

Nicoll, Allardyce: *A History of English Drama, 1660–1900, Vol. VIII: Late Eighteenth-Century Drama, 1750–1800* (Cambridge, 1952)

Roberts, Jane: *Views of Windsor: Watercolours by Thomas and Paul Sandby* (London, 1995)

Rogers, Pat: *Samuel Johnson* (Oxford, 1993)

——*The Samuel Johnson Encyclopedia* (Westport, Connecticut, 1996)

Schama, Simon: *Citizens: A Chronicle of the French Revolution* (London, 1989)

——*Landscape and Memory* (London, 1996)

Scouten; Arthur H. (editor): *The London Stage, 1660–1800: A Calendar of Plays, Entertainments & Afterpieces, Together with Casts, Box-Receipts and Contemporary Comment, Compiled from* the Playbills, Newspapers and Theatrical Diaries of the Period. Part III: 1729–47 (Carbondale, Illinois, 1961)

Sermoneta, Duchess of: *The Locks of Norbury: The Story of a Remarkable Family in the XVIIIth and XIXth Centuries* (London, 1940)

Shute, Nerina: *Georgian Lady: A Conversation Piece of the Eighteenth Century* (London, 1948): a fictionalised life of Fanny Burney, based on her diaries

Simond, Charles: *Paris de 1800 à 1900 D'après les Estampes et les Mémoires du Temps. Volume I: 1800–1830, Le Consulat; Le Premier Empire; La Restauration* (Paris, 1900)

Stone, George Winchester, Jr (editor): *The London Stage, 1660–1800: A Calendar of Plays, Entertainments & Afterpieces, Together with Casts, Box-Receipts and Contemporary Comment, Compiled from the Playbills, Newspapers and Theatrical Diaries of the Period, Part IV: 1747–76* (Carbondale, Illinois, 1962)

Stone, Lawrence: *Broken Lives: Separation and Divorce in England, 1660–1857* (Oxford, 1993)

Tillyard, Stella: *Aristocrats: Caroline, Emily, Louisa and Sarah Lennox, 1740–1832* (London, 1994)

Tomalin, Claire: *The Life and Death of Mary Wollstonecraft* (London, 1974)

——*Mrs Jordan's Profession* (London, 1993)

——*Jane Austen: A Life* (London, 1997)

Walker, Richard: *Regency Portraits* (National Portrait Gallery, London, 1985)

Woolf, Virginia: 'Dr Burney's Evening Party', *The Common Reader* (second series, London, 1986), pp. 108–25

Yalom, Marilyn: *A History of the Breast* (New York, 1997)

Typically high-flown language of her
later years — 8

pompous style — conservative and
sanctimonious streak — 174

never lost the child-like desire to be her
father's favorite girl — 220

prudish Fanny — "vestal sister who
has ventured on sea of matrimony" . . .
conquering hero who has thawed Fanny's
ice" — 172